PERSPECTIVES
ON PAUL

PERSPECTIVES ON PAUL

FIVE VIEWS

EDITED BY

SCOT McKNIGHT

AND

B. J. OROPEZA

Baker Academic
a division of Baker Publishing Group
Grand Rapids, Michigan

Published by Baker Academic
a division of Baker Publishing Group
PO Box 6287, Grand Rapids, MI 49516-6287
www.bakeracademic.com

Printed in the United States of America

Library of Congress Cataloging-in-Publication Data
Names: McKnight, Scot, editor. | Oropeza, B. J., 1961– editor.
Title: Perspectives on Paul : five views / Scot McKnight and B. J. Oropeza, eds.
Description: Grand Rapids, Michigan : Baker Academic, a division of Baker Publishing Group, 2020. | Includes index.
Identifiers: LCCN 2020011318 | ISBN 9781540960757 (paperback) | ISBN 9781540963482 (hardcover)
Subjects: LCSH: Bible. Epistles of Paul—Criticism, interpretation, etc. | Bible. Epistles of Paul—Theology.
Classification: LCC BS2650.52 .P47 2020 | DDC 227/.06—dc23

20   21   22   23   24   25   26   7   6   5   4   3   2   1

To Jimmy
(October 21, 1939–June 26, 2020)

Contents

Preface

We have a common heritage in Pauline studies—namely, our doctoral supervisor, James D. G. Dunn. Yet, B. J. did work under him in Pauline studies, while Scot did work on the Gospel of Matthew. Scot was studying with Dunn just after the original lecture about the New Perspective on Paul—in fact, before it was "The New Perspective"—and has watched the whole unfold. We wish to express our sadness that our beloved professor, Jimmy, passed away on June 26, 2020, after a short battle with cancer. Future generations of biblical exegetes and theologians will recognize him as one of the greatest biblical scholars of the late twentieth and early twenty-first centuries. Every page of this book—and countless others—shows the presence of the formidable proposals Dunn offered scholarship on the apostle Paul.[1]

In many ways, the decisive impetus for each of the perspectives here was the 1977 book by E. P. Sanders, *Paul and Palestinian Judaism*. The book sought to demolish the typical stereotype of Judaism at work in much scholarship, but at the same time, and only in tentative ways, it opened the door to fresh analysis of Paul in light of Sanders's reconstruction of Judaism. These studies, even A. Andrew Das's traditional view, have taken new shape and angles because of Sanders.

This book is for professors, students, and pastors who want to know what is going on in recent Pauline scholarship and want to see civil engagement about the apostle Paul's theology in its context. There has been much mudslinging,

---

1. See the following for our commemorations of James D. G. Dunn: Scot McKnight, "Rest in Peace, Jimmy," *Jesus Creed* (blog), *Christianity Today*, June 26, 2020, https://www.christianity today.com/scot-mcknight/2020/june/rest-in-peace-jimmy.html; B. J. Oropeza, "Memories of My Doktorvater, James D. G. Dunn (1939–2020)," *In Christ* (blog), Patheos, June 26, 2020, https://www .patheos.com/blogs/inchrist/2020/06/memories-of-my-doktorvater-james-d-g-dunn-1939-2020/.

begun among some who thought Sanders's view of Judaism and the New Perspective itself (though there is really no such thing, since it is more new *perspectives*) undermined what they thought Paul was saying, and some of the criticism has landed and some of it is little more than repeating the mudslingers. Our hope is that this volume will help the whole church better come to terms with the apostle Paul and his great letters, which, we need to remind ourselves, are at the foundation of so much theology at work in the history of the church.

We are grateful for those who made this project possible, and we wish to thank especially Bryan Dyer at Baker. Next, we would like to thank the contributors for their willingness to present their views and respond to the other contributors in timely fashion. Also, Scot would like to acknowledge Northern Seminary and the Board of Trustees, and B. J. would like to acknowledge Azusa Pacific University, particularly the Department of Biblical and Religious Studies (Bobby Duke and Robert Mullins, dean and chair, respectively), as well as the Office of Research and Grants (Yvonne Rodriguez), which awarded him a Faculty Research Grant in view of this project.

Scot McKnight
B. J. Oropeza

Abbreviations

Books by E. P. Sanders

PALLT	*Paul: The Apostle's Life, Letters, and Thought*
PLJP	*Paul, the Law, and the Jewish People*
PPJ	*Paul and Palestinian Judaism: A Comparison of Patterns of Religion*

General Abbreviations

NPP	New Perspective on Paul
STJ	Second Temple Judaism

Bible Versions and Translations

AT	Author's translation
LXX	Septuagint
NEB	New English Bible
NET	New English Translation
NIV	New International Version
NRSV	New Revised Standard Version
RSV	Revised Standard Version

Primary Sources

Deuterocanonical Works and Septuagint

Tob.	Tobit
Jdt.	Judith
Add. Esth.	Additions to Esther
Sir.	Sirach
1–4 Macc.	1–4 Maccabees

Old Testament Pseudepigrapha

Apoc. Ab.	Apocalypse of Abraham
Jos. Asen.	Joseph and Aseneth
Jub.	Jubilees
LAB	Liber antiquitatum biblicarum (Pseudo-Philo)
Let. Aris.	Letter of Aristeas
Pss. Sol.	Psalms of Solomon
T. Ab.	Testament of Abraham

Dead Sea Scrolls

1QapGen	Genesis Apocryphon
1QS	Rule of the Community
4QMMT	4QHalakhic Letter
CD	Cairo Genizah copy of the Damascus Document

Philo

Abr.	De Abrahamo (On the Life of Abraham)
Congr.	De congressu eruditionis gratia (On the Preliminary Studies)
Deus	Quod Deus sit immutabilis (That God Is Unchangeable)
Ebr.	De ebrietate (On Drunkenness)
Flacc.	In Flaccum (Against Flaccus)
Fug.	De fuga et inventione (On Flight and Finding)
Her.	Quis rerum divinarum heres sit (Who Is the Heir?)
Leg.	Legum allegoriae (Allegorical Interpretation)
Legat.	Legatio ad Gaium (On the Embassy to Gaius)
Migr.	De migratione Abrahami (On the Migration of Abraham)
Mos.	De vita Mosis (On the Life of Moses)
Mut.	De mutatione nominum (On the Change of Names)
Post.	De posteritate Caini (On the Posterity of Cain)
Praem.	De praemiis et poenis (On Rewards and Punishments)
QG	Quaestiones et solutiones in Genesin (Questions and Answers on Genesis)
Sacr.	De sacrificiis Abelis et Caini (On the Sacrifices of Cain and Abel)
Sobr.	De sobrietate (On Sobriety)
Somn.	De somniis (On Dreams)
Spec.	De specialibus legibus (On the Special Laws)
Virt.	De virtutibus (On the Virtues)

Josephus

Ant.	Jewish Antiquities
J.W.	Jewish War
Life	The Life

Rabbinic Works

b. Sanh.	Babylonian Talmud, Sanhedrin
m. ʿAbod. Zar.	Mishnah, ʿAbodah Zarah

m. Ber.   Mishnah, Berakot
m. Demai   Mishnah, Demai
m. Ḥul.   Mishnah, Ḥullin
m. 'Ohol.   Mishnah, 'Oholot
t. 'Abod. Zar. Tosefta, 'Abodah Zarah

Greek and Latin Works

AELIAN
Var. hist.   *Varia historia (Various History)*

AELIUS THEON
Prog.   *Progymnasmata*

ARISTOTLE
Eth. nic.   *Ethica nicomachea (Nicomachean Ethics)*
Rhet.   *Rhetorica (Rhetoric)*

AUGUSTINE
Civ.   *De civitate Dei (The City of God)*

DIO CASSIUS
Hist. rom.   *Historia romana (Roman History)*

EPICTETUS
Diatr.   *Diatribai (Discourses)*

QUINTILIAN
Inst.   *Institutio oratoria (Institutes of Oratory)*

SENECA
Ep.   *Epistulae morales (Moral Epistles)*

THUCYDIDES
Hist.   *Historiai (Histories)*

Secondary Sources

AB   Anchor Bible
ACW   Ancient Christian Writers
APB   *Acta Patristica et Byzantina*
APR   Ancient Philosophy and Religion
AYBRL   Anchor Yale Bible Reference Library
BBR   *Bulletin for Biblical Research*
BDAG   Baur, Walter, Frederick W. Danker, William F. Arndt, and F. Wilbur Gingrich.
            Greek-English Lexicon of the New Testament and Other Early Christian Lit-
            erature. 3rd ed. Chicago: University of Chicago Press, 2000
BECNT   Baker Exegetical Commentary on the New Testament
Bib   *Biblica*
BibInt   *Biblical Interpretation*

BJRL	*Bulletin of the John Rylands University Library of Manchester*
BNTC	Black's New Testament Commentaries
BR	*Biblical Research*
BSac	*Bibliotheca Sacra*
BTS	Biblical Tools and Studies
BWANT	Beiträge zur Wissenschaft vom Alten und Neuen Testament
BZ	*Biblische Zeitschrift*
BZNW	Beihefte zur Zeitschrift für die neutestamentliche Wissenschaft
CanTR	*Canadian Theological Review*
CBQ	*Catholic Biblical Quarterly*
CBR	*Currents in Biblical Research*
CC	Continental Commentaries
CCSS	Catholic Commentary on Sacred Scripture
ConBNT	Coniectanea Biblica: New Testament Series
ConcC	Concordia Commentary
ConcJ	*Concordia Journal*
COQG	Christian Origins and the Question of God
CRINT	Compendia rerum iudaicarum ad Novum Testamentum
CTJ	*Calvin Theological Journal*
CTR	*Criswell Theological Review*
DSSSE	*The Dead Sea Scrolls: Study Edition.* Edited by Florentino García Martínez and Eibert J. C. Tigchelaar. 2 vols. Leiden: Brill; Grand Rapids: Eerdmans, 1997–98
EC	*Early Christianity*
ETL	*Ephemerides theologicae lovanienses*
EvQ	*Evangelical Quarterly*
ExpTim	*Expository Times*
FC	Fathers of the Church
HBT	*Horizons in Biblical Theology*
HTKNT	Herders theologischer Kommentar zum Neuen Testament
HTR	*Harvard Theological Review*
HTSTS	*HTS Teologiese Studies / Theological Studies*
IBC	Interpretation: A Bible Commentary for Teaching and Preaching
ICC	International Critical Commentary
IJRR	*Interdisciplinary Journal of Research on Religion*
Int	*Interpretation*
JAET	*Journal of Asian Evangelical Theology*
JAOC	Judaïsme ancien et origines du christianisme
JBL	*Journal of Biblical Literature*
JEBS	*Journal of European Baptist Studies*
JETS	*Journal of the Evangelical Theological Society*
JJMJS	*Journal of the Jesus Movement in Its Jewish Setting*
JMT	*Journal of Ministry and Theology*
JSJ	*Journal for the Study of Judaism*
JSNT	*Journal for the Study of the New Testament*
JSNTSup	Journal for the Study of the New Testament Supplement Series
JSOTSup	Journal for the Study of the Old Testament Supplement Series

JSPL	*Journal for the Study of Paul and His Letters*
JSSR	*Journal for the Scientific Study of Religion*
JTI	*Journal of Theological Interpretation*
KI	*Kirche und Israel*
KNNE	Kontexte und Normen neutestamentlicher Ethik / Contexts and Norms of New Testament Ethics
LNTS	Library of New Testament Studies
LPS	Library of Pauline Studies
LQ	*Lutheran Quarterly*
LTJ	*Lutheran Theological Journal*
NCBC	New Century Bible Commentary
NIB	*The New Interpreter's Bible*. Edited by Leander E. Keck. 12 vols. Nashville: Abingdon, 1994–2004
NICNT	New International Commentary on the New Testament
NIGTC	New International Greek Testament Commentary
NIVAC	NIV Application Commentary
NovT	*Novum Testamentum*
NovTSup	Supplements to Novum Testamentum
NPNF[1]	*Nicene and Post-Nicene Fathers*, Series 1
NSD	New Studies in Dogmatics
NTM	New Testament Monographs
NTR	New Testament Readings
NTS	*New Testament Studies*
NTT	New Testament Theology
OECS	Oxford Early Christian Studies
OTP	*Old Testament Pseudepigrapha*. Edited by James H. Charlesworth. 2 vols. New York: Doubleday, 1983–85
PBM	Paternoster Biblical Monographs
PFES	Publications of the Finnish Exegetical Society
PNTC	Pillar New Testament Commentary
RHCS	Romans through History and Cultures Series
SBET	*Scottish Bulletin of Evangelical Theology*
SBL	Studies in Biblical Literature
SBLDS	Society of Biblical Literature Dissertation Series
SBLECL	Society of Biblical Literature Early Christianity and Its Literature
SBLSP	Society of Biblical Literature Seminar Papers
SBLTT	Society of Biblical Literature Texts and Translations
SEÅ	*Svensk exegetisk årsbok*
SFSHJ	South Florida Studies in the History of Judaism
SJLA	Studies in Judaism in Late Antiquity
SJT	*Scottish Journal of Theology*
SNTSMS	Society for New Testament Studies Monograph Series
SP	Sacra Pagina
ST	*Studia Theologica*
TECC	Theological Explorations for the Church Catholic
Them	*Themelios*
TL	*Theology & Life*

TR	*Theological Review*
TS	*Theological Studies*
TSAJ	Texte und Studien zum antiken Judentum
TynBul	*Tyndale Bulletin*
TZ	*Theologische Zeitschrift*
VIOT	Veröffentlichungen des Instituts für Orthodoxe Theologie
WBC	Word Biblical Commentary
WTJ	*Westminster Theological Journal*
WUNT	Wissenschaftliche Untersuchungen zum Neuen Testament
ZTK	*Zeitschrift für Theologie und Kirche*

Paul in Perspective

An Overview of the Landscape More Than Forty Years after Paul and Palestinian Judaism

B. J. OROPEZA AND SCOT McKNIGHT

More than forty years have passed since the publication of E. P. Sanders's *Paul and Palestinian Judaism: A Comparison of Patterns of Religion,* a study that would revolutionize the way biblical scholars and theologians interpret Paul and the Judaism of his day.[1] Sanders worked through the "patterns of religion" in the Palestinian literature on Second Temple Judaism and in Paul's undisputed letters.[2] One of his primary aims was "to destroy the view of Rabbinic Judaism which is still prevalent in much, perhaps most, New Testament scholarship."[3] Sanders's perspective in this monograph, along with

---

1. Philadelphia: Fortress, 1977; London: SCM, 1977. For Sanders's own description of this study, see E. P. Sanders, *Comparing Judaism and Christianity: Common Judaism, Paul, and the Inner and the Outer in Ancient Religion* (Minneapolis: Fortress, 2016), 1–27.

2. Romans, 1–2 Corinthians, Galatians, Philippians, 1 Thessalonians, Philemon.

3. *PPJ,* xii. Prior to Sanders, some prominent forerunners included George Foot Moore, "Christian Writers on Judaism," *HTR* 14 (1921): 197–254; Moore, *Judaism in the First Centuries of the Christian Era: The Age of the Tannaim,* 3 vols. (Cambridge, MA: Harvard University Press, 1927); C. G. Montefiore, *Judaism and St. Paul: Two Essays* (New York: Dutton, 1915); H. J. Schoeps, *Paul: The Theology of the Apostle in the Light of Jewish Religious History,* trans. Harold Knight (Philadelphia: Westminster, 1961); W. D. Davies, *Paul and Rabbinic Judaism: Some Rabbinic Elements in Pauline Theology,* 4th ed. (1948; Philadelphia: Fortress, 1980). See further examples in *PPJ,* 1–12; Preston M. Sprinkle, "The Old Perspective on the New Perspective: A Review of Some 'Pre-Sanders' Thinkers," *Them* 30 (2005): 21–31; Jay E. Smith, "The New Perspective on Paul: A Select and Annotated Bibliography," *CTR* 2 (2005): 91–111.

his follow-up book, *Paul, the Law, and the Jewish People*,[4] presented a different perspective than the Lutheran-Protestant interpretation of Paul and the Judaism of his time. An entire generation of scholars has been influenced by, or made its point of departure from, Sanders and the New Perspective on Paul that followed from his studies.[5] In this introductory chapter, then, a brief "history of interpretation" is in order that covers Sanders, the New Perspective on Paul, critics of the New Perspective, and some of the major perspectives that followed.[6]

4. Philadelphia: Fortress, 1983.

5. Of course, we are not suggesting that these are the only perspectives on Paul on the market. Our focus centers on traditions and criticisms engaging with Sanders and the New Perspective on Paul.

6. For further surveys and bibliographies, consult Stephen Westerholm, *Perspectives Old and New on Paul: The "Lutheran" Paul and His Critics* (Grand Rapids: Eerdmans, 2004), 101–248; Westerholm, "The 'New Perspective' at Twenty-Five," in *Justification and Variegated Nomism*, vol. 2, *The Paradoxes of Paul*, ed. D. A. Carson, Peter T. O'Brien, and Mark A. Seifrid, WUNT 2/181 (Tübingen: Mohr Siebeck; Grand Rapids: Baker Academic, 2004), 1–38; Westerholm, "The New Perspective in Review," *Direction* (2015): 4–15; Michael F. Bird, "Bibliography on the New Perspective on Paul," in *The Saving Righteousness of God: Studies on Paul, Justification and the New Perspective*, PBM (Milton Keynes: Paternoster, 2007), 196–211; Don Garlington, "The New Perspective on Paul: Two Decades On," in *Studies in the New Perspective on Paul: Essays and Reviews* (Eugene, OR: Wipf & Stock, 2008), 1–28 (= "The New Perspective on Paul: An Appraisal Two Decades Later," *CTR* [2005]: 17–38); Jay E. Smith, "The New Perspective on Paul: A Select and Annotated Bibliography," *CTR* 2 (2005): 91–111; James D. G. Dunn, "The New Perspective: Whence, What and Whither?," in *The New Perspective on Paul*, rev. ed. (Grand Rapids: Eerdmans, 2008), 1–97; Kent L. Yinger, *The New Perspective on Paul: An Introduction* (Eugene, OR: Cascade, 2011); Magnus Zetterholm, *Approaches to Paul: A Student's Guide to Recent Scholarship* (Minneapolis: Fortress, 2009); N. T. Wright, *Paul and His Recent Interpreters: Some Contemporary Debates* (Minneapolis: Fortress, 2015); Steven E. Enderlein, "Justification in Contemporary Debate," in *Justification: Five Views*, ed. James K. Beilby and Paul Rhodes Eddy (Downers Grove, IL: IVP Academic, 2011), 53–82; Murray J. Smith, "Paul in the Twenty-First Century," in *All Things to All Cultures: Paul among Jews, Greeks, and Romans*, ed. Mark Harding and Alanna Nobbs (Grand Rapids: Eerdmans, 2013), 1–33; Mark A. Chancey, foreword to *Paul and Palestinian Judaism: A Comparison of Patterns of Religion*, by E. P. Sanders, 40th anniversary ed. (Minneapolis: Fortress, 2017), xi–xxvi; Mark M. Mattison, "A Summary of the New Perspective on Paul," *The Paul Page*, October 16, 2009, http://www.thepaulpage.com/a-summary-of-the-new-perspective-on-paul/; see also the bibliography on *The Paul Page*, http://www.thepaulpage.com/new-perspective/bibliography/. *The Paul Page* website continues to provide updates on relevant sources and links.

For earlier surveys, see Donald A. Hagner, "Paul and Judaism: Testing the New Perspective," in Peter Stuhlmacher, *Revisiting Paul's Doctrine of Justification: A Challenge to the New Perspective* (Downers Grove, IL: InterVarsity, 2001), 75–105, esp. nn. 64, 79; Christian Strecker, "Paulus aus einer 'neuen Perspektive': der Paradigmenwechsel in der jüngeren Paulusforschung," *KI* (1996): 3–18; A. J. Bandstra, "Paul and the Law: Some Recent Developments and an Extraordinary Book," *CTJ* 25 (1990): 249–61; Stephen Westerholm, *Israel's Law and the Church's Faith: Paul and His Recent Interpreters* (Grand Rapids: Eerdmans, 1988); F. F. Bruce, "Paul and the Law in Recent Research," in *Law and Religion: Essays on*

E. P. Sanders's Perspective

Sanders's *Paul and Palestinian Judaism* and *Paul, the Law, and the Jewish People* featured a number of tenets that would become pivotal in biblical scholarship, not least his calling into question the historical integrity of much New Testament scholarship.

First, his examination of Palestinian Second Temple Judaism, the Dead Sea Scrolls, and Tannaitic literature led him to conclude that the Judaism of Paul's day was not typified by work-righteousness or legalism; it did not seek to secure divine approval by human merit.[7] Contrary to what Lutheran-Protestant scholars had assumed, ancient Judaism was a religion of grace.[8] The Jews held to what Sanders called *covenantal nomism*: "Briefly put, covenantal nomism is the view that one's place in God's plan is established on the basis of the covenant and that the covenant requires as the proper response of man his obedience to its commandments, while providing means of atonement for transgression."[9] A covenant relationship with God and adherence to Mosaic law were central to understanding rewards and punishments from God. For

the *Place of the Law in Israel and Early Christianity*, ed. Barnabas Lindars (Cambridge: James Clarke, 1988), 115–25; Douglas J. Moo, "Paul and the Law in the Last Ten Years," *SJT* 40 (1987): 287–307; John M. G. Barclay, "Paul and the Law: Observations on Some Recent Debates," *Them* 12 (1986): 5–15. Some basic overviews (some amiable, some not) can be found in James E. Allman, "Gaining Perspective on the New Perspective on Paul," *BSac* 170 (2013): 51–68; Solomon H. F. Wong, "Paul Revisited: New Perspective on Paul," *TL* 32 (2009): 145–80; Douglas C. Bozung, "The New Perspective: A Survey and Critique—Part I," *JMT* 9 (2005): 95–114; Michael B. Thompson, *The New Perspective on Paul* (Cambridge: Grove Books, 2002); James A. Meek, "The New Perspective on Paul: An Introduction for the Uninitiated," *ConcJ* 27 (2001): 208–33. For a systematic theological assessment, see Michael Scott Horton, *Justification*, 2 vols., NSD (Grand Rapids: Zondervan, 2018), esp. 2:17–55.

7. E.g., *PPJ*, 233–34; cf. 33.

8. E.g., *PPJ*, 543. Sanders also addresses Jewish-Hellenistic Second Temple sources in "The Covenant as a Soteriological Category and the Nature of Salvation in Palestinian and Hellenistic Judaism," in *Jews, Greeks, and Christians: Religious Cultures in Late Antiquity; Studies in Honor of William David Davies*, ed. Robert Hamerton-Kelly and Robin Scroggs, SJLA 21 (Leiden: Brill, 1976), 11–44; Sanders, *Judaism: Practice and Belief, 63 BCE–66 CE* (London: SCM; Philadelphia: Trinity Press International, 1992), 262–78. Prior to *PPJ*, see Sanders, "Patterns of Religion in Paul and Rabbinic Judaism: A Holistic Method of Comparison," *HTR* 66 (1973): 455–78.

9. *PPJ*, 75; cf. 180. Sanders writes, "The 'pattern' or 'structure' of covenantal nomism is this: (1) God has chosen Israel and (2) given the law. The law implies (3) God's promise to maintain the election and (4) the requirement to obey. (5) God rewards obedience and punishes transgression. (6) The law provides for means of atonement, and atonement results in (7) maintenance or re-establishment of the covenantal relationship. (8) All those who are maintained in the covenant by obedience, atonement, and God's mercy belong to the group which will be saved. An important interpretation of the first and last points is that election and ultimately salvation are considered to be by God's mercy rather than human achievement" (422).

God's elect people, the aspect of "getting in" a covenant relationship with God happened as a sheer act of grace. The people, moreover, were to keep the Torah in obedience to God, which constituted their "staying in" that covenant relationship.[10] Works are thus the condition of staying in, "*but they do not earn salvation.*"[11] For Sanders, then, Israel's salvation is by grace, and judgment is according to works.

Second, when Paul became a Christ-follower, his experience led him from solution to plight. He started with God's redemption in Christ (solution) and then attempted to explain why humans were in need of salvation (plight).[12] This makes it unlikely that what is at stake with the Torah for Paul is that it is impossible to obey or that it leads to self-righteousness.[13] The issue that Paul faces is how gentiles could be on equal footing with Jews rather than being second-class citizens.[14] Prior to Sanders, Krister Stendahl came to a similar conclusion after arguing that a troubled conscience, exemplified by Luther and Western sentiments, was not Paul's struggle. As a Pharisee, Paul could claim to have confidence in his status and considered himself "blameless" regarding righteousness in the Torah (Phil. 3:4–6).[15]

Third, for Sanders, when transgressions and other shortcomings took place among Torah adherents, the Torah provided its own means of expiating such violations through cultic sacrifices (e.g., Lev. 4–6; 16). This assisted in maintaining and restoring Israel's covenant relationship with God.[16] Israel's atonement already provided a remedy for guilt and sin prior to Christ.

Fourth, Paul's negativity toward the Torah in his letters resulted from his conclusion that faith in Christ was the only way to salvation.[17] Thus, he ob-

---

10. *PPJ*, 420, 543.

11. *PPJ*, 543 (emphasis original).

12. *PPJ*, 442–47, 474–76.

13. *PLJP*, 150–51.

14. *PLJP*, 153–54.

15. Krister Stendahl, "The Apostle Paul and the Introspective Conscience of the West," *HTR* 56 (1963): 199–215, esp. 200–206; reprinted in *Paul among Jews and Gentiles* (London: SCM, 1976), 76–96. Stendahl presented an earlier version as an address at the American Psychological Association (September 1961), a summary of which is published in *JSSR* 1 (1962): 261–63. The introduction states that "Professor Stendahl reports that a fuller statement has appeared in Swedish: 'Paulus och Samvetet,' *Svensk Exegetisk [Årsbok]*, 25 (1960)" (261). Sanders (*PPJ*, 436–37) claims that a forerunner to Stendahl is Lucien Cerfaux, *Le chrétien dans la théologie paulinienne* (Paris: Cerf, 1962); ET, *The Christian in the Theology of St. Paul*, trans. Lilian Soiron (New York: Herder & Herder, 1967), 375–76. See also Dunn, *New Perspective*, 469–90; N. T. Wright, *Paul and the Faithfulness of God*, COQG 4 (Minneapolis: Fortress, 2013), 2:988–89.

16. *PPJ*, 442.

17. *PLJP*, 47; *PPJ*, 519.

jected to the law because it attempts another way of righteousness. It is not that Judaism is legalistic; rather,"*This is what Paul finds wrong in Judaism: it is not Christianity.*"[18] God chose another way to save without the law; it is through faith in Jesus Christ,[19] and gentiles simply "cannot live by the law."[20] This either-or approach of Sanders can be seen along the axes of either apocalyptic disruption or salvation-historical fulfillment.

Fifth, whereas justification for Jews meant to live according to the Torah and so retain covenant membership, justification for Paul involves salvation through Christ. Sanders prefers to interpret the verb δικαιόω (*dikaioō*) as "to righteous" rather than "to justify." Stress is then placed not on the forensic aspect of God's declaration of acquittal but on a person being "righteoused" by participation in Christ. The righteoused person is transferred over into the community of God's people in Christ.[21]

Sixth, for Paul, to remain a member of God's covenant people, God's will is to be fulfilled not by particularisms of observing things such as Sabbath and food laws but by loving one's neighbor.[22] Here we see that Sanders maintains a "getting in" and "staying in" covenantal pattern not only for Second Temple Judaism but also for Paul.

Sanders's perspective, though criticized on certain points, received praise as a milestone in scholarship from early reviewers such as Nils A. Dahl, Philip King, G. B. Caird, and Samuel Sandmel.[23] In more recent years, Sanders's *Comparing Judaism and Christianity: Common Judaism, Paul, and the Inner and the Outer in Ancient Religion*[24] collects a number of his previous essays and unpublished papers, and his massive *Paul: The Apostle's Life,*

18. *PPJ*, 552 (emphasis original).

19. *PPJ*, 550.

20. *PPJ*, 496.

21. Regarding a deeper explanation of what participation in Christ means, Sanders (*Paul: The Apostle's Life, Letters, and Thought* [Minneapolis: Fortress, 2015], 724–25) defers to Richard B. Hays, "What Is 'Real Participation in Christ'? A Dialogue with E. P. Sanders on Pauline Soteriology," and Stanley K. Stowers, "What Is 'Pauline Participation in Christ'?," both in *Redefining First-Century Jewish and Christian Identities: Essays in Honor of Ed Parish Sanders*, ed. Fabian E. Udoh et al. (Notre Dame, IN: University of Notre Dame Press, 2008), 336–51 and 352–71, respectively. And now see Michael J. Gorman, *Participating in Christ: Explorations in Paul's Theology and Spirituality* (Grand Rapids: Baker Academic, 2019); Gorman, *Becoming the Gospel: Paul, Participation, and Mission* (Grand Rapids: Eerdmans, 2015); Gorman, *Inhabiting the Cruciform God: Kenosis, Justification, and Theosis in Paul's Narrative Soteriology* (Grand Rapids: Eerdmans, 2009); Gorman, *Cruciformity: Paul's Narrative Spirituality of the Cross* (Grand Rapids: Eerdmans, 2001).

22. *PLJP*, 93–135.

23. See Chancey, foreword to *Paul and Palestinian Judaism*, xiv–xv.

24. Minneapolis: Fortress, 2016.

Letters, and Thought covers the apostle's undisputed letters. In these works, inter alia, Sanders reaffirms and expands on his interpretation of Paul and covenantal nomism. Sanders says of *Paul: The Apostle's Life, Letters, and Thought*, "I have summed up my views after a career as an interpreter of the apostle."[25] The Society of Biblical Literature (SBL) also recently dedicated a session in honor of Sanders and the fortieth anniversary of *Paul and Palestinian Judaism*. The articles presented at the session were revised and reprinted in the *Journal of the Jesus Movement in Its Jewish Setting*.[26] In the journal's introduction the editor-in-chief writes, "In 1977, E. P. Sanders published a book that would change the way that New Testament scholarship approached both Judaism and, in consequence, the NT texts themselves. . . . As the reader will discover on the pages that follow, this quest shows no signs of slowing down. On the contrary, it has entered a new level of intensity and strength."[27]

The New Perspective of James D. G. Dunn and N. T. Wright

Scholars influenced by Sanders, particularly James D. G. Dunn and N. T. Wright, made their own points of departure from Sanders when it came to interpreting Paul. "The New Perspective on Paul" was minted from the title of Dunn's Manson Memorial Lecture in Manchester (November 4, 1982), which was published the year after in the *Bulletin of the John Rylands Library*.[28] Dunn, however, mentions that Wright used the term earlier in his 1978 article "The Paul of History and the Apostle of Faith," and in the pre-Sanders era, Stendahl used the term in his famous "Introspective Conscience" article.[29] In any case, Dunn claims that the New Perspective

25. E. P. Sanders, "Preface to the 40th Anniversary Edition," in *Paul and Palestinian Judaism* (2017), xxvii–xxviii, n. 1. But as one reviewer states of this work, "Readers may wish to know what Sanders makes of the apocalyptic Paul, intertextuality, rhetorical criticism, 'empire' criticism, or even the various permutations of the 'new perspective on Paul' that Sanders himself is credited with launching. Yet none of this factors significantly in the book's discourse." Garwood Anderson, review of *Paul: The Apostle's Life, Letters, and Thought*, by E. P. Sanders, *Int* 71 (2017): 434–36, here 435.

26. Issue 5 (2018).

27. Anders Runesson, "*Paul and Palestinian Judaism*: A Milestone in New Testament and Early Jewish Studies," *JJMJS* 5 (2018): 1–3.

28. "The New Perspective on Paul," *BJRL* 65 (1983): 95–122; reprinted in Dunn, *Jesus, Paul, and the Law: Studies in Mark and Galatians* (Louisville: Westminster John Knox, 1990), chap. 7; and in Dunn, *New Perspective*, chap. 2.

29. N. T. Wright, "The Paul of History and the Apostle of Faith," *TynBul* 29 (1978): 61–88, here 64; Stendahl, "Introspective Conscience," 214; cf. Dunn, *New Perspective*, 7n24.

on Paul (NPP) is not really new at all, since it is Paul's own perspective[30] that highlights teachings he considered central to justification and that largely had been ignored among contemporary perceptions of Paul.[31] Not only do Wright and Dunn disagree with Sanders's Paul, but also they do not agree with each other on various points.[32] Discussions and criticisms on the NPP, then, must take into account both the similarities and differences among its authors.

Dunn in his NPP article, and again in his other publications that followed,[33] proposed that Sanders's conclusion regarding Second Temple Judaism (STJ) was correct though overstated. Contrary to Sanders, however, Dunn asserts that Paul maintained a sense of continuity with his Jewishness. Paul's language of law and justification is to be understood within the social context of his gentile mission. The central point of his letters regarding these issues was that the gospel is about salvation in Christ for all, Jews and gentiles, and the latter are not to be excluded from belonging to God's people, despite their nonobservance of Jewish customs. For Dunn, Paul's mentioning of the "works of the law" centers on boundary markers related to Jewish pride and exclusivism, such as circumcision and food laws. These markers became important in the Maccabean era during Hellenist attacks on the Jews, and as such they focused on "Israel's distinctiveness and made visible Israel's claims to be a people set apart, [and they] were the clearest points which differentiated the Jews from the nations. The law was coterminous with Judaism."[34] For Paul's opponents, to be elect as a Jew meant to take

30. Affirmed in the recent study by Matthew J. Thomas, *Paul's "Works of the Law" in the Perspective of Second Century Reception*, WUNT 2/468 (Tübingen: Mohr Siebeck, 2018).

31. James D. G. Dunn, "A New Perspective on the New Perspective," *EC* 4 (2013): 157–82, here 157.

32. See, e.g., James D. G. Dunn, "An Insider's Perspective on Wright's Version of the New Perspective on Paul," in *God and the Faithfulness of Paul: A Critical Examination of the Pauline Theology of N. T. Wright*, ed. Christoph Heilig, J. Thomas Hewitt, and Michael F. Bird, WUNT 2/413 (Tübingen: Mohr Siebeck, 2016; Minneapolis: Fortress, 2017), 347–58; N. T. Wright, foreword to *Jesus and Paul: Global Perspectives in Honor of James D. G. Dunn for His 70th Birthday*, ed. B. J. Oropeza, C. K. Robertson, and Douglas C. Mohrmann, LNTS 414 (London: T&T Clark, 2009), xv–xx. Dunn and Wright engage each other in in "An Evening Conversation on Paul with James D. G. Dunn and N. T. Wright," ed. Mark M. Mattison, *The Paul Page*, October 16, 2009 (updated March 25, 2016), http://www.thepaulpage.com/an-evening-conversation-on -paul-with-james-d-g-dunn-and-n-t-wright/. On Wright's ambivalence about the New Perspective, see, e.g., N. T. Wright, "Communion and *Koinonia*: Pauline Reflection on Tolerance and Boundaries," in *Pauline Perspectives: Essays on Paul, 1978–2013* (Minneapolis: Fortress, 2013), 257; Chancey, foreword to *Paul and Palestinian Judaism*, xxii–xxiii.

33. A number are reprinted in Dunn, *New Perspective*.

34. Dunn, "Works of the Law and the Curse of the Law (Galatians 3.10–14)," *NTS* 31 (1985): 526; this essay is reprinted in Dunn, *Jesus, Paul, and the Law*, 215–41. Garlington, who

one's righteousness for granted, and the apostle comes against this attitude by proclaiming salvation by faith in Christ alone and that his gentile converts do not need to become Jewish proselytes in order to be saved. Even so, Dunn has repeatedly clarified that "works of the law" has a broader meaning than the boundary markers; this term refers to "what the law requires, the conduct prescribed by the Torah; whatever the law requires to be done can be described as 'doing' the law, as work of the law."[35] The clarification is important since repeated characterizations of his position wrongly limit his meaning to "boundary markers." In the context of gentile mission, when gentiles are being compelled to become Jews, however, the works of the law more specifically center on that which divides Jews from gentiles, and hence boundary markers come to the foreground.[36]

In his monumental *The Theology of Paul the Apostle*,[37] Dunn, along with doing other things, reaffirms and elaborates on the New Perspective, suggesting that interpreting Paul in this light helps combat that type of racism and nationalism that has "distorted and diminished Christianity past and present."[38] More recently he writes that the NPP does not seek to replace the "Old Perspective" but endeavors to have all factors be included and carefully considered in Paul's theology of justification. This includes four prominent points. First, the "new perspective" on Judaism views it in terms of covenantal nomism—though with an accent on the "nomism." Second, although it emphasizes the inclusion of gentiles with Jews, Paul's gospel mission was for all who believe. Third, in the history of Christian faith, Paul initially set justification in opposition to works of the law as a result of Jewish believers requiring gentile believers to live like Jews. And fourth, the *whole* gospel should be featured in relation to Pauline soteriology, "warts and all," not just parts that do not create tensions or inconsistences for the interpreter. Such aspects include (1) justification by faith *in* Christ (rather than Christ's faith); (2) readiness with Paul to cut through the "letter" (surface reference) of the law to the principles underlying it that determine faith's conduct; (3) attention to justification according to works, which encourages good works while warning against moral failure and holding final salvation in some sense contingent upon faithfulness; and (4) a holding

---

draws attention to this point, adds that such markers "became *the acid tests of one's loyalty to Judaism.*" Garlington, "The New Perspective on Paul," 4 (emphasis original).

35. Dunn, *New Perspective*, 23–24; cf. 25–28.

36. See Dunn, "New Perspective on the New Perspective," 174–75.

37. Grand Rapids: Eerdmans, 1998.

38. Summary from Dunn, *New Perspective*, 16–17.

together of both the imagery of forensic justification and participation in Christ.[39]

N. T. Wright generally concurs with Sanders's assessment of STJ, and he argues that Paul's problem with the Judaism that he encounters involves a social dimension. It was caught up in "national righteousness," an expression also used by Dunn; it held that "fleshly Jewish descent guarantees membership of God's true covenant people."[40] Wright describes his "Romans" moment in 1976: He was reading particularly Romans 10:3, where Paul says that his fellow Jews, not knowing God's righteousness, seek to establish their own righteousness. Wright considered that "their own righteousness" was not "in the sense of a *moral* status based on the *performance* of Torah and the consequent accumulation of a treasury of merit, but an *ethnic* status based on the *possession* of Torah as the sign of automatic covenant membership."[41] He agrees with Dunn that "works of the law" identifies Jew over gentile with badges such as Sabbath, circumcision, and food laws.[42] He also finds that justification in Paul normally appears in the context of Jew and gentile coming together and/or his criticism of Judaism.[43]

Valuing the role that Scripture plays in Paul's thinking, Wright posits that God had established a covenant with Abraham as the proper venue to deal with evil, but Abraham's family tragically shared in the evil. Israel was to be the light of the world and deal with what is wicked, but instead of fulfilling this role to the nations, the people treated their vocation as their exclusive privilege.[44] This became for the people a sin, and Torah enticed Israel to national righteousness.[45] Hence, the Israel of Paul's day is suffering exile based on prophetic declarations, and due to their being in sin,

---

39. Dunn, "New Perspective on the New Perspective," 157–82. On this final aspect along with stress on the Holy Spirit, see Dunn, "The Gospel according to St. Paul," in *The Blackwell Companion to Paul*, ed. Stephen Westerholm (Chichester: Wiley-Blackwell, 2014), 139–53.
40. Wright, "The Paul of History," 65. A collection of Wright's essays conveniently appears in Wright, *Pauline Perspectives*. See also *NTWrightPage*, http://www.ntwrightpage.com.
41. N. T. Wright, "New Perspectives on Paul," paper presented at the 10th Edinburgh Dogmatics Conference, Rutherford House, August 25–28, 2003, 1–17, here 2 (emphasis original, though the quotation was posed as a question).
42. Wright, "New Perspectives"; cf. N. T. Wright, *The Climax of the Covenant: Christ and the Law in Pauline Theology* (Edinburgh: T&T Clark, 1991; Minneapolis: Fortress, 1992), 242–43; Wright, *What Saint Paul Really Said: Was Paul of Tarsus the Real Founder of Christianity?* (Grand Rapids: Eerdmans, 1997), 132; Wright, *Paul and the Faithfulness of God*, 2:1034–35.
43. Wright, "New Perspectives," 3.
44. N. T. Wright, *Paul: In Fresh Perspective* (Minneapolis: Fortress, 2005), 36–37.
45. Wright, *Climax of the Covenant*, 242–43.

they are under covenant curse (Deut. 27–30). Jewish occupation by Rome is a constant reminder of this.[46] But Jesus the Messiah is to be the people's restorer in whom the blessing of covenant renewal takes place and extends to the nations. His death on the cross deals the final blow to sin and the curse of the people; he is their representative.[47] Christ is also to be ruler of the world, causing political implications with the Roman Empire and its imperial ideology.

For Wright, righteousness (δικαιωσύνη, *dikaiosynē*) can be interpreted along the lines of covenant membership,[48] and to be justified identifies the believing person as a covenant member of God's family, a single people of all nations inclusive of Israel. This is God's verdict on whoever is genuinely God's people.[49] Wright adds further that final judgment is on the basis of works, which are to be taken seriously; these works are things showing that one is "in Christ" and obedient to the Spirit's leading.[50] Justification by faith, then, is courtroom language of the "*anticipation in the present* of the justification which will occur in the future,"[51] on the ground of "the entirety of the life led."[52] Wright clarifies:

> Justification is not "how someone becomes a Christian." It is God's declaration about the person who has just become a Christian. And, just as the final declaration will consist, not of words so much as of an event, namely the resurrection of the person concerned into a glorious body like that of the risen Jesus, so the present declaration consists, not so much of words, though words there may be, but of an event, the event in which one dies with the Messiah and rises to new life with him, anticipating that final resurrection. In other words, baptism.[53]

---

46. See, e.g., Wright, *Paul and the Faithfulness of God*, 1:150; 2:1036, 1165; cf. 1:139–63; Wright, *Climax of the Covenant*, 141.

47. See, e.g., Wright, *Climax of the Covenant*, 141, 154; cf. Wright, *What Saint Paul Really Said*, 51; Wright, *Paul and the Faithfulness of God*, 2:943–44, 999–1000.

48. Wright, *Climax of the Covenant*, 203. "Righteousness of God" is understood by Wright as "God's covenant faithfulness" ("New Perspectives," 5). See also Wright, *Justification: God's Plan and Paul's Vision* (London: SPCK, 2009), 116, 133–34.

49. Wright, *Justification*, 116, 121; Wright, *Paul and the Faithfulness of God*, 2:960–61. On Rom. 4:3–5 interpreted along this line, see N. T. Wright, "Paul and the Patriarch: The Role of Abraham in Romans 4," *JSNT* 35 (2013): 207–41.

50. Indeed, justification is grounded in Christ; see N. T. Wright, "Justification: Yesterday, Today, Forever," *JETS* 54 (2011): 49–63, here 62.

51. Wright, "New Perspectives," 9–10 (emphasis original); further, Wright, *Paul and the Faithfulness of God*, 2:1030–32.

52. Dunn and Wright, "An Evening Conversation," 4; similarly, Wright, *Justification*, 251; Wright, *Paul: In Fresh Perspective*, 57.

53. Wright, "New Perspectives," 14.

In response to assumptions that Wright considers works as the basis (rather than evidence) of salvation and thus makes "faith alone" questionable,[54] Wright insists that his view is in accord with traditional Protestant Reformed theology.[55] He also clarifies that how a person is saved or justified should not be polarized against how Jews and gentiles may come together without necessity of the latter being circumcised. Likewise, there is both juridical and participatory ("in Christ") language in Paul.[56]

Some common tenets generally shared by New Perspective scholars are as follows.[57] First, there is sensitivity toward Judaism and how it is to be perceived by Christians. Second, STJ is generally perceived not in terms of legalism but in terms of grace, election, and covenantal nomism. Third, the pre-Damascus Paul had problems with pride and privilege rather than inner struggles with guilt and sin. Fourth, the social dimension of Paul's mission to the gentiles is featured. Fifth, whereas distinctive practices such as circumcision demarcated STJ, Paul rejected such particularisms for his gentile churches in favor of righteousness, faith, love, and obedience. Sixth, there is interest in highlighting righteousness related to participation in Christ. Seventh, New Perspective scholars insist that interpretations based on biblical and ancient historical examination carry more weight than traditional and theological dogmas when it comes to interpreting Paul. In addition, six benefits related to studying the NPP are worth repeating:[58] (1) a better understanding of Paul's Letters; (2) avoidance of individualistic Western perception; (3) reduction of anti-Semitism and anti-Judaism; (4) more continuity between Old Testament and New Testament; (5) more continuity between Jesus and Paul; (6) more continuity between Roman Catholics and Protestants over justification.

54. E.g., John Piper, *The Future of Justification: A Response to N. T. Wright* (Wheaton: Crossway, 2007); see further Alan P. Stanley, introduction to *Four Views on the Role of Works at the Final Judgment*, by Robert N. Wilkin et al., ed. Alan P. Stanley (Grand Rapids: Zondervan, 2013), 9–24, here 20; also discussion in Michael F. Bird, "What Is There between Minneapolis and St. Andrews? A Third Way in the Piper-Wright Debate," *JETS* 54 (2011): 299–309.

55. Wright, *Justification*; Wright, "Justification"; see further Stanley, introduction to *Four Views on the Role of Works*, 20–23.

56. Dunn and Wright, "An Evening Conversation," 7; cf. Wright, *Paul and the Faithfulness of God*, 2:1038–39.

57. Different and overlapping lists are also given in Brendan Byrne, "Interpreting Romans Theologically in a Post-'New Perspective' Perspective," *HTR* 94 (2001): 227–41, here 228–29; Byrne, "Interpreting Romans: The New Perspective and Beyond," *Int* 58 (2004): 241–51, here 245–47.

58. On these benefits, see Yinger, *New Perspective*, 87–93.

Responses to the New Perspective: Positive and Negative

A complete survey of supporters and works sympathetic toward the New Perspective is beyond the scope of this study.[59] Even so, three influential scholars are worth mentioning in this category. Terence L. Donaldson, who agrees with Sanders's covenantal nomism, advances studies on the gentiles and Paul's core convictions that provide the framework for his thinking.[60] Don Garlington stresses the obedience of faith and the importance of perseverance for followers of Christ needed during the "now and not yet" interim of justification and final judgment.[61] Kent Yinger focuses on the importance of final judgment in relation to justification, and he addresses the issues of Jewish legalism and synergism as factors in the debate between Old and New Perspectives.[62] Such studies represent a continued interest in scholarship over issues related to Paul and the gentile problem,[63] and covenant nomism and the pattern of "getting in" and "staying in" in light of

59. For supporters, see, e.g., scholars mentioned in Westerholm, "The 'New Perspective' at Twenty-Five," 13–17; on *The Paul Page*, see "Bibliography," http://www.thepaulpage.com/new -perspective/bibliography/; "From the New Perspective," http://www.thepaulpage.com/new -perspective/around-the-web/articles-from-the-new-perspective/. On recent ethical, ethnic, and gender studies related to the NPP, see, e.g., Scot McKnight and Joseph B. Modica, eds. *The Apostle Paul and the Christian Life: Ethical and Missional Implications of the New Perspective* (Grand Rapids: Baker Academic, 2016); Jens-Christian Maschmeier, "Justification and Ethics: Theological Consequences of a New Perspective on Paul," *TR* 38 (2017): 35–53; Maschmeier, *Rechtfertigung bei Paulus: Eine Kritik alter und neuer Paulusperspektiven*, BWANT 189 (Stuttgart: Kohlhammer, 2010); Kobus Kok, "The New Perspective on Paul and Its Implication for Ethics and Mission," *APB* 21 (2010): 3–17; Friedrich Wilhelm Horn, "Die Darstellung und Begründung der Ethik des Apostels Paulus in der *new perspective*," in *Jenseits von Indikativ und Imperativ*, ed. Friedrich Wilhelm Horn and Ruben Zimmermann, KNNE 1, WUNT 238 (Tübingen: Mohr Siebeck, 2009), 213–31; Tet-Lim N. Yee, *Jews, Gentiles, and Ethnic Reconciliation: Paul's Jewish Identity and Ephesians*, SNTSMS 130 (Cambridge: Cambridge University Press, 2005); Kathy Ehrensperger, *That We May Be Mutually Encouraged: Feminism and the New Perspective in Pauline Studies* (London: T&T Clark, 2004).

60. Terence L. Donaldson, *Paul and the Gentiles: Remapping the Apostle's Convictional World* (Minneapolis: Fortress, 1997). More recently, see Donaldson, *Judaism and the Gentiles: Jewish Patterns of Universalism (to 135 CE)* (Waco: Baylor University Press, 2007); Donaldson, "'Gentile Christianity' as a Category in the Study of Christian Origins," *HTR* 106 (2013): 433–58.

61. Don Garlington, *"The Obedience of Faith": A Pauline Phrase in Historical Context*, WUNT 2/38 (Tübingen: Mohr Siebeck, 1991); Garlington, *Faith, Obedience, and Perseverance: Aspects of Paul's Letter to the Romans*, WUNT 79 (Tübingen: Mohr/Siebeck, 1994); Garlington, *Studies in the New Perspective*.

62. Kent L. Yinger, *Paul, Judaism, and Judgment according to Deeds*, SNTSMS 105 (Cambridge: Cambridge University Press, 1999); Yinger, "The Continuing Quest for Jewish Legalism," *BBR* 19 (2009): 375–91; Yinger, "Reformation Redivivus: Synergism and the New Perspective," *JTI* 3 (2009): 89–106; Yinger, *New Perspective*.

63. See, e.g., our discussion of Paul within Judaism below.

tensions between divine and human agencies,[64] perseverance and apostasy,[65] justification and final judgment.[66]

Nevertheless, the NPP has gained many critics over the years.[67] Critics frequently come from traditional Protestant backgrounds that place emphasis on

64. E.g., John M. G. Barclay and Simon J. Gathercole, eds., *Divine and Human Agency in Paul and His Cultural Environment*, LNTS 335 (London: T&T Clark, 2007); Preston M. Sprinkle, *Paul and Judaism Revisited: A Study of Divine and Human Agency in Salvation* (Downers Grove, IL: IVP Academic, 2013); Kyle B. Wells, *Grace and Agency in Paul and Second Temple Judaism: Interpreting the Transformation of the Heart*, NovTSup 157 (Leiden: Brill, 2015); Jason Maston, *Divine and Human Agency in Second Temple Judaism and Paul: A Comparative Study*, WUNT 2/297 (Tübingen: Mohr Siebeck, 2010); Yinger, "Reformation Redivivus"; Paul A. Rainbow, *The Way of Salvation: The Role of Christian Obedience in Justification*, PBM (Milton Keynes: Paternoster, 2005).

65. E.g., B. J. Oropeza, *Jews, Gentiles, and the Opponents of Paul: The Pauline Letters*, vol. 2 of *Apostasy in the New Testament Communities* (Eugene, OR: Cascade; Wipf & Stock, 2012); Oropeza, *Paul and Apostasy: Eschatology, Perseverance, and Falling Away in the Corinthian Congregation*, WUNT 2/115 (Tübingen: Mohr Siebeck, 2000; Eugene, OR: Wipf & Stock, 2007); Judith M. Gundry Volf, *Paul and Perseverance: Staying In and Falling Away*, WUNT 2/37 (Tübingen: Mohr Siebeck, 1990; Louisville: Westminster John Knox, 1991); Andrew Wilson, *The Warning-Assurance Relationship in 1 Corinthians*, WUNT 2/452 (Tübingen: Mohr Siebeck, 2017).

66. Chris VanLandingham, *Judgment and Justification in Early Judaism and the Apostle Paul* (Peabody, MA: Hendrickson, 2006); Wilkin et al., *Four Views on the Role of Works*; Oropeza, *Jews, Gentiles, and the Opponents of Paul*; Christian Stettler, *Das Endgericht bei Paulus: Framesemantische und exegetische Studien zur paulinischen Eschatologie und Soteriologie*, WUNT 371 (Tübingen: Mohr Siebeck, 2017); Stettler, "Paul, the Law and Judgment by Works," *EvQ* 76 (2004): 195–215; James B. Prothro, *Both Judge and Justifier: Biblical Legal Language and the Act of Justifying in Paul*, WUNT 2/461 (Tübingen: Mohr Siebeck, 2018); Kyoung-Shik Kim, *God Will Judge Each One according to Works: Judgment according to Works and Psalm 62 in Early Judaism and the New Testament*, BZNW 178 (Berlin: de Gruyter, 2010); John M. G. Barclay, "Believers and the 'Last Judgment' in Paul: Rethinking Grace and Recompense," in *Eschatologie—Eschatology: The Sixth Durham-Tübingen Research Symposium; Eschatology in Old Testament, Ancient Judaism, and Early Christianity (Tübingen, September 2009)*, ed. Hans-Joachim Eckstein, Christof Landmesser, and Hermann Lichtenberger, WUNT 272 (Tübingen: Mohr Siebeck, 2011), 195–208; Dane C. Ortlund "Justified by Faith, Judged according to Works: Another Look at a Pauline Paradox," *JETS* 52 (2009): 323–39.

67. For a sampling (some more polemical than others), see Gitte Buch-Hansen, "Beyond the New Perspective: Reclaiming Paul's Anthropology," *ST* 71 (2017): 4–28; Yongbom Lee, "Getting In and Staying In: Another Look at 4QMMT and Galatians," *EvQ* 88 (2016/17): 126–42; Charles Lee Irons, *The Righteousness of God: A Lexical Examination of the Covenant-Faithfulness Interpretation*, WUNT 2/386 (Tübingen: Mohr Siebeck, 2015); Jordan Cooper, *The Righteousness of One: An Evaluation of Early Patristic Soteriology in Light of the New Perspective on Paul* (Eugene, OR: Wipf & Stock, 2013); Michael Morson, "Reformed, Lutheran, and 'New Perspective': A Dialogue between Traditions Regarding the Interpretation of 'Works of the Law' in Galatians," *CanTR* 1 (2012): 61–67; Andrew Hassler, "Ethnocentric Legalism and the Justification of the Individual: Rethinking Some New Perspective Assumptions," *JETS* 54 (2011): 311–27; Mark Seifrid, "The Near Word of Christ and the Distant Vision of N. T. Wright," *JETS* 54 (2011): 279–97; Thomas R. Schreiner, "An Old Perspective on the New Perspective," *ConcJ* 35 (2009): 140–55; Gerhard H. Visscher, *Romans 4 and the New Perspective on Paul: Faith Embraces the Promise*, SBL 122 (New

justification by grace through faith and the inability to secure divine approval by human merit or submission to divine law.[68] There are three prominent categories of these responses.

York: Peter Lang, 2009); Cornelis P. Venema, *The Gospel of Free Acceptance in Christ: An Assessment of the Reformation and New Perspectives on Paul* (Edinburgh: Banner of Truth Trust, 2006); Peter T. O'Brien, "Was Paul a Covenant Nomist?," in Carson, O'Brien, and Seifrid, *Justification and Variegated Nomism*, 2:249–96; Donald Macleod, "The New Perspective: Paul, Luther and Judaism," *SBET* 22 (2004): 4–31; Paul F. M. Zahl, "Mistakes of the New Perspective on Paul," *Them* 27 (2001): 5–11; Friedrich Avemarie, "Die Werke des Gesetzes im Spiegel des Jakobusbriefs: A Very Old Perspective on Paul," *ZTK* 98 (2001): 282–309; David Abernathy, "A Critique of James D. G. Dunn's View of Justification by Faith as Opposed to the 'Works of the Law,'" *LTJ* 35 (2001): 139–44; R. Barry Matlock, "Almost Cultural Studies? Reflections on the 'New Perspective' on Paul," in *Biblical Studies / Cultural Studies: The Third Sheffield Colloquium*, ed. J. Cheryl Exum and Stephen D. Moore, JSOTSup 266 (Sheffield: Sheffield Academic Press, 1998), 433–59; Timo Eskola, "Paul, Predestination and 'Covenantal Nomism': Re-Assessing Paul and Palestinian Judaism," *JSJ* 28 (1997): 390–412; Michael Bachmann, "Rechtfertigung und Gesetzeswerke bei Paulus," *TZ* 49 (1993): 1–33; C. E. B. Cranfield, "'The Works of the Law' in the Epistle to the Romans," *JSNT* 43 (1991): 89–101; Moisés Silva, "The Law and Christianity: Dunn's New Synthesis," *WTJ* 53 (1991): 339–53; Robert H. Gundry, "Grace, Works, and Staying Saved in Paul," *Bib* 66 (1985): 1–38; John M. Espy, "Paul's 'Robust Conscience' Re-Examined," *NTS* 31 (1985): 161–88. In addition, we counted 139 critiques from *Monergism* (www.monergism.com). In 2011, Yinger (*New Perspective*, 39) counted 108.

68. See, e.g., Westerholm, *Perspectives Old and New*, 408–45; cf. 88–97; more specifically on justification, Westerholm, *Justification Reconsidered: Rethinking a Pauline Theme* (Grand Rapids: Eerdmans, 2013). For recent responses from Lutheran sources, see, e.g., Stephen J. Hultgren, "The 'New Perspective on Paul': Exegetical Problems and Historical-Theological Questions, *LTJ* 50 (2016): 70–86; Michael Bachmann, "Lutherische oder Neue Paulusperspektive? Merkwürdigkeiten bei der Wahrnehmung der betreffende exegetischen Diskussionen," *BZ* 60 (2016): 73–101; Bachmann, ed., *Lutherische und neue Paulusperspektive: Beiträge zu einem Schlüsselproblem der gegenwärtigen exegetischen Diskussion*, WUNT 182 (Tübingen: Mohr Siebeck, 2005); Timothy J. Wengert, "The 'New' Perspective on Paul at the 2012 Luther Congress in Helsinki," *LQ* 27 (2013): 89–91; Jens Schröter, "'The New Perspective on Paul'— eine Anfrage an die lutherische Paulusdeutung?," *Lutherjahrbuch* 80 (2013): 142–58; Notger Slenczka, "Die neue Paulusperspektive und die Lutherische Theologie," *Lutherjahrbuch* 80 (2013): 184–96; David C. Ratke, ed., *The New Perspective on Paul* (Minneapolis: Lutheran University Press, 2012); Erik M. Heen, "A Lutheran Response to the New Perspective on Paul," *LQ* 24 (2010): 263–91.

For responses from other churches/denominations (whether constructive, critical, or polemical), see, e.g., Lekgantshi C. Tleane, "N. T. Wright's New Perspective on Paul: What Implications for Anglican Doctrine?," *HTSTS* 74 (2018): 1–9; Athanasios Despotis, ed., *Participation, Justification, and Conversion: Eastern Orthodox Interpretation of Paul and the Debate between "Old and New Perspectives on Paul,"* WUNT 2/442 (Tübingen: Mohr Siebeck, 2017); Despotis, *Die "New Perspective on Paul" und die griechisch-orthodoxe Paulusinterpretation*, VIOT 11 (St. Ottilien: EOS-Verlag, 2014); Tara Beth Leach, "A Symphonic Melody: Wesleyan-Holiness Theology Meets New-Perspective Paul," in *The Apostle Paul and the Christian Life: Ethical and Missional Implications of the New Perspective*, ed. Scot McKnight and Joseph B. Modica (Grand Rapids: Baker Academic, 2016), 153–78; Sungkook Jung, "The New Perspective on Paul and Korean Evangelical Responses: Assessment and Suggestions," *JAET* 19 (2015): 21–41; Thomas D. Stegman, "Paul's Use of *dikaio-* Terminology: Moving beyond N. T. Wright's Forensic Interpretation," *TS* 72 (2011): 496–524; S. M. Baugh, "The New Perspective, Mediation,

First, there are criticisms related to Sanders's interpretation of Second Temple Judaism.[69] Contrary to Sanders's tendency for the nationalistic election and salvation of Israel, Mark Adam Elliott argues from STJ, minus rabbinic literature, that the sources often provide evidence only for a remnant of Israel being saved.[70] Simon J. Gathercole takes issue with Sanders's lack of focusing on *final* vindication when STJ sources bear out the importance of obedience as the condition and ground for Jewish confidence at final judgment. Romans 1–5 is then said to criticize a soteriology related to keeping the law to be saved at the eschaton.[71] Chris VanLandingham contests Sanders's connection between grace and election for STJ. What is evident in these sources is "reward for obedience to God's will, not the unmerited gift of God's grace."[72] The two-volume compilation edited by D. A. Carson, Peter T. O'Brien, and Mark A. Seifrid, *Justification and Variegated Nomism*,[73] is perhaps the most ambitious response of this sort. The contributors in volume 1 set out to examine STJ to assess whether various texts teach covenant nomism as Sanders proposes. Volume 1 assesses various theological aspects relevant to the NPP. The conclusion of this work asserts that STJ is more variegated than Sanders had proposed. Although several of the contributors found covenant nomism to be a useful category for the sources they examined, the conclusion of the monograph has it that Sanders is "wrong when he tries to establish that his category is right everywhere."[74] More recently, John Barclay concedes to grace being pervasively found in STJ, though quite more diverse than Sanders proposed. For Barclay, grace is everywhere present in the literature but not everywhere the same.[75]

and Justification," in *Covenant, Justification, and Pastoral Ministry: Essays by the Faculty of Westminster Seminary California*, ed. R. Scott Clark (Phillipsburg, NJ: P&R, 2007), 137–63; Guy Prentiss Waters, *Justification and the New Perspectives on Paul: A Review and Response* (Phillipsburg, NJ: P&R, 2004); Theodor Stoychev, "Is There a New Perspective on St. Paul's Theology?," *JEBS* 11 (2001): 31–50.

69. See also, e.g., Friedrich Avemarie, *Tora und Leben: Untersuchungen zur Heilsbedeutung der Tora in der frühen rabbinischen Literatur*, TSAJ 55 (Tübingen: Mohr Siebeck, 1996); A. Andrew Das, *Paul, the Law, and the Covenant* (Peabody, MA: Hendrickson, 2001), 1–69; Das, "Paul and Works of Obedience in Second Temple Judaism: Romans 4:4–5 as a 'New Perspective' Case Study," *CBQ* 71 (2009): 795–812; Sigurd Grindheim, *The Crux of Election: Paul's Critique of the Jewish Confidence in the Election of Israel*, WUNT 2/202 (Tübingen: Mohr Siebeck, 2005); Charles L. Quarles, "The New Perspective and Means of Atonement in Jewish Literature of the Second Temple Period," *CTR* 2 (2005): 39–56.

70. Mark Adam Elliott, *The Survivors of Israel: A Reconsideration of the Theology of Pre-Christian Judaism* (Grand Rapids: Eerdmans, 2000).

71. Simon J. Gathercole, *Where Is Boasting? Early Jewish Soteriology and Paul's Response in Romans 1–5* (Grand Rapids: Eerdmans, 2002), 33, 90, 159, 194, 214–15.

72. VanLandingham, *Judgment and Justification*, 333.

73. Tübingen: Mohr Siebeck; Grand Rapids: Baker Academic, 2001, 2004.

74. D. A. Carson, "Conclusion," in *Justification and Variegated Nomism*, 2:543.

75. John M. G. Barclay, *Paul and the Gift* (Grand Rapids: Eerdmans, 2015), e.g., 319.

Second, a number of critiques focus on the New Perspective's interpretation of Paul's Letters. Stephen Westerholm categorizes scholarly criticisms into five groups.[76] One group of interpreters argues that Paul's own view is contradictory or distorts Jewish evidence.[77] Another set believes that Paul's view may be compatible with certain Jewish traditions, and both Paul and these traditions determine that other Jews did not live up to covenant requirement for righteousness.[78] Others argue that Christ's atonement either added reality behind Judaic atonement or invalidated it.[79] Others emphasize anthropological pessimism; humans who are not transformed are simply too corrupt to be obedient and contribute to salvation.[80] A final group believes that "Paul found it important *in principle* that human beings rely exclusively on divine goodness for all their needs—and he deemed Judaism, in its reliance on 'works,' to have departed from this principle."[81] Westerholm himself argues that righteousness in Paul is not primarily about covenant language; righteousness by faith is about what sinners lack and what is unmerited. Romans 4:4–6 and 5:7–9, for example, cannot be about what humans have done; what they have done is sinned, and transgression brings about curse, since none can obey all that is written in the law. Paul insists that humans "are sinners who do not, and cannot, do the good that the law demands of its subjects."[82] As such, Paul "based his case not on the impracticability of imposing Jewish practices on Gentiles, nor indeed on a charge of ethnocentricity brought against the Jews who thought Gentiles ought to live as they did, but on the inability of

76. Westerholm, "The 'New Perspective' at Twenty-Five," 17–18.

77. Heikki Räisänen, *Paul and the Law*, 2nd ed., WUNT 29 (Tübingen: Mohr Siebeck, 1986); Kari Kuula, *The Law, the Covenant, and God's Plan*, vol. 2, *Paul's Polemical Treatment of the Law in Galatians*, PFES 85 (Göttingen: Vandenhoeck & Ruprecht, 1999).

78. Frank Thielman, *From Plight to Solution: A Jewish Framework for Understanding Paul's View of the Law in Galatians and Romans*, NTS 41 (Leiden: Brill, 1989); Timo Eskola, *Theodicy and Predestination in Pauline Soteriology*, WUNT 2/100 (Tübingen: Mohr Siebeck, 1998).

79. Thomas R. Schreiner, *The Law and Its Fulfillment: A Pauline Theology of Law* (Grand Rapids Baker, 1993); Das, *Paul, the Law, and the Covenant*. But technically, Das opts for a "newer" perspective (see below, his essay "The Traditional Protestant Perspective on Paul"), which arguably can place him among proponents of the more recent trend below.

80. E.g., Mark A. Seifrid, *Justification by Faith: The Origin and Development of a Central Pauline Theme*, NovTSup 68 (Leiden: Brill, 1992); Seifrid, *Christ, Our Righteousness: Paul's Theology of Justification* (Downers Grove, IL: InterVarsity, 2000); Peter Stuhlmacher, *Revisiting Paul's Doctrine of Justification: A Challenge to the New Perspective* (Downers Grove, IL: InterVarsity, 2001); Timo Laato, *Paul and Judaism: An Anthropological Approach*, trans. T. McElwain, SFSHJ 15 (Atlanta: Scholars Press, 1995).

81. Westerholm, "The 'New Perspective' at Twenty-Five," 18 (emphasis original). See, e.g., Seyoon Kim, *Paul and the New Perspective: Second Thoughts on the Origin of Paul's Gospel* (Grand Rapids: Eerdmans, 2002).

82. Westerholm, *Perspectives Old and New*, 444; similarly 333.

the law to cope with human sin."[83] Gentiles and Jews "are declared righteous by faith in Jesus Christ *apart from* the law (cf. Gal. 2:21; 5:4; Rom. 3:1) and its works (Gal. 2:16; Rom. 3:20, 28)."[84] Even so, Westerholm concedes with the NPP that ancient Judaism on its own terms did not seem to "promote a self-righteous pursuit of salvation by works,"[85] and he affirms that the NPP has made an important contribution to Pauline studies.[86]

A third manner of critique involves monographs or journals in which other scholars evaluate NPP topics or a work by a NPP proponent, who then responds.[87] The monograph *God and the Faithfulness of Paul: A Critical Examination of the Pauline Theology of N. T. Wright*[88] assesses Wright's tome *Paul and the Faithfulness of God*. In the final chapter of the critique Wright responds to the contributors. Similarly, various scholars assess Wright's view of Israel remaining in exile in *Exile: A Conversation with N. T. Wright*.[89] Wright contributes two chapters to the volume, the second one a response. Similarly, various essays in German or English assess the NPP in *Lutherische und Neue Paulusperpektive* (Lutheran and new Pauline perspective).[90] James Dunn responds in the final chapter. In the *Journal for the Study of the New Testament* Barry Matlock and Douglas Campbell write critiques of Dunn's *Theology of the Apostle Paul*, and Dunn responds.[91] A common misconception about the NPP is that it is attempting to overthrow Lutheran, Reformed, or Reformation theology. Both Wright and Dunn deny this.[92] Rather, as biblical scholars, they endeavor to refine Paul's theology through the rigors of their discipline rather than simply adhere to dogmas that may not be properly sustainable in Paul's Letters.

83. Westerholm, *Perspectives Old and New*, 441.
84. Westerholm, *Perspectives Old and New*, 442 (emphasis original).
85. Westerholm, *Perspectives Old and New*, 444.
86. Westerholm, *Perspectives Old and New*, 445.
87. Apart from the main text, other important NPP responses to critics include Dunn, *New Perspective*, esp. 1–97; Garlington, *Studies in the New Perspective*; Yinger, *New Perspective*, 47–80. For various contributor viewpoints (both for and against the NPP), see James D. G. Dunn, ed., *Paul and the Mosaic Law*, WUNT 89 (Tübingen: Mohr Siebeck, 1996); Wilkin et al., *Four Views on the Role of Works*; Beilby and Eddy, *Justification: Five Views*.
88. Christopher Heilig, J. Thomas Hewitt, and Michael F. Bird, eds., WUNT 2/413 (Tübingen: Mohr Siebeck, 2016; Minneapolis: Fortress, 2017).
89. James M. Scott, ed. (Downers Grove, IL: IVP Academic, 2017). See also Wright's interaction with various contributors in Nicholas Perrin and Richard B. Hays, eds. *Jesus, Paul and the People of God: A Theological Dialogue with N. T. Wright* (Downers Grove, IL: IVP Academic, 2011).
90. Michael Bachmann, ed., subtitled *Beiträge zu einem Schlüsselproblem der gegenwärtigen exegetischen Diskussion*, WUNT 182 (Tübingen: Mohr Siebeck, 2005).
91. *JSNT* 21 (1998): 67–90 (Matlock); 91–111 (Campbell); 113–20 (Dunn).
92. See, e.g., Wright, *Justification*; Dunn, *New Perspective*, 18–23; Dunn and Wright, "An Evening Conversation," 2. Further questions about the NPP are recently answered by various scholars in "The New Perspective on Paul," *Overthinking Christian*, www.overthinkingchristian.com/?s=new+perspective.

In an overlooked rapprochement, Dunn and Westerholm wrote back-to-back essays commending each other's viewpoints, entitled, respectively, "What's Right about the Old Perspective on Paul" and "What's Right about the New Perspective on Paul."[93] For Dunn, Luther's rediscovering of the saving righteousness of God, his reasserting of faith's essential role in human-divine relationships, and his emphasis that humans cannot achieve that relationship with God on their own efforts are among positive "Old Perspective" features. For Westerholm, the importance of grace in Judaism, emphasis on the social setting of Jew/gentile relationships, and sensitivity regarding the practical implications of justification, such as with class, gender, and ethnicity, are among the positive NPP features.

Post-New Perspectives

While NPP advocates and critics remain, its influence presses other scholars to reconceptualize relevant Pauline texts and make their own points of departure or rapprochement. This more recent development has been identified as "post-new perspective" or "beyond new perspective."[94] We now turn to some significant examples.

The "Paul within Judaism Perspective," also called the "radical" new perspective on Paul,[95] is promoted by scholars such as Mark Nanos,[96] Paula

93. In *Studies in the Pauline Epistles: Essays in Honor of Douglas J. Moo*, ed. Matthew S. Harmon and Jay E. Smith (Grand Rapids: Zondervan, 2014), 214–29 (Dunn); 230–42 (Westerholm).
94. The term is used by, e.g., Garlington, *Studies in the New Perspective*, 1; Byrne, "Interpreting Romans Theologically in a Post-'New Perspective' Perspective"; Michael F. Bird, "When the Dust Finally Settles: Reaching a Post-New Perspective," *CTR* 2 (2005): 57–69, though the latter two change their terminology in later publications to "beyond new perspective": Byrne, "Interpreting Romans: The New Perspective and Beyond"; Bird, *Saving Righteousness*, chap. 5, "When the Dust Finally Settles: Beyond the New Perspective."
95. Mark D. Nanos, introduction to *Paul within Judaism: Restoring the First-Century Context to the Apostle*, ed. Mark D. Nanos and Magnus Zetterholm (Minneapolis: Fortress, 2015), 1–29, here 1; Pamela Eisenbaum, "Paul, Polemics, and the Problem with Essentialism," *BibInt* 13 (2005): 224–38, here 232–33. For surveys, see Daniel R. Langton, *The Apostle Paul in the Jewish Imagination: A Study in Modern Jewish-Christian Relations* (Cambridge: Cambridge University Press, 2010); Langton, "The Myth of the 'Traditional View of Paul' and the Role of the Apostle in Modern Jewish-Christian Polemics," *JSNT* 28 (2005): 69–104; Kathy Ehrensperger, "The New Perspective and Beyond," in *Modern Interpretations of Romans: Tracking Their Hermenuetical/Theological Trajectory*, ed. Daniel Patte and Christina Grenholm, RHCS 10 (London: Bloomsbury T&T Clark, 2013), 191–219; Philip La Grange Du Toit, "The Radical New Perspective on Paul, Messianic," *HTSTS* 73 (2013): 1–8; Zetterholm, *Approaches to Paul*, 127–64; Michael F. Bird and Preston M. Sprinkle, "Jewish Interpretation of Paul in the Last Thirty Years," *CBR* 6 (2008): 355–76.
96. Mark Nanos, *The Mystery of Romans: The Jewish Context of Paul's Letter* (Minneapolis: Fortress, 1996); Nanos, *The Irony of Galatians: Paul's Letter in First-Century Context*

Fredriksen,[97] Pamela Eisenbaum,[98] Matthew Thiessen,[99] Magnus Zetterholm,[100] and others.[101] Although not uniform in all of their beliefs, supporters generally maintain that Paul always considered himself a Jew and never left Judaism or its practices after encountering Jesus as the Messiah. Paul started a reformed movement or Jewish sect within Judaism, and he was not a law-free apostle. His teachings are directed at non-Jewish followers of Christ, whom he instructs to live in consistency with Judaism, and yet he respects their identity as non-Jews. Although this perspective affirms its indebtedness to Sanders, Dunn, and Stendahl—and it rejects caricatures of Judaism as a religion of works righteousness—it does not consider itself to be "*within* the New Perspective paradigm or in reaction *against* it," but it endeavors to place Paul "within his most probable first-century context, Judaism," before having him converse with other contexts or interpretations.[102] "Paul within Judaism" disagrees with the NPP, for instance, when the latter claims that Paul found "something wrong with and in Judaism itself, something essentially different from Paul's 'Christianity' (however labeled)"; it also rejects the NPP notion

---

(Minneapolis: Fortress, 2002); and now the multivolume set subtitled *Collected Essays of Mark Nanos* (Eugene, OR: Cascade, 2017–18).

97. Paula Fredriksen, *Paul: The Pagans' Apostle* (New Haven: Yale University Press, 2017); Fredriksen, "How Jewish Is God? Divine Ethnicity in Paul's Theology," *JBL* 137 (2018): 193–212.

98. Pamela Eisenbaum, *Paul Was Not a Christian: The Original Message of a Misunderstood Apostle* (New York: HarperCollins, 2009); Eisenbaum, "Jewish Perspectives: A Jewish Apostle to the Gentiles," in *Studying Paul's Letters: Contemporary Perspectives and Methods*, ed. Joseph A. Marchal (Minneapolis: Fortress, 2012), 135–53.

99. Matthew Thiessen, *Paul and the Gentile Problem* (Oxford: Oxford University Press, 2016); Thiessen, "Conjuring Paul and Judaism Forty Years after *Paul and Palestinian Judaism*," *JJMJS* 5 (2018): 6–20. See also Rafael Rodríguez and Matthew Thiessen, eds., *The So-Called Jew in Paul's Letter to the Romans* (Minneapolis: Fortress, 2016).

100. Magnus Zetterholm, "Paul within Judaism: The State of the Questions," in Nanos and Zetterholm, *Paul within Judaism*, 31–51; Magnus Zetterholm, "'Will the Real Gentile-Christian Please Stand Up!' Torah and the Crisis of Identity Formation," in *The Making of Christianity: Conflicts, Contacts, and Constructions; Essays in Honor of Bengt Holmberg*, ed. Magnus Zetterholm and Samuel Byrskog, ConBNT 47 (Winona Lake, IN: Eisenbrauns, 2012), 391–411; Zetterholm, "Jews, Christians, and Gentiles: Rethinking the Categorization within the Early Jesus Movement," in *Reading Paul in Context: Explorations in Identity Formation; Essays in Honour of William S. Campbell*, ed. Kathy Ehrensperger and J. Brian Tucker, LNTS 428 (London: Bloomsbury T&T Clark, 2010), 242–54.

101. Fredriksen (*Paul: The Pagans' Apostle*, 177) adds recently Gabriele Boccaccini and Carlos Segovia, eds., *Paul the Jew: Reading the Apostle as a Figure of Second Temple Judaism* (Minneapolis: Fortress, 2016); John G. Gager, *Who Made Early Christianity? The Jewish Lives of the Apostle Paul* (New York: Columbia University Press, 2015); Joshua Garroway, *Paul's Gentile-Jews: Neither Jew nor Gentile, but Both* (London: Palgrave Macmillan, 2012); J. Albert Harrill, *Paul the Apostle: His Life and Legacy in Their Roman Context* (Cambridge: Cambridge University Press, 2012).

102. Nanos, introduction to *Paul within Judaism*, 2, 6 (emphasis original).

of Paul finding Judaism wrong with regard to ethnocentrism, nationalism, and related terms.[103] An apocalyptic motivation may be viewed behind Paul's urgency for gentiles against the law.[104]

If Paul within Judaism moves further away from traditional Protestantism than the NPP, another trend moves in the opposite direction by holding to a *via media* between the Old and New Perspectives on Paul. Bruce Longenecker reflects this position when writing that Lutheran and NPP advocates "make claims which suggest that if one approach has merit, the other does not. . . . However, there is good reason to think that the situation may not be so clear cut, and that the 'either-or' that marks out current polemic in Pauline scholarship might best be laid to rest."[105] He agrees with the NPP that the Galatian concern is centered not on meriting salvation through works but on community identity: "To be excluded was a form of ethnocentrism rather than self-righteousness."[106] He also agrees with the Traditional Protestant Perspective, for example, when Paul says that the law is not a proper way to life, "since human inability rendered it impossible to do the law perfectly, and since the law is powerless to correct that situation."[107] Michael Bird, in *The Saving Righteousness of God*, argues that Reformed and NPP readings of Paul provide a complementary and fuller picture of the apostle's soteriology. Bird endorses both forensic and covenantal aspects of justification, and for him "incorporated" righteousness captures justification in relation to a believer's union in Christ. More recently, Garwood Anderson's *Paul's New Perspective: Charting a Soteriological Journey* studies the disputed and undisputed Pauline letters together—and his theory depends on dating the letters of Paul—to conclude that both Old and New Perspectives are right, "but not all the time."[108] Paul's view developed from one that was compatible with the NPP regarding "works of the law" in his earlier letters (e.g., Galatians) to "works" as human effort in his later letters (e.g., Pastoral Letters). Stephen Chester's *Reading Paul with the Reformers: Reconciling Old and New Perspectives*[109] argues, inter alia, that early Reformers generally came to the same exegetical interpretation as Stendahl: the pre-Damascus Paul was *not* plagued by a guilty conscience. Such a view developed later on in the tradition. Likewise,

103. Nanos, introduction to *Paul within Judaism*, 6–7.
104. A central tenet, e.g., in Eisenbaum, "Jewish Perspectives."
105. Bruce W. Longenecker, *The Triumph of Abraham's God: The Transformation of Identity in Galatians* (Edinburgh: T&T Clark, 1998), 179; cf. Longenecker, "Lifelines: Perspectives on Paul and the Law," *Anvil* 16 (1999): 125–30.
106. Longenecker, *Abraham's God*, 180.
107. Longenecker, *Abraham's God*, 180–81.
108. Downer's Grove, IL: IVP Academic, 2016 (quotation, p. 5).
109. Grand Rapids: Eerdmans, 2017.

for Reformers, union with Christ and interest in transformation were held together with Luther's alien righteousness.[110]

Differently than both perspectives, Francis Watson's *Paul, Judaism, and the Gentiles: A Sociological Approach*[111] originally was complimentary of the NPP and against the Lutheran view, but in a revision of this work—newly subtitled *Beyond the New Perspective*—he is also critical of the former.[112] Watson argues, for example, that divine agency "plays a more direct and immediate role in the Pauline 'pattern of religion' than in the Judaism" opposed by Paul, and works of the law are not boundary markers but a distinctive "way of life" for Jewish communities.[113] Paul's antithetical statements in Romans—faith / works of law—may reflect the antithesis of the church's separation from the synagogue, and this separation helps give account for why faith in Christ is "incompatible with works of the law."[114] Watson still claims, against the Lutheran view, that Judaism as legalism or works righteousness is misleading, but then again, so is the NPP notion of "Judaism as a religion of grace."[115]

Douglas Campbell's point of departure stresses an apocalyptic and participatory reading of Paul, presented most extensively in *The Deliverance of God*.[116] Among other things, he argues that Paul typically has been misread.

---

110. Chester, *Reading Paul with the Reformers*, 136–37, 360–61, 368–77, 421–22. Union with Christ is another recently recognizable theological trend: e.g., Constantine R. Campbell, *Paul and Union with Christ: An Exegetical and Theological Study* (Grand Rapids: Zondervan, 2012); Grant Macaskill, *Union with Christ in the New Testament* (Oxford: Oxford University Press, 2013); J. Todd Billings, *Union with Christ: Reframing Theology and Ministry for the Church* (Grand Rapids: Baker Academic, 2011); Robert Letham, *Union with Christ: In Scripture, History, and Theology* (Phillipsburg, NJ: P&R, 2011); Michael S. Horton, *Covenant and Salvation: Union with Christ* (Louisville: Westminster John Knox, 2007). See also Michael Gorman's works, e.g., *Participating in Christ*, and notice that the NPP, especially Sanders, reflects this perception.

111. SNTSMS 56; Cambridge: Cambridge University Press, 1986.

112. Grand Rapids: Eerdmans, 2007.

113. Watson, *Paul, Judaism, and the Gentiles* (2007), 25.

114. Watson, *Paul, Judaism, and the Gentiles* (2007), 98; cf. 60.

115. Watson, *Paul, Judaism, and the Gentiles* (2007), 346.

116. Subtitled *An Apocalyptic Reading of Justification in Paul* (Grand Rapids: Eerdmans, 2009); see also Campbell, "Beyond Justification in Paul: The Thesis of the Deliverance of God," *SJT* 65 (2012): 90–104; Campbell, "An Apocalyptic Rereading of 'Justification' in Paul," *ExpTim* 123 (2012): 182–93; Campbell, "Christ and the Church: A 'Post-New Perspective' Account," in *Four Views on the Apostle Paul*, ed. Michael F. Bird (Grand Rapids: Zondervan, 2012); and Campbell's responses in Chris Tilling, ed., *Beyond Old and New Perspectives on Paul: Reflections on the Work of Douglas Campbell* (Eugene, OR: Cascade, 2014). Prior to *The Deliverance of God*, see Campbell, *The Quest for Paul's Gospel: A Suggested Strategy*, JSNTSup 274 (London: T&T Clark, 2005). Reading Paul apocalyptically, as advanced in the last century by scholars such as Ernst Käsemann, J. Christiaan Beker, J. Louis Martyn, and Martinus de Boer, remains

This misreading, which Campbell associates with "Justification theory," focuses on retributive justification, a contractual mode of salvation, and conditional human faith rather than a liberating justification, unconditionality, and the faithfulness of Christ. For Campbell, Romans 1:17, citing Habakkuk 2:4, is not to be understood as "The righteous shall live by faith," but rather, "The Righteous One [Messiah = Jesus] by faithfulness shall live," intimating the resurrection of Christ, Christ's eschatological centrality in salvation, and his faithfulness as the means to the deliverance of God. The following passages in Romans 1–4 are said to characterize "Justification theory," and as such, they reflect mostly the beliefs of Paul's opponents, representative of a Jewish Christian "Teacher." In Campbell's view, Paul uses speech-in-character (*prosopopoeia*) here so that, for example, Romans 1:18–32 reflects the Teacher's words, which Paul contests beginning in 2:1, and the Teacher then responds to Paul, and an exchange continues from there. Paul's own view stands out prominently in Romans 5–8, which, inter alia, highlights a Triune God known through the act of redemption.

Finally, newly called "the Gift Perspective" for the present volume (see chapter 5), John Barclay presents his own view distilled from his recent work *Paul and the Gift*.[117] In that study, which has already sparked much discussion,[118] Barclay agrees with the NPP when it comes to the context of Paul's theology of justification grounded in gentile mission and "the constructions of communities that crossed ethnic (as well as social) boundaries."[119] At the same time, Barclay parts company with the NPP by locating the root of Paul's theology in the incongruous grace of the "Christ-gift that shapes his appeals to the Abrahamic promises, to the experience of the Spirit, and to the oneness of God"; in relation to the gentile mission it "demolishes old criteria of worth and clears space for innovative communities that inaugurate new patterns of social existence."[120] Barclay concludes that his reading harmonizes with neither Augustinian-Lutheran tradition nor NPP, but reshapes both.[121]

---

an important point of view in the new millennium: e.g., Joshua B. Davis and Douglas Harink, eds., *Apocalyptic and the Future of Theology: With and beyond J. Louis Martyn* (Eugene, OR: Wipf & Stock, 2012); Beverly Roberts Gaventa, ed., *Apocalyptic Paul: Cosmos and Anthropos in Romans 5–8* (Waco: Baylor University Press, 2013); Ben C. Blackwell, John K. Goodrich, and Jason Maston, eds., *Paul and the Apocalyptic Imagination* (Minneapolis: Fortress, 2016).

117. Grand Rapids: Eerdmans, 2015.

118. See, e.g., article reviews by Joel Marcus and Margaret Mitchell, and Barclay's response, in *JSNT* 39, no. 3 (2017). The entire issue of *EvQ* 89, no. 4 (2018), is also dedicated to Barclay's view.

119. Barclay, *Paul and the Gift*, 572.

120. Barclay, *Paul and the Gift*, 572.

121. Barclay, *Paul and the Gift*, 573.

Perspectives on Paul

We now present *Perspectives on Paul: Five Views*, which incorporates some of the most influential perspectives above. Five well-recognized scholars present their respective positions. Since the New Perspective responded to the "Old Perspective"—the traditional Protestant perspective influenced by Luther and other Reformers—and Luther, in turn, made his point of departure from Roman Catholicism, it is important for us to include these perspectives in the current discussion. Our first contributor, Brant Pitre, presents the Roman Catholic Perspective on Paul. Our second contributor, A. Andrew Das, presents the Protestant Perspective. Then James D. G. Dunn presents the New Perspective. Magnus Zetterholm then presents the Paul within Judaism Perspective, and finally, John Barclay finishes our viewpoints with the Gift Perspective. They each present their position, and then the other contributors provide a critique of each position. After this, each presenter concludes by replying back to these critiques. After this, Dennis Edwards concludes our study by evaluating the various perspectives from a pastoral point of view.

We hope that these stimulating perspectives and exchanges will challenge every reader to think more deeply, and perhaps even differently, about Paul and salvation.

1

The Roman Catholic Perspective on Paul

BRANT PITRE

Introduction

The current debate over the "New Perspective" on Paul arguably was launched in 1977 by E. P. Sanders's book *Paul and Palestinian Judaism*.[1] Over the years, one fascinating feature of this debate is that Sanders's interpretation has sometimes been criticized for being too "Catholic." For example, Kent Yinger points out that critics of the New Perspective on Paul (NPP) contend that it "blurs the distinction between Roman Catholic and Protestant soteriology."[2] In particular, Sanders's concept of "covenantal nomism" is singled out as dangerously close to a Catholic perspective: "*Covenantal nomism and NPP versions of salvation seem closer to Roman Catholic views than to Luther's.* They certainly highlight the role of obedience more than 'by grace alone through faith alone' would seem to do. . . . Such ecumenical union sounds to many like the clearest signal that the gains of the Reformation are being lost."[3]

---

1. E. P. Sanders, *Paul and Palestinian Judaism: A Comparison of Patterns of Religion* (Minneapolis: Fortress, 1977); 40th anniversary ed. (Minneapolis: Fortress, 2017).
2. Kent L. Yinger, *The New Perspective on Paul: An Introduction* (Eugene, OR: Cascade, 2011), 80.
3. Yinger, *New Perspective*, 80 (emphasis added).

Sanders himself was the first to draw a connection between nineteenth-century Protestant caricatures of Judaism as a legalistic religion of "works righteousness" and similar views of Catholicism: "One must note in particular the projection on to Judaism of the view which Protestants find most objectionable in Roman Catholicism: the existence of a treasury of merits established by works of supererogation. We have here the retrojection of the Protestant-Catholic debate into ancient history, with Judaism taking the role of Catholicism and Christianity the role of Lutheranism."[4]

In this essay I will seek to show that Sanders's interpretation of Paul is in fact very close to Catholic soteriology on several key points. As a Catholic, I do not see this as a weakness of Sanders's position. Instead, I would argue that Sanders's reading of Paul coheres with Catholic readings over the centuries because both are based on compelling interpretations of what Paul himself actually says. By way of illustration, my essay will have three objectives.

First, I will focus on key passages in Paul that are foundational for Catholic exegesis. Space does not permit me to address every aspect of the Catholic doctrine of justification. Instead, I will limit myself to four central issues: (1) justification as forgiveness and real participation "in Christ"; (2) initial justification by grace through faith alone; (3) the meaning of "works of the law"; and (4) final justification according to works and not by faith alone.[5]

Second, I will give a brief overview of how these key passages in Paul have been interpreted in the Catholic tradition. On the one hand, this will entail surveying what individual commentators have said in the patristic, medieval, and modern periods. On the other hand, since I have been tasked with summarizing "*The* Roman Catholic perspective on Paul," we will also need to pay attention to official Catholic teaching on justification, which can be found in three key places: (1) the Council of Trent's *Decree on Justification* (1547);[6] (2) the official *Catechism of the Catholic Church*'s article on "Grace and Justification" (1992);[7] and (3) the General Audiences of Pope Benedict XVI on Saint Paul (2008–9).[8] For readers unfamiliar with the Catholic perspective, I

---

4. *PPJ*, 57.

5. Due to limited space, I will follow Sanders in focusing on the seven undisputed Pauline Epistles.

6. All translations of the Council of Trent herein are from Heinrich Denzinger, *Compendium of Creeds, Definitions, and Declarations on Matters of Faith and Morals*, ed. Peter Hünermann, 43rd ed. (San Francisco: Ignatius, 2012), 374–88.

7. *Catechism of the Catholic Church*, 2nd ed. (Vatican City: Libreria Editrice Vaticana, 1997), nos. 1987–2029. All references to the *Catechism* herein are by paragraph numbers.

8. Pope Benedict XVI, *Saint Paul: General Audiences, July 2, 2008–February 4, 2009* (San Francisco: Ignatius, 2009).

cannot overemphasize the importance of reading these documents firsthand, with specific attention to how they interpret Paul.[9]

Third, I will highlight key areas of overlap between the Catholic perspective on Paul and the work of E. P. Sanders. One prominent Lutheran exegete recently described Sanders's work as an "assault" on "the Lutheran Paul."[10] As I hope to show, one reason Sanders has been accused of undermining the Protestant Reformation is that his exegesis of Paul unintentionally arrived at several of the same conclusions as patristic and medieval Catholic interpreters of Paul, as well as the Council of Trent. As far as I know, this kind of close comparison of Sanders and the Catholic perspective has never been done. My hope is that it will highlight common ground in the task of "rereading Paul together."[11]

Justification as Forgiveness and Real Participation "in Christ"

The first aspect of the Catholic perspective on Paul that needs to be emphasized is that justification involves both the remission of sins and a real participation in the death and resurrection of Christ. Through faith and baptism, a person is both reputed to be righteous and transformed from being a slave of sin "in Adam" to being a child of God "in Christ."

The Apostle Paul: Justification, Baptism, and Being "in Christ"

In support of this view, consider the following passages in which Paul links justification and dying and rising "in Christ," especially through baptism:[12]

> The law was our custodian until Christ came, that we might be *justified* by faith. . . . For *in Christ Jesus* you are all sons of God, through faith. For as many of you as were *baptized into Christ* have put on Christ. (Gal. 3:24–27)

9. Unfortunately, I cannot address the Lutheran World Federation and the Roman Catholic Church, *Joint Declaration on the Doctrine of Justification* (Grand Rapids: Eerdmans, 2000). Although very significant, due to its inherent complexity as a joint statement, I am unable to do justice to it here. Readers familiar with the final version will see multiple points of overlap with my conclusions. See esp. *Joint Declaration*, nos. 22, 25, 31, 37–38; Annex, nos. 2A, 2C, 2E.

10. John Reumann, "Justification by Faith in Pauline Thought: A Lutheran View," in *Rereading Paul Together: Protestant and Catholic Perspectives on Justification*, ed. David E. Aune (Grand Rapids: Baker Academic, 2006), 111.

11. See the important essay by my *Doktorvater*, David E. Aune, "Recent Readings of Paul Relating to Justification by Faith," in Aune, *Rereading Paul Together*, 188–245, esp. 241.

12. For the sake of clarity, I will follow Sanders herein in utilizing the RSV for quotations of Scripture, unless otherwise noted. All emphasis is added.

You were *washed*, you were *sanctified*, you were *justified* in the name of the
Lord Jesus Christ and in the Spirit of our God. . . . He who is *united to the
Lord* becomes one spirit with him. (1 Cor. 6:11, 17)

If any one is *in Christ, he is a new creation*. . . . All this is from God, who *through
Christ reconciled us to himself*. . . . For our sake he made him to be sin who knew no
sin, so that *in him we might become the righteousness of God*. (2 Cor. 5:17–18, 21)

As one man's trespass led to condemnation for all men, so one man's act of
righteousness leads to *acquittal and life for all men*. For as by one man's disobedience many were *made sinners*, so by one man's obedience many will be
made righteous. (Rom. 5:18–19)

Do you not know that all of us who have been *baptized into Christ Jesus* were
baptized into his death? We were buried therefore with him by baptism into
death, so that as Christ was raised from the dead by the glory of the Father,
we too might walk in newness of life. . . . *For he who has died is justified from
sin*. (Rom. 6:3–4, 7)

We will return to the specific role of faith below. For now, three observations are necessary. First, Paul repeatedly connects the noun "righteousness"
(δικαιοσύνη, *dikaiosynē*) and/or the verb "justify" (δικαιόω, *dikaioō*) with
being "in Christ" (ἐν Χριστῷ, *en Christō*) or "united to" Christ (Gal. 3:24,
26; 1 Cor. 6:11, 17; 2 Cor. 5:17, 21; Rom. 6:1–11). Second, Paul also connects
being "in Christ" with being "baptized" (βαπτίζω, *baptizō*) (Gal. 3:27; Rom.
6:3). In one case, he clearly links being "washed" in baptism with being
"sanctified" and "justified" (1 Cor. 6:11).[13] Third, justification seems to bring
about both the forgiveness of an individual's trespasses and a real change
in those who are justified. For example, just as those who engage in sexual
immorality, adultery, idolatry, theft, and so forth are actually "unrighteous"
(ἄδικοι, *adikoi*) (1 Cor. 6:9–10), so too those washed in baptism are actually
"justified" or "made righteous" (ἐδικαιώθητε, *edikaiōthēte*) (1 Cor. 6:11).
Along similar lines, just as those who are in Adam are actually "made sinners" (ἁμαρτωλοὶ κατεστάθησαν, *hamartōloi katestathēsan*), so too those
who are in Christ are actually "made righteous" (δίκαιοι κατασταθήσονται,
dikaioi katastathēsontai) (Rom. 5:19).[14] Perhaps the strongest statement of

13. See Isaac Morales, "Baptism and Union with Christ," in *"In Christ" in Paul: Explorations
in Paul's Theology of Union and Participation*, ed. Michael J. Thate, Kevin J. Vanhoozer, and
Constantine R. Campbell (Grand Rapids: Eerdmans, 2018), 151–79, here 166–68.
14. See Thomas D. Stegman, "Paul's Use of *dikaio*- Terminology: Moving beyond N. T.
Wright's Forensic Interpretation," *TS* 72 (2011): 496–524.

all is when Paul says that those who have been "reconciled" to God in Christ "become the righteousness of God" (γενώμεθα δικαιοσύνη θεοῦ, *genōmetha dikaiosynē theou*) (2 Cor. 5:21).[15] Significantly, Paul's statements about being "made righteous" (Rom. 5:19) come immediately in the wake of his discussion of the effects of "the transgression of Adam" (Rom. 5:14). In context, then, being "made righteous" involves not only the forgiveness of personal transgressions but also a transferal from the state of being in Adam to the state of being in Christ. As Paul says elsewhere, "For as *in Adam* all die, so also *in Christ* shall all be made alive" (1 Cor. 15:22).

Patristic and Medieval Interpreters: Believers "Become Righteous" in Christ

In light of such passages, several influential patristic and medieval Catholic interpreters of Paul conclude that justification involves both the forgiveness of sins and a real participation in Christ. Consider the following:[16]

> [Christ] himself is the righteousness through which all *become righteous*. . . . What [Paul] has said, "The love of God has been shed abroad into our hearts" [Rom. 5:5], needs to be carefully pondered. . . . From the fullness of the Spirit, the fullness of love is *infused into the hearts* of the saints in order to receive *participation* in the divine nature. (Origen, *Commentary on the Epistle to the Romans* 3.6.5; 4.10.11–12)[17]

> So does God also love [the believer], though deserving to suffer for countless sins, *not in freeing him from punishment only, but even by making him righteous*. (John Chrysostom, *Homilies on Romans* 8.2)[18]

> It is by "putting on Christ" through faith that all are *made sons*—not by nature (as is the case with the only Son, who is indeed the Wisdom of God). . . . Rather, *we are made sons by participation* in Wisdom. (Augustine, *Commentary on Galatians* 3.27)[19]

15. See Edith Humphrey, "Becoming the Righteousness of God: The Potency of the New Creation in the World (2 Cor. 5:16–21)," in Thate, Vanhoozer, and Campbell, *"In Christ" in Paul*, 125–58.

16. Unless otherwise noted, emphasis in block quotations of patristic and medieval sources is added.

17. Origen, *Commentary on the Epistle to the Romans*, trans. Thomas P. Scheck, 2 vols., FC 103, 104 (Washington, DC: Catholic University of America Press, 2001–2), 1:205, 292.

18. John Chrysostom, *Homilies on the Acts of the Apostles and the Epistle to the Romans*, NPNF[1] 11:386 (archaic English adapted throughout).

19. Augustine, *Augustine's Commentary on Galatians*, trans. Eric Plumer, OECS (Oxford: Oxford University Press, 2003), 173.

"That we might be made the justice of God *in him*" [2 Cor. 5:21], i.e., that *we, who are sinners, might be made not only just,* but justice itself. . . . But he says, "of God," to exclude man's justice, by which a man trusts in his own merits. . . . "In him," namely, *in Christ.* (Thomas Aquinas, *Commentary on 2 Corinthians* 5.5.202)[20]

Notice that it is the *Greek* church father John Chrysostom who interprets "justify" (*dikaioō*) in Romans as not merely forensic but transformative: "to make [someone] righteous" (δίκαιον ποιῆσαι, *dikaion poiēsai*).[21] In light of such evidence, the common claim that the transformative interpretation is based on a Latin mistranslation of the Greek word should be abandoned.[22] Notice also that both Origen and Augustine use the language of "participation" (Latin *participatio/nem*) to describe what justification "in Christ" entails. As recent studies have shown, the notion of participated righteousness plays an important role in patristic interpretation of Paul.[23]

The Council of Trent and Today: The Baptized Are Both "Reputed" and "Made Righteous"

When we turn to the sixteenth-century Council of Trent, the official Catholic *Decree on Justification* describes justification as follows:

The justification of the sinner . . . [is] *a transition* from *the state in which man is born* a son of the first Adam to *the state of grace and adoption* as sons of God (Rom. 8:15) through the second Adam, Jesus Christ our Savior. (Council of Trent, *Decree on Justification*, chap. 4)[24]

Justification . . . is *not only the remission of sins* but the sanctification and renewal of the interior man through the voluntary reception of grace and of

---

20. Thomas Aquinas, *Commentary on the Letters of Saint Paul to the Corinthians*, trans. F. R. Larcher, B. Mortensen, and D. Keating, ed. J. Mortensen and E. Alarcón (Lander, WY: Aquinas Institute for the Study of Sacred Doctrine, 2012), 486–87.

21. John Chrysostom, *Homilies on Romans* 8.2. See also Thomas P. Scheck, *Origen and the History of Justification: The Legacy of Origen's Commentary on Romans* (Notre Dame, IN: University of Notre Dame Press, 2008), 13–62, esp. 32–38.

22. E.g., Alister E. McGrath, *Iustitia Dei: A History of the Christian Doctrine of Justification*, 3rd ed. (Cambridge: Cambridge University Press, 2005), 20. Unfortunately, McGrath completely ignores both Origen and Chrysostom on this point.

23. See Athanasios Despotis, ed., *Participation, Justification, and Conversion: Eastern Orthodox Interpretation of Paul and the Debate between "Old and New Perspectives on Paul,"* WUNT 2/442 (Tübingen: Mohr Siebeck, 2017); Ben C. Blackwell, *Christosis: Engaging Paul's Soteriology with His Patristic Interpreters* (Grand Rapids: Eerdmans, 2016).

24. Denzinger, *Compendium of Creeds*, no. 1524. Unless otherwise noted, all emphasis in quotations from Trent herein is added.

the gifts, where from unjust *man becomes just.* . . . Thus, *not only are we considered just*, but we are truly called just and *we are just.* . . . By the merit of the same most holy Passion, "God's love is *poured* through the Holy Spirit into the hearts" (Rom. 5:5) of those who are being justified and *inheres in them.* (Council of Trent, *Decree on Justification*, chap. 7)[25]

Three points need to be underscored here. First, for Trent, justification is not just the forgiveness of a person's sins. It is also the "transition" (Latin *translatio*) from the "state" of being in Adam to the "state" of being in Christ. Second, contrary to what many assume, according to Trent, the "gift" of justification is *both forensic and transformative*: a person who is in Christ is both "considered" or "reputed" (*reputamur*) to be righteous and actually "becomes just" (*fit iustus*).[26] Indeed, those who are in Christ "truly . . . are just" (*vere iusti*).[27] Third, note well that Trent, like Origen, grounds the claim of a real, infused righteousness in Paul's statement about the indwelling of divine "love" in the human heart: "God's love [ἀγάπη, *agapē*] has been *poured into our hearts* through the Holy Spirit which has been given to us" (Rom. 5:5). If the Spirit of God can actually dwell in believers, then so can the righteousness of God.

If we fast-forward to modern times, we discover that Catholic exegetes continue to emphasize that justification for Paul involves both the forensic declaration of forgiveness and a real participation in Christ. Consider, for example, the words first of Joseph Fitzmyer and then of Frank Matera:

"All are justified freely" [Rom. 3:24]. . . . I.e., "made upright" gratuitously through God's powerful declaration of acquittal. . . . The sinful human being is not only "declared upright," but is "made upright" (as in [Rom.] 5:19), for the sinner's condition has changed.[28]

Although justification is a forensic metaphor, the effect of God's work in Christ includes some form of transformation, . . . in the sense that they become a new creation in Christ and are being transformed into the image of Christ.[29]

Along similar lines, Pope Benedict XVI has recently emphasized that being "in Christ" entails a transformative righteousness by which the believer is

25. Denzinger, *Compendium of Creeds*, nos. 1528, 1530.
26. Council of Trent, *Decree on Justification*, chap. 7.
27. Council of Trent, *Decree on Justification*, chap. 7.
28. Joseph A. Fitzmyer, *Romans: A New Translation with Introduction and Commentary*, AB 33 (New York: Doubleday, 1993), 347; cf. 421.
29. Frank J. Matera, *God's Saving Grace: A Pauline Theology* (Grand Rapids: Eerdmans, 2012), 106n27.

actually made just: *"Being just simply means being with and in Christ....
We are just by being united with him and in no other way.... Transformed
by his love*, by the love of God and neighbor, *we can truly be just in God's
eyes."*[30] In sum, from a Catholic perspective, justification is not only the forensic declaration of the forgiveness of sins but also the transition from being
a slave to sin in Adam to being an adopted son of God in Christ. Catholic
interpreters of Paul, from Augustine to Aquinas to Benedict XVI, agree that
justification is a real participation in Christ, so that believers are both reputed
and made righteous. In the words of the official *Catechism of the Catholic
Church*, "Justification consists in both victory over the death caused by sin
and a new participation in grace.... By the gift of grace ... adoptive filiation
gains us a real participation in the life of the only Son."[31]

E. P. Sanders: Justification as Real "Participation,"
Not "Mere Imputation"

When we turn to the work of E. P. Sanders, we are immediately struck by
two points of overlap with Catholic interpretation of Paul.

First, Sanders insists that for Paul, justification is not a counterfactual
declaration of imputed righteousness:

> The idea of fictional, imputed righteousness had not occurred to [Paul], but
> had it done so he would have raged against it.[32]

> *Fictional* or *imputed righteousness* ... is a bulwark of Protestant exegesis of
> Paul. Thus in this interpretation, supported by the inadequate synonym of *jus-
> tify*, *nothing happens to the person*; rather, he or she is simply declared innocent,
> not guilty, even though he or she continues to perform acts that make one guilty.
>   Paul thought that Christians were *changed*. . . .
>   It would be closer to Paul's meaning to translate the passive phrase "to be
> righteoused by faith" as "faith in Christ *makes a person righteous*."[33]

These statements are strikingly similar to the Catholic perspective on justification. Just as the Council of Trent rejected the idea of justification by
"imputation alone" (Latin *sola imputatione*),[34] so too Sanders rejects the idea

---

30. Benedict XVI, *Saint Paul*, 82–83 (emphasis added).

31. *Catechism of the Catholic Church*, no. 654 (slightly adapted).

32. E. P. Sanders, *Paul: A Very Short Introduction* (1991; Oxford: Oxford University Press,
2001), 81; cf. 85. See also *PPJ*, 492n57.

33. *PALLT*, 506 (emphasis original).

34. See Council of Trent, *Canons on Justification*, no. 11.

of "mere imputation."[35] And just as Trent said that justification referred to both a forensic decree of "reputed" righteousness and actually being "made righteous,"[36] so too Sanders concludes that for Paul, justification in Christ has a "forensic character,"[37] but it also actually "makes a person righteous."[38]

Second, Sanders interprets Paul's statement that "he who has died is justified from sin" (Rom. 6:7) as evidence that "'righteousness' is primarily *a transfer term* in Paul."[39] This transferal is real, not counterfactual:

> It seems to me best to understand Paul as saying what he meant and meaning what he said: Christians really are one body and Spirit with Christ, . . . Christians really are being changed from one stage of glory to another [2 Cor. 3:18], . . . and those who are in Christ really will be transformed.
>
> But what does this mean? How are we to understand it? We seem to lack a category of "reality"—*real participation in Christ*.[40]

Remarkably, just as the Council of Trent described justification as being "translated" from being in Adam to being in Christ, so too Sanders describes righteousness in Paul as a "transfer" term.[41] Perhaps most astonishing of all: just as the official *Catechism of the Catholic Church* speaks of justification as a "real participation" (Latin *participationem realem*) in Christ,[42] so too Sanders thinks that for Paul justification entails a "real participation in Christ."[43]

Initial Justification by Grace through Faith Alone

The second aspect of the Roman Catholic perspective on Paul that needs to be emphasized is that no one can do anything to merit the initial grace of justification at the beginning of life in Christ. Although it may come as a surprise to some readers, there are in fact patristic, medieval, and modern Catholic interpreters—including Thomas Aquinas and Benedict XVI—who affirm that initial justification is by grace through "faith alone," meaning "faith apart from works."

35. *PALLT*, 457.
36. Council of Trent, *Decree on Justification*, chap. 7.
37. *PPJ*, 536.
38. *PPJ*, 470–71.
39. *PPJ*, 501.
40. *PPJ*, 522 (emphasis added).
41. Council of Trent, *Decree on Justification*, chap. 4.
42. *Catechism of the Catholic Church*, no. 654 (my translation).
43. Significantly, after a lifetime of study, Sanders quotes his original statements about "real participation" (*PPJ*, 522) on the last pages of *PALLT*, 723–24.

The Apostle Paul: Justification by "Grace" through "Faith" apart from "Works"

In support of this view, consider two key passages from Paul's Letter to the Romans:

> But now the righteousness of God has been manifested apart from law, . . . the righteousness of God *through faith in Jesus Christ* for all who believe. For there is no distinction; since all have sinned and fall short of the glory of God, they are *justified by his grace as a gift.* (3:21–24)

> Has God rejected his people? By no means! . . . At the present time there is a remnant, *chosen by grace.* But if it is by grace, *it is no longer on the basis of works; otherwise grace would no longer be grace.* (11:1, 5–6)

We will return to the issue of what exactly Paul means by "works" below. For now, we simply want to focus on Paul's insistence that a person is "justified" (δικαιόω, *dikaioō*) by "grace" (χάρις, *charis*) through "faith" (πίστις, *pistis*) (Rom. 3:24, 26, 28; Gal. 2:16 [2x]).[44] In the first passage, Paul himself unequivocally declares that because "all" human beings have "sinned," it follows that they are "justified" (δικαιούμενοι, *dikaioumenoi*) by his "grace" (τῇ χάριτι, *tē chariti*) as a "gift" (δωρεάν, *dōrean*) (Rom. 3:24). In other words, because all human beings have sinned, righteousness in Christ is not something earned, but a divine gift. Indeed, even Paul's fellow Israelites who belong to the "remnant" who believe in Jesus have been chosen "by grace" (χάριτι, *chariti*), and not "from works" (ἐξ ἔργων, *ex ergōn*) (Rom. 11:6). Here Paul delivers perhaps his strongest statement on the primacy of grace: if righteousness were in any way "from works" (ἐξ ἔργων, *ex ergōn*), then "grace would no longer be grace" (ἡ χάρις οὐκέτι γίνεται χάρις, *hē charis ouketi ginetai charis*) (Rom. 11:6).

Patristic and Medieval Interpreters: Justified by "Grace" through "Faith Alone"

In light of such passages, prominent patristic and medieval Catholic interpreters of Paul hold that the initial justification of a sinner is by grace

---

44. See Fitzmyer (*Romans*, 137–38), who stresses that for Paul, "faith is a gift of God" (e.g., Rom. 3:24–25; 6:14; 12:3). Moreover, faith "is not merely an intellectual assent to the proposition, 'Jesus is Lord,' but also a vital, personal dedication of the whole person to God in Christ. . . . ["Faith" is] a confidence in the promises of God and his assisting grace, and a trust upon which Christian hope is built."

through "faith alone"—that is, apart from any works whatsoever.[45] Consider the following:

> [All] are *justified through the grace* and redemption which is in Christ Jesus. . . . [Paul] is saying [in Rom. 3:28] that the justification of *faith alone* suffices, so that the one who only believes is justified, even if he has not accomplished *a single work.* (Origen, *Commentary on the Epistle to the Romans* 3.9.2)[46]

> [Paul] adds also righteousness; and righteousness, not your own, but that of God. . . . For *you do not achieve it by toilings and labors,* but you receive it by *a gift* from above, contributing *one thing only* from your own store, "*believing.*" (John Chrysostom, *Homilies on Romans* 2)[47]

> Paul in this letter says . . . "through the Law comes knowledge of sin" (Rom. 3:20), but not the removal of sin, which comes through *grace alone.* (Augustine, *Propositions from the Epistle to the Romans* 13–18)[48]

> It can be truthfully said that the commandments of God pertain to *faith alone,* provided that the faith which is meant is not a dead faith but that living faith which works through love. (Augustine, *On Faith and Works* 22.4)[49]

> Works indeed come after someone has been justified and not before he is justified; but *a person is made just by faith alone without preceding works.* (*Glossa Ordinaria,* on Rom. 3:28)[50]

> The Apostle [Paul] seems to be speaking of the moral precepts. . . . *[But] the hope of justification must not be placed in them,* but in *faith alone:* "we account a man to be justified by faith, without the works of the law" (Rom. 3:28). (Thomas Aquinas, *Commentary on 1 Timothy* 1.3.21)[51]

45. For more examples, see Fitzmyer, *Romans,* 359–62.

46. Origen, *Commentary on the Epistle to the Romans,* 1:226.

47. John Chrysostom, *Homilies on the Acts of the Apostles and the Epistle to the Romans,* NPNF[1] 11:349. See also John Chrysostom, *Homilies on Romans* 9, NPNF[1] 11:396.

48. Paula Fredriksen Landes, trans., *Augustine on Romans: Propositions from the Epistle to the Romans, Unfinished Commentary on the Epistle to the Romans,* SBLTT 23 (Chico, CA: Society of Biblical Literature, 1982), 5–7.

49. Augustine, *On Faith and Works,* trans. Gregory J. Lombardo, ACW 48 (New York: Newman, 1988), 46.

50. *The* Glossa Ordinaria *on Romans,* trans. Michael Scott Woodward (Kalamazoo: Medieval Institute Publications, Western Michigan University, 2011), 59.

51. Thomas Aquinas, *Commentary on the Letters of Saint Paul to the Philippians, Colossians, Thessalonians, Timothy, Titus, and Philemon,* trans. F. R. Larcher, ed. J. Mortensen and E. Alarcón (Lander, WY: Aquinas Institute for the Study of Sacred Doctrine, 2012), 251. Nor is this the only time Aquinas uses *sola fide.* Note Aquinas, *Commentary on Romans* 4.1.330:

Three points are in order here. First, both patristic and medieval Pauline commentators spoke of justification by "grace alone" (Latin *sola gratia*) (Augustine) through "faith alone" (Latin *sola fide*)—that is, apart from works (Origen, Augustine, *Glossa Ordinaria*, Aquinas). Second, when read in their wider context, it is clear that all of the commentators cited above are speaking specifically about the *initial* grace of justification at the beginning of life in Christ. Below we will turn to what these same commentators say about the role of works *after* baptism. Third and finally—and this cannot be overemphasized—the patristic idea of initial justification by grace through "faith alone" *does not disappear during the Middle Ages*. If anything, it becomes more prominent by being utilized in the annotations to Romans in the massively influential twelfth-century *Glossa Ordinaria*—*the* medieval Catholic "Bible Commentary."[52] Initial justification *sola fide* also appears in the thirteenth-century Pauline commentaries of Thomas Aquinas, which were delivered as lectures at the University of Paris.[53]

In other words, centuries before the time of Martin Luther and John Calvin there was already in place a medieval Catholic tradition of interpreting Paul as teaching initial justification by grace through "faith alone."[54]

The Council of Trent and Today: "Nothing" Merits the Initial Grace of Justification

When we turn to the sixteenth-century Council of Trent, we discover that while the *Decree on Justification* does not employ the patristic and medieval expression "faith alone" to summarize Paul's teaching, it does insist that

---

"'His faith is reputed' [Rom. 4:5], i.e., faith alone without outward works [*fides . . . sola sine operibus*]."

52. See Lesley Smith, *The Glossa Ordinaria: The Making of a Medieval Bible Commentary*, Commentaria 3 (Leiden: Brill, 2009). *Sola fide* also appears in the twelfth-century work of Bernard of Clairvaux, *Sermons on the Song of Songs* 22.8: "Therefore the man who through sorrow for sin hungers and thirsts for justice, let him trust in the One who changes the sinner into a just man (Rom 4:5), and judged righteous in terms of *faith alone*, he will have peace with God (Rom 5:1)." See Bernard of Clairvaux, *On the Song of Songs*, vol. 2, trans. Kilian Walsh, Cistercian Fathers (Kalamazoo, MI: Cistercian Publications, 1976), 20.

53. See Thomas Weinandy, *Aquinas on Scripture: An Introduction to His Biblical Commentaries* (London: T&T Clark, 2005).

54. Unfortunately, many studies ignore the medieval Catholic affirmation of initial justification *sola fide* in the *Glossa Ordinaria* on Romans and Thomas Aquinas's commentaries on Paul, as if neither existed. See, e.g., Michael Scott Horton, *Justification*, 2 vols., NSD (Grand Rapids: Zondervan, 2018); Stephen J. Chester, *Reading Paul with the Reformers: Reconciling Old and New Perspectives* (Grand Rapids: Eerdmans, 2017); Thomas Schreiner, *Faith Alone: The Doctrine of Justification; What the Reformers Taught . . . and Why It Still Matters* (Grand Rapids: Zondervan, 2015); McGrath, *Iustitia Dei*.

nothing can merit the initial grace of justification. Moreover, Trent explicitly anchors this teaching in Paul's Letter to the Romans:

> When the apostle [Paul] says that man is justified "through faith" and "gratuitously" (Rom. 3:22, 24), those words are to be understood in the sense in which the Catholic Church has held and declared them with uninterrupted unanimity, namely, that we are said to be *justified through faith* because "faith is the beginning of man's salvation," the foundation and root of all justification. . . . *And we are said to be justified gratuitously because nothing that precedes justification, neither faith nor works, merits the grace of justification*; for "if it is by grace, it is no longer on the basis of works; otherwise (as the same apostle [Paul] says) grace would no longer be grace" (Rom. 11:6). (Council of Trent, *Decree on Justification*, chap. 8)[55]

Three features of the Council of Trent's reading of Paul stand out as important. First, Trent interprets Romans 3:24 as teaching initial justification by "grace" (Latin *gratis*). Indeed, the *Decree on Justification* is unequivocal that "nothing" (*nihil*)—"neither faith nor works" (*sive fides, sive opera*)—can earn or merit the "grace [*gratia*] of justification" at the "beginning" (*initium*) of salvation. Second, Trent interprets Romans 3:22 as teaching justification "through faith" (*per fidem*). It even insists that faith is the "foundation" (*fundamentum*) and "root" (*radix*) of all justification. It is crucial to underscore that, like Augustine, when Trent speaks of justification by "faith," it does *not* mean "faith without hope and charity," which would be dead, but faith enlivened by love.[56] In support of this, Trent quotes Paul's statements that "God's love [*caritas Dei*] has been poured into our hearts through the Holy Spirit" (Rom. 5:5) and that what matters is not "circumcision" but "faith working through love" (Gal. 5:6).[57] Third and finally, Trent interprets Romans 11:6 as denying that "works" (*opera*) play *any role* in justification at the beginning of life in Christ. Indeed, Trent directly quotes Paul in support of this point: "no longer on the basis of works [*non ex operibus*], otherwise grace would no longer be grace [*non est gratia*]" (Rom. 11:6). In sum, although Trent does not use the patristic and medieval terminology of "faith alone," the council clearly teaches that *initial justification is by grace through faith apart from any works or merits whatsoever.*

55. Denzinger, *Compendium of Creeds*, no. 1532.
56. Council of Trent, *Decree on Justification*, chap. 7.
57. Council of Trent, *Decree on Justification*, chap. 7: "By the merit of the same most holy Passion, 'God's love is poured through the Holy Spirit into the hearts' (Rom 5:5) of those who are being justified and inheres in them." See Denzinger, *Compendium of Creeds*, no. 1530.

If we turn to the modern period, we discover that contemporary Catholic interpreters of Paul are equally emphatic about initial justification by unmerited grace through faith apart from works.[58] Consider the words first of Joseph Fitzmyer, SJ, arguably the most prolific Catholic Pauline scholar in the last century, and then of Pope Benedict XVI, the first pope in history to compose a book-length treatment of Paul:

> "All are justified freely" [Rom. 3:24]. . . . I.e., are "made upright" gratuitously through God's powerful declaration of acquittal. . . . This status is not achieved by something within their own power or measured by their own merits. It comes to humanity through an unmerited dispensation of God himself, who has taken the initiative.[59]

> Following Saint Paul, we have seen that man is unable to "justify" himself with his own actions, but can only truly become "just" before God because God confers his "justice" upon him, uniting him to Christ his Son. And man obtains this union through faith. In this sense, Saint Paul tells us: not our deeds, but rather "faith" renders us just. . . . This faith is communion with Christ, which the Lord gives to us.[60]

Most striking of all, both Fitzmyer and Benedict XVI agree that the expression "faith alone" is an apt summary of Paul's teaching in Romans 3:

> The qualification "apart from deeds of (the) law" [in Rom. 3:28] shows that in this context Paul means "by faith alone." Only faith appropriates God's effective declaration of uprightness for a human being.[61]

> Being just simply means being with Christ and in Christ. And this suffices. Further observances are no longer necessary. *For this reason Luther's phrase: "faith alone" is true, if faith is not opposed to charity, to love.*[62]

Note well that neither Fitzmyer nor Benedict XVI is abandoning the Council of Trent's doctrine of justification in favor of a "peculiarly Protestant"

58. See, e.g., Frank J. Matera, *Romans*, Paideia (Grand Rapids: Baker Academic, 2010), 263; Jerome Murphy-O'Connor, *Paul: A Critical Life* (Oxford: Oxford University Press, 1996), 153.
59. Fitzmyer, *Romans*, 347; see also 605.
60. Benedict XVI, *Saint Paul*, 84.
61. Fitzmyer, *Romans*, 363.
62. Benedict XVI, *Saint Paul*, 82 (emphasis added). I have slightly adapted the final line of the English translation here to more accurately reflect the original Italian "se non si oppone la fede alla carità, all'amore." My thanks to John Sehorn for this point.

exegesis.[63] Rather, they are simply reviving *a patristic and medieval Catholic tradition* of summarizing Paul's teaching on initial justification in Romans. Notice also that, as Benedict XVI emphasizes, when Catholics speak of "faith alone," they mean faith enlivened by the gift of "God's love" (ἀγάπη, *agapē*) (Rom. 5:5)—or, as Paul puts it elsewhere, "faith working through love" (πίστις δι' ἀγάπης ἐνεργουμένη, *pistis di' agapēs energoumenē*) (Gal. 5:6).[64]

In sum, especially in the wake of Pope Benedict XVI's interpretation of Paul, it should be clear that there is a patristic, medieval, and modern Catholic perspective that affirms initial justification by grace through "faith alone"— provided that by *sola fide* one means "faith apart from works," not "faith without the gift of God's *agapē*."

E. P. Sanders: "Getting In" by Unmerited Grace through "Faith Alone"

How does the Catholic perspective on initial justification square with E. P. Sanders's interpretation?

First, it coheres quite well with Sanders's concept of "covenantal nomism,"[65] which he defines as follows: "Covenantal nomism is the view that one's place in God's plan is established on the basis of the covenant. . . . *Obedience maintains one's position in the covenant, but it does not earn God's grace as such.*"[66] Elsewhere, Sanders puts it more simply: "getting in" the covenant takes place by "God's grace in election," while "staying in" is contingent on "obedience."[67] We will look at obedience below. For now, the upshot is that no one can merit the initial grace of "getting in" to the people of God. Like Catholic interpreters before him, Sanders holds that the initial grace of justification cannot be earned.

Second, although some critics have suggested that Sanders undermines Paul's teaching on justification through "faith alone,"[68] a close look at his works shows otherwise:

> Gentiles who enter the people of God must do so on the basis of faith alone and . . . the law must not be a condition of their admission.[69]

63. So Michael Bird, "Progressive Reformed" response in *Justification: Five Views*, ed. James K. Beilby and Paul Rhodes Eddy (Downers Grove, IL: IVP Academic, 2011), 296. Bird uses this phrase with specific reference to Fitzmyer, *Romans*, 307.

64. Here Benedict is specifically following Augustine's reading of Gal. 5:6. See Augustine, *On Faith and Works* 22.4 (quoted above).

65. See E. P. Sanders, "Covenantal Nomism Revisited," in *Comparing Judaism and Christianity: Common Judaism, Paul, and the Inner and Outer in Ancient Religion* (Minneapolis: Fortress, 2016), 51–84.

66. *PPJ*, 75, 420 (emphasis original).

67. E. P. Sanders, *Judaism: Practice and Belief, 63 BCE–66 CE* (London: SCM; Philadelphia: Trinity Press International, 1992), 262.

68. See examples of this criticism of the NPP in Yinger, *New Perspective*, 73–77.

69. *PLJP*, 29; cf. 30, 57n64.

If one asks, how can one enter the body of Christ, Paul will answer, "by faith alone, not by observing the Jewish law and becoming Jewish."[70]

Notice here that when Sanders uses "faith alone," he always does so with reference to "admission" or "getting in" to the body of Christ (i.e., initial justification). Notice also the inescapably *corporate* dimension of initial justification: it is not just about individual salvation, but about entering the "people of God." Finally, whenever Sanders speaks of faith alone, like Augustine and Benedict XVI, he does not mean faith without charity. Instead, Sanders interprets Paul's reference to "faith working through love" (Gal. 5:6) to mean that for Paul, "*only faith in Christ*, or being in Christ . . . , *plus love*, are all that really matters."[71]

In sum, just as Sanders insists that "*Sola fide*, 'by faith alone'" was "crucially important to Paul's view of Christianity,"[72] so too Augustine, Aquinas, and Benedict XVI can speak of initial justification by grace through "faith alone." And just as Sanders holds that for Paul, initial justification as "life" in Christ "can be received only as a gift,"[73] so too the *Catechism of the Catholic Church* teaches, "Since the initiative belongs to God in the order of grace, *no one can merit the initial grace of forgiveness and justification*, at the beginning of conversion."[74]

"Works of the Law" ≠ "Good Works"

The third aspect of the Catholic perspective on justification involves what Paul means by "works of the law." On this issue, there is no official Catholic position. Instead, over the centuries, Catholic interpreters have debated whether Paul refers (1) exclusively to circumcision, Sabbath keeping, and the Mosaic food laws; or (2) to any work of the law of Moses, including the Ten Commandments. With that said, there is widespread agreement that when Paul speaks of "works of the law," he is not referring to "good works" done by those who are already in Christ.

The Apostle Paul: Justification Is Not by "Works of the Law"

In order to see this clearly, we need to look briefly at the passages in which Paul speaks of justification apart from "works of the law":

70. *PALLT*, 573.
71. *PALLT*, 704 (emphasis added); cf. 552.
72. *PALLT*, 722.
73. *PALLT*, 509; cf. 517, 447.
74. *Catechism of the Catholic Church*, no. 2010 (emphasis added).

We ourselves, who are Jews by birth and not Gentile sinners, yet who know that a man is *not justified by works of the law* but through faith in Jesus Christ, even we have believed in Christ Jesus, in order to be justified by faith in Christ, and *not by works of the law*, because *by works of the law shall no one be justified*. (Gal. 2:15–16)

For *no human being* will be *justified* in his sight by *works of the law*, since through the law comes knowledge of sin. . . . Then what becomes of our boasting? It is excluded. On what principle? On the principle of works? No, but on the principle of faith. For we hold that a man is *justified* by faith *apart from works of law*. (Rom. 3:20, 27–28)

For our purposes here, only two brief observations are necessary. On the one hand, in both Galatians and Romans, Paul clearly uses the expression "works of the law" (ἔργα νόμου, *erga nomou*) (Gal. 2:16 [3x]; Rom. 3:20, 28) in the contexts of discussions about the specific role of "circumcision."[75] On the other hand, there are times when Paul's use of "works of the law" seems to refer to the entire Mosaic law, including the Ten Commandments. For example, when Paul says that "no human being will be justified in his sight by works of the law [ἐξ ἔργων νόμου, *ex ergōn nomou*], since through the law [διὰ νόμου, *dia nomou*] comes knowledge of sin" (Rom. 3:20), he is hardly specifying the law of circumcision. Instead, he seems to have the Decalogue in mind, as when he later says that he would not have "known sin" if "the law" had not said, "You shall not covet" (Rom. 7:7 [cf. Exod. 20:17]). Likewise, when Paul rejects the idea that "Abraham was justified by works [ἐξ ἔργων, *ex ergōn*]" (Rom. 4:2), he seems to be speaking of "human labor" that would be owed a "wage" (μισθός, *misthos*) (Rom. 4:4), and not simply of an entry rite such as circumcision.[76]

Patristic and Medieval Interpreters: "Works of the Law" ≠ "Good Works"

What does Paul mean by "works of the law"? Over the centuries, interpreters have taken different positions.

On the one hand, some patristic and medieval interpreters of Paul contend that the expression refers to circumcision, the Mosaic food laws, and Sabbath observance:

The works that Paul repudiates and frequently criticizes are *not the works of righteousness* that are commanded in the law, but . . . the *circumcision* of the

75. Cf. Gal. 2:12; 5:6, 11; 6:15; Rom. 2:25–29; 3:1, 30; 4:9–12.
76. Cf. Yinger, *New Perspective*, 65.

flesh, the sacrificial rituals, the observance of Sabbaths or new moon festivals. (Origen, *Commentary on the Epistle to the Romans* 8.7.6)[77]

I should ask about what is at hand [in Gal. 3:2]: whether it was *works of the law*, observance of *the Sabbath*, the superstition of *circumcision*, and new moons. . . . Let us consider carefully what [Paul] does *not* say, "I want to learn from you" whether you "receive the Spirit" by works, but instead "by the works of the law." (Jerome, *Commentary on Galatians* 1.3.2)[78]

Paul's object [in Gal. 2:16] . . . was pointed at the disciples; and not only at the Galatians, but also at others who labor under the same error with them. For though few are now *circumcised*, yet, by fasting and observing the sabbath with the Jews, they equally exclude themselves from grace. (John Chrysostom, *Homilies on Galatians*, on Gal. 2:17)[79]

The works of the law [in Rom. 3:20] are those that were instituted with the law, and they were ended since they were ceremonial and figurative. . . . Understand this according to *the ceremonial, not the moral laws*, which certainly justify and are perfected in the Gospel. (*Glossa Ordinaria*, on Rom. 3:20)[80]

Significantly, none of these interpreters of Paul are obscure figures. Nor are they limited to a particular place or time. The idea that "works of the law" refers specifically to circumcision, Sabbath, and food laws can be found in eastern and western, Greek and Latin, patristic and medieval Pauline interpreters.[81]

Other patristic and medieval commentators, however, argue that Paul uses "works of the law" to refer to *all* the commands of the Mosaic Torah. Consider, for example, the words first of Augustine and then of Thomas Aquinas:

Although, therefore, the apostle [Paul] seems to reprove and correct those who were being persuaded to be circumcised, in such terms as to designate by the word "*law*" circumcision itself and other similar legal observances, . . . he at the same time nevertheless would have it to be clearly understood that *the law, by which he says no man is justified* [Rom. 3:20], *lies not merely in those sacramental institutions which contained promissory figures, but also in those works by which whosoever has done them lives holily*, and amongst which

77. Origen, *Commentary on the Epistle to the Romans*, 2:159.
78. *St. Jerome's Commentaries on Galatians, Titus, and Philemon*, trans. Thomas P. Scheck (Notre Dame, IN: University of Notre Dame Press, 2010), 114.
79. John Chrysostom, *Homilies on the Epistles to the Galatians, Ephesians, Philippians, Colossians, Thessalonians, Timothy, Titus, and Philemon*, NPNF[1] 13:21.
80. *The* Glossa Ordinaria *on Romans*, 54–55.
81. See further Matthew J. Thomas, *Paul's "Works of the Law" in the Perspective of Second Century Reception*, WUNT 2/468 (Tübingen: Mohr Siebeck, 2018).

occurs this prohibition: "Thou shalt not covet." . . . It is summed up in these ten commandments, in which there is no precept about circumcision. (Augustine, *On the Spirit and the Letter* 23)[82]

[A] work of the law is of two kinds: one is peculiar to the Mosaic law, as the observance of ceremonial precepts; the other is a work of the law of nature, because it pertains to the natural law, as "you shall not kill, you shall not steal," etc. Now some take the Apostle's [Paul's] words as referring to the first works, namely, that the ceremonials did not confer the grace through which men are made just. But this does not seem to be the Apostle's intent, for he immediately adds: "for by the law is the knowledge of sin" (Rom. 3:20). But it is clear that sins are made known through prohibitions contained in the moral precepts. Consequently, the Apostle intends to say that by no works of the Law, even those commanded by the moral precepts, is man justified in the sense that justice would be caused in him by works, because, as he states below: "and if by grace, it is not now by works" (Rom. 11:6). (Thomas Aquinas, *Commentary on Romans* 3.2.297)[83]

Both Augustine and Aquinas are clearly aware of the more restrictive interpretation of "works of the law," but they reject it as too limited. Moreover, both specify that this broader interpretation includes the Ten Commandments.[84] Finally, it is significant that Aquinas disagrees with the restrictive view on *exegetical* grounds: it does not seem to be "the Apostle's intent" (Latin *intentio Apostoli*).

The Council of Trent and Today: "Works of the Law" ≠ "Good Works"

As I mentioned above, the Council of Trent did not promulgate an official Catholic interpretation of "works of the law" in Paul. Regarding the Mosaic law, it says,

So completely were [human beings] the slaves of sin [Rom. 6:20] and under the power of the devil and of death that not only the Gentiles by means of the power of nature but even the Jews by means of *the letter of the law of Moses* were unable to liberate themselves and to rise from that state. (Council of Trent, *Decree on Justification*, chaps. 1, 4)[85]

82. Augustine, *Anti-Pelagian Writings*, NPNF[1] 5:93.
83. Thomas Aquinas, *Commentary on the Letter of Saint Paul to the Romans*, trans. F. R. Larcher, ed. J. Mortensen and E. Alarcón (Lander, WY: Aquinas Institute for the Study of Sacred Doctrine, 2012), 99.
84. See likewise Aquinas, *Commentary on Romans* 3.4.317.
85. Denzinger, *Compendium of Creeds*, no. 1521.

Notice here that Trent never says anything about Judaism being "legalistic." It simply states that keeping "the letter of the Law of Moses" (Latin *litteram Legis Moysi*) does not have the power to "liberate" (Latin *liberari*) from the state of "sin" and "death" that afflicts all human beings because of "the sin of Adam" (Rom. 5:12).[86] In short, neither keeping the natural moral law (for gentiles) nor keeping the Mosaic law (for Jews) has the power to transfer a person from being in Adam to being in Christ.[87]

As a result, the Catholic debate over the meaning of "works of the law" in Paul continues. Some contemporary Catholic exegetes hold that Paul uses the expression to refer to circumcision, Sabbath keeping, and food laws.[88] Others argue that "works of the law" refers to the entire Mosaic Torah, including the Decalogue.[89] What they all seem to agree on, however, is that *Paul is not polemicizing against "good works" done in Christ*. For example, although Joseph Fitzmyer takes the broader view, he insists that for Paul, "these are not simply 'good deeds,' but those performed in obedience to the law."[90]

In light of this debate, it is significant that in the year 2008 Pope Benedict XVI weighed in on what Paul means by "works of the law." On the one hand, Benedict XVI seems to follow Augustine and Aquinas in not restricting "works of the law" to circumcision, Sabbath, and food laws: "So what does the Law from which we are liberated and which does not save mean? For Saint Paul, as for all his contemporaries, *the word "Law" meant the Torah in its totality*, that is, the five books of Moses."[91]

On the other hand, Benedict XVI also insists that Paul is not arguing against "good works" done in Christ:

86. Denzinger, *Compendium of Creeds*, no. 1521.

87. Denzinger, *Compendium of Creeds*, no. 1523.

88. E.g., Scott W. Hahn, *Kinship by Covenant: A Canonical Approach to the Fulfillment of God's Saving Promises*, AYBRL (New Haven: Yale University Press, 2009), 274–76; Luke Timothy Johnson, *The Letter of James: A New Translation with Introduction and Commentary*, AB 37A (New York: Doubleday, 1995), 62; Frank J. Matera, *Galatians*, SP 9 (Collegeville, MN: Liturgical Press, 1992), 94.

89. E.g., Ronald D. Witherup, "Galatians," in *The Paulist Biblical Commentary*, ed. José Enrique Aguilar Chiu et al. (Mahwah, NJ: Paulist Press, 2018), 1389; Jean-Noël Aletti, *Justification by Faith in the Letters of Saint Paul: Keys to Interpretation*, trans. Peggy Manning Meyer (Rome: Gregorian and Biblical Press, 2015), 68; Joseph Fitzmyer, "Justification by Faith in Pauline Thought: A Catholic View," in Aune, *Rereading Paul Together*, 88; Brendan Byrne, *Romans*, SP 6 (Collegeville, MN: Liturgical Press, 1996), 121; Fitzmyer, *Romans*, 338. It is worth noting that in his more recent work Frank Matera has changed his view to the broader interpretation. See Matera, *God's Saving Grace*, 105. Compare Scott W. Hahn, *Romans*, CCSS (Grand Rapids: Baker Academic, 2017), 49–53, who leaves the question open.

90. Fitzmyer, *Romans*, 337.

91. Benedict XVI, *Saint Paul*, 80–81 (emphasis added).

First, we must explain what is this "Law" from which we are freed and what are those "works of the Law" that do not justify. The opinion that was to recur systematically in history already existed in the community at Corinth. This opinion consisted in thinking that it was a question of *moral law* and that the Christian freedom thus consisted in the liberation from ethics. Thus in Corinth the term "Πάντα μοι ἔξεστιν" (I can do what I like) was widespread [1 Cor. 6:12]. *It is obvious that this interpretation is wrong*: Christian freedom is not libertinism; *the liberation of which Saint Paul spoke is not liberation from good works.*[92]

Although Benedict XVI's statements here are not intended to be a definitive statement of Catholic doctrine,[93] they nevertheless constitute a papal contribution to the Catholic perspective on "works of the law" in Paul.

E. P. Sanders: "Works of the Law" ≠ "Good Works"

When we turn once again to E. P. Sanders's interpretation of "works of the law," we find further overlap with Catholic exegesis of Paul.

On the one hand, like Origen, Jerome, Chrysostom, and the *Glossa Ordinaria* on Romans, Sanders takes the more restrictive view that Paul is primarily referring to circumcision, Sabbath keeping, and food laws. On the other hand, like Joseph Fitzmyer and Pope Benedict XVI, Sanders insists that when Paul speaks about justification through faith "apart from works" of the law, he is *not* polemicizing against "good deeds."[94] Consider the following:

> The erroneous view that Paul was opposed to good deeds and reward is the result of identifying those "works of law" that he opposed (especially circumcision of gentiles) with good deeds. Actually, "works of law" (becoming and being Jewish) are in a separate category from "good deeds." *Good deeds were not works of law, and works of law were not good deeds.*[95]

> "Works of the law" do not qualify as good deeds or charitable actions for other people. When he uses that term, Paul had in mind principally circumcision.[96]

Whether or not one agrees with Sanders's more restrictive interpretation of "works of the law," it can hardly be dismissed as novel when similar views were

---

92. Benedict XVI, *Saint Paul*, 80 (emphasis added).
93. General Audiences are basically weekly papal homilies. While they are part of the ordinary papal magisterium, they are not the normal venue for defining doctrine, usually done in the decrees of an Ecumenical Council, Papal Encyclical, or Apostolic Constitution.
94. See *PLJP*, 18; *PALLT*, 497, 513–14.
95. *PALLT*, 561 (emphasis altered).
96. *PALLT*, 562.

held by Origen, Chrysostom, and Jerome. In any case, just as Benedict XVI insists that Paul is not speaking about "liberation from good works,"[97] so too Sanders insists that Paul is not "opposed" to "good deeds."[98] As we will see momentarily, this distinction will prove crucial for understanding how Paul can affirm both that a person "is justified [δικαιοῦσθαι, *dikaiousthai*] by faith apart from works of the law" (Rom. 3:28) and that "the doers of the law . . . will be justified [δικαιωθήσονται, *dikaiōthēsontai*]" (Rom. 2:13).

Final Judgment according to Works, Not by Faith Alone

The fourth and final aspect of the Catholic perspective on Paul that merits our attention is this: while initial justification is by unmerited grace through faith apart from works, final justification on the day of judgment is according to works and *not* by faith alone. To use Sanders's language, while good works are not necessary for "getting in" to the body of Christ, they *are* necessary for "staying in" Christ and receiving the reward of eternal life.

The Apostle Paul: Final Judgment/Justification according to "Works"

In support of this view of final judgment by works, consider the following passages:[99]

I am sure that *he who began a good work in you* will bring it to completion at the day of Christ Jesus. (Phil. 1:6)

But *let each one test his own work*, and then his reason to boast will be in himself alone. . . . *Whatever a man sows, that he will also reap.* For he who sows to his own flesh from the flesh *will reap destruction*; but he who sows to the Spirit from the Spirit *will reap eternal life*. And let us not grow weary in *doing good*, for in due season we shall reap, *if we do not lose heart*. So then, as we have opportunity, *let us work good* to all men. (Gal. 6:4, 7–10)[100]

I [Paul] planted, Apollos watered, but God gave the growth. . . . *Each shall receive his wages according to his labor.* For we are God's *coworkers*, you are

---

97. Benedict XVI, *Saint Paul*, 80.

98. *PALLT*, 561.

99. Because many English translations obscure or eliminate positive uses of "work" (ἔργον, *ergon*) in Paul's Letters, I will translate the key phrases as literally as possible, following *PALLT*, 571–74 (emphasis added).

100. When Paul speaks of boasting in one's "work" (Gal. 6:4), the NIV changes "work" to "actions."

God's field, God's building. . . . Now if any one builds on the foundation with gold, silver, precious stones, wood, hay, straw—*each man's work* will become manifest; for the Day will disclose it, because it will be revealed with fire, and *the fire will test what sort of work each one has done*. If *the work* which any man has built on the foundation survives, he will receive *a wage*. If any man's *work* is burned up, *he will be punished*, though *he himself will be saved, but only as through fire*. (1 Cor. 3:6, 8–9, 12–15)[101]

[Satan's] servants also disguise themselves as servants of righteousness. Their end will be *according to their works*. (2 Cor. 11:15)[102]

For [God] will *repay* each person *according to his works*: to those who by patience in *good work* seek for glory and honor and immortality, he will give *eternal life*; but for those who are factious and do not obey the truth, but obey wickedness, there will be *wrath and fury*. There will be tribulation and distress for every human being who *works evil*, the Jew first and also the Greek, but glory and honor and peace for every one who *works good*, the Jew first and also the Greek. (Rom. 2:6–10)[103]

For it is not the hearers of the law who are righteous before God, but *the doers of the law* who *will be justified*. When Gentiles who have not the law *do* by nature *the things that are of the law*, they are a law to themselves, even though they do not have the law. They show that *the work of the law* is written on their hearts, while their conscience also bears witness and their conflicting thoughts accuse or perhaps excuse them on that day when, according to my gospel, God judges the secrets of men by Christ Jesus. (Rom. 2:13–16)[104]

Entire books have been written on judgment according to works in Paul.[105] Space permits only four brief observations.

First, Paul uses the verb "justify" (δικαιόω, *dikaioō*) (Rom. 2:13; 1 Cor. 4:4) to describe what will happen on the future "day" of judgment (Rom. 2:16; 1 Cor. 3:13; cf. Phil. 1:6). In other words, justification is a future as well as past reality, so that final justification and final judgment are two ways of referring to the same reality.

101. For good "work" (1 Cor. 3:14), both the NRSV and the NIV omit the word "work."

102. For "works" (2 Cor. 11:15), the NRSV has "deeds"; the NIV changes "works" to "actions."

103. For "works" (Rom. 2:6), the NRSV has "deeds" and the NIV (1984) "what he has done." For "good work" (Rom. 2:7), the NRSV, NIV, and NEB delete the word "work."

104. For "work of the law" (Rom. 2:15), the NRSV has "what the law requires" and the NIV (1984) "requirements of the law."

105. E.g., Kent L. Yinger, *Paul, Judaism, and Judgment according to Deeds*, SNTSMS 105 (Cambridge: Cambridge University Press, 1999).

Second, while Paul insists that initial justification takes place apart from works, he is equally emphatic that final justification will be to "each according to his works" (ἑκάστῳ κατὰ τὰ ἔργα αὐτοῦ, *hekastō kata ta erga autou*) (Rom. 2:6), "according to his own labor" (κατὰ τὸν ἴδιον κόπον, *kata ton idion kopon*) (1 Cor. 3:8), or "according to their works" (κατὰ τὰ ἔργα αὐτῶν, *kata ta erga autōn*) (2 Cor. 11:15). Notice here that it is Paul himself who emphasizes the individual (and not just corporate) nature of the final judgment. He even insists that it is "the doers of the law [οἱ ποιηταὶ νόμου, *hoi poiētai nomou*] who will be justified" (Rom. 2:13). In light of such texts, there should be no hesitation in affirming that for Paul, final judgment indeed is according to works.

Third, this means that individuals who do not remain in Christ but persist in doing *evil works* will be punished with wrath and destruction. That is what Paul means when he says that each believer should "test his own work [ἔργον, *ergon*]" (Gal. 6:4) and warns that whoever engages in "works [ἔργα, *erga*] of the flesh" (Gal. 5:19) will "not inherit the kingdom of God" (Gal. 5:21) but will "reap" the fruit of "destruction" (Gal. 6:8). Likewise, all who "work [κατεργάζομαι, *katergazomai*] evil" will bring upon themselves "wrath and fury" (Rom. 2:8–9).[106]

Fourth, conversely, those who persist in doing *good works in Christ* will merit the reward or wage of eternal life. That is what Paul means when he says that those who "work [ἐργάζομαι, *ergazomai*] good" and do not "grow weary" will "reap" (θερίζω, *therizō*) the fruit of "eternal life" (Gal. 6:8–10). Notice here that Paul's agricultural image of "reaping" presupposes *human cooperation* with God's grace. (Only someone who has never worked a garden or field could imagine a harvest where no human effort is necessary!) Likewise, he whose "work" (ἔργον, *ergon*) is built on the "foundation" of Christ will receive a "reward" or "wage" (μισθός, *misthos*) as recompense (1 Cor. 3:8,

---

106. Note well that Paul insists elsewhere that believers can be "severed from Christ" and "fall away from grace" (Gal. 5:4), and that those who will "reap" the fruit of "eternal life" will do so *only* "if" they do not "lose heart" (Gal. 6:9). Likewise, if believers do not "remain" in the kindness of God, they too will be "cut off" (Rom. 11:22). Although Paul clearly considers himself as being "in Christ," he readily admits that just because he is not "aware" of anything against himself, he is "not thereby justified" (1 Cor. 4:4), and he "pommels" his body so that in the race for the "imperishable" wreath he himself will not be "disqualified" (1 Cor. 9:25, 27). Compare *PPJ*, 517–18: "Paul did not mean [in Rom. 11:22; 1 Cor. 6:9–11; Gal. 5:21] that not sinning in the specified ways, but behaving correctly, would earn salvation . . . ; but wilful or heinous disobedience would exclude one from salvation." In this regard, note well that Paul's declaration that nothing "will be able to separate us from the love of God in Christ Jesus" (Rom. 8:39) *does not list sins*. He does not say, "neither adultery, nor idolatry, nor theft, etc." What Paul says is that neither *sufferings* ("tribulation, distress, famine") nor *evil powers* ("angels," "principalities," "powers") can separate believers from Christ.

14). Perhaps most striking of all, those who persist in "good work" (ἔργου ἀγαθοῦ, *ergou agathou*) will be "paid back" or "recompensed" (ἀποδίδωμι, *apodidōmi*) with "eternal life" itself (Rom. 2:6–7).[107] Apparently, this is what Paul means when elsewhere he refers to the "fruits of justification" (καρπὸν δικαιοσύνης, *karpon dikaiosynēs*) (Phil. 1:11) or "the harvest of justification" (τὰ γενήματα τῆς δικαιοσύνης, *ta genēmata tēs dikaiosynēs*) (2 Cor. 9:10).

But how can Paul speak of good works as being "rewarded" or "paid back" with eternal life? Because for him, there is *no competition* between God's work and good works done *in Christ*. For Paul, it is God who begins the "good work" (ἔργον ἀγαθόν, *ergon agathon*) in believers and will bring it to "completion" on the "day" of judgment (Phil. 1:6; cf. Phil. 2:13), and it is Christ himself who "achieves" or "accomplishes" (κατεργάζομαι, *katergazomai*) his good work "through" them (Rom. 15:18). For this reason, those who are in Christ are truly "coworkers" (συνεργοί, *synergoi*) who "work together" (συνεργέω, *synergeō*) with "the grace of God" (1 Cor. 3:9–10; 2 Cor. 6:1).

Patristic and Medieval Interpreters: Judgment according to Works, Not by "Faith Alone"

In light of such passages in Paul, the very same patristic and medieval interpreters who held that initial justification was by grace through "faith alone" are equally insistent that final justification is according to "works" and *not* by faith alone. Consider the following:

> Let believers be edified so as to not entertain the thought that, *because they believe, this alone can suffice for them.* On the contrary, they should know that God's righteous judgment pays back each one *according to his own works.* (Origen, *Commentary on the Epistle to the Romans* 2.5.7)[108]

> If any man have an ill life with a right faith, his faith shall not shelter him from punishment, his work being burnt up. . . . Wherefore [Paul] said, . . . "but he himself shall be saved, but so as by fire" (1 Cor. 3:15). (John Chrysostom, *Homilies on 1 Corinthians* 9.5)[109]

> [The faithful] would endanger the salvation of their souls if they acted on the false assurance that *faith alone is sufficient for salvation* or that *they need not perform good works to be saved.* . . . When St. Paul says, therefore, that man is justified by faith and not by the observance of the law, *he does not mean that*

---

107. On *apodidōmi*, see BDAG 109–10.
108. Origen, *Commentary on the Epistle to the Romans*, 1:112.
109. John Chrysostom, *Homilies on the Epistles of Paul to the Corinthians*, NPNF[1] 12:51.

*good works are not necessary or that it is enough to receive and profess the faith
and no more.* What he means rather . . . is that man can be justified by faith,
even though he has not previously performed any works of the law. *For the
works of the law are meritorious not before but after justification.* (Augustine,
On Faith and Works 14.21)[110]

"Without the works of the law" [Rom. 3:28]. Without preceding works, *not without subsequent works*, apart from which faith would be empty, as James says:
"Faith without works is dead" (James 2:17). (*Glossa Ordinaria*, on Rom. 3:28)[111]

"Without works of the law" [Rom. 3:28]. . . . This, of course, means without
works prior to becoming just, but *not without works following it*, because, as
is stated in James: "faith without works" (James 2:26), i.e., *subsequent works*,
"is dead." (Thomas Aquinas, *Commentary on Romans* 3.4.317)[112]

The idea that faith alone is not sufficient for the final judgment, but must
ordinarily be accompanied by good works, is present in eastern and western,
Greek and Latin, patristic and medieval commentators on Paul. Significantly,
several assert that Paul's teaching on judgment by works coheres with James's
declaration that "a man is justified by works [ἐξ ἔργων δικαιοῦται, *ex ergōn
dikaioutai*] and not by faith alone [οὐκ ἐκ πίστεως μόνον, *ouk ek pisteōs
monon*]" (James 2:24). The reason: both Paul and James are referring to the
role of works *after* initial justification.

The Council of Trent and Today: Judgment according to Works, Not by "Faith Alone"

With this patristic and medieval background in mind, we can now interpret
the Council of Trent's famous rejection of "faith alone" (Latin *sola fide*) in
its proper context:

Nobody should flatter himself with *faith alone*, thinking that *by faith alone
he is made an heir and will obtain the inheritance, even if he does not "suffer
with Christ* in order that he may also be glorified with him" (Rom. 8:17). . . .
That is why the Apostle [Paul] himself admonishes the justified, saying: ". . . I
pommel my body and subdue it, *lest* after preaching to others I myself should
be disqualified" (1 Cor. 9:24–27). (Council of Trent, *Decree on Justification*,
chap. 11)[113]

110. Augustine, *On Faith and Works*, 28–29.
111. *The* Glossa Ordinaria *on Romans*, 59.
112. Aquinas, *Saint Paul to the Romans*, 106.
113. Denzinger, *Compendium of Creeds*, no. 1538.

In these references to *sola fide* the Council of Trent is *not* rejecting the patristic and medieval Catholic tradition of *initial* justification by unmerited grace through "faith alone." Instead, as the passages from Paul quoted by Trent make clear, the council is specifically rejecting the idea that when it comes to *final* justification, "nothing else is required by way of cooperation"[114] and that a believer can "obtain the inheritance" of eternal life without willingly suffering with Christ (Rom. 8:17; 1 Cor. 9:27). For Trent, faith alone is not sufficient for the final justification of those who are already "in Christ."[115]

A quick glance at contemporary Catholic interpretation of Paul shows a continued emphasis on final judgment according to works. Consider once again the words first of Joseph Fitzmyer and then of Pope Benedict XVI:

> Paul seems to say that one is justified by faith, but *judged by works*. . . . It is only in the light of divine judgment according to human deeds that the justification of the sinner by grace through faith is rightly seen. Hence there is no real inconsistency in Paul's teaching about justification by faith and *judgment according to deeds*.[116]

> It is important that Saint Paul, in the same Letter to the Galatians, radically accentuates, on the one hand, the freely given nature of justification that is not dependent on our works, but which *at the same time* also emphasizes the relationship between faith and charity, *between faith and works*: "In Christ Jesus neither circumcision nor uncircumcision counts for anything, but only *faith working through love*" (Gal. 5:6). . . . Justified through the gift of faith in Christ, we are called to live in the love of Christ for neighbor, because *it is on this criterion that we shall be judged at the end of our lives*.[117]

Along similar lines, in a recent essay on judgment by works, Michael Barber clarifies why Paul thinks that good works done in Christ are not only fitting but will receive a reward:

> Works performed by those in union with Christ have meritorious value. They cannot *not* have meritorious value. Why? Because they are the result of Christ's work. The believer says, "It is no longer I who live, but Christ who lives within me" (Gal. 2:20).

114. Council of Trent, *Canons on Justification*, no. 9.
115. As Trent states elsewhere, "faith without works [*fidem sine operibus*], is dead and unprofitable (James 2:17, 20)" because "in Christ Jesus [*in Christo Iesu*] neither circumcision nor uncircumcision is of any avail, but faith working through love" (Gal. 5:6; cf. 6:15) (Council of Trent, *Decree on Justification*, chap. 7). Denzinger, *Compendium of Creeds*, no. 1531.
116. Fitzmyer, *Romans*, 306, 307 (emphasis added).
117. Benedict XVI, *Saint Paul*, 85–86 (emphasis added).

The good works of the believer *are* the good works accomplished by Christ in him or her. *To insist that the believer's works lack meritorious value is to claim that Christ's work lacks meritorious value.*[118]

From a Catholic perspective, there is no contradiction between Paul's doctrine of initial justification by grace through faith alone and final justification according to works and not by faith alone. For Paul, when God rewards good works done by believers who are in Christ, he is rewarding the "good work" (ἔργον ἀγαθόν, *ergon agathon*) of *Christ himself* (Phil. 1:6), who "lives in" them and is "at work" (ἐνεργῶν, *energōn*) in them (Gal. 2:20; Phil. 2:13).

E. P. Sanders: Judgment according to Works; "Rewards" for "Good Works" in Christ

At this point, the reader will not be surprised to learn that E. P. Sanders and the Catholic perspective on judgment by works in Paul cohere remarkably well.

First, Sanders interprets Paul's statement that the "doers of the law . . . will be justified" (Rom. 2:16) as evidence that final justification will be according to works:

> If there is any passage in Paul that is aberrant, it is Rom. 2.12–16, but not because it mentions judgment on the basis of works. The curiosity is rather that it mentions *righteousness by works*, which Paul otherwise insists must be by faith and not by works. *The solution to this difficulty seems to reside in the future tense of the verb, will be justified.* . . . Righteousness or being justified here has to do with whether or not one is punished on *the day of judgment.*[119]

Sanders sees no contradiction here, since Paul is speaking in one instance of initial justification (Rom. 3:28) and in the other about "eschatological" justification (Rom. 2:12–16).[120]

Second, Sanders stresses that "in Paul's letters 'work' is usually a positive good."[121] He even argues that for Paul "good works" can be performed in Christ in the hope of receiving a "reward." For example, regarding Paul's statements that "every man will receive his commendation (ἔπαινος, *epainos*)

118. Michael P. Barber, "A Catholic Perspective: Our Works are Meritorious at the Final Judgment Because of Our Union with Christ by Grace," in Robert N. Wilkin et al., *Four Views on the Role of Works at Final Judgment*, ed. Alan P. Stanley (Grand Rapids: Zondervan, 2013), 161–84, here 180 (emphasis altered).
119. *PPJ*, 516 (emphasis altered).
120. *PPJ*, 516.
121. *PALLT*, 572.

from God" (1 Cor. 4:5), and that those who do good will "reap eternal life" (Gal. 6:8–9), Sanders writes,

> Salvation by grace is not incompatible with punishment and reward for deeds.[122]

> Because of the Protestant horror at the thought that there are rewards for *deeds*, I shall quote Gal. 6:7–10: ". . . If you sow to the Spirit, you will reap eternal life from the Spirit. So let us not grow weary in doing what is right. . . . " *Thus it is not true that Paul was opposed to doing good deeds in the hope of reward.* Since God is just, he rewards good deeds and punishes evil.[123]

In sum, just as the *Catechism of the Catholic Church* can speak of "God's eternal reward for the good works accomplished with the grace of Christ,"[124] so too Sanders can speak of Paul's support for "good deeds" done "in the hope of reward."[125] Likewise, just as the *Catechism* upholds "the merit of good works" done "in Christ" through "the grace of God,"[126] so too Sanders attributes to Paul the idea of "reward for deeds" and even "the concept of merit."[127]

Conclusion

Just over forty years ago, E. P. Sanders stated that one of his "chief aims" in *Paul and Palestinian Judaism* was to "destroy" the caricature of Judaism as a religion of "legalistic works-righteousness."[128] It is high time someone destroyed the parallel caricature of Catholicism. In this essay, I have at least tried to correct it in three ways.

First, I hope to have shown *the absolutely central role played by Paul—* especially his Letter to the Romans—in Catholic soteriology. Unfortunately, one sometimes gets the impression that Scripture itself (to say nothing of Paul's Letters) plays little or no role in the Catholic perspective on justification. For example, in his important book *Justification: God's Plan and Paul's Vision*, N. T. Wright states, "Luther and Calvin answered from Scripture; the Council of Trent responded by insisting on tradition."[129] I am genuinely

122. *PPJ*, 517.
123. *PALLT*, 560 (emphasis original in the first sentence, added in the final sentence).
124. *Catechism of the Catholic Church*, no. 1821.
125. *PALLT*, 560.
126. *Catechism of the Catholic Church*, no. 2008.
127. *PPJ*, 517n3.
128. *PPJ*, xxxi; cf. 33–59.
129. N. T. Wright, *Justification: God's Plan & Paul's Vision* (Downers Grove, IL: IVP Academic, 2009), 23. Compare McGrath (*Iustitia Dei*, 338–44), who mentions that Trent's "decree

at a loss to explain how the Council of Trent's *Decree on Justification*, which quotes Paul over fifty times and the Bible over one hundred times, could be described this way. By all means we should discuss whether Trent *misinterprets* Paul, but it is historically incorrect to describe the *Decree on Justification* as simply insisting on "tradition." Whether or not one agrees with it, the Catholic doctrine of justification is explicitly rooted in Scripture, and in Paul in particular.

Second, I also hope to have shed some light on the fact that, long before Luther and Calvin, there was a *medieval Catholic tradition* of summarizing Paul's teaching on initial justification as being by grace through "faith alone." To be sure, *sola fide* is *just a tradition*, since Paul himself never uses the expression.[130] At the same time, it did not happen in a corner. Instead, *sola fide* was utilized by two of the most important medieval Catholic commentators on Paul: the *Glossa Ordinaria* on Romans and Thomas Aquinas. In light of such evidence, and especially in the wake of Benedict XVI's teaching on Paul, I hope it is clear that the Catholic Church affirms *initial* justification by grace through "faith alone"—meaning "faith apart from works."[131] Catholic interpretation of Paul is not Pelagian. At the same time, it is also not antinomian. Hence, the real point of disagreement seems to be over whether Paul taught that *final* justification was also by faith alone, without works. Here the Council of Trent, citing both Romans 2:6 and James 2:24, gave a resounding no.[132] As we saw above, when it comes to the final judgment, Paul himself declares that each individual will be "repaid" according to "works" and thereby "reap" the reward of "eternal life" (Rom. 2:6–7; Gal. 6:8–9).

Finally, I have tried to show that the New Perspective on Paul—at least as represented by E. P. Sanders—is in fact remarkably similar to patristic, medieval, and modern Catholic interpretations of Paul, including the Council of Trent.[133] How do we explain this, when Sanders himself says that he writes

---

on justification" is "notable for its marked preference to appeal directly to Scripture" (338), but says absolutely nothing about which biblical passages Trent draws on, much less how the council interprets Paul.

130. In the New Testament, "by faith alone" (ἐκ πίστεως μόνον, *ek pisteōs monon*) only occurs in James 2:24, where it is rejected.

131. Strikingly, both Horton (*Justification*) and Schreiner (*Faith Alone*) completely ignore the affirmation of initial justification *sola fide* in the *Glossa Ordinaria*, Thomas Aquinas, and Pope Benedict XVI.

132. Council of Trent, *Decree on Justification*, chaps. 7, 11, 16. Compare James Dunn, "New Perspective View," in Beilby and Eddy, *Justification: Five Views*, 199, rightly noting that "one of the most disturbing features of the new perspective for many" is its attention to "Paul's teaching on final judgment."

133. This does not mean that Sanders lines up with the Catholic perspective on every point. For example, Catholic teaching is more emphatic than Sanders that one not only "gets in" to

as "a liberal, modern, secularized Protestant"?[134] To my mind, the simplest explanation is that, with regard to the four topics we have covered here, Sanders's interpretation of Paul is largely *correct*. This would at least explain why commentators on Paul writing in different languages and different cultures over the course of two thousand years keep coming to the same conclusions as he. With that said, I do hope that more work will be done on Sanders's concept of "new" covenantal nomism:

> One can see already in Paul how it is that Christianity is going to become *a new form of covenantal nomism*, a covenantal religion which one enters by baptism, membership in which provides salvation, which has a specific set of commandments, obedience to which (or repentance for the transgression of which) keeps one in the covenantal relationship, while repeated or heinous transgression removes one from membership.[135]

As I have argued elsewhere, a compelling case can be made that Paul himself was a "new covenant Jew," and early Christianity can accurately be described as "new covenantal nomism."[136] Seen in this light, the parallels between Sanders's perspective and the Catholic perspective on Paul will hopefully stimulate future dialogue between all who share the goal of understanding the life and letters of the man known in the Catholic tradition as "*the* Apostle."[137]

Christ by grace, but also one "stays in" and does good works by grace. See, e.g., *Catechism of the Catholic Church*, nos. 2007–8, 2011.

134. E. P. Sanders, *Jesus and Judaism* (Philadelphia: Fortress, 1985), 334.

135. *PPJ*, 513 (emphasis added).

136. See Brant Pitre, Michael P. Barber, and John A. Kincaid, *Paul, A New Covenant Jew: Rethinking Pauline Theology* (Grand Rapids: Eerdmans, 2019). As we point out, Sanders claims that for Paul himself, "covenantal categories" are inadequate (*PPJ*, 513), but the reasons he gives are not convincing, especially in light of the centrality of the "new covenant" in the Lord's Supper (1 Cor. 11:25; cf. 2 Cor. 3:6–18).

137. The Council of Trent always uses the expression "the Apostle" to refer to Paul (not Peter). See Denzinger, *Compendium of Creeds*, e.g., nos. 1521, 1532, 1538.

Traditional Protestant Perspective Response to Pitre

A. ANDREW DAS

The sixteenth-century Lutherans confessed that genuine faith necessarily produces good works as evidence of what God has done (Formula of Concord, Epitome IV.2, 10). The necessary presence of good works adorning the Christian at the last day and vindicating God as just Judge should not, however, be considered a basis for salvation or justification. An individual is not saved or justified by works.

Professor Pitre relies heavily on parallelism: Paul links justification to baptism and being "in Christ" (Gal. 3:24–27; 1 Cor. 6:11, 17). Pitre writes, "In context, then, being 'made righteous' involves not only the forgiveness of personal transgressions but also a transferal from the state of being in Adam to the state of being in Christ" (29). As Charles Lee Irons demonstrated, *parallelism does not prove identity*.[1] No interpreter would dispute the *relationships* between righteousness, union with Christ, and transformation. Certainly justification and sanctification cannot be neatly separated in Christian experience.[2] The question is whether justification is to be *defined* in these terms. Getting that definition right is imperative to understanding what transpires at the last day. Paul does not treat justification as both forensic *and*

---

1. Charles Lee Irons, *The Righteousness of God: A Lexical Examination of the Covenant-Faithfulness Interpretation*, WUNT 2/386 (Tübingen: Mohr Siebeck, 2015), 65–68, 142–56, 274.

2. Note the title of A. Andrew Das, "Oneness in Christ: The *Nexus Indivulsus* between Justification and Sanctification in Paul's Letter to the Galatians," *ConcJ* 21 (1995): 173–86.

transformative/participatory. Justification is not to be confused with the *larger category* of God's activity for/in believers.[3]

The verb "justify" is consistently employed as an action taken and/or a declaration made during a *contention*.[4] As for the noun, "righteousness" is a gift "from God" and *not* Paul's own (Phil. 3:9), a construction paralleling the gift of righteousness in Romans 10:3–5. "Righteousness" is a genitive of source, a gift, in Romans 1:17 and 3:21–22. For righteousness to be a gift in some places but transformation in others would confuse the reader and require an explanation that Paul does not provide. For believers to "become the righteousness of God" in 2 Corinthians 5:21 is to enjoy the forgiveness of sins just mentioned in 5:19.

The apostle *consistently distinguishes* being justified or saved "by," "from," or "through" (ἐκ, *ek*; διά, *dia*) faith from being judged "according" (κατά, *kata*) to works (Rom. 3:22, 25; 5:1; Gal. 2:16; cf. Eph. 2:8; Col. 2:12 versus Rom. 2:6; 2 Cor. 11:15; cf. Rom. 2:2; 2 Tim. 4:14). "Justification is *contingent upon* faith; judgment is *congruent with* obedience."[5] In other words, contra Pitre, one is judged according to works *and* justified by faith apart from works.

Not only are believers justified "by" or "through" faith; such faith is regularly contrasted with works (Rom. 1:17; 3:22, 26; 4:3; 5:9, 13; 9:30; 10:4; Gal. 2:16; 3:6, 11; 5:5; Phil. 3:9). In Romans 4:4–5 it is not those who *work* but those who *believe* who are righteous before God! As Paul just explained, it is impossible to be righteous before God by works because *all* people have fallen short (Rom. 3:23). Thus, it must be a gift on the basis of belief rather than on the basis of doing. Faith relies on Christ's death for forgiveness (Rom. 3:21–26; 4:25). Righteousness must be *counted* (λογίζομαι, *logizomai*) to believers because it is not native to them (Rom. 3:28; 4:3–6, 8–11, 22–24; 9:8; Gal. 3:6). Righteousness is regularly linked with *forgiveness* (e.g., Rom. 4:25; 8:32–33). Likewise, the verb "justify" (δικαιόω, *dikaioō*) and forgiveness are frequently linked. Note in Romans 4:1–8 how David's forgiveness *is* his justification before God. God forgives *sinners*! He does not "count" sin against those who believe in Christ (2 Cor. 5:19). This righteousness is a *free gift*

---

3. James Barr cautioned against wrongly reading into a word what is a function of the context and not the word itself, in *The Semantics of Biblical Language* (Oxford: Oxford University Press, 1961), 218, 221–22.

4. As demonstrated by James B. Prothro, *Both Judge and Justifier: Biblical Legal Language and the Act of Justifying in Paul*, WUNT 2/461 (Tübingen: Mohr Siebeck, 2018), the verb frequently expresses the action of a judge in taking the side of the guilty (with forgiveness), or for the other party's dropping a charge.

5. Dane C. Ortlund, "Justified by Faith, Judged according to Works: Another Look at a Pauline Paradox," *JETS* 52 (2009): 323–39, here 332 (emphasis original).

(Rom. 5:17). Paul never describes a process of earning God's justification, whether initial or final.[6]

No one disputes that judgment according to works is a major motif in Paul (Gal. 5:21; 6:8, 10; 1 Cor. 6:9–10; 9:24–27; Eph. 5:5–6; Col. 3:5–6). Works are necessary at the judgment, but, again, one is not saved or justified *by* the law's works (Gal. 2:16; 3:2, 5, 10) or works in general. Paul never claims that.[7] In Romans 2:6 Paul says, "God will repay each person according to his works," but what of Romans 2:13, "It is not the hearers of the law who are justified before God, but the doers of the law who will be justified"? Does this contradict Paul's assertions that no one obeys God's law (Gal. 3:10; Rom. 7:7–25 [cf. Rom. 3:23])? Paul says in Romans 3:20, "For no one *will* be justified in his sight by [ἐξ] the works of the law, because the knowledge of sin comes through the law." In Romans 3:28 he says, "A person is justified by faith [dative: πίστει, *pistei*], apart from the works of the law." Elsewhere, in Galatians 2:16, he says, "By [ἐξ, *ex*] the works of the law no human being will be justified." Does Paul contradict himself? He never says that "the doers of the law" have *fully* done the law, let alone that they are justified "by" their works. Pitre never considers another, more likely approach to Romans 2:13: the doers of the law will be justified, *not* because they merited justification or salvation by good works; rather, those justified on the sole basis of faith in Christ are, in the end, doers of the law by virtue of what the Spirit brings forth (and of what Christ's saving work has erased [Rom. 3:21–26; 5:6–11]). Paul does not identify Christians in Romans 2:13 (as he focuses on Jew and gentile in general), but they are not far from mind.

Paul explains in the next paragraph that circumcision is of value only if there is a simultaneous "doing" of the law (Rom. 2:25).[8] Obedience is the criterion: if one transgresses the law, circumcision becomes uncircumcision; if the uncircumcised does the "just requirement of the law," that person will be regarded as circumcised (v. 26). In verse 27 the circumcised transgressor will be judged by the uncircumcised who keeps (τελοῦσα, *telousa*) the law. Verses

---

6. Pitre inserts good works into a "new covenant" context that includes blessings for obedience. On Paul's discomfort with and modifications of covenantal categories, especially in their emphasis on obedience, see A. Andrew Das, "Rethinking the Covenantal Paul," in *Paul and the Stories of Israel: Grand Thematic Narratives in Galatians* (Minneapolis: Fortress, 2016), 65–92.

7. For why "works of the law" cannot be limited to circumcision or Jewish distinctives but applies more broadly, see A. Andrew Das, *Paul, the Law, and the Covenant* (Peabody, MA: Hendrickson, 2001), 145–267; Das, "Galatians 3:10: A 'Newer Perspective' on an Omitted Premise," in *Unity and Diversity in the Gospels and Paul: Essays in Honor of Frank J. Matera*, ed. Christopher W. Skinner and Kelly R. Iverson, SBLECL 7 (Atlanta: Society of Biblical Literature, 2012), 203–23.

8. For a more detailed discussion of Rom. 2:25–29, see Das, *Paul, the Law, and the Covenant*, 184–88.

28–29 conclude that outward circumcision does not make one a Jew, but rather inward circumcision that comes through the Spirit does. There are gentiles circumcised in heart who do what is good before God's impartial judgment.

The description of the gentile as true Jew draws on language that Paul later uses to describe *Christians*. The just requirements of the law (δικαιώματα τοῦ νόμου, *dikaiōmata tou nomou*) in Romans 2:26 is the same phrase in the singular in Romans 8:4, where those who walk by the Spirit fulfill the law's requirement (cf. disobedience of God's decree [δικαίωμα, *dikaiōma*] in 1:32). The contrast between "Spirit" and "letter" in 2:29 recurs in Romans 7:5–6; 8:1–4 (cf. 2 Cor. 3:6–7). Paul contrasts the new situation of those in Christ with the Spirit with those in the letter of the law without the Spirit. In Romans 2:26 the uncircumcised are "reckoned" as circumcised, language used throughout Romans 3 and 4 for those reckoned righteous on the basis of faith (3:28; 4:3, 4, 5, 6, 8, 9, 10, 11, 22, 23, 24; 9:8; cf. Gal. 3:6; 2 Cor. 5:19). Circumcision is a sign of *faith* in Romans 4. Those who worship in the Spirit are the "true circumcision" (Phil. 3:3).

If Paul has in mind gentile *Christians* in Romans 2:25–29, why not identify them as such? Paul does not turn to Christ's work until 3:21–26. His point in Romans 2 is more limited: God's judgment is impartial. Nor does Paul definitively assert that there *are* such gentiles. He does not actually identify anyone falling into the category of the good in 2:25–29 or in 2:6–10. He says "if" in 2:25 and leaves matters at the level of suggestion, although he does say in 2:27 that such people will "judge" the Jew, a function of Christians (1 Cor. 6:2). Ultimately, Paul is using language that anticipates himself. As he proceeds, it will become clear that those gentiles judged righteous on the final day are gentiles *in Christ*.

As he continues, Paul carefully qualifies the "doers of the law" from Romans 2:13. He conspicuously drops all reference to doing the law. He describes Christians repeatedly as *fulfilling* the law.[9] After lamenting how the "I" under the law simply cannot "do" it (Rom. 7:14–25, with a variety of synonyms for "doing": πράσσω, *prassō* [7:15, 19]; ποιέω, *poieō* [7:15, 16, 19, 20, 21]; κατεργάζομαι, *katergazomai* [7:15, 17, 18, 20]), he turns to the law as taken hold of by the Spirit. The "just requirement of the law" is "fulfilled" in those walking according to the Spirit (8:4). The Spirit abolishes the futile struggle to do the law's enslaving obligations and empowers behavior that fulfills all that the law originally required.

After listing several of the Ten Commandments in Romans 13:9a, Paul adds in 13:9b–10 that these commandments "and any other commandment,

9. Here I am relying on what is argued in greater detail in A. Andrew Das, *Paul and the Jews*, LPS (Peabody, MA: Hendrickson, 2003), 166–86; Stephen Westerholm, "On Fulfilling the Whole Law (Gal. 5:14)," *SEÅ* 51–52 (1987): 229–37.

are summed up in this word, 'Love your neighbor as yourself.' Love does no wrong to a neighbor; therefore, love is the fulfilling of the law." Paul conspicuously avoids any notion of setting out to *do* the law. In fact, he contrasted doing the law with believing earlier in Romans 10:5–8, citing Leviticus 18:5 (in v. 5) and Deuteronomy 9:4; 30:12–14 (in vv. 6–8), and conspicuously deleting Deuteronomy 30:12–14's original threefold emphasis on "observing" the law. The "doers of the law" in Romans 13:8–10 are, ironically, not those who set out to "do" it but those who, led by the Spirit, *fulfill* it. Again, what follows Romans 2:13 qualifies it and not vice versa.

Paul's Letter to the Galatians offers confirmation. The Galatian Christians were trying to complete for themselves what the Spirit began by returning to the flesh with the works of the law (Gal. 3:2–5). The law cannot justify (2:15–16), and Paul assumes that no one "does" it (3:10). Galatians 3:23–4:7 emphasizes the temporal limitations: *slavery* under the law and its curse is relegated to the age prior to Christ's coming. Christian existence is so radically new and discontinuous that Paul can describe it as the dawning of a new world, a new creation (6:15). No longer is the Christian "under the law."

Paul couches his positive construal of the Christian life within two polemical thrusts against the law (Gal. 5:2–12; 6:11–16). One must obey the *entire* law (5:3); Paul faults those who obey God's law only in part (6:12–13). The law does not offer the Galatian *believers* (!) a viable path to justification before God: "You who want to be justified by [ἐν, *en*] the law have cut yourselves off from Christ; you have fallen away from grace" (5:4). The two warning sections (5:2–12; 6:11–16) enclose the apostle's own approach to the Christian life (5:13–6:10).[10] Love in action (5:13) is precisely what the law had promoted: "For the whole law is summed up [literally, "fulfilled"] in a single commandment, 'You shall love your neighbor as yourself'" (Gal. 5:14). Paul's fulfillment of the "whole law" (ὁ πᾶς νόμος, *ho pas nomos* [5:14]) responds to the obligation to obey the entire law (ὅλος ὁ νόμος, *holos ho nomos* [5:3]). For an audience so eager to live according to the law, the apostle sets forth an alternate path, the way of love, ironically couched in the law's own words: "You shall love your neighbor as yourself" (Lev. 19:18, cited in Gal. 5:14). Christians *fulfill* the whole law—taken hold of by Christ (Gal. 6:2)—by their love.

While the Christian is no longer in bondage to the law, the path of the Spirit is not in any way contrary to what the law enjoins (Gal. 5:23b). The fruit of the Spirit fully satisfies the law. The law had enjoined such virtues (cf. love as a fruit of the Spirit in 5:22 with the law's summary in Lev. 19:18 // Gal.

---

10. Frank J. Matera, "The Culmination of Paul's Argument to the Galatians: Gal. 5.1–6.17," *JSNT* 32 (1988): 79–91.

5:14). Paul has already interpreted love through Jesus's self-sacrifice for the sake of others (2:20). Now Christians are to bear one another's burdens (6:2); Christ's self-sacrificial example offers the pattern. In other words, by setting out to follow their Lord and his example, the Christian will consequently be fulfilling the law interpreted through the prism of Christ's love—without ever setting out to "do" it. The requirements of the law take care of themselves as the "fruit" of the Spirit. The focus is always on Christ, not on deeds (3:1)!

In Philippians 2:12–13 Paul says, "Work out your salvation with fear and trembling; for it is *God who is at work* in you, enabling you both to will and to work for his good pleasure." Paul envisions a Spirit-created fruit. Without ever having set out to "do" the law, in following Christ the Spirit-filled believer serves as a foil to the Jew who fails to do what God's law requires. The Holy Spirit enters the heart by faith in Christ as a free gift, and the consequent works are equally miraculous and gracious. Salvation is not awarded on the basis of works, but no one will be saved without them. In short, works are not a means to salvation but serve as evidence of God's just judgment, as many Pauline specialists have recognized over the years. The Christian's obedience is not perfect, but it is significant, substantial, and observable—and the blood of Christ (Rom. 3:21–26; 2 Cor. 5:19–21) removes all sin. God's justification at the last day is no less generous or gracious than a person's initial justification.

New Perspective Response to Pitre

JAMES D. G. DUNN

I was very impressed by Brant Pitre's essay. His demonstration of what he describes as "the parallels between Sanders's perspective and the Catholic perspective on Paul" (55) is very well worth reading. As an example of drawing together viewpoints and attitudes that traditionally have been contrasted and set in opposition, it is something of a model for ecumenical dialogue. The attempt to draw a "close comparison of Sanders and the Catholic perspective" (27) is well done and intriguing, and I have little to question or would wish to add to what he says about justification, baptism, and being "in Christ." The appeal for those from the Protestant side to listen more carefully to the spokesmen (I would have liked to add "and spokeswomen") of Catholic tradition is justified and well made. However, the essay raised a few questions, the chief of which can be summed up as a concern as to whether the sweeping breadth of review ignores the historical contexts of the particular issues and disagreements that came to focus on the Pauline texts at the center of the debate.

First, does it need to be said once more that the issue of faith and not works of the law arose in a particular historical context, a context that largely determined the terms of the issue debated? When the debate expanded over subsequent generations, of course the terms expanded too, as Brant illustrates. But if we want to know the terms of the issue that confronted Paul in the first century, we need to set to one side the evidence as to how the debate was conducted in later centuries. And the crucial point in exegesis of first-century Christian documents was the emergence of a distinctive Christianity from the parental Judaism within which it came to birth. It is that context which determines what Paul had in mind when he set faith in Christ over against works of the law in Galatians 2. Since I was first attracted to the issue at the heart of the Antioch incident (Gal. 2:11–16), it has always troubled me that the second half of Galatians 2 has so often in effect been separated from the first half of the chapter. It is when we read Galatians 2 as a whole that it becomes clear that the issue of faith and not works began as Paul's insistence that gentile converts did not need to be circumcised or to observe Jewish food laws. It was precisely this insistence that made clear that the faith proclaimed by Paul could not be regarded simply as a form of Judaism, that those converted by his message were not to be regarded simply as Jewish proselytes. Brant alludes to this, but simply as a matter of Catholic debate, and without following it up. In short, if we misunderstand the Antioch incident, we misunderstand both the thoroughly Jewish roots of Christianity and why Christianity had to emerge as distinctive from Judaism.

Second, it is all very well to highlight the careful statements of leading Catholic theologians and councils through the centuries and till today. Should it be pointed out, however, that if these statements expressed formal beliefs, historically and consistently expressed in appropriate actions, there would have been no cause for a Reformation in the first place? The Reformation was a reformation of the church. Simply to ignore the issue of whether a reformation was desirable or necessary is hardly to face the theological issue that evidently was foremost for Luther, as it had been for Paul. Was Luther unjustified in claiming that Rome had in effect distorted the gospel by its practice of selling indulgences, that it was in effect saying, "No! Faith plus works are *both* necessary for salvation"? If the issues that caused the Reformation are simply ignored and glossed over, are we not in danger of ignoring those aspects of history that make us uncomfortable, and also ignoring the lessons that emerged from these controversies? *Semper reformanda* is a slogan for the whole church, is it not?

Third, sad to confess, in this whole area of debate I often find myself wondering whether there is a danger of losing sight of the whole picture. A slogan I often turn to is "already and not yet," another way of expressing the difference between root and fruit. The point, of course, is that, as Brant recognizes, good works are not to be dismissed from the discussion. They are the fruit that a life rooted in faith should be expected to display. But the basis of such a life is faith, or should I say faith alone? It is rooted in the recognition that we can do nothing to earn or warrant salvation, that even to think we could somehow earn salvation or prove ourselves worthy of salvation is to ignore or downplay the indescribable gulf between God and humankind. But at the same time it is to recognize that the very purpose of a renewed relationship with God is to live a life approved by God, living by the values expressed by Jesus, living primarily for his praise. This is where the Spirit comes in—a crucial part of the whole story that I think Brant's essay does not give enough attention to. It is one of the problems of focusing the issue of faith and works too narrowly on justification. To include the gift of the Spirit in the discussion is immediately to recognize that conversion/ justification is just the beginning of the life of faith, that the gift of the Spirit is the first installment. It is when we set the fruit of the Spirit, as in Galatians 5:22–23, over against works of the law, we begin to see the balance that Paul's theology of salvation set out: a life rooted in faith (alone), enabled and empowered by the Spirit of God, will necessarily and inevitably produce the fruit of transformed character expressed in good works.

Paul within Judaism Perspective
Response to Pitre

MAGNUS ZETTERHOLM

It should be noted that the contribution by Brant Pitre differs from the other essays in this volume in a significant way. While James Dunn, John Barclay, Andrew Das, and I present *scholarly* positions, Pitre has been entrusted with the task of presenting a *theological* one—the Catholic perspective on Paul. Thus, it is rather the reception of Paul and Pauline scholarship within a faith community that is on the table here. Although I greatly appreciate Pitre's essay, I need to stress that it is not a completely natural mix of perspectives and is one that resembles comparing apples and oranges. The idea of a "Catholic (or Protestant) perspective" highlights the very close connection between Pauline scholarship and normative theology—a connection not without problems as New Testament studies have long been colonized by Christian normative theology in a way that would not have been acceptable in any other research discipline. Is it, for instance, really a concern to take seriously in the academic study of Paul whether Sanders's reconstruction constitutes a threat to Protestant soteriology? And is the assessment of a historical investigation dependent on the extent to which it supports a certain theological position? I think not, but I realize that this is a minority position within this discipline.

In my view, the first task that Pauline scholars are facing is to try to figure out what Paul was communicating in the socio-religious-political situation in which he lived,[1] *no matter the consequences for normative theology.* I realize that the present situation is the result of a long historical development, but I also believe that the relevance of New Testament studies goes way beyond the interest of the Christian church—getting Paul right is part of correctly understanding the history and development of Western society with implications for global development as well.

Having said that, I recognize, of course, that it is a legitimate scientific task to investigate how Pauline scholarship is related to normative theology. In that respect, Pitre's essay is highly interesting, and I have very few objections to his analysis. Pitre makes a convincing case for something I have long suspected: Catholic soteriology comes closer to the historical Paul than does Protestant. And I sometimes joke with my students that if only I could find just a bit of religiosity in me, I would convert to Judaism—or Catholicism.

Pitre brings up the important, but often misinterpreted, relation between "faith" and "works" in Paul. As I hint at in my responses to John Barclay and Andrew Das, I understand Paul to argue that God's gift (to the nations) is indeed by grace, apart from the Torah (if we disregard that the promise to the nations is in the Torah, according to Paul), but non-Jews in Christ (who are Paul's main concern) are expected to adopt a Jewish lifestyle of sorts. They are, among other things, to refrain from "idolatry," forbidden sexual relations (πορνεία, *porneia*), and the consumption of "food offered to idols." It may even be the case—but this is admittedly more or less a conjecture built on Acts 15—that Paul expected non-Jews only to eat food acceptable to Jews, avoiding "whatever has been strangled and from blood" (τοῦ πνικτοῦ καὶ τοῦ αἵματος, *tou pniktou kai tou haimatos*) (Acts 15:20). Consider also the possibility of disobedience as a reason for being expelled from the *ekklēsia* (1 Cor. 5:1–5). Thus, if we define covenantal nomism as certain obedience in a covenantal context, Paul surely would represent that, and I agree with Pitre that this seems to cohere with both Sanders and "the Catholic perspective."[2]

However, in Pitre's presentation there is a certain emphasis on the forgiveness of an individual's sins as someone turns to Christ and becomes "justified." Pitre states, "Justification seems to bring about both the forgiveness of an individual's trespasses and a real change in those who are justified" (28).

---

1. I have no intention of engaging in the discussion regarding authorial intent and the prospect of reconstructing the author's intended meaning from a text. I have to conclude that most New Testament scholars appear to assume that it is possible. In principle, I would agree, but since many relevant circumstances are unknown to us, or hard to verify, our reconstructions exhibit varying degrees of probability.

2. See E. P. Sanders, *Paul and Palestinian Judaism: A Comparison of Patterns of Religion* (Minneapolis: Fortress, 1977), 422, and Pitre's essay in this volume, 25.

Regarding the latter aspect—a real change—I completely agree, but the idea of forgiveness of sins needs some modification to become truly Pauline, as I see it. As Krister Stendahl pointed out long ago, "Forgiveness is the term for salvation which is used least of all in the Pauline writing."[3] Paul, it seems, is mainly interested in categories. His central problem is how the category "nations" is to be saved from the wrath that "is revealed [ἀποκαλύπτεται, *apokalyptetai*] from heaven against all ungodliness and wickedness" (Rom. 1:18). The principal problem of the "nations" is not that they sin—so do Jews ("All have sinned and fall short of the glory of God" [Rom. 3:23])—but that they are "Gentile sinners" by nature (Gal. 2:15). By turning to Christ and through baptism—and here Pitre gets it right—non-Jews undergo a transition from the category "sinner" to the category "holy and pure": washed, sanctified, justified "in the name of the Lord Jesus Christ and in the Spirit of our God" (1 Cor. 6:11). Thus, as I point out in my response to John Barclay, while not becoming Israel, non-Jews become *as* Israel and the same conditions apply: obedience to the covenantal norms makes them maintain their position in the covenant. The individualization both of sins and of salvation may be part of the "Catholic perspective," but I doubt it is Pauline. In general, however, it seems that the Catholics got it right.

I also find Pitre's discussion of the meaning of the "works of the law" (ἔργων νόμου, *ergōn nomou*) (Gal. 2:15–16; 3:2, 5, 10; Rom. 3:20, 28) illuminating. For obvious reasons, these passages appear frequently in this volume, because the meaning is far from clear, which allows for interpretations with rather different theological implications. At the center of the contemporary discussion is the question of whether Paul refers to the Torah in its entirety or only certain aspects, as argued by adherents of the position of the so-called New Perspective on Paul. Nothing, however, is new under the sun. In his excellent monograph *Paul and the Gentile Problem*, Matthew Thiessen concludes that the "radical perspective on Paul," aka the "Paul within Judaism perspective," is neither new nor radical; already Luke portrayed Paul as a Torah-observant Jew, and Acts evidently was incorporated into the authoritative canon of the Christian church.[4] Something similar appears to be true regarding the idea that "works of the law" refers only to certain Jewish identity markers, like circumcision (Sanders's view). I have to admit that I was unaware of the fact that this idea originated during the patristic period, and one has to agree with Pitre that this idea can hardly be dismissed as novel.

3. Krister Stendahl, "The Apostle Paul and the Introspective Conscience of the West," *HTR* 56 (1963): 199–215, esp. 202.

4. Matthew Thiessen, *Paul and the Gentile Problem* (Oxford: Oxford University Press, 2016), 169.

However, as for the historical Paul, I would assume that Paul refers to the Torah in general. As Pitre notices, in Romans 3:20 Paul seems to have something more wide-ranging in mind than Jewish identity markers. The simplest explanation, as I suggest in my response to Andrew Das, is that Paul encountered non-Jews who wrongly believed that Torah observance on Jewish terms would make them righteous before Israel's god. Jews in general, however, knew that also the righteous among them had to reckon with God's grace, since "a person is justified not by the works of the law but through faith in Jesus Christ" (Gal. 2:16). Christ, the τέλος (*telos*, fulfillment) of the Torah (Rom. 10:4), is accordingly the personification of God's grace, "for everyone who believes" (Rom. 10:4).[5]

What I miss in Pitre's presentation of the "Catholic perspective" is what is usually missing: a discussion of the relation between Israel and the nations in the new economy of salvation brought about by the Christ event. Even in *Nostra aetate*, the up-to-now most radical attempt to define the relationship of the church to the Jewish people, there is a certain triumphalist, not to say supersessionist, tendency. Now, all religions (even Judaism) tend to become supersessionist—what is new is better than what is old—and in general I have no problem with that: all religions (even Christianity) should be entitled to develop their own theology.

However, if one claims to be "explicitly rooted in Scripture, and in Paul in particular" (54), as Pitre does (admittedly with regard to the Catholic doctrine of justification), it should be pointed out that Paul always recognized the primacy of Israel: he certainly is not ashamed of the gospel—"it is the power of God for salvation to everyone who has faith, *to the Jew first* and also to the Greek" (Rom. 1:16). Thus, a Catholic (or Protestant) perspective on (the historical) Paul would need to appreciate that the church has been grafted into Paul's Judaism, indeed by grace, but indeed by the god of *Israel*.

Most "Paul within Judaism" scholars probably would be in general agreement with Sanders on those aspects that Pitre here uses for presenting the "Catholic perspective" on soteriology. But in other areas—Paul's Jewish identity and his relation to the Torah, for instance—Pauline scholarship has moved on during the last decades in ways that go far beyond Sanders's reading of Paul. My impression is that there is quite a lot for Catholic theologians to explore in the Paul within Judaism Perspective.

In conclusion, I contend that Pitre has convincingly shown that there is a close connection between the historical Paul and "the Catholic perspective on Paul," at least with regard to soteriology. This is, of course, quite ironic: Paul, the great hero of Protestantism, turns out to have been the first real Catholic.

---

5. Magnus Zetterholm, "Paul and the Missing Messiah," in *The Messiah: In Early Judaism and Christianity*, ed. Magnus Zetterholm (Minneapolis: Fortress, 2007), 33–55.

Gift Perspective Response to Pitre

JOHN M. G. BARCLAY

Brant Pitre helpfully reminds us that the Catholic Church has always been engaged in serious study of Paul, and that its doctrinal statements are shot through with references to Pauline texts. He dispels several Protestant misconceptions of Catholic theology, even finding some verbal resonance with Protestant theology ("faith alone"). Pitre's remit was complex, as he says, since *the* Roman Catholic perspective is to be distilled from a plethora of sources: a diverse range of patristic authors (Origen, Chrysostom, Jerome, Augustine) is here mixed with the medieval *Glossa Ordinaria*, and with Trent, the Catholic Catechism, and Pope Benedict XVI. But clear lines of continuity are drawn, sufficient to create a coherent picture.

As for every stream in the history of reception of Paul, what matters is not only which Pauline texts are cited but also what larger theological (or ideological) frame they are placed within. The same Pauline text can sound different when located in a differing matrix of co-texts and underlying presumptions concerning God, humanity, salvation, and grace. As my Catholic colleague Karen Kilby has recently pointed out, Catholics and Protestants tend to place grace within different theological pairings: the Catholic pairing of grace and nature creates a different thematic pattern (and thus different readings of Paul) from the Protestant pairing of grace and sin.[1] If grace perfects human nature, which is marred by sin, but capable of virtue once infused by grace,

---

1. Kilby's remarks on this topic are contained in an essay-response to my book *Paul and the Gift* (Grand Rapids: Eerdmans, 2015), to be published shortly in the *International Journal of Systematic Theology*.

this gives a different nuance to grace than that found in the absolute contrast between grace and the sinner, which is characteristic of Protestantism. What we mean by "grace," "faith," "justification," and "participation in Christ" reflects not just our reading of this or that Pauline text, but the whole theological matrix in which these themes are placed.

One of the intriguing elements of Pitre's essay is his analysis of the ways in which E. P. Sanders's reading of Paul coheres with the Catholic tradition. Since Pitre takes Sanders to be a good reader of Paul (and of Second Temple Judaism), this, for him, confirms the correctness of Catholic interpretation. For others, who question Sanders's reading of Paul, an opposite conclusion will be drawn. This is particularly significant in the overlap between Sanders's distinction between "getting in" (by unmerited grace) and "staying in" (by obedience) and Pitre's Catholic differentiation between "initial justification" by faith and "final justification" by works. In fact, Sanders's model of "getting in" and "staying in" is not without its critics. In relation to Second Temple Judaism this sequential model, basic to Sanders's "covenantal nomism," has seemed both limited and overly rigid.[2] And in relation to Paul, I consider both Sanders's "getting in"/"staying in" model and Pitre's distinction between "initial justification" and "final justification" highly problematic.[3]

Pitre traces in the Catholic tradition a clear emphasis on "initial" justification by faith, with grace unmerited by previous works (drawing out what I would call the "incongruity" of grace).[4] But much depends on what we mean by "faith." If faith is a human "contribution" (see Chrysostom, cited by Pitre, 35) or an assent to propositions about God or Christ, the focus rests wrongly on the human believer. For Paul, faith in the Christian era means *faith in Christ* (or better, *trust in Christ*): it represents a declaration of bankruptcy on the part of the human, a total and utter reliance on the death and resurrection of Christ.[5] Faith in this sense constitutes not just the beginning but the whole of the Christian life. As Paul puts it, "I have been crucified with Christ; it

2. For critiques, see, e.g., Simon J. Gathercole, *Where Is Boasting? Early Jewish Soteriology and Paul's Response in Romans 1–5* (Grand Rapids: Eerdmans, 2002); Barclay, *Paul and the Gift*, 151–58.

3. Pitre himself recognizes a deficiency in Sanders at this point ("Catholic teaching is more emphatic than Sanders that one not only 'gets in' to Christ by grace, but also one 'stays in' and does good works by grace," 54n133), but still he utilizes this analogy between Sanders and the Catholic tradition.

4. See Barclay, *Paul and the Gift*.

5. For the Protestant Reformers, *sola fide* was inseparable from *sola gratia* and *solus Christus*. See Stephen J. Chester, *Reading Paul with the Reformers: Reconciling the Old and New Perspectives* (Grand Rapids: Eerdmans, 2017).

is no longer I who live, but Christ who lives in me; and *the life I now live in the flesh I live by faith* in the Son of God, who loved me and gave himself for me" (Gal. 2:19–20). This suggests that the whole Christian life, from start to finish, is suspended from the saving act and saving presence of Christ; it is *all* a life of faith, in the sense of utter dependence on a grace sourced continuously from elsewhere.[6]

As Pitre rightly insists, salvation for Paul entails, centrally, "participation in Christ," a point emphasized as much in the Protestant as in the Catholic tradition.[7] But the question remains: What does this mean? Are the attributes of Christ (holiness, righteousness, etc.) "transferred" to believers such that they become, in some sense, "their own"? Or do believers live always an "excentric" existence, permanently dependent on the risen life of Christ and the living presence of the Spirit, on which they draw in every breath and act, but which can never be said to "inhere" in them? This is the larger question behind the disputed translation of δικαιόω (*dikaioō*), which Pitre takes to mean "make righteous." Despite Chrysostom (cited by Pitre, 29), most modern interpreters of Paul, both Catholic and Protestant, would consider that a questionable translation of the verb, both in Paul and elsewhere, since it turns a relational act ("to consider someone in the right") into an act of moral alteration ("to make someone morally righteous").[8]

Paul does expect moral transformation in the believer, even if he does not express this by the verb δικαιόω. As Pitre insists, and as I have emphasized in my book *Paul and the Gift*, the incongruous gift of grace is designed to effect necessary changes in the lives and communities of believers, creating a kind of fit, or congruity, between believers and the will of God (Rom. 12:1–2). The incongruous grace of God elicits an obedient response, as the Spirit received through adoption bears its fruit. This congruity is not an addition to faith, a sequel to a status realizable in other terms; it is the expression of faith in Christ, the enactment of a life in Christ that can otherwise make no claim to be alive. But for this reason, it is inseparable from Christ and

6. This utter trust in Christ is certainly active in love, but Paul's πίστις δι' ἀγάπης ἐνεργουμένη (*pistis di' agapes energoumenē*) in Gal. 5:6 can hardly be translated (as Pitre does) as "faith enlivened by love."

7. Chester, *Reading Paul with the Reformers*, highlights this point. As he shows, it is therefore absurd for Sanders (or others) to represent Luther's "forensic" justification as "fictional." For the Reformers, there is nothing fictional about the justification that believers have "in Christ," but it is Christ's righteousness, and not their own ("the righteousness of God *in him* [Christ]" [2 Cor. 5:21]).

8. The literature on this is, of course, immense. For an important recent contribution, see James B. Prothro, *Both Judge and Justifier: Biblical Legal Language and the Act of Justifying in Paul*, WUNT 2/461 (Tübingen: Mohr Siebeck, 2018).

from grace; walking in the Spirit is, at every moment and in every facet, grounded in grace, in the miraculous, incongruous grace that creates the life from which the believer now lives. To put this another way, we may ask: Who is the "I" who does the works of love that issue from faith? Is it the old "I" enhanced or supplemented by grace, now "cooperating" with grace with an agency placed alongside that of God? Or is it a new "I," a new creation in Christ (2 Cor. 5:17)—"no longer I who live, but Christ who lives in me" (Gal. 2:20)—founded in the resurrection (Rom. 6:1–11) and dependent, at each moment, on the life given by the Spirit (Gal. 5:25)? Since the Spirit is the source and energy of believers' lives, the life of Christ within (Gal. 4:19), there remains to the end a permanent incongruity between the believers' "natural" existence and their existence "in Christ." Although Romans 7:7–25 cannot, I think, be read convincingly as a description of the Christian life (and thus as a depiction of life *simul justus et peccator*, at the same time justified and a sinner), Paul is everywhere clear that the new life that bears fruit for God is created by "the newness of the Spirit" (Rom. 7:6), so that every work of the believer is persistently and wholly constituted by an incongruous grace.

I am not convinced that "synergism," "assistance," or "cooperation" are helpful terms here; they suggest that the believer has an agency in some sense separable from that of God, which can be added to that of God, and works alongside it.[9] The reason there is, as Pitre says, "*no competition* between God's work and good works done *in Christ*" (49) is not because there is good collaboration between them but because the works of the believer are *situated within* the agency of Christ who "began a good work in you" and "will bring it to completion" (Phil. 1:6).[10] I have suggested that "energism" is a more helpful label than either "synergism" or "monergism," since Paul certainly expects the believer to work, but that work is both grounded in and energized by the persisting grace of God "in which we stand" (Rom. 5:1).[11] And I do not think that Paul imagines grace to be something "infused" into the believer (even if a liquid metaphor can be used of the love of Christ [Rom. 5:5]), since grace is not a substance but a relation—not an object transferable from God to believers so as to "inhere" within them but a relationship in which they are

9. The Pauline texts that Pitre cites for this notion (1 Cor. 3:9–10; 2 Cor. 6:1) do not seem to me apposite (they are about human agents working together); 1 Cor. 15:10 might be more relevant, but even here Paul complicates notions of agency so much as to question the use of the label "synergism."

10. For the language of "collaboration," see *Catechism of the Catholic Church*, nos. 2001, 2003, 2008, 2025; cf. "cooperation" (nos. 1993, 2001), "assistance" (no. 2008), and "help" (nos. 1996, 2021).

11. See Barclay, *Paul and the Gift*, 441–42.

held.[12] Here, underlying structures of thought concerning the relation between nature and grace influence the Catholic reading of Paul, with nature perfected by a supernatural addition. Paul has a more dynamic sense of grace in which believers are not only re-created by grace but also ever dependent on the life of Christ, which is in a deep sense never their own.[13]

This is the context in which to understand judgment by works. Like Pitre, I think that the Pauline statements on this topic should be taken seriously, but I take Paul to mean not that the works of the believer merit a second and final gift (an eschatological justification distinguishable from an initial justification) but that the final judgment tests the integrity of the gift and its necessary actualization and brings the one incongruous gift of new creation to its proper completion.[14] Eternal life is not a prize to be earned: it is the gift (χάρισμα, *charisma*) of God (Rom. 6:23) from start to finish. There will indeed be some congruity between the completion of this gift and the behavior of those "who by patiently doing good seek for glory and honor and immortality" (Rom. 2:7); but they are able to "seek" only because of the law written on the heart (Rom. 2:15), the hidden circumcision of the heart effected by the Spirit (Rom. 2:29). In other words, the good works themselves are the product of God's gift, effected in Christ.[15] Inasmuch as they draw from the life of Christ, they cannot be attributed *separably* to the believer, and cannot be the basis for a *second* act of saving justification, distinguishable from the grace in which they were effected. Such a two-stage justification, where "staying in" operates on a different basis from "getting in," runs contrary to everything Paul says about grace, the Spirit, and participation in Christ, even if these operate in past, present, and future tenses. To be sure, the believer can fall out of grace and be cut off from Christ (Gal. 5:4), or from the root of mercy by which she lives (Rom. 11:17–24). But inasmuch as she stands in grace (Rom. 5:1) and belongs to Christ (2 Cor. 13:5), building on the foundation that is Christ (1 Cor. 3:11), the judgment will not determine whether she has done enough to

12. For "infusion," note *Catechism*, no. 2023: "Sanctifying grace is the gratuitous gift of his life that God makes to us; it is infused by the Holy Spirit into the soul to heal it of sin and to sanctify it."

13. Note the distinction in the *Catechism* between "actual graces" (such as the grace "at the beginning of conversion") and "habitual grace" which is "a stable and supernatural disposition that perfects the soul itself to enable it to live with God, to act by his love" (no. 2000; cf. no. 2024).

14. See my reading of Rom. 2 in *Paul and the Gift*, 463–71, which avoids either sidelining this text or treating it as a hypothetical scenario.

15. This point is repeatedly emphasized in the *Catechism*, but the principle of "merit" is necessary to preserve both justice and equality (no. 2006). Pitre's distinction is summarized in no. 2027: "No one can merit the initial grace which is at the origin of conversion. Moved by the Holy Spirit, we can merit for ourselves and for others all the graces needed to attain eternal life, as well as necessary temporal goods."

merit eternal life; it will only (but still significantly) test and reveal the works that have flowed from the gift of the Spirit that constitutes the Christian life. The "reward" here is not a distinct act of grace, definitive for final salvation, but is the proper crowning of the effects of an unmerited gift that has created and defined the life of the believer from the start.

The Trojans learned to fear the Greeks, even when they brought gifts. Whatever support Sanders offers to certain Catholic ways of reading Paul, his schematic distinction between "getting in" and "staying in" is, I believe, one of his least helpful contributions to Pauline studies. In *Paul and the Gift* I have offered a close analysis of "grace" that enables an integrated reading of Paul, incorporating Pitre's strong points concerning transformation, participation in Christ, and judgment by works, without resorting to an un-Pauline distinction between an initial justification by faith and a final justification by works. Faith, as self-abandoning trust in Christ, is as definitive on the "day of Christ" as it is on the day of baptism; without it, works are without meaning and value. And inasmuch as believers are held by (and therefore stand in) the grace of Christ, they may run with confidence the race that is set before them, knowing that the one who began a good work in them will bring it (the same good work) to completion (Phil. 1:6; 3:12–14).

Roman Catholic Perspective
Reply to the Respondents

BRANT PITRE

Let me begin by saying what a privilege it has been to contribute to this volume. I have learned much from the essays by Andrew Das, James Dunn, Magnus Zetterholm, and John Barclay. In grateful dialogue, I would like to reply briefly to each of their responses to my essay.

A. Andrew Das—Traditional Protestant Perspective

I admit that Das left me wondering: What does he think of my actual arguments? His response contains very little engagement with my essay. This is unfortunate, since I was looking forward to seeing what he would make of the overlap between E. P. Sanders and the Catholic interpretation of Paul. With that said, two brief points:

1. *Affirmations versus denials.* It seems to me that, overall, Das tends to be right in what he affirms and wrong in what he denies. For example, Das correctly affirms that for Paul, "the focus is always on Christ," but he incorrectly insists that Paul's focus is "not on deeds" (61). Over and over again, Paul does emphasize deeds:

> [God] will repay according to each one's deeds [κατὰ τὰ ἔργα αὐτοῦ, *kata ta erga autou*]. (Rom. 2:6)

75

The doers of the law [οἱ ποιηταὶ νόμου, *hoi poiētai nomou*] . . . will be justified. (Rom. 2:13)

All of us must appear before the judgment seat of Christ, so that each may receive recompense for what has been done [ἃ ἔπραξεν, *ha epraxen*]. (2 Cor. 5:10)

All must test their own work [ἔργον, *ergon*]. (Gal. 6:4)

Let us not grow weary in doing good [καλὸν ποιοῦντες, *kalon poiountes*], for we will reap at harvest time, if we do not give up. (Gal. 6:9 AT)

Likewise, Das correctly affirms that "righteousness is a *free gift* (Rom. 5:17)" (58). However, he incorrectly insists that Paul "never" uses the language of "earning" with reference to "final" justification (58). But Paul does in fact use the language of "wages" and "reward" with reference to final judgment:

He will repay [ἀποδώσει, *apodōsei*] according to each one's deeds. (Rom. 2:6)

Each will receive wages [μισθόν, *misthon*] according to the labor of each. (1 Cor. 3:8)

If the work which any man has built on the foundation survives, he will receive a wage [μισθόν, *misthon*]. (1 Cor. 3:14 AT)

I highlighted these passages in my essay. Unfortunately, Das never discusses Paul's language of final repayment and wages.

2. *"Faith" in Paul: not just "belief."* Along similar lines, when Das says justification "must be a gift on the basis of belief rather than on the basis of doing" (57), he gives the impression that for Paul, πίστις (*pistis*) is mere "belief." However, a case can be made that "while Paul does employ *pistis* to signify belief in particular propositions as well as trust, he also employs the term to signify true faithfulness or fidelity."[1] For example:

The scripture, foreseeing that God would justify the Gentiles by faith, declared the gospel beforehand to Abraham, saying, "All the Gentiles shall be blessed in you." For this reason, those who believe [οἱ ἐκ πίστεως, *hoi ek pisteōs*] are blessed with faithful Abraham [τῷ πιστῷ Ἀβραάμ, *tō pistō Abraam*]. (Gal. 3:8–9 AT)

1. Brant Pitre, Michael P. Barber, and John A. Kincaid, *Paul, A New Covenant Jew: Rethinking Pauline Theology* (Grand Rapids: Eerdmans, 2019), 185, citing 1 Thess. 1:3, 8–10; 3:2–10; 5:8; Gal. 5:6; Rom. 1:5; 3:31; 16:26. See also Teresa Morgan, *Roman Faith and Christian Faith: Pistis and Fides in the Early Roman Empire and Early Churches* (Oxford: Oxford University Press, 2015), 36–175.

Here Paul talks about "faith" (πίστις, *pistis*) as bound up with "faithfulness" (πιστός, *pistos*)![2] *"Pauline 'faith,' then, is a radical, all-encompassing virtue."*[3] Indeed, scholars of very different perspectives agree that "the word has this fuller sense for Paul."[4] Perhaps that is why Paul describes his mission as bringing about "the obedience of faith" (ὑπακοὴν πίστεως, *hypakoēn pisteōs*) (Rom. 1:5; 16:26).

One strength of the Catholic perspective is that it is able to affirm what Paul says about "faith" without downplaying or explaining away what he says about "deeds," "works," "obedience," and "faithfulness."

James D. G. Dunn—New Perspective

Three aspects of James Dunn's incisive response stood out to me.

1. *The history of Pauline interpretation.* I wholeheartedly agree with Dunn that exegetes should understand "the terms of the issue that confronted Paul in the first century" (62). I myself have written elsewhere that the first task is "to interpret Paul *on his own terms*."[5] However, I do not agree that "we need to set to one side the evidence" from "later centuries" (62). On the contrary, if contemporary Pauline exegesis is to advance, it needs to become *more familiar*—not less—with the *entire* history of Pauline interpretation. This is particularly important when commentators from multiple eras (patristic, medieval, modern), multiple languages (Greek, Latin, German, English), and multiple continents (Africa, Asia Minor, Europe, North America) interpret Paul in similar ways. One reason I chose to compare patristic, medieval, and modern Catholic interpreters with the work of E. P. Sanders is precisely that Sanders, as far I know, has no firsthand knowledge of the Catholic tradition. Yet, on the basis of a close exegesis of Paul, Sanders arrives at remarkably *similar* conclusions. This demands an explanation. One possible explanation (to which I am inclined) is that they are all reading Paul well.

2. Pitre, Barber, and Kincaid, *Paul, A New Covenant Jew*, 191–92.

3. Pitre, Barber, and Kincaid, *Paul, A New Covenant Jew*, 185, following Joseph A. Fitzmyer, *Paul and His Theology: A Brief Sketch* (Englewood Cliffs, NJ: Prentice Hall, 1987), 84–85 (emphasis original).

4. Pitre, Barber, and Kincaid, *Paul, A New Covenant Jew*, 185, citing Thomas R. Schreiner, *Paul, Apostle of God's Glory in Christ: A Pauline Theology* (Downers Grove, IL: IVP Academic, 2001), 211; Matthew Bates, *Salvation by Allegiance Alone: Rethinking Faith, Works, and the Gospel of Jesus the King* (Grand Rapids: Baker Academic, 2017), 20–22, 98–99; Douglas Campbell, *The Quest for Paul's Gospel: A Suggested Strategy* (London: T&T Clark, 2005), 186.

5. Pitre, Barber, and Kincaid, *Paul, A New Covenant Jew*, 7 (emphasis original).

2. *The meaning of "works of the law."* Dunn rightly points out that I avoided addressing the "Catholic debate" over "works of the law" (63). Let me do so now. As I have stated elsewhere, in my view, for Paul, the expression "works of the law" refers *quintessentially but not exclusively* to circumcision, food laws, and Sabbath observance.[6] It seems clear that in his first use of "works of the law," Paul is speaking primarily of circumcision and other boundary markers (Gal. 2:15–16).[7] On the other hand, other passages suggest a wider range of meaning. For example, shortly after declaring that "a person is justified by faith apart from works of the law [ἔργων νόμου, *ergōn nomou*]" (Rom. 3:28), Paul cites the example of David:

> So also David speaks of the blessedness of those to whom God reckons righteousness apart from works: "Blessed are those whose iniquities are forgiven, and whose sins are covered; blessed is the one against whom the Lord will not reckon sin." (Rom. 4:6–8)

As Jewish Scripture makes clear, circumcision and food laws were not where David failed! Instead, he committed adultery and murder (2 Sam. 11:1–25; cf. Exod. 20:13–14). Hence, in context, when Paul uses David as an example of how God "justifies" (δικαιόω, *dikaioō*) the "ungodly" who are "without works" (μὴ ἐργαζομένῳ, *mē ergazomenō*) (Rom. 4:5), the works in view seem to involve keeping the Ten Commandments.[8]

3. *Was Luther's claim justified?* Finally, Dunn asks whether Luther was justified in claiming "that Rome had in effect distorted the gospel by its practice of selling indulgences" (63). On this point, I think so. That is why the Council of Trent decreed that "all base gain for securing indulgences, which has been the source of *abundant abuses* among the Christian people, should be *totally abolished*."[9] At the same time, Luther also initiated a division that has endured to this day. Just as we should not ignore abuses in medieval Christianity, we also need to weigh Luther's solution against what Paul says about schism: "Now I appeal to you, brothers and sisters, by the name of our Lord Jesus Christ, that all of you be in agreement and that *there be no divisions* [σχίσματα, *schismata*] among you" (1 Cor. 1:10).

6. See Pitre, Barber, and Kincaid, *Paul, A New Covenant Jew*, 53–54.
7. See James D. G. Dunn, *The New Perspective on Paul*, rev. ed. (Grand Rapids: Eerdmans, 2008), 1–120.
8. See Pitre, Barber, and Kincaid, *Paul, A New Covenant Jew*, 53.
9. Council of Trent, *Decree on Indulgences* (December 4, 1563) (emphasis added). See *Decrees of the Ecumenical Councils*, ed. Norman P. Tanner, 2 vols. (Washington, DC: Georgetown University Press, 1990), 2:797.

Hence, when Dunn writes, "*Semper reformanda* is a slogan for the whole church, is it not?" (63), I would say yes![10] However, there is a difference between always reforming and always dividing. It is my hope that books such as this one will help heal the rifts that still impede Paul's vision of a united church.

Magnus Zetterholm—Paul within Judaism

I was happy to see several points of agreement with Magnus Zetterholm. Here I address two of his critiques.

1. *The forgiveness of sins.* Zetterholm suggests that "the idea of forgiveness of sins needs some modification to become truly Pauline" (67), because, as Krister Stendahl has pointed out, "forgiveness is the term for salvation which is used least of all in the Pauline writing." Given the occasional nature of Paul's Letters, however, frequency is only one index of a term's importance. Another is where Paul deploys it. For Paul emphasizes atonement for sin in a central passage:

> Since all have sinned and fall short of the glory of God; they are now justified by his grace as a gift, through *the redemption that is in Christ Jesus, whom God put forward as a sacrifice of atonement by his blood*, effective through faith. (Rom. 3:23–25)

A case can be made that when Paul speaks of "redemption" (ἀπολύτρωσις, *apolytrōsis*) (Rom. 3:24), he means redemption "from sin."[11] Likewise, when Paul speaks of "a sacrifice of atonement" (ἱλαστήριον, *hilastērion*) (Rom. 3:25), he is alluding to the Jewish feast of Yom Kippur, when the atoning blood was sprinkled on the "mercy seat" (*hilastērion*) (Lev. 16:13–15 LXX).[12] If the forgiveness of sins is not truly "Pauline," why does Paul use imagery from the Day of Atonement to describe what happens when someone is "justified" (Rom. 3:24)?

2. *The salvation of the individual.* Zetterholm also suggests, "The individualization both of sins and salvation may be part of the 'Catholic perspective,'

---

10. For a Catholic perspective, see Yves Congar, *True and False Reform in the Church*, trans. Paul Philibert (Collegeville, MN: Liturgical Press, 2011).

11. Mark D. Nanos, "The Letter of Paul to the Romans," in *The Jewish Annotated New Testament: New Revised Standard Version Bible Translation*, ed. Amy-Jill Levine and Marc Zvi Brettler, 2nd ed. (Oxford: Oxford University Press, 2017), 293.

12. See Daniel Stökl Ben Ezra, *The Impact of Yom Kippur on Early Christianity: The Day of Atonement from Second Temple Judaism to the Fifth Century*, WUNT 2/163 (Tübingen: Mohr Siebeck, 2003), 197–205.

but I doubt it is Pauline" (67). Again, I demur. For Paul himself speaks in strikingly individual terms:

> So also David speaks of the blessedness of those to whom God reckons righteousness apart from works: "Blessed are those whose iniquities are forgiven, and whose sins are covered; *blessed is the one against whom the Lord will not reckon sin.*" (Rom. 4:6–8)

> *I* have been crucified with Christ; and it is no longer *I* who live, but it is Christ who lives in *me*. And the life *I* now live in the flesh *I* live by faith in the Son of God, who loved *me* and gave himself for *me*. (Gal. 2:19–20)

Notice here that Paul describes justification in terms of David's *individual* "iniquities" (ἀνομίαι, *anomiai*) and "sins" (ἁμαρτίαι, *hamartiai*) being "forgiven" (ἀφίημι, *aphiēmi*) and "covered" (ἐπικαλύπτω, *epikalyptō*) (Rom. 4:8). As for Galatians 2, I would invite Zetterholm to find a more individualistic description of sin and salvation in all of Second Temple Jewish literature. I for one cannot think of one.

Thus, I stand by my description of justification in Paul. After all, Paul was a Jew, and in first-century Judaism forgiveness of sin involved both corporate sacrifices, such as on Yom Kippur (Lev. 16:13–15), and individual sacrifices, such as the countless "sin offerings" and "guilt offerings" of individual Jews in the temple (Lev. 4:1–7:10). As the Torah says, "Thus the priest shall make atonement on his behalf for his *sin*, and he shall be *forgiven*" (Lev. 4:26).

This is another example of how a Catholic "both-and" approach is helpful for reading Paul. For Paul the Jew, forgiveness of sin is both corporate and individual.[13]

John M. G. Barclay—Gift Perspective

John Barclay's rich response makes an adequate reply difficult. Thankfully, I have published elsewhere on several issues he raises. I encourage the reader to consult the chapter "New Covenant Justification through Divine Sonship" that I coauthored with Michael Barber and John Kincaid.[14]

1. *Grace and the "intertwining of agencies."* I think that Barclay may have misconstrued my position when he suggests that I posited an "old 'I' . . . now 'cooperating' with grace with an agency placed alongside that of God," instead of "a new 'I,' a new creation in Christ (2 Cor. 5:17)" (72). Of course there

---

13. See Pitre, Barber, and Kincaid, *Paul, A New Covenant Jew*, 211–50.
14. See Pitre, Barber, and Kincaid, *Paul, A New Covenant Jew*, 162–210.

is a "new 'I,'" but that does not stop Paul himself from *distinguishing*—not separating—his own "work" from the "grace" of God acting in him: "But *by the grace of God* I am what I am, and his grace toward me has not been in vain. On the contrary, *I worked harder than any of them*—though *it was not I, but the grace of God* that is with me" (1 Cor. 15:10).

Indeed, even after baptism, Paul continues to speak both of "Christ" living in him and Paul himself as "living": "*It is no longer I who live*, but it is *Christ who lives in me*. And the life *I now live* in the flesh *I live by faith* in the Son of God" (Gal. 2:20).

To be sure, Paul himself "is not the source of this new life"; at the same time, "this does not mean that Paul is no longer an acting subject. Christ has not canceled out the believer's role. . . . Paul himself is working and his work is effective, but *only* because Christ is working within him."[15] This, I would suggest, is what Barclay has helpfully described as "the intertwining of agencies."[16] For Paul, human agency is transformed and empowered—but not eradicated—through grace.[17]

2. *"Grace" as an indwelling "power."* Barclay also objects to the idea of grace as "something 'infused' into the believer," insisting that "grace is not a substance but a relation" (72). I agree that Paul never describes grace as a "substance" or "object," but neither did I! However, Paul does describe grace as a "power" that dwells in the believer: "'My *grace* is sufficient for you, for *power* is made perfect in weakness.' So, I will boast all the more gladly of my weaknesses, so that *the power of Christ* may dwell in me" (2 Cor. 12:9).

Notice here the parallelism between "grace" (χάρις, *charis*) and the indwelling "power" (δύναμις, *dynamis*) of Christ. For Paul, then, *charis* is both a relationship into which believers are grafted and "the power of Christ" (ἡ δύναμις τοῦ Χριστοῦ, *hē dynamis tou Christou*) dwelling in them. In short, "Paul views grace in terms of divine empowerment."[18]

3. *"Justification": both a "relational act" and an "act of moral alteration."* Barclay objects to any suggestion that for Paul, the verb "justify" (δικαιόω, *dikaioō*) can mean "make righteous." For him, this "turns a relational act ('to consider someone in the right') into an act of moral alteration ('to make someone righteous')" (71). I think that this is an unnecessary dichotomy. While I agree that *dikaioō* in Paul is forensic, I would suggest that this declaration

---

15. Pitre, Barber, and Kincaid, *Paul, A New Covenant Jew*, 169 (emphasis original).

16. John Barclay, "Grace and the Transformation of Agency in Christ," in *Redefining First-Century Jewish and Christian Identities: Essays in Honor of Ed Parish Sanders*, ed. Fabian E. Udoh et al. (Notre Dame, IN: University of Notre Dame Press, 2008), 372–89, here 383–84.

17. Pitre, Barber, and Kincaid, *Paul, A New Covenant Jew*, 169.

18. Pitre, Barber, and Kincaid, *Paul, A New Covenant Jew*, 168.

is morally realistic and not exclusively counterfactual.[19] Barclay himself puts this realism well when he writes, "If this 'considering righteous' is *not mere pretense that sinners are righteous*, it represents either a performative state-ment (*making people 'in the right' when it announces them so*) or the decla-ration of *a new reality*."[20]

Barclay is right to suggest this, since Paul uses the verb "justify" (*dikaioō*) to signify being "conformed" to Christ: "For those whom he foreknew he also predestined to be *conformed* to the image of his Son. . . . And those whom he predestined he also called; and those whom he called he also *justified*; and those whom he *justified* he also glorified" (Rom. 8:29–30). If Paul does not see justification as involving "moral alteration," why does he describe those who have been "justified" (δικαιόω, *dikaioō*) (Rom. 8:30) as being "conformed" (σύμμορφος, *symmorphos*) to "the image of the Son" (Rom. 8:29)? I submit that for Paul, "the decree of justification could be seen as *both* forensic *and* transformative of moral character."[21]

In Paul's theology of what may be called "cardiac righteousness," a per-son "believes with the heart and so is justified" (καρδίᾳ γὰρ πιστύεται εἰς δικαιοσύνην, *kardia gar pisteuetai eis dikaiosynēn*) (Rom. 10:10). That is, through the indwelling of the "Spirit" (cf. Rom. 5:5; Gal. 4:6), the "heart" (καρδία, *kardia*) is truly changed and a person is thus truly justified—that is, he or she *is* righteous.[22]

---

19. Pitre, Barber, and Kincaid, *Paul, A New Covenant Jew*, 163, 186n66, 205, where we too draw on the excellent work of James B. Prothro, *Both Judge and Justifier: Biblical Legal Language and the Act of Justifying in Paul*, WUNT 2/461 (Tübingen: Mohr Siebeck, 2018).

20. John M. G. Barclay, *Paul and the Gift* (Grand Rapids: Eerdmans, 2015), 476 (emphasis added). We cite this page in Pitre, Barber, and Kincaid, *Paul, A New Covenant Jew*, 209n128.

21. Pitre, Barber, and Kincaid, *Paul, A New Covenant Jew*, 209 (emphasis original).

22. For more on "cardiac righteousness," see Pitre, Barber, and Kincaid, *Paul, A New Cov-enant Jew*, 172–88, 208–9.

2

The Traditional Protestant Perspective on Paul

A. ANDREW DAS

Traditional Protestant readings are diverse but typically include three inter-related claims: (1) Second Temple Jews adhered to a religion of works righteousness and legalism; (2) Paul, in response, emphasized God's free grace over against human works; (3) that emphasis on sheer grace exclusive of works is characteristic of God's saving, justifying activity. Ferdinand Weber, for instance, a nineteenth-century German Lutheran scholar, declared Judaism to be a religion of works righteousness, a religion of law, against which Paul posited the free grace of God in the gospel of Jesus Christ. After the Shoah, modern interpreters began to conclude that the theological proclivities of interpreters had influenced their interpretation and that Paul, read on his own terms and in his own religious milieu, should be understood differently. Terence Donaldson describes a paradigm shift in modern scholarship away from the Reformation and its Lutheran roots and away from the traditional opposition of grace/justification and human works/guilt.[1] A short essay reaffirming the traditional position will hardly be adequate to the task. The criticism, while often dismissive, has its reasons.

1. Terence L. Donaldson, *Paul and the Gentiles: Remapping the Apostle's Convictional World* (Minneapolis: Fortress, 1998), 4–6; cf. ix.

In the 1980s, while I was attending a conservative Lutheran seminary, my class on Romans was designed to conclude after chapter 8. Romans 9–11 and the remainder of the letter were relegated to a rarely offered elective. The professor spent much of his time on the great doctrines of the faith: Christology, justification, and sanctification. I struggled to understand how certain features of the letter that we had neglected figured into those doctrinal emphases. Paul says repeatedly that his gospel is to the Jew *first* and also to the Greek. He returns to the circumcised and the uncircumcised in Romans 4. Looking ahead to the seminary elective's chapters, I was not surprised, then, that Romans 9–11 continues with the inclusion of the gentiles in God's saving activity on behalf of Israel.

Later, in a graduate seminar on Galatians with J. Louis Martyn, I reported on James D. G. Dunn's essay on Galatians 3:10–14.[2] Dunn had placed Jew and gentile back into the mix. In fact, he contended that it was central to the letter. Much of what he wrote made sense and was helpful. At the same time, the inclusion of the gentiles into God's people struck me as so central to Dunn's thinking that justification by faith had become somewhat secondary. Dunn had not interpreted works in Paul in terms of the law-gospel dialectic so familiar to me as a Lutheran. E. P. Sanders had convinced Dunn that Second Temple Judaism was a religion of grace and atonement. What, then, was Paul's polemic against "works" about if not a response to works righteousness? By the phrase "works of the law," Dunn's Paul had in mind the entire law, but especially those aspects of the law that serve as ethnic boundary markers. Paul's contrast of the works of the law with faith in Christ was a component of his argument for the *inclusion of the gentiles* into God's people—a new perspective on Paul.

Although representing for this volume the traditional view of Paul, I was largely convinced by Sanders's *Paul and Palestinian Judaism*;[3] and John M. G. Barclay has nuanced the varied elements of grace in Second Temple Judaism even further.[4] I took as my starting point Sanders's description of covenantal nomism, although I prefer the label "*elective* nomism" since Sanders demonstrated the centrality of Israel's election in Second Temple Judaism, not any particular covenant conception.[5] Sanders demonstrated, for instance, that the

---

2. James D. G. Dunn, "Works of the Law and the Curse of the Law (Gal. 3.10–14)," in *Jesus, Paul, and the Law: Studies in Mark and Galatians* (Louisville: Westminster John Knox, 1990), 215–41; originally published in *NTS* 31 (1985): 523–42.

3. E. P. Sanders, *Paul and Palestinian Judaism: A Comparison of Patterns of Religion* (Philadelphia: Fortress, 1977).

4. John M. G. Barclay, *Paul and the Gift* (Grand Rapids: Eerdmans, 2015).

5. See the chapter "Rethinking the Covenantal Paul" in A. Andrew Das, *Paul and the Stories of Israel: Grand Thematic Narratives* (Minneapolis: Fortress, 2016), 65–92: e.g., one covenant

Second Temple Jewish document Jubilees requires strict, even perfect obedience of God's law, but that demand for perfect obedience is embedded within a gracious framework inclusive of God's gracious election of a people and provision for sin and failure through atoning sacrifice.[6] I proposed a "newer" perspective—that Paul reasons christologically—paralleling in some ways Sanders's "solution to plight" proposal. If God's salvation takes place through faith in/of Christ, it is not through observing the law. From this I contended that Paul's advocacy for the inclusion of the gentiles stems from his christological convictions. If God saves through Christ and not the law of Moses, why foist Moses's law upon the gentiles for their salvation? It struck me that Dunn's emphases placed the cart before the horse. My "newer perspective" granted Sanders's basic insights on Second Temple Judaism but launched from Sanders in a different, "newer" trajectory that does not deny or fail to appreciate "New Perspective" elements in Pauline texts. It is simply not an "either-or": again, if God saves on the basis of faith in/of Jesus Christ, then salvation is not on the basis of the law or its works. If so, there is no reason to exclude Christ-believing non-Jews from God's salvation. The ethnic element in Paul's argument flows *from* the soteriological claim that God saves on the basis of faith in/of Christ.

Despite my advocacy of a "newer perspective" on Paul—and Magnus Zetterholm's essay offers a still "newer" perspective—I am representing for this volume the traditional view, and that includes the claim that Paul was responding to a legalistic or works-based perspective on the part of his Jewish peers. Traditionalists would maintain that Paul's doctrine of salvation by faith in Christ stands over against an affirmation of works on the part of his Jewish peers *at some level*.[7] Not all Second Temple Jews affirmed a legalistic or works-based approach, but at least some did, and Paul is responding to that claim. Although I have denied that Paul is responding to legalism, admittedly, Galatians includes a pivotal section in which Paul turns to Abraham in the context of an intra-Jewish Christian dispute and affirms Abraham's faith, while excluding works.

---

as a will in Gal. 3:16, two Abrahamic covenants side by side in Gal. 4:21–31, an old covenant and a new one in 2 Cor. 3—contingent responses to how covenant and law were conjoined in Second Temple Judaism.

6. *PPJ*, 381: "Perfect obedience is specified"; but, as Sanders then explains, this perfect obedience of the law is effectively mitigated within Jubilees' gracious framework. For an appropriation and corrective of Sanders, see A. Andrew Das, *Paul, the Law, and the Covenant* (Peabody, MA: Hendrickson, 2001), chaps. 1–2: e.g., the practical result of a system inclusive of election, covenant, and atoning sacrifice for failure.

7. E.g., D. A. Carson, Peter T. O'Brien, and Mark A. Seifrid, eds., *Justification and Variegated Nomism*, vol. 1, *The Complexities of Second Temple Judaism*, WUNT 2/140 (Tübingen: Mohr Siebeck; Grand Rapids: Baker Academic, 2001).

Abraham as a Model of Obedience in Second Temple Judaism and Paul's Approach in Galatians

Abraham figured prominently in Second Temple Jewish discourse as a model for conversion from paganism. As a Chaldean, he had come to realize the truth of monotheism and the error of his family's idolatry (Philo, *Virt.* 39.212–19; Jub. 11.3–5, 7–8, 16–17; 12.1–8, 12–13.1; Josephus, *Ant.* 1.154–57; Apoc. Ab. 1–8; Jdt. 5:6–9; Philo, *Migr.* 176–86; *Abr.* 60–88; *QG* 3.1; *Somn.* 1.41–60; *Her.* 96–99; LAB 6.3–4, 16–17; 23.5). Gentile conversion to Judaism would reenact Abraham's journey. As Jewish Christian teachers attempted to influence the Galatian gentiles to adopt Jewish observances, Abraham would be Exhibit A.

Abraham was Exhibit A in another respect as well. Equally widespread, if not even more ubiquitous, was the praise of Abraham's obedience. This was no mere hagiography; Abraham served as a *model*. Josephus recognizes Abraham's submission to God's will "in everything" (ἅπαντα, *hapanta*) (Josephus, *Ant.* 1.225). For the author of Jubilees, Abraham proved "faithful" in each of the six times he was tested (Jub. 17.15 [2x], 17, 18 [2x]; 18.16), whether with famine, the lack of land, the pain of circumcision, temptation in the face of royal wealth, or the loss of loved ones, but especially his immediate obedience in response to God's command to offer his son as a sacrifice (17.18; 18.3, 9). God told Abram in 15.3 to "be pleasing before me and be perfect." Abraham is then praised in 23.10 as "perfect in all of his actions with the Lord and . . . pleasing through righteousness all of the days of his life."[8] In 24.11, "All of the nations of the earth will bless themselves by your seed because your father [Abraham] obeyed me and observed my restrictions and my commandments and my laws and my ordinances and my covenant." Abraham's exemplary or even perfect obedience was a common motif in Second Temple Judaism. In the Prayer of Manasseh 8, "You, therefore, O Lord, God of the righteous, did not appoint grace for the righteous, such as Abraham, . . . who did not sin against you."

Philo (*Abr.* 3–6) praises, as a model of piety for subsequent generations, the patriarch's observance, with ease, of the unwritten law—whether divine laws corresponding to Sinai or the pre-Sinaitic expression of the law of Moses. Those who observe the written Torah would therefore find themselves behaving as Abraham did. Philo presents Abraham as the *embodiment* of the as-yet-unwritten law (*Abr.* 275–76)! Second Baruch 57.1–3 refers to the unwritten law and commandments accomplished by Abraham. In the Damascus Document (CD) column 3, lines 2–3, "Abraham . . . was counted as a friend for keeping

---

8. Old Testament Pseudepigrapha translations are from *OTP*.

God's precepts and not following the desire of his spirit."[9] In the later Mishnah Qiddushin 4.14, "And we find that Abraham our father had performed the whole Law before it was given. . . . *Abraham obeyed my voice and kept my charge, my commandments, my statutes, and my laws.*"[10]

Abraham's apparent failure in Genesis 12 in pawning off Sarah as his sister to Pharaoh was not perceived as such in Second Temple interpretation. In the Genesis Apocryphon (1QapGen XIX.14–16; XX.2–15), for instance, Sarah is so beautiful in the eyes of the Egyptians that they could not resist describing her to Pharaoh. Pharaoh would have killed Abraham had the ruler suspected Sarah of being Abraham's wife. Abraham had no choice but to deceive Pharaoh, and he remained a man of supreme faith, as his occasional anxiety and fear were placed in a different light and rationalized.

One Jewish author even seems to be *reacting* to the widespread tradition of Abraham's exemplary obedience. The Testament of Abraham begins with the standard description of Abraham's righteousness, piety, hospitality, and kindness toward strangers and the needy (T. Ab. [A] 1.1–2, 5). The angel Michael pleads with God on behalf of Abraham, since he is a man like no one else on earth in refraining from evil and in his mercy, truthfulness, justice, and hospitality (T. Ab. [A] 4.6). A voice from heaven agrees that up to that point, "Abraham has *not sinned*" (T. Ab. [A] 10.13 [emphasis added]). Surprisingly, the reader learns that Abraham fears death, and so God permits him a tour of the otherworldly realms. When Death finally demands Abraham's soul, the patriarch continues to resist. Death eventually resorts to trickery. The Testament of Abraham questions popular estimations and "the elevation of this patriarch to the status of an ideal model, perfect beyond the capacity of emulation."[11]

Sirach 44:20 narrates, "When he was tested he proved faithful." The language of Abraham's *testing* (נסה, *nsâ*) derives from Genesis 22:1. The note of *faithfulness*, however, is not from Genesis 22 but may be traced to Nehemiah 9:8: "you found his heart *faithful* [אמן, *'mn*] before you." Nehemiah 9:7–9 recounts God's choice of Abraham, Abraham's departure from Ur, his name change, the covenant to give him the land, but nothing on the Aqedah. Nehemiah 9:8's "faithful" derives rather from Genesis 15:6; reference to Abraham's faithfulness in both contexts is followed by the covenant promise of the land.

9. Dead Sea Scrolls translations are from *DSSSE*.

10. Translation from Herbert Danby, *The Mishnah: Translated from the Hebrew with Introduction and Brief Explanatory Notes* (Oxford: Clarendon, 1933) (emphasis original).

11. Annette Yoshiko Reed, "The Construction and Subversion of Patriarchal Perfection: Abraham and Exemplarity in Philo, Josephus, and the *Testament of Abraham*," *JSJ* 40 (2009): 185–212, here 208–9.

Sirach 44:20 is therefore conflating Abraham's faith(fulness) in Genesis 15 with Genesis 22's testing of him, the ultimate example of faithfulness. "Already in Sirach the future blessings of Israel are contingent on Abraham's obedience, particularly that of his greatest trial in Genesis 22."[12] As an author of wisdom literature, ben Sira is ultimately admonishing his readers to the same faithful obedience as the basis for God's further blessing.

Similarly, the Dead Sea Scolls document 4QMMT 117 (4Q398 frag. 2, col. 2; 4Q399 frag. 1, col. 2) echoes the language of Genesis 15:6 and interprets that language not in terms of Abraham's believing trust but rather of his good deeds: "It shall be reckoned to you [plural] as justice when you do what is upright and good before him, for your good and that of Israel." Mattathias in 1 Maccabees 2:52 reminds his sons, "Was not Abraham found faithful [εὑρέθη πιστός, *heurethē pistos*] when tested [in his willingness to sacrifice Isaac, Gen. 22], and it was reckoned [ἐλογίσθη, *elogisthē*] to him as righteousness [εἰς δικαιοσύνην, *eis dikaiosynēn*]?" The 1 Maccabees text attests to the tradition of interpreting the reckoning of Abraham's "faith" in Genesis 15:6 not in terms of his believing God's promises but in terms of his "faithfulness" in the near sacrifice of Isaac. Paul will interpret Genesis 15:6 differently.

As many have observed, Paul seems to use the term "children of Abraham" in Galatians 3:7 in an unannounced, unexpected way—as if he were *responding* to the use of the phrase in someone else's argument, an argument befitting the rival teachers, who were encouraging the Galatians to become children of Abraham.[13] In stark, perhaps even deliberate, contrast to that widespread tradition in Second Temple Judaism, Paul stresses in Galatians 3:6–9 Abraham's believing trust. Paul sets forth Abraham in Genesis 15:6 as one who believed God, and it was credited to him for righteousness. He conspicuously does not refer in those verses to Abraham's obedience. The debate between Paul and the rival teachers at Galatia may be interpreted in light of the contemporary reflections on the patriarch's faithfulness.

At least in Galatians 3:6–9 Paul defines πίστις (*pistis*) strictly in terms of faith or trust in God without reference to faithfulness. Galatians 3:6 quotes Genesis 15:6: Abraham "believed" (ἐπίστευσεν, *episteusen*) God. Galatians 3:6 is unpacking the contrast in verse 5 between works of the law and the hearing of faith (ἀκοῆς πίστεως, *akoēs pisteōs*). Immediately after the verb in verse 6 for Abraham's believing trust, "those of faith" (οἱ ἐκ πίστεως, *hoi ek pisteōs*) in verse 7 should be taken as those who believe or place their trust in God as

12. Bradley C. Gregory, "Abraham as the Jewish Ideal: Exegetical Traditions in Sirach 44:19–21," *CBQ* 70 (2008): 66–81, here 76–77; see also 73–75, 79–80.
13. E.g., J. Louis Martyn, *Galatians: A New Translation with Introduction and Commentary*, AB 33A (New York: Doubleday, 1997), 299.

did Abraham in verse 6; thus verse 7's ἄρα (*ara*, "then") represents a genuine conclusion or inference from verse 6. Πίστις is defined by Abraham's believing trust in verse 6 and not by reference to his faithfulness. Those "of faith" believe or trust God just as Abraham did. Verse 7 then serves as a premise for a syllogism in verses 7–9 that is anchored in the Galatians' faith/trust. Faithfulness, whether to the law or its works, or the Abrahamic tradition of obedience is excluded.

Although Paul does not employ a formulaic introduction in Galatians 3:8, that he is quoting would have been clear to the ancients from his mention of the Scriptures (ἡ γραφή, *hē graphē*) and from the pronominal shift to the second person in the citation itself. The problem is that Genesis uses this language, or variations of it, on *multiple* occasions, including Genesis 12:3 but then again at the Aqedah, the near sacrifice of Isaac in Genesis 22. The question, then, is whether Paul is drawing on the language of Genesis 12:3 in *conjunction* with Genesis 22 and Abraham's obedient faithfulness, or whether Paul is *avoiding* reference to Genesis 22 and Abraham's obedience.

Although Paul is primarily quoting Genesis 12:3, he changes 12:3's "tribes of the earth" (αἱ φυλαὶ τῆς γῆς, *hai phylai tēs gēs*) to the word "nations" (τὰ ἔθνη, *ta ethnē*). Paul typically uses "gentiles" (τὰ ἔθνη) opposite the Jewish people (e.g., Gal. 1:16; 2:2, 8, 9, 12, 14, 15). Here Paul is stressing the inclusion of the non-Jews in these blessings. So he bypasses "all the families or tribes of the earth" in favor of "nations" (τὰ ἔθνη). Commentators have disagreed on whether the word "nations" is from Genesis 18:18 or from Genesis 22:18 (see table 1).

Table 1. The Language of Genesis in Galatians 3:8

Gal. 3:8	ἐνευλογηθήσονται	ἐν σοὶ	πάντα τὰ ἔθνη
	eneulogēthēsontai	*en soi*	*panta ta ethnē*
	will be blessed	in you	all the nations
Gen. 12:3	ἐνευλογηθήσονται	ἐν σοὶ	πᾶσαι αἱ φυλαὶ τῆς γῆς
	eneulogēthēsontai	*en soi*	*pasai hai phylai tēs gēs*
	will be blessed	in you	all the tribes of the earth
Gen. 18:18	ἐνευλογηθήσονται	ἐν αὐτῷ	πάντα τὰ ἔθνη τῆς γῆς
	eneulogēthēsontai	*en autō*	*panta ta ethnē tēs gēs*
	will be blessed	in him [Abraham]	all the nations of the earth
Gen. 22:18	ἐνευλογηθήσονται	ἐν τῷ σπέρματί σου	πάντα τὰ ἔθνη τῆς γῆς
	eneulogēthēsontai	*en tō spermati sou*	*panta ta ethnē tēs gēs*
	will be blessed	in your seed	all the nations of the earth

Gen. 26:4	ἐνευλογηθήσονται	ἐν τῷ σπέρματί σου	πάντα τὰ ἔθνη τῆς γῆς
	eneulogēthēsontai	*en tō spermati sou*	*panta ta ethnē tēs gēs*
	will be blessed	in your seed	all the nations of the earth
Gen. 28:14	ἐνευλογηθήσονται	ἐν σοὶ	πᾶσαι αἱ φυλαὶ τῆς γῆς καὶ ἐν τῷ σπέρματί σου
	eneulogēthēsontai	*en soi*	*pasai hai phylai tēs gēs kai en tō spermati sou*
	will be blessed	in you [Jacob]	all the tribes of the earth and in your seed

Favoring the view that Paul conflated Genesis 12:3 with 22:18 (and the Aqedah), some interpreters disqualify any use of Genesis 18:18 since the promise there was not spoken *to* Abraham as is the promise in Galatians 3:6, Genesis 12:3, and Genesis 22:18. This contention remains problematic. Genesis commentators have long recognized that Genesis 18:18 is referring back to Genesis 12:3 and is to be interpreted in view of Genesis 12:3. As a narratival recap, the third-person reference to Abraham is to be *expected*. Thus, Genesis 18:18's "in him [Abraham]" is in reference to Genesis 12:3's "in you." Such internal soliloquy in Genesis 18:18 demonstrates the earlier divine disclosure to Abraham in 12:1–3 to be "*authentic*, unadulterated and truthful."[14]

After the near sacrifice of Isaac, God promised to Abraham the blessing of the nations in connection with Abraham's *seed* (Gen. 22:18). A reference to Abraham's seed is conspicuously absent in Galatians 3:8, leaving a reference to Genesis 22:18 unlikely. Paul could easily have included the word "seed," and it would have served as an introduction and anticipation of his discussion of the "seed" in the next paragraph. He *avoided* the language of Genesis 22. The majority of commentators have therefore concluded that Paul adapts Genesis 12:3 with language from Genesis 18:18. Rightly, James D. G. Dunn says, "It may be significant that Paul cites the first two expressions of the promise, with the implication that the promise had a universal aspect from the first."[15] The later instances of the promise in Genesis 22:18 and 26:4–5 are associated with Abraham's obedient faithfulness rather than with his faith in the promises—the subject of these verses of Galatians. Paul is not alluding to the Aqedah or to Abraham's later faithfulness here. For Paul, there is only the believing trust of Abraham and the foundational

14. Roger Lapointe, "Divine Monologue as a Channel of Revelation," *CBQ* 32 (1970): 161–81, here 179 (emphasis original); cf., e.g., Claus Westermann, *Genesis 12–36*, CC (Minneapolis: Augsburg, 1995), 288.

15. James D. G. Dunn, *The Epistle to the Galatians*, BNTC (Peabody, MA: Hendrickson, 1993), 164.

promise that the gentiles would be included. God saves by faith and not by works or obedience.

This stress on Abraham's believing trust begged discussion of Isaac, the promised seed, and Genesis 22. Paul does turn to Abraham's Seed in Galatians 3:16 and mentions that the promises were to Abraham but also to his Seed. Shockingly, Paul completely ignores Isaac and bypasses him (and Gen. 22) in favor of the one Seed as Jesus Christ instead. By the end of the chapter in 3:27–29, those who place their faith in Christ have become one with him and therefore enjoy the promises that were to Abraham and to his one and only Seed, Jesus Christ.

In the course of Paul's reasoning, obedient works are excluded from any role. As Galatians 3:10–14 points out, it is by faith and not by the law's works that this takes place. Galatians 3:12 clarifies that the law is based on *doing* what it requires, not faith. Here faith is anything but faithfulness or obedience or works; it is believing trust. Whereas the Jews often had interpreted faithfulness in terms of the Mosaic Torah, Paul wants to stress from these texts Abraham's faith in the promises long before the near sacrifice of Isaac. The promises are enjoyed not through the works of the law but through faith (in Christ). This does not rule out a reference to the faithfulness of Christ or God's own faithfulness elsewhere in Paul, but in Galatians 3:6–9 the focus is exclusively on believing trust as the basis for enjoying blessing with Abraham.

Perfect Obedience?

Traditional interpreters have affirmed that, from Paul's perspective, the law demands strict, perfect obedience. Thus the apostle juxtaposes faith in Christ over against a futile attempt at obeying the law. E. P. Sanders provided an impetus for a different understanding. He interprets obedience of the law within the gracious framework of God's election of the Jewish people, their covenant, and atoning sacrifices for forgiveness. The practical result is that individual law observance need not be perfect or rigorous since God provides already in the law for failure. Following Sanders's lead, Dunn comments on Galatians 3:10, "The righteousness of the law included use of the sacrificial cult and benefit of the Day of Atonement."[16] Paul could therefore describe

16. Dunn, *Galatians*, 171. Likewise, for instance, N. T. Wright, *The Climax of the Covenant: Christ and the Law in Pauline Theology* (Minneapolis: Fortress, 1991), 146: "The Torah does not envisage that all Jews will be perfect all the time, and it therefore makes provision for sin, through repentance and sacrifice, so that atonement may be made."

his law observance as "blameless" (Phil. 3:6). Dunn appealed to the gracious context of "covenantal nomism" to mitigate its embedded demand: "The mistake, once again, has been to read into the argument the idea that at this time the law would be satisfied with nothing less than sinlessness, unblemished obedience."[17] Norman Young made the same claim: "Judaism made no such demand" "to obey the whole law without failure."[18] Richard Hays called any supposed critique of a failure to obey God's law perfectly "a ridiculous caricature of Judaism" since "the rival Missionaries could easily have refuted [Paul] by pointing out that the Law makes ample provision for forgiveness of transgressions through repentance, through the sacrificial system, and through the solemn annual celebration of the Day of Atonement."[19] "Transgressions were dealt with according to the Law's provisions."[20] Galatians 3:10 remains a stumbling block to the New Perspective.

In Galatians 3:10 Paul seizes a passage from Deuteronomy that pronounces a curse upon those who do not observe the law. In a surprising twist, the apostle concludes that those who adopt the path of the law will *themselves* suffer its curse:

> Premise: Cursed is everyone who does not abide by everything that is written in this book of the law to do them.
>
> Conclusion: As many who are of (ἐκ, *ek*) the works of the law are under a curse.[21]

Omitted premises are a regular feature of Paul's writing.[22] The implied premise, reconstructed from the stated premise and conclusion, would literally read, "As many who are of the works of the law do not abide by everything that is written in this book of the law to do them."

Without the implied premise, Paul would be saying that those who obey the law are under a curse since the law pronounces a curse on everyone who does not obey it—a non sequitur. Ancient rhetoricians commended as a matter of style the omission of premises in enthymemes that would have been clear or obvious (Aristotle, *Rhet.* 1.2.13 [1357a]; 2.22.3 [1395b]; 3.18.2, 4 [1419a];

---

17. Dunn, *Galatians*, 171.

18. Norman H. Young, "Who's Cursed—And Why? (Galatians 3:10–14)," *JBL* 117 (1988): 79–92, here 83.

19. Richard B. Hays, "The Letter to the Galatians," *NIB* 11:181–348, here 257.

20. Hays, "Letter to the Galatians," 257; see also 312.

21. On the translation of ἐκ, see the corrective by Jan Lambrecht, "Critical Reflections on Paul's 'Partisan ἐκ' as Recently Presented by Don Garlington," *ETL* 85 (2009): 135–41.

22. E.g., John D. Moores, *Wrestling with Rationality in Paul: Romans 1–8 in a New Perspective*, SNTSMS 82 (Cambridge: Cambridge University Press, 1995).

Epictetus, *Diatr.* 1.8.1–4; Quintilian, *Inst.* 5.14.24; 5.10.3; Aelius Theon, *Prog.* 3.99–100). Paul is assuming in Galatians 3:10 that law observers simply do not do all that is written in the law. Its adherents have not attained, at least from Paul's experience, the comprehensive, perfect obedience that it demands. Traditional commentators have frequently concluded from Galatians 3:10 that Paul was reminding the Galatians of the perfect standard of Moses's law. In 1977 E. P. Sanders's *Paul and Palestinian Judaism* ushered in a new paradigm. Judaism in the Second Temple and Tannaitic eras, as Sanders explained, was never a pattern of religion devoid of God's grace without the merciful provision for failure. Paul could hardly have assumed a contentious premise with which his rivals would have disagreed. Scholars were left searching for other ways to understand Galatians 3:10.

This widespread skepticism of an assumption that people fail to obey God's law perfectly is unwarranted. Deuteronomy, including the verse(s) Paul cites, repeatedly lamented Israel's failure to obey the law. The implied premise in Galatians 3:10 supports Paul's apocalyptic perspective that the law only brings about an enslaving curse because of disobedience. God's saving work is associated strictly with the Abrahamic promises and not Mount Sinai. The promises are realized only in Jesus Christ.[23]

What is really at issue is the *means* by which those who transgress may be righteous before God according to the apostle. Paul, for his part, never mentions animal sacrifice as efficacious for God's mercy or forgiveness in his letters. He speaks instead of the efficacy of *Christ's* death. The covenantal curse that the law places on those who fail to obey its commands (3:10) is resolved only by the one who became a "curse" on humanity's behalf (3:13). Jesus Christ "gave himself for our sins" (1:4). If this verse represents pre-Pauline material, as many suspect, then Paul could assume that his rivals would agree that the only effective means for addressing sin was Jesus Christ. The law may "imprison" and "guard" (3:23), but it does not offer help with transgression (2:21; 3:21). Christ's Spirit, not the law, counteracts the flesh in Galatians 5–6.

In Sanders's paradigm, atoning sacrifice functioned as part of the framework of God's gracious election and covenant relationship with the people of Israel. What of Paul? In Galatians 6:16 he invokes the "Israel of God." Most interpreters have identified the "Israel of God" as those Jews and gentiles

---

23. See A. Andrew Das, "Galatians 3:10: A 'Newer Perspective' on an Omitted Premise," in *Unity and Diversity in the Gospels and Paul: Essays in Honor of Frank J. Matera*, ed. Christopher W. Skinner and Kelly R. Iverson; SBLECL 7 (Atlanta: Society of Biblical Literature, 2012), 203–23. On the various rather problematic attempts to explain away the Gal. 3:10 enthymeme, see Das, *Paul, the Law, and the Covenant*, 145–70.

who follow Paul's rule that circumcision and uncircumcision do not count for anything in light of the cross of Christ. The "Israel of God" would therefore consist of those in Christ rather than those under the law. A minority of interpreters have proposed that Paul is speaking of two *separate* groups: those who follow his rule as well as "the Israel of God." The apostle closes the letter in 6:10–16 as he opened it in 1:6–9, on a fiercely polemical note. He may have coined the phrase "Israel of God" in opposition to the false "Israel" in the Galatians' midst who were promoting gentile circumcision.[24] In either interpretive approach, the Israel of God would recognize the irrelevance for salvation of Jewish ethnic identity. God's elect people are defined by their oneness and faith in Christ, whether Jew *or gentile* (3:27–29). Paul therefore sees Abraham's "covenant" availing only through the one "seed," Jesus Christ (3:15–17, 29)—a *new* covenant (e.g., 2 Cor. 3:6). The gracious elements in Second Temple Judaism—the election of a people, the covenant, provision for failure—are all understood by Paul in terms of Christ. If the only solution for sin is in Jesus Christ (cf. Gal. 2:21; 3:21), then the law offers no viable provision in itself for transgression. Without a useful mechanism to receive God's mercy and forgiveness, transgression of the law would be, from Paul's standpoint, a serious problem for those "under the law." Paul therefore recognized that his "blameless" law observance as a Jew was of little value in view of what God had done in Christ (Phil. 3:3–11).[25] The law's commands are sundered by Paul from their gracious and merciful context within Second Temple Judaism.

What has been widely overlooked are the implications of this reconceptualization for the New Perspective. The New Perspective interpreter cannot appeal to animal sacrifice, Israel's election, or any other mechanism of repentance or atonement apart from faith in Christ. In this "newer" perspective, Paul's emphasis on perfect obedience of the law is not necessarily a commentary on the Second Temple Judaism of his day but rather a consequence of his christological emphases.

"Works of the Law" Focused Especially on Nationalism and Boundary Markers?

Galatians 3:10 places the emphasis on obeying *everything* in the law. A New Perspective interpreter would respond that "works of the law" should be

24. See the discussion in A. Andrew Das, *Galatians*, ConcC (St. Louis: Concordia, 2014), 644–52.

25. "Blameless" in view of the law's own provisions, *not* perfect; cf. the inability and failure of those under the law to obey in Rom. 7:14–25.

taken as shorthand for the whole law, but especially those aspects of the entire law that demarcate God's people from others.[26] The emphasis on the entire law would be targeting not perfection but rather adherence to the entirety of the law, whether or not one's obedience was rigorous. Dunn and others have stressed the phrase "works of the law" as the law from the point of view, especially, of its boundary markers.

Paul, however, continues in Galatians 2:21: "For if justification comes through the law, then Christ died for nothing." Paul's statement here parallels his claim a few verses earlier that no one is justified by the "works of the law." Likewise 2:19: "For through the law I died to the law, so that I might live to God." Paul's elaboration in the ensuing verses seems to have more to do with the law as a whole than with a focus on only a part of the law.[27] Paul's point is that the law *as such* cannot justify. A better approach would begin not with the boundary-marking features of the law but with the law in its entirety: obedience to the law requires obedience of *all* that it commands, which certainly would include those aspects that distinguish the Jews from the gentiles. Again, a critique of the gentiles' adopting Jewish customs follows *from* Paul's soteriological convictions.

Paul does not fault the Galatian rivals for promoting merely the sectarian aspects of the law. He faults them for requiring the law itself of the gentiles (4:21). The ritual laws may not be separated from the remainder of the law (5:3, 14). The law acted as a guardian in the old era until the fullness of time came with Christ (3:24–25; 4:4–5). "Works of the law" "most naturally" means "deeds or actions which the law requires."[28] Moses is to teach the Israelites God's "statutes and instructions and make known to them the way they are to go and the things they are to do" (Exod. 18:20).[29] Paul therefore

26. New Perspective interpreters in the mold of James D. G. Dunn or N. T. Wright offer an alternative by tracing the apostle's critique in Gal. 3:10 to the "works of the law"—that is, to the law's ethnic boundary-marking features as, in Paul's view, a mistaken nationalism. See Dunn, "Works of the Law"; Wright, *Climax of the Covenant*, 3, 150.

27. Heikki Räisänen writes, "The problem of the 'identity markers' may well once have been the starting point for Paul's theologizing about the law, but finally he arrived at very negative statements on the law *as such* and *as a whole*." Räisänen, "Galatians 2.16 and Paul's Break with Judaism," in *Jesus, Paul and Torah: Collected Essays*, trans. David E. Orton, JSNTSup 43 (Sheffield: JSOT Press, 1992), 122.

28. Dunn, *Galatians*, 135.

29. With Robert L. Brawley, "Meta-Ethics and the Role of Works of Law in Galatians," in *Lutherische und neue Paulusperspektive: Beiträge zu einem Schlüsselproblem der gegenwärtigen exegetischen Diskussion*, ed. Michael Bachmann and Johannes Woyke, WUNT 182 (Tübingen: Mohr Siebeck, 2005), 135–59, here 147: "It is difficult to maintain that ἔργα is strictly confined to 'regulations' at a meta-ethical level when the phrase ἔργα νόμου arises in connection with the ethical level of the behavior of Cephas, Barnabas, and the other Jews."

refers sometimes to "works of the law" but in other places to the law in general (e.g., 2:21; 3:11; 5:3–4). He uses "law" and "works of the law" synonymously (e.g., 2:16 and 2:21; 3:10 and 3:11).

4QMMT, one of the Dead Sea Scrolls, offers a parallel to Paul's "works of the law" (ἔργα νόμου, *erga nomou*). 4QMMT lists various sectarian legal rulings that serve to distinguish the Qumran community. Dunn flagged 4QMMT C 27 with the full phrase "works of the law" (מעשי תורה, *m'śê tôrâ*) in support of his position that the phrase, or the shortened "works," always refers to those aspects of the law that distinguished the sectarian community. 4QMMT C 23, within the same paragraph, however, employs "works" (מעשיהם, *m'śêhm*) in relation to the actions of the kings of Israel, including David as "a man of good deeds" (איש חסדים, *'îš ḥsdîm*). When 4QMMT C 26 mentions the forgiveness of David, his adulterous affair would have immediately come to mind for Second Temple Jews (e.g., CD col. 5, ll. 5b–6a; 2 Sam. 12:13; 1 Kings 15:5; note also the proximity to C 27 of C 23–26). These references in the immediate context to the general behavior or "works" of the kings must be factored into the interpretation of the full phrase "works of the law" (מעשי תורה) in C 27.[30] Taking "works of the law" in the broader sense of the entirety of the law, apart from a *necessary* notion of separation, neatly avoids the problems that 4QMMT C 23 poses, since the full phrase "works of the law" alternates with "works" in relation to the moral, non-boundary-marking aspects of the law. Joseph Fitzmyer wrote about 4QMMT,

> Yet it is now seen in the light of this Qumran text that "works of the law" cannot be so restricted [to those aspects of the law serving as ethnic identity markers]. The text of 4QMMT does single out about twenty halakhot, but they are not limited to circumcision and food laws; they are moreover associated by the Jewish leader who wrote this letter with the status of "righteousness" before God. There are, indeed, food regulations among the precepts singled out, but they include many others, e.g., regulations about sacrifices, about the

---

30. See James D. G. Dunn, "4QMMT and Galatians," in *The New Perspective on Paul: Collected Essays*, WUNT 185 (Tübingen: Mohr Siebeck, 2005), 333–39, esp. 336–37. Dunn thinks that C 27's use of the phrase "some of the works of the Torah" should be interpreted alongside B 2, but this connection is not rendered explicit by 4QMMT. Too much of the original context of B 2 has been lost to be sure of Dunn's reasoning. Dunn and others have *assumed* that "works" in B 2 is a noun. It may just as well be a Qal active masculine plural participle. B 2 could be reconstructed in a parallel fashion to C 23's "contemplate their deeds": "contemplate the deeds which we have performed" [התבנן ב]מעשים שא א[נ]ח[נ]ו עשינו] ([*htbnn b*] *m'śîm š' '*[*n*]*ḥ*[*nû 'śînû*]) (cf. Gen. 20:9; 1 Sam. 8:8; 2 Kings 23:19; Jer. 7:13; Eccles. 1:14); see Jacqueline C. R. de Roo, *"Works of the Law" at Qumran and in Paul*, NTM 13 (Sheffield: Sheffield Phoenix, 2007), 91.

impurity of members, tithes to be paid, etc. In fact, it makes explicit mention of "the Book of Moses and the words of the prophets and David." Given such a broad outlook, it is difficult to see how the restriction of the phrase that Paul uses can be understood in Dunn's sense.[31]

Fitzmyer then adds that the slogan-like phrase had a legalistic connotation since righteousness in God's sight depended on observance of these precepts (see especially the epilogue to the document, 4QMMT[f] [4Q399]). Fitzmyer repeatedly emphasizes throughout his article that "works of the law" at Qumran must be taken as those works that the law requires in a general sense.[32] That same alternation takes place in Paul, as Romans 3:27–4:5 shows. A "both-and" reading is more likely than an approach that remains primarily focused on the ethnic or sectarian demands of the law.

Romans 4:4–5 as Support for the Traditional Reading

Romans 3:27–29 is a centerpiece for the New Perspective reading of Paul and the law. In verse 28 the apostle categorically denies any justification by the "works of the law" and then in the very next breath asks, "Is God the God of Jews only?" (v. 29). "Works of the law" here distinguishes the Jew from the gentile. The concern with Jewish ethnocentrism continues in the next chapter when Paul emphasizes the testimony of the Jews' own law to the primacy of faith for all humanity, regardless of ethnicity. Abraham, *prior to* his circumcision, was justified by faith in the same manner as the gentiles of Paul's day (4:10–11). Since the Jews' "ancestor according to the flesh" (4:1) was justified apart from circumcision, no one can object to the inclusion of uncircumcised gentiles in God's people. Abraham is the father of both the circumcised and the uncircumcised (4:10–18), of both law-observant and non-law-observant Christ-believers (4:14: οἱ ἐκ νόμου, *hoi ek nomou*; cf. v. 16).

Romans 4 explicates key concepts from the end of chapter 3: "justification" (δικαιοσύνη, *dikaiosynē*) (3:20, 21, 22, 24, 25, 26, 28, 30; 4:2, 3, 5, 6); "grace" (χάρις, *charis*) (3:24; 4:4, 16); faith/faithfulness (πίστις/πιστεύω, *pistis/pisteuō*) (3:22, 26, 27; 4:3, 5, 11–13, 16–17); circumcision/uncircumcision (3:20; 4:9–12); Christology (3:25–26; 4:25); boasting (3:27; 4:2); abolishing the law / rendering the promise void (3:31; 4:14). In Romans 4 Paul also builds on the tension internal to the law—between its requirements and its witness to

---

31. Joseph A. Fitzmyer, "Paul's Jewish Background and the Deeds of the Law," in *According to Paul: Studies in the Theology of the Apostle* (Mahwah, NJ: Paulist Press, 1993), 18–35, here 23.
32. Fitzmyer, "Paul's Jewish Background," 19–24.

faith—which he introduced in 3:27, 31 by presenting Abraham as an instance of the law's own testimony to the primacy of faith.

In that explication, Romans 4:4–5 has proven difficult for New Perspective interpreters, because Paul defines "works" (ἔργα, *erga*) in these verses not in terms of Jewish ethnic identity or nationalism but rather in the broader terms of human activity: "work" merits the reward of wages. God's reckoning, on the other hand, is as a gracious "gift" (cf. 3:24: δωρεάν, *dōrean*) and not as "something due" (4:4). Thus, 4:4–5 places a reckoning according to "works" (ἐξ ἔργων, *ex ergōn*), "working" (ἐργάζομαι, *ergazomai*), or "according to debt" (κατὰ ὀφείλημα, *kata opheilēma*) in opposition to a reckoning "according to grace/gift" (κατὰ χάριν, *kata charin*) by "faith" (ἡ πίστις, *hē pistis*). The contrast between "works" and "grace"/"faith" is recurrent throughout this section of Romans (e.g., 3:20–22, 27; 4:4–5) and appears to be central to the developing argument.[33] The antithesis of gift (χάρις) and obligation (ὀφείλημα) was an ancient *topos* (e.g., Thucydides, *Hist.* 2.20.4; Aristotle, *Eth. nic.* 1165a3). Likewise, the image of "one who works" (τῷ ἐργαζομένῳ, *tō ergazomenō*) is contrasted with "one who does not work" (τῷ μὴ ἐργαζομένῳ, *tō mē ergazomenō*). Paul's discussion of "wages" (ὁ μισθός, *ho misthos*) in verse 4 is embedded in *this* context and should be understood accordingly.[34] Following on the heels of 3:27–29, Paul is explaining that "works of the law" should be understood in terms of works in general. As Stephen Westerholm says, "Since the issue ('works of law' *versus* 'faith in Jesus Christ') permits restatement in terms of a general distinction between 'works' and 'faith,' the point of the attack cannot be limited to statutes in the law which served as Jewish 'identity markers.'"[35] Paul's critique broadens at this point to treating works in opposition to God's grace in Christ.

Later in the letter Paul confirms that the "works" of Romans 4:4–5 should be interpreted more generally. Romans 6:23 contrasts the "wages" of sin with the "free gift" of God. Dunn, in his Romans commentary, surmised that Paul may have been hearkening back to 4:4: "If the talk is to be of something earned, then only death is in view."[36] Paul employs the same language again in 9:11–12: "Even before [Esau and Jacob] had been born or had done anything good or

33. Contra Michael Cranford, "Abraham in Romans 4: The Father of All Who Believe," *NTS* 41 (1995): 71–88, here 80, who claims that it is "accidental," and N. T. Wright, "Paul and the Patriarch: The Role of Abraham in Romans 4," *JSNT* 35 (2013): 207–41, here 234, who amazingly sees no contrast with human effort.

34. Contra Wright, "Paul and the Patriarch," 233, who overloads μισθός, an instance of the linguistic error of illegitimate totality transfer of a covenant instrument (cf. μισθός in Gen. 15:1, within a chapter where God later enters into a covenant with Abraham).

35. Stephen Westerholm, *Israel's Law and the Church's Faith: Paul and His Recent Interpreters* (Grand Rapids: Eerdmans, 1988), 119 (emphasis original).

36. James D. G. Dunn, *Romans 1–8*, WBC 38A (Dallas: Word, 1988), 357.

bad (so that God's purpose of election might continue, not by works but by his call) . . ." Here "works" are defined in terms of doing good or bad. Likewise in 9:16: "So it depends not on human will or exertion, but on God who shows mercy." Again, the language remains more generally expressed in terms of effort. Or in 11:6: "But if it is by grace, it is no longer on the basis of works, otherwise grace would no longer be grace." Paul's repeated contrast of human effort or works with God's merciful gift confirms such a contrast in 4:4–5.[37]

New Perspective interpreters have responded. Michael Cranford contends that ethnocentrism does indeed remain a central factor in Romans 4:4–9: αἱ ἀνομίαι (hai anomiai, "lawless deeds") and αἱ ἁμαρτίαι (hai hamartiai, "sins") in verse 7 are terms "typically associated with Gentiles."[38] Ἀνομία (anomia, "lawless") and ἁμαρτωλός (hamartōlos, "sinner") indicate actions "outside the covenant."[39] Similarly, τὸν ἀσεβῆ (ton asebē, "ungodly") in 4:5 refers to those "excluded from the covenant," "gentiles."[40] On the other hand, ἀνομία (anomia) and ἁμαρτωλός (harmartōlos) were used in reference to "sinfulness" in general and could characterize a Jew (e.g., ἁμαρτωλός: Sir. 11:32; 15:12; 27:30; 32:17; 1 Macc. 2:44, 48, 62 [note "gentiles" as a separate category]; ἀνομία: Philo, Sobr. 48 [in relation to Exod. 20:5]; Mut. 150 [the opposite of virtue]; Spec. 1.188; 1.279). Psalm 32 employs just such terminology for the author himself. Likewise, Paul's condemnation of ἀσέβεια (asebeia, "ungodliness") in Romans 1:18–32 is not limited to the gentiles but includes the Jews. Romans 1:23 cites a passage that censures Israel's idolatry. Paul frames 1:16–2:10 with an inclusio that emphasizes God's impartial relations with all humanity. The list of sins at the end of Romans 1 includes several of a moral nature that would include both Jews and gentiles. Romans 11:26 cites the prophet who declared that God would remove "ungodliness from Jacob" (ἀσέβειας ἀπὸ Ἰακώβ, asebeias apo Iakōb)! In Romans 5:6 Paul applies the term ἀσεβής (asebēs) to the beneficiaries of Christ's death in general. The use of ἀσεβής ("ungodly") should therefore be taken as a general indictment of sin that could apply to both gentiles and Jews. Nothing in Romans 4:4–5 indicates that ἀσεβής should be taken in a narrower sense of idolatry or a specific violation of Torah.[41]

---

37. See the discussion of Rom. 9:11, 16; 11:6 in Das, Paul, the Law, and the Covenant, 237–41.

38. Cranford, "Abraham in Romans 4," 82.

39. Cranford approvingly quotes Dunn (Romans 1–8, 206) on this point; followed by Wright, "Paul and the Patriarch," 218n33.

40. Cranford, "Abraham in Romans 4," 82, again following Dunn, Romans 1–8, 204–5. In fact, Wright's logic ("Paul and the Patriarch," 218) in Rom. 4 depends on ἀσεβής referring to gentiles, a claim that does not work elsewhere in Romans.

41. With Robert Jewett, Romans: A Commentary, Hermeneia (Minneapolis: Fortress, 2007), 314.

John M. G. Barclay minimized Romans 4:4–5's contrast between works and grace as "some subsidiary generalized comments about 'faith as such' and 'works as such'" that show the "absence or insufficiency of works underlines human inadequacy."[42] Paul Achtemeier, another interpreter sympathetic to the New Perspective, was more candid with the problem posed by these verses: "It is I think one of the ironies of interpreting Romans that the passage that most clearly points to works of the law as a Jewish boundary marker is juxtaposed to the passage (4:4–5) that seems most clearly to point to works as human accomplishment about which one may boast."[43] A better interpretation would incorporate the contribution of Romans 4:4–5 to Paul's unfolding argument. Paul poses "works" as the antithesis of "faith" in 4:4–5 immediately after he contrasts the "law of faith" and the "law of works" in 3:27. Paul's understanding of "works" in 4:4–5 must therefore influence the interpretation of the "law of works" in 3:27. The "works of the law" in 3:27–28 cannot, then, be limited to those aspects of the law that serve as boundary markers for the Jewish people.

The widespread Second Temple tradition of viewing Abraham as a model of faithful (πιστός, *pistos*), obedient conduct[44] required Paul to deny saving significance to Abraham's faithfulness. Paul interprets "faith" (πίστις, *pistis*) in terms of belief (or trust) apart from human activity (ἔργων, ἐργάζομαι, *ergōn, ergazomai*). After repeatedly asserting justification apart from works in Romans 3:21–31 and again in 4:2, Paul says in 4:4, "Now to the one who works, wages are not reckoned as a gift but as something due." Paul describes Abraham's God in 4:5 as one who "justifies the ungodly [τὸν ἀσεβῆ, *ton asebē*]." The description implies that when Abraham received the promise and believed, he was "ungodly."[45] Paul's citation from the Davidic psalm in 4:7–8 speaks of the sinner whose sins are forgiven and not reckoned. Paul connects the psalmist's language to those "to whom God reckons righteousness apart from works" (v. 6). In verses 9–10 Paul applies the language of the psalm to *Abraham*. The implication is that Abraham is one whose sins have been forgiven and not reckoned.[46] The psalm citation, in speaking of sins of a *moral* nature (cf. the psalm's association with David and 2 Sam. 11–12), implies

42. John M. G. Barclay, *Obeying the Truth: Paul's Ethics in Galatians* (Minneapolis: Fortress, 1988), 246–47.

43. Paul J. Achtemeier, "Unsearchable Judgments and Inscrutable Ways: Reflections on the Discussion of Romans," in *1995 SBL Seminar Papers*, ed. Eugene H. Lovering Jr., SBLSP 34 (Atlanta: Scholars Press, 1995), 521–34, esp. 533n44.

44. A glaring nonfactor in Wright's analysis ("Paul and the Patriarch").

45. Anthony Tyrrell Hanson, "Abraham the Justified Sinner," in *Studies in Paul's Technique and Theology* (London: SPCK, 1974), 52–66, here 53.

46. Hanson, "Abraham," 53.

that Abraham may have been guilty of such sins as well.[47] Even "faithful Abraham" was not faithful enough. God justifies *apart* from human activity or faithfulness. Abraham the "justified sinner" may therefore serve as a model for gentile conversion.

N. T. Wright has offered a helpful essay explaining how Paul draws on Genesis 15 to prove that the gentiles are included in the Abrahamic promises and family on the basis of faith in Romans 3:27–31 and 4:9–25 (the inclusion of the gentiles is absent in 4:1–8).[48] One may affirm much of what Wright contends as not exclusive of the traditional reading. The issue in verses 4–5 is *how* one becomes Abraham's child: by God's gracious gift apart from human activity. Thus Paul returns to the contrast between "works" and "grace" quite frequently in the letter. The proper interpretation of Romans 4:4–5 is not an "either-or" matter: either Paul's problem with the law is that it requires gentiles to become Jewish, as is the case in 3:28–29 and 4:9–15, or Paul's problem is that the law leads people to confidence in empty human accomplishments or works (4:4–5). Romans 4:4–5 provides a *supporting* argument for the inclusion of the gentiles in God's salvation, an argument that was necessary given the Second Temple emphasis on Abraham's obedience, bordering on the meritorious. The discussion of works in general forms the basis for Paul's conclusions in 4:9 (οὖν, *oun*) with regard to circumcision—that is, implications for ethnocentrism. The Mosaic law, which previously had divided humanity, is fundamentally a human endeavor with no saving significance. Paul cites Abraham, who was justified as a sinner apart from works by faith, as proof that God surely can justify the uncircumcised, *gentile* sinner on the same basis of faith.

Jouette Bassler highlighted Galatians 3:10 and Romans 4:4–5 as passages that do not conform to the New Perspective approach.[49] These passages "yield more naturally to the old perspective."[50] Nevertheless, she faults recent critics

---

47. C. E. B. Cranfield, "'The Works of the Law' in the Epistle to the Romans," *JSNT* 43 (1991): 89–101, esp. 97. Hanson ("Abraham," 55–56) developed the parallels between Rom. 4 and Ps. 32 as further evidence that Abraham ought to be understood in terms of the psalm. Ἀσεβής (*asebēs*) in v. 5 is a rare word in Paul but may be occasioned by Ps. 32:5 in the Septuagint (31:5). Psalm 32:3 has "my body wasted away"; cf. Rom. 4:19. In Ps. 32:10 "steadfast love surrounds those who trust in the Lord"; cf. Rom. 4:18. Compare Ps. 32:7 and Gen. 15:1, and Ps. 32:8 and Gen. 15:7.

48. Wright, "Paul and the Patriarch," joins Cranford and others in arguing against the traditional position but overlooked the most recent traditional articulation in A. Andrew Das, "Paul and Works of Obedience in Second Temple Judaism: Romans 4:4–5 as a 'New Perspective' Case Study," *CBQ* 71 (2009): 795–812, which answered Cranford's and others' earlier arguments on which Wright relied.

49. Jouette M. Bassler, *Navigating Paul: An Introduction to Key Theological Concepts* (Louisville: Westminster John Knox, 2007), 15–16.

50. Bassler, *Navigating Paul*, 15.

of the New Perspective for lapsing into a legalistic view of Second Temple Judaism: "All of these explanations . . . fail to account for the central role of divine mercy, forgiveness, and atonement in first-century Judaism."[51] Apparently unaware of any other alternative in the debate, Bassler concludes, "We are left, then, with an apparent stalemate. Legalistic (soft or hard) interpretations of Paul's criticism of 'works of the law' fail to do justice to the realities of Second Temple Judaism or to the thrust of Paul's argument in several crucial passages. The New Perspective, on the other hand, requires strained exegesis of some other crucial passages [Rom. 4:1–5; Gal. 3:10–14]."[52]

A solution to the impasse was readily available at the time of Bassler's essay.[53] Again, scholars have been wrong in assuming that Paul viewed the "divine mercy, forgiveness, and atonement in first-century Judaism" as effective for the salvation of an individual. Paul never grants that an animal sacrifice, as prescribed by the law, can offer the forgiveness of sins that comes solely in Christ's death (Gal. 1:4; 3:13).[54] Reconciliation to God has taken place in Christ. Paul never grants to Israel an election that avails to salvation apart from Christ (e.g., Gal. 3:27–29: "*Jew* or Greek"; Gal. 6:14–16: "Israel of God"; Rom. 10:9–13: "all"). If the law could save by means of its provisions for failure, then Christ's death would have been unnecessary (Gal. 2:21; 3:21).

Paul can therefore describe the "wretched" plight of the "I" under the law who is incapable of obeying its commands (Rom. 7:7–25). This is underscored by the variation of terms: κατεργάζομαι, ποιέω, πράσσω (*katergazomai, poieō, prassō*). While the "I" wants to "do" what is good, sin and the flesh prevent it. Ethnic boundaries figure nowhere in this futile struggle. The apostle has sundered strict obedience from God's election and mercy toward ethnic Israel. One searches in vain in Romans 7:7–25 for an atoning mechanism that avails for sin apart from Christ (vv. 24–25).[55] To follow the law is to engage in a merely human endeavor, an exercise in empty exertion or "works." This "newer perspective" neatly resolves the stalemate. A more positive appraisal

51. Bassler, *Navigating Paul*, 16.
52. Bassler, *Navigating Paul*, 17.
53. Das, *Paul, the Law, and the Covenant*.
54. In fact, many Second Temple texts suggest a shift away from sacrifice as a means of atonement. See Tob. 12:9; Sir. 3:3, 30; 45:23; 4 Macc. 17:22; Pss. Sol. 3:8. The Qumran community likewise viewed its good works as a substitute means of atonement in the place of the temple (e.g., 1QS 3:6–12; 8:3, 6, 10; 9:4–7); see Mark A. Seifrid, *Justification by Faith: The Origin and Development of a Central Pauline Theme*, NovTSup 68 (Leiden: Brill, 1992), 93–108. On the lack of atoning sacrifice in Paul, see Das, *Paul, the Law, and the Covenant*, chap. 5.
55. See the discussion of this text in Das, *Paul, the Law, and the Covenant*, 222–28. For a detailed critique of the two-covenant or *Sonderweg* approach with its special path to God for the Jews apart from Christ, see Das, *Paul and the Jews*, LPS (Peabody, MA: Hendrickson, 2003), 96–106.

of Second Temple Judaism and a recognition of Paul's intense concern with the inclusion of the gentiles in God's salvation are perfectly compatible with a reading of Galatians 3:10 and Romans 4:4–5 in the manner that Bassler and others have seen as most natural.

The Gift of Justification

Modern Pauline scholarship is rife with controversy over justification, and yet a position is unavoidable since the apostle weaves justification into the fabric of his thought. He connects justification to Christ's saving death (Rom. 5:9; Gal. 2:21) and baptism (Rom. 6:7; 1 Cor. 6:11). He connects it to God's own grace and righteousness (Rom. 3:21–26; 5:16–21), numbering even gentiles with the Jews in God's promises (Rom. 3:28–30). Paul discusses justification while looking forward to the final judgment (Rom. 2:13–16; 1 Cor. 4:4–5) and eternal life (Rom. 5:18). Consonant with a more traditional understanding of Paul and the law, a contrast between human effort and divine activity is characteristic of Paul's approach to justification/righteousness—although, as the other authors of this volume will note, this leaves much unaddressed (inevitably for a short essay).[56]

In Philippians 3:9 Paul contrasts the righteousness of God (ἡ ἐκ θεοῦ δικαιοσύνη, *hē ek theou dikaiosynē*), the righteousness of faith (ἡ [δικαιοσύνη] διὰ πίστεως Χριστοῦ . . . ἐπὶ τῇ πίστει, *hē [dikaiosynē] dia pisteōs Christou . . . epi tē pistei*), with his *own* righteousness from the law (ἐμὴ δικαιοσύνη ἡ ἐκ νόμου, *emē dikaiosynē hē ek nomou*).[57] Righteousness is thus a gift from God, unlike human righteousness based on the Mosaic law. Philippians 3:9 is helpful for understanding Romans, especially Romans 10:3 in its immediate context: the righteousness of God (ἡ τοῦ θεοῦ δικαιοσύνη . . . ἡ δικαιοσύνη τοῦ θεοῦ, *hē tou theou dikaiosynē . . . hē dikaiosynē tou theou* [10:3]), which is the righteousness of faith (ἡ δικαιοσύνη ἡ ἐκ πίστεως, *hē dikaiosynē hē ek pisteōs*; ἡ ἐκ πίστεως δικαιοσύνη, *hē ek pisteōs dikaiosynē* [9:30; 10:6]), stands over against Israel's *own* righteousness (ἡ ἰδία δικαιοσύνη, *hē idia dikaiosynē* [10:3]) from the law (νόμος δικαιοσύνης, *nomos dikaiosynēs*; ἡ δικαιοσύνη

---

56. See, e.g., *Justification: Five Views*, ed. James K. Beilby and Paul Rhodes Eddy (Downers Grove, IL: IVP Academic, 2011).

57. Paul regularly contrasts what is "of God" versus what is "of human beings"; e.g., 2 Cor. 4:7: the power of God for salvation (cf. 4:1–6). In 2 Cor. 3:5 humans are not sufficient of themselves (ἀφ' ἑαυτῶν, *aph' heautōn*) to reckon anything as from themselves (ἐξ ἑαυτῶν, *ex heautōn*); rather, sufficiency comes from God (ἐκ τοῦ θεοῦ, *ek tou theou*). Compare Sadducean doctrine according to Josephus (*Ant.* 13.172–73), where all things are within our power (ἅπαντα δὲ ἐφ' ἡμῖν αὐτοῖς κεῖσθαι, *hapanta de eph' hēmin autois keisthai*).

ἡ ἐκ νόμου, *hē dikaiosynē hē ek nomou* [9:31; 10:5]). Even as righteousness is from God in Philippians 3:9, so it is also in Romans 10:5. In both texts the opposite is for people to seek a righteousness of their own through the Mosaic law. The same contrast is likely at work earlier in the letter in Romans 3:21 when Paul describes the righteousness of God through faith in/of Christ as apart from the law (χωρὶς νόμου, *chōris nomou*) (cf. Rom. 1:17).[58]

The gift character of the noun "righteousness" (δικαιοσύνη, *dikaiosynē*) in these passages is understandable in view of how the cognate verb (δικαιόω, *dikaioō*) functions. Whereas in secular Greek literature the verb indicated punishment or condemnation (Dio Cassius, *Hist. rom.* 40.54.1; Aelian, *Var. hist.* 5.18), for the Jews—as is clear from the Septuagint and Second Temple Jewish literature—the verb refers only to a judicial act *in favor* of a person.[59] Paul at times employs the verb while citing or alluding to the Scriptures (Ps. 143:2 [142:2 LXX] in Rom. 3:20 and Gal. 2:16; and Isa. 50:8 in Rom. 8:33–34), and the Jewish pattern of usage informs his thinking. Jewish literature uses the verb δικαιόω in contexts of bilateral or trilateral contention, a pattern that Paul follows: δικαιόω serves as an antonym to verbs of condemnation (Rom. 5:16–19) where charges or accusations (Rom. 2:15; 8:33–34) are being lodged, witnesses called upon, defenses given (Rom. 1:20; 2:1; cf. 2:15), and judgments rendered (1 Cor. 4:2–5).

When two parties contend over a perceived wrong, whether individuals or groups, one confronts the other with accusations, appealing to witnesses, with a goal to be reconciled. The accused party may counteraccuse (e.g., Gen. 38:25–26) or may admit guilt and acknowledge the other party as in the right through a confession (e.g., Gen. 44:16), a gesture, or silence. The accused would then provide reconciliatory gifts or make pacts. Unreconciled parties may submit the complaint to a third party for a trilateral contention. The third party or sovereign restores the community by administering justice, condemning the guilty, and "justifying" the righteous (e.g., 2 Sam. 15:2, 4). The third party "justifies" by actively taking the side of the one against the other (1 Kings 8:32). This help consists not only of clearing the one party's name but also of providing assistance (2 Sam. 14:4–11). When God is the other party in a bilateral contention or is acting as a third party to resolve a dispute, no one may properly be justified (Ps. 143:2 [142:2 LXX]; Sir. 7:5;

---

58. Thomas R. Schreiner, *New Testament Theology: Magnifying God in Christ* (Grand Rapids: Baker Academic, 2008), 357–58; followed by Charles Lee Irons, *The Righteousness of God: A Lexical Examination of the Covenant-Faithfulness Interpretation*, WUNT 2/386 (Tübingen: Mohr Siebeck, 2015), 334–36.

59. James B. Prothro, *Both Judge and Justifier: Biblical Legal Language and the Act of Justifying in Paul*, WUNT 2/461 (Tübingen: Mohr Siebeck, 2018), 3–5.

18:2; 1 Cor. 4:4 [in the face of God's judgment]; Gal. 2:16), but God may nevertheless choose to pardon/forgive and justify the contrite, guilty party (e.g., Ps. 51:3–4 [50:5–6 LXX]; 130:3–4 [129:3–4 LXX]; Isa. 43:22–28). In a trilateral contention God may justify the one party and condemn the other (e.g., Israel and the nations in Add. Esth. 10:8–12 [10:3e–i LXX]; Isa. 50:7–9). The Lord "justifies" the righteous and takes away their sins (Isa. 53:10–12). God's actions on behalf of the "justified" sinner bear the character of a gift (1 Cor. 6:11), unlike the righteousness that is due (Rom. 2:13).[60] Not surprisingly, then, Paul uses δικαιοσύνη θεοῦ (*dikaoisynē theou*, "righteousness of God") for the gift of the God who justifies.

Paul repeatedly describes the gracious gift character of justification with nouns such as δωρεά, δώρημα, χάρισμα (*dōrea, dōrēma, charisma*).

"They are now justified by his grace as a gift [δωρεάν, *dōrean*]." (Rom. 3:24)

"But the free gift [τὸ δώρημα, *to dōrēma*] is not like the trespass. . . . Much more surely have the grace of God [ἡ χάρις τοῦ θεοῦ, *hē charis tou theou*] and the free gift [ἡ δωρεά, *hē dōrea*] in the grace of the one man, Jesus Christ, abounded for the many." (5:15)

"The free gift [τὸ χάρισμα, *to charisma*] is not like the effect of the one man's sin. . . . The free gift [τὸ χάρισμα, *to charisma*] following many trespasses brings justification." (5:16)

"Much more surely will those who receive the abundance of grace and the free gift of righteousness [οἱ τὴν περισσείαν τῆς χάριτος καὶ τῆς δωρεᾶς τῆς δικαιοσύνης λαμβάνοντες, *hoi tēn perisseian tēs charitos kai tēs dōreas tēs dikaiosynēs lambanontes*] exercise dominion in life through the one man, Jesus Christ." (5:17)

"The free gift of God [τὸ χάρισμα τοῦ θεοῦ, *to charisma tou theou*] is eternal life in Christ Jesus our Lord." (6:23)

Righteousness is that free gift of God in 5:17 and, with it, eternal life (6:23).[61]

60. Prothro's work, *Both Judge and Justifier*, applies to Paul the pattern of usage of δικαιόω in contexts of bilateral and trilateral contention, as developed, especially, by Pietro Bovati, *Re-Establishing Justice: Legal Terms, Concepts and Procedures in the Hebrew Bible*, trans. Michael J. Smith, JSOTSup 105 (Sheffield: JSOT Press, 1994).

61. Irons, *The Righteousness of God*, 316. Irons's study offers a very helpful critique of Hermann Cremer's relational approach to righteousness, especially in terms of covenant faithfulness—that is, not according to a divine standard of right and wrong. Cremer applied what is now known as a linguistic error: illegitimate totality transfer; contra, e.g., Wright,

The gracious gift of righteousness is by faith/faithfulness. To return to Philippians 3:9, Paul contrasts "my" righteousness, which is from the law, with the righteousness of God by faith/faithfulness—the same contrast as in Romans 10:3–4. The righteousness of God must therefore be revealed and is from faith/faithfulness (Rom. 1:17). This righteousness of God is for all who believe (Rom. 3:22). In Christ humans *become* the righteousness of God (2 Cor. 5:21). Gifted righteousness contrasts with God's distributive righteousness as judge in Romans 3:5, 25–26. To appeal to the verb again, when the other party drops the claim against a truly guilty party in a bilateral contention, or when a third party takes the side of the truly guilty in a trilateral contention, the guilty enjoy a gifted status of righteousness. Such righteousness is not merited by the guilty party. It is "reckoned" to them (Rom. 4:3–9, 22) as God does not "count" trespasses (2 Cor. 5:19).

Conclusion

Obedience of the law is a genuine problem for the law-observant since forgiveness and salvation are located, for Paul, solely in Christ. Attempts to enjoy a right status with God by means of the law and its works are failed human endeavors. Consonant with Paul's understanding of Israel's law, the gift of righteousness is apart from human activity or efforts, in which case God may include gentiles. Paul has reconceptualized God's grace in terms of Christ.

"Paul and the Patriarch." Cremer read covenantal contexts, in the few instances where they are present in the Hebrew Bible, *into* the noun δικαιοσύνη. Irons tracks the Septuagintal instances and finds that the terminology is used judicially or ethically. For a recent critique of covenantal approaches to the apostle Paul, see the chapter "Rethinking the Covenantal Paul," in Das, *Paul and the Stories of Israel*, 65–92.

Roman Catholic Perspective
Response to Das

BRANT PITRE

Given the centuries-old debate between Catholics and Lutherans over how to interpret Paul regarding justification, some readers may be surprised to discover that I find much to agree with in Andrew Das's robust and thought-provoking essay.

E. P. Sanders—Underemphasizing the Role of "Works" in Early Judaism

For one thing, Das makes very clear that though he writes from a Lutheran perspective, he is not "anti-Sanders" (see 84–85). In this essay and his earlier work Das pays close attention to the real gains made by Sanders.[1] However, Das also rightly points out that in Sanders's attempt to destroy the nineteenth- and twentieth-century Protestant caricature of Judaism as a legalistic religion of "works righteousness," Sanders ended up *underemphasizing* the role of good works in early Judaism. In my view, Das is also correct when he insists, "Paul was responding to a legalistic or works-based perspective on the part of his Jewish peers," "*at some level*" (85). Otherwise, certain passages in Paul which speak of "righteousness" based on "works" are difficult to explain, such as the following: "What then are we to say? Gentiles, who did not strive

---

1. See A. Andrew Das, *Paul, the Law, and the Covenant* (Peabody, MA: Hendrickson, 2001).

for righteousness, have attained it, that is, righteousness through faith; but *Israel, who did strive for the righteousness that is based on the law*, did not succeed in fulfilling that law. *Why not? Because they did not strive for it on the basis of faith, but as if it were based on works*" (Rom. 9:30–32).

It is quite telling that Sanders himself struggles to provide a compelling exegesis of this passage. Not only does he admit that it constitutes a "difficulty"; in the end, he is forced to fall back on the rather underwhelming conclusion that "Paul's meaning [in Rom. 9:30–32] is not sufficiently clear for anyone to hang anything of weight on the passage."[2] This is just one example of Sanders's tendency to overemphasize the role of grace and underemphasize the necessity of works when painting his portrait of Second Temple Judaism. Other examples could be given.[3] In short, Das is right to argue that Sanders swung the pendulum too far in the other direction in his portrait of Second Temple Judaism: instead of overemphasizing works to the exclusion of grace, Sanders overemphasizes grace and underplays the meritorious role of good works.[4]

"Works of the Law" = Both "Boundary Markers" and the Whole Torah

I also agree with Das's view that while Paul's starting point for the formulation of justification by faith was likely the controversy over circumcision and food laws (Gal. 2:11–13; cf. Gen. 17:1–14; Lev. 11:1–47), Paul finally arrives at the conclusion that "the law *as such* cannot justify" (95). Although (as I showed in my essay) there is a centuries-old debate in the Catholic tradition over how to interpret "works of the law," I am personally inclined to the view that Paul uses the expression *both* with specific reference to circumcision and food laws *and* as a synonym for the whole Torah. In this regard, the work of the Jesuit exegete Joseph Fitzmyer is extremely helpful. As Fitzmyer has shown, the one Dead Sea Scroll we possess that uses the Hebrew equivalent of Paul's expression—"works of the Torah" (*mʿśê tôrâ*)—does not limit its meaning: "It is now seen in the light of this Qumran text that 'works of the law' cannot be so restricted. The text of 4QMMT does single out about twenty halakhot, but *they are not limited to circumcision and food laws. . . . They*

2. *PALLT*, 677–79.
3. See, e.g., Das, *Paul, the Law, and the Covenant*, 234–67.
4. To be fair to Sanders, it should be noted that, taken on its own the term "covenantal nomism" maintains a healthy balance between grace and works: one "gets in" through grace (covenant), but one "stays in" through works of obedience to the law (nomism). The grace of the covenant may have priority, but Sanders's formula makes clear that "works" are still necessary for remaining in "righteousness." Even on Sanders's own terms, then, it is quite accurate to describe Second Temple Judaism as a religion of "grace" *and* "works."

include many others, e.g., regulations about sacrifices, about the impurity of members, tithes to be paid, etc."[5]

I agree, though I would strengthen Fitzmyer's case by pointing out among the "works of the Torah" that are "reckoned" as "righteousness," the Dead Sea Scroll specifically mentions (1) not being "a slanderer and a blasp[he]mer" (4QMMT^c col. 3, l. 10), (2) not engaging in "fornications" (4QMMT^c col. 4, ll. 4, 11), and (3) the "sins" for which "David" was "forgiven" (4QMMT^c frags. 14–17, col. 2, ll. 1–2). It should go without saying that circumcision and food laws were not the "works of the law" that David failed to obey (cf. 2 Sam. 11; Ps. 51)! Following the work of Fitzmyer, Das comes to the very reasonable conclusion that, in Paul's first-century Jewish context, "a 'both-and' reading is more likely than an approach that remains primarily focused on the ethnic or sectarian demands of the law" (97).

"Works" and "Wages" in Romans: Not Just "Boundary Markers"

Third, I also agree with Das's argument that in several key passages in Romans, "Paul defines 'works' (ἔργα, *erga*) . . . not in terms of Jewish ethnic identity or nationalism but rather in the broader terms of human activity: 'work' merits the reward of wages" (98). Consider the following passages:

> Now to one who *works*, *wages* are not reckoned as a gift but as something due. But to one who *without works* trusts him who justifies the ungodly, such *faith* is reckoned as righteousness. So also David speaks of the blessedness of those to whom God reckons *righteousness apart from works*. (4:4–6)

> Even before they [Jacob and Esau] had been born or had *done anything good or bad* (so that God's purpose of election might continue, *not by works* but by his call) she [Rebecca] was told, "The elder shall serve the younger." (9:11–12)

> So too at the present time there is a remnant, chosen by grace. But if it is by grace, it is *no longer on the basis of works*, otherwise grace would no longer be grace. (11:5–6)

In such passages, phrases such as "righteousness apart from works" (δικαιοσύνην χωρὶς ἔργων, *dikaiosynēn chōris ergōn*) (Rom. 4:6) and "not by works" (οὐκ ἐξ ἔργων, *ouk ex ergōn*) (Rom. 9:12) and "no longer on the basis of works" (οὐκέτι ἐξ ἔργων, *ouketi ex ergōn*) (Rom. 11:6) seem to refer

---

5. Joseph A. Fitzmyer, *According to Paul: Studies in the Theology of the Apostle* (Mahwah, NJ: Paulist Press, 1993), 23 (emphasis added).

to "works" of obedience to the Torah in ways that cannot be restricted to just "boundary markers." In light of such texts, Das concludes that "Paul's repeated contrast of human effort or works with God's merciful gift confirms such a contrast in [Romans] 4:4–5" (99). Not only do I agree, but also I think it important to emphasize that, in saying this, Das is at one with the Council of Trent's interpretation of Romans: "And we are said to be justified gratuitously because *nothing that precedes justification*, neither faith nor works, *merits the grace of justification*; for 'if it is by grace, it is no longer on the basis of works; otherwise (as the same apostle [Paul] says) grace would no longer be grace' (Rom. 11:6)" (Council of Trent, *Decree on Justification*, chap. 8).[6] Notice here that it is Romans 11:6 that lays the foundation for the Catholic doctrine that no human being can do *anything* to merit the initial grace of justification. From a Catholic perspective, it is not just circumcision or obedience to the food laws that do not merit the initial grace of justification, but any human activity.

With these points of agreement in mind, there are several questions that I have about Das's essay.

Final "Justification" and "Judgment" according to "Works"

First, Das seems to follow the traditional Protestant view that Paul's soteriology is one of "sheer grace exclusive of works" (83). However, on multiple occasions, Paul insists that one's "work" (ἔργον, *ergon*) will play a key role at the final judgment:

> All must test *their own work*; then *that work*, rather than their neighbor's work, will become a cause for boasting. . . . So let us not grow weary in *doing good*, for we will reap at harvest time, if we do not give up. So then, whenever we have an opportunity, let us *work good* for all. (Gal. 6:4, 9–10 NRSV adapted)[7]

> For *all of us* must appear before the judgment seat of Christ, so that each may *receive recompense* for *what has been done in the body*, whether good or evil. (2 Cor. 5:10)

> For he will *repay according to each one's works*: to those who by patience in *good work* seek for glory and honor and immortality, he will give *eternal life*; while for those who are self-seeking and who obey not the truth but wickedness,

---

6. Heinrich Denzinger, *Compendium of Creeds, Definitions, and Declarations on Matters of Faith and Morals*, ed. Peter Hünermann, 43rd ed. (San Francisco: Ignatius, 2012), no. 1532.

7. I have adapted the NRSV in the Galatians and Romans quotations to translate key phrases as literally as possible.

there will be *wrath and fury*. There will be anguish and distress for everyone who *works evil*, the Jew first and also the Greek, but glory and honor and peace for everyone who *works good*, the Jew first and also the Greek. . . . For it is not the hearers of the law who are righteous before God, but *the doers of the law* who *will be justified*. When Gentiles, who have not the law, do by nature the things that are of the law, they are a law to themselves, even though they do not have the law. They show that *the work of the law* is written on their hearts, while their conscience also bears witness and their conflicting thoughts accuse or perhaps excuse them on that day when, according to my gospel, God judges the secrets of men by Christ Jesus. (Rom. 2:6–10, 13–16 NRSV adapted)

Notice here that Paul over and over again declares in no uncertain terms that people will be judged according to "their own work [ἔργον, *ergon*]" (Gal. 6:4), for "doing good" (καλὸν ποιοῦντες, *kalon poiountes*) (Gal. 6:9), for "what has been done [ἃ ἔπραξεν, *ha epraxen*], whether good or evil" (2 Cor. 5:10), "according to his works" (κατὰ τὰ ἔργα αὐτοῦ, *kata ta erga autou*) (Rom. 2:6). He even says that God will "repay" (ἀποδώσει, *apodōsei*) each person who does "good work" (ἔργου ἀγαθοῦ, *ergou agathou*) with the gift of "eternal life" (ζωὴν αἰώνιον, *zōēn aiōnion*) itself (Rom. 2:6–7). Perhaps most striking of all, Paul declares that it is "the doers of the law" (οἱ ποιηταὶ νόμου, *hoi poiētai nomou*)—those who have "the work of the law" (τὸ ἔργον τοῦ νόμου, *to ergon tou nomou*) written on their hearts—who "will be justified" (δικαιωθήσονται, *dikaiōthēsontai*) on the day of judgment (Rom. 2:13, 15).

In his essay, Das claims that "obedient works are excluded from any role" in Paul's reasoning about justification by faith in Galatians 3 (91). Granted, insofar as Paul is speaking about *initial* justification by faith apart from works, I am in full agreement.[8] I am still left wondering: How would Das account for the relationship between initial justification apart from works and final justification according to works? Would Das agree that for Paul, initial justification is by grace through faith apart from any works, but final judgment *is* according to works and not by faith alone?

Paul and the "Wages" of Good "Works"

Finally, as I mentioned above, Das is right to emphasize that by using the language of "wage" (μισθός, *misthos*) in Romans 4, Paul seems to be contrasting

---

8. For more on initial justification and final judgment, see Brant Pitre, Michael P. Barber, and John A. Kincaid, *Paul, a New Covenant Jew: Rethinking Pauline Theology* (Grand Rapids: Eerdmans, 2019), 201–10. For a similar distinction between "(initial) justification and final judgment," see James D. G. Dunn, *The New Perspective on Paul*, rev. ed. (Grand Rapids: Eerdmans, 2008), 75–76.

justification by faith with "the broader terms of human activity: 'work' merits the reward of wages" (98). I agree. But I wonder if Das would say the same thing about Paul's use of "work" (ἔργον, *ergon*) and "wage" (μισθός, *misthos*) in 1 Corinthians, in which Paul speaks of the righteous being rewarded with wages for the good works they have done in Christ:

> *Each will receive wages according to the labor of each.* For we are God's co-workers; you are God's field, God's building. *According to the grace of God given to me,* like a skilled master builder I laid a foundation, and someone else is building on it. Each builder must choose with care how to build on it. For no one can lay any foundation other than the one that has been laid; that foundation is Jesus Christ. Now if anyone builds on the foundation with gold, silver, precious stones, wood, hay, straw—*each one's work* will become visible, for the Day will disclose it, because it will be revealed with fire, and the fire will test *what sort of work each has done.* If *the work which anyone has built on the foundation survives, that one will receive a wage.* If anyone's *work* is burned up, that one will suffer loss; he himself will be saved, but only as through fire. (3:8–15 NRSV adapted)[9]

Notice here that Paul not only speaks about final judgment according to "what sort of work each has done" (ἑκάστου τὸ ἔργον ὁποῖον, *hekastou to ergon hopoion*) (3:13); he even goes so far as to say that "each will receive wages [μισθόν, *misthon*] according to the labor of each [κατὰ τὸν ἴδιον κόπον, *kata ton idion kopon*]" (3:8). Most striking of all, he speaks of a "wage" (*misthos*) received for "labor" (*kopos*) or good "work" (*ergon*) not once, but twice (3:8, 14)! Although for Paul, initial justification is by faith apart from any good work, final judgment is so clearly according to works that Paul can even describe the eschatological reward as a "wage" (*misthos*) earned for the "work" (*ergon*) done in Christ.[10]

In sum, despite the many strengths of his essay, it seems to me that Das makes the same mistake with reference to Paul that Sanders made with reference to Second Temple Judaism. Just as Sanders overemphasized the importance of grace and underemphasized the role of good works in early Judaism, so too Das's exclusive focus on the role of grace seems to lead him to neglect Paul's language of "wages" for good "works" done in Christ.

Now, to be fair, Das may well agree with me on the role of good works done in Christ in final justification. However, I cannot tell from his essay,

---

9. The NRSV is problematic here because in places it obscures the presence of the words "work" (*ergon*) and "wage" (*misthos*).

10. Note Raymond F. Collins, *1 Corinthians*, SP 7 (Collegeville, MN: Liturgical Press, 1999), 159: "Paul uses 'wages' (*misthos*) as a metaphor for eschatological reward; elsewhere it indicates pay for a job well done (Rom 4:4; cf. 1 Cor 9:17, 18)."

since he never discusses (or even mentions) the multiple passages in which Paul speaks of judgment according to works.[11] So my questions for Das are these: If "sheer grace exclusive of works" is an accurate description of Paul's soteriology (83), why does Paul himself repeatedly emphasize that those who are in Christ ("we") will be "judged" according to what they have "done" (2 Cor. 5:10)? In addition, how would Das interpret Paul's economic language of being "rewarded" or "repaid" or "recompensed" for the good "works" done by those who are "in Christ" (1 Cor. 3:8–15)? Perhaps by clarifying these two points, we will be able to find even more common ground between Lutheran and Catholic readings of Paul.

---

11. As far as I can tell, Paul's statements about final judgment by "works" also receive no substantial discussion in Das, *Paul, the Law, and the Covenant*. There, Das mentions "judgment according to works" in Rom. 2:16 in passing in a footnote (180n27), but he does not explain what it means or how to reconcile it with justification by "faith alone."

New Perspective Response to Das

JAMES D. G. DUNN

I enjoyed Andrew Das's essay, the breadth of its coverage, and particularly the final section, "The Gift of Justification." I was somewhat surprised, however, by the concluding thought that "forgiveness and salvation are located, for Paul, solely in Christ" (106), since so much of Paul's discussion focuses on and depends on the fact that Abraham was justified by faith—that justification was known and experienced already without works of the law, or specifically circumcision.

Which leads to my opening question: Does Andrew give enough attention to the original context that prompted Paul for the first time, so far as our written record tells us, to formulate his insistence on faith and not works? For Andrew to express his aim in terms of "reaffirming the traditional position" (83) on faith/grace and works seems somewhat odd, when the issue is precisely whether the traditional interpretation had been more or too much influenced by the sixteenth-century context than by the first-century context. Again, I have to insist on the importance of reading in its original historical context what appears to be Paul's first written statement of how the gospel that he proclaimed came to effect in practice. To read and expound Galatians 2:16 without reference to its context in Galatians 2 is to easily lose sight of the situation that provoked Paul's words and to set it in a later and different context of Reformation exegesis and application. It is this failure or unwillingness (what is the right word?) to set Galatians 2:16 in its original context to which I object. How can we so ignore the fact that 2:16 was Paul's reaction and response to the attempt made by his fellow Jewish Christians in Antioch to insist that gentile believers should observe the food laws, rules that were distinctively Jewish and in practice served to keep Jews and gentiles apart? To set the issue in terms of "legalism" may be justifiable in terms of the debate that came later to focus on this verse, but it is basically an unfair expression of the issues that Paul confronted in Galatians 2. For Paul, these were straightforward: Are only those who observe the distinctively Jewish laws to be reckoned as justified? The faith/works issue was an expression of this deeper issue—how freely is the gospel to be offered to non-Jews?—and if we lose sight of that, we miss the chief point that Paul was seeking to make in Galatians 2.

Second, I would have to insist that Romans 4 is not simply a repetition of Galatians 2 and should not be imposed on the interpretation of Galatians 2. Paul's Letter to the Galatians comes down to us as his first formulation of what became or had already become a key expression of his gospel. Romans 4 is both a reaffirmation of that key insight and a broadening out of its implications. Of course, justification through faith (alone) has several corollaries that Paul goes on to spell out, but that does not affect its primary point for Paul as the justification for a law-free gentile mission. And anyway, is enough emphasis given to Paul's insistence in Romans 4 on the priority of Abraham's faith? He was justified by faith before and independently of circumcision.

Something that puzzled me is Andrew's insistence that Galatians 3:10 "remains a stumbling block to the New Perspective" (92). I confess that when that passage is read in context, I fail to see any stumbling block—perhaps because unwittingly I have stumbled over it? I am equally puzzled by his assertion that Paul "never mentions animal sacrifice as efficacious for God's mercy or forgiveness" (93). Is Andrew giving enough weight to the fact that Paul has no hesitation in using the sacrifice of atonement as the key image for understanding the efficacy of the death of Jesus? I am equally puzzled by his assertion that "the law's commands are sundered by Paul from their gracious and merciful context within Second Temple Judaism" (94). I expect that Paul himself would have been highly indignant at the charge. Is this all again because the original context of Paul's initial assertion has been ignored or set aside to give later theological contexts the primary weight in interpretation— the original context of a protest against the assumption that gentiles had in effect to become Jews if they were to be justified? To broaden the discussion to "the law as a whole," "the law in its entirety" (95), is again to ignore the specific context of the issue (faith and not works) as it first arose for Paul, as indicated in Galatians 2. Paul's subsequent reflections on the law as a whole did indeed go further, but if we miss the fact that his treatment in Galatians 2 was primarily about the openness of the gospel to gentiles as such, gentiles as well as Jews, we have missed or lost the Pauline roots of this key Christian teaching. I would have to echo Das's quotation of Joseph Fitzmyer in this critique: to root the discussion of "works of the law" in 4QMMT is fine when 4QMMT is the primary context for understanding the phrase. But for understanding Paul's use of the phrase in Galatians 2, the context of Galatians 2 must surely be the primary context.

Paul within Judaism Perspective Response to Das

MAGNUS ZETTERHOLM

Scholarship should always be assessed on at least two basic levels: the first step is to determine to what extent a specific analysis is coherent with regard to the fundamental assumptions used; the second step is to scrutinize the assumptions themselves. With regard to the first aspect, it has to be concluded that Andrew Das's presentation of the Traditional Protestant Perspective on Paul makes sense. If the postulation that Paul considers Torah observance to be a problem since forgiveness and salvation are located only in Christ is correct, Das's analysis appears coherent, even convincing.

This applies to most studies written from a traditional perspective—the reason scholars, in my view, arrive at a less probable view of the historical Paul is not because of their exegesis per se but because their presuppositions are wrong. This, I believe, is also the case with the so-called New Perspective on Paul, and on this Das and I seem to be in agreement. Thus, I appreciate his extensive critique of the idea that Paul mainly reacted against those aspects of the Torah that functioned as identity markers, and I concur with Das that Paul's discussion of the role of the Torah seems to involve the Torah in its entirety (whatever that means), not certain aspects.

I also find Das's interpretation of Paul's use of Abraham as a model quite convincing. It seems obvious that Paul downplays Abraham's "obedience" while emphasizing the patriarch's "believing trust." And Das certainly is correct in pointing out that Paul creates a dichotomy between "works" and "faith," as in Galatians 3:10–14. The question is why, and this is where "assumptions" become decisive, which can easily be demonstrated by examining a text that Das mentions in his essay, Galatians 6:16: ὅσοι τῷ κανόνι τούτῳ στοιχήσουσιν, εἰρήνη ἐπ' αὐτοὺς καὶ ἔλεος καὶ ἐπὶ τὸν Ἰσραὴλ τοῦ θεοῦ (*hosoi tō kanoni toutō stoichēsousin, eirēnē ep' autous kai eleos kai epi ton Israēl tou theou*). The conundrum here is the translation of the second καί in the latter part of the verse: Is Paul wishing peace and mercy over one or over two groups? If the first alternative is to be preferred, καί has to be taken to mean "that is," and "those who will follow this rule" are identified with "the Israel of God," which could imply that Paul equates the church with "Israel." According to the second alternative, καί simply means "and," and Paul addresses two groups: "those who will follow this rule" and "the Israel of God."[1] Philology is of little help when trying to decide what Paul is communicating here. Instead, what ultimately decides which interpretative path is chosen is the individual scholar's general understanding of Paul, his relation to Israel, and his view on the relation between Jews and members of the nations within the Jesus movement.

Das assumes that Paul's idea of excluding Torah observance as a prerequisite for salvation stems from his christological convictions, an idea, as Das admits, that comes close to Sanders's notion "from solution to plight"; that is, since God has chosen to save the world through Christ, observing the Torah would be counterproductive.[2] Das's argument runs similarly: "If God's salvation takes place through faith in/of Christ, it is not through observing the law." This has important implications for the inclusion of non-Jews, according to Das: "If God saves through Christ and not the law of Moses, why foist Moses's law upon the gentiles for their salvation?" (85).

This argument rests upon the assumption that Paul's opponents really believed that there was a simple connection between Torah observance and salvation, and Das acknowledges his belief that "Paul was responding to a legalistic or works-based perspective on the part of his Jewish peers" (85). This is a presumption that can indeed be questioned. Now, it is, of course, not impossible that Paul's opponents believed that "perfect" Torah observance led to salvation and that Paul reacted against this by arguing that salvation

---

1. For two opposing views, see Ben Witherington III, *Conflict and Community in Corinth: A Socio-Rhetorical Commentary on 1 and 2 Corinthians* (Grand Rapids: Eerdmans, 1995), 451–53; Peter Richardson, *Israel in the Apostolic Church*, SNTSMS 10 (Cambridge: Cambridge University Press, 1969), 74–84.

2. E. P. Sanders, *Paul and Palestinian Judaism: A Comparison of Patterns of Religion* (Minneapolis: Fortress, 1977), 442–43.

from now on is possible only through Christ. The question is whether that is plausible.

The problem is that there is scarce evidence to substantiate the claim that there existed groups advocating strict Torah observance as a prerequisite for salvation. Sanders's review of the sources led him to the conclusion that the various texts from different periods and from different groups reveal a common theme: salvation cannot be earned. "The theme of God's mercy as being the final reliance even of the righteous appears in all the literature surveyed except IV Ezra."[3] Fourth Ezra is, firstly, generally thought to be a reaction to a very specific incident—the destruction of the temple—and, secondly, is consequently demonstrably later than Paul's Letters. It is, of course, feasible that similar ideas were known to Paul and his opponents, but the fact remains: even if we (rightly) grant Sanders's critics that he may have oversimplified the relation between deeds and grace,[4] and that his analysis may be in need of all sorts of nuance, it is still conspicuously difficult to argue that the idea of a one-to-one relation between "perfect" Torah observance and salvation was a dominant theme in Second Temple Judaism, as Das seems to do by referring to Abraham as a model for perfect obedience. To me, this seems to be too shaky a ground to be used as a hermeneutical key for understanding Paul.

A Paul within Judaism Perspective changes the game drastically. As I hint in my presentation of that perspective, I do believe that Torah observance constituted a problem for Paul, but only with regard to members of the nations. As mentioned above, Das believes that Paul's "christological convictions" are connected to the "inclusion of the gentiles" (85), but this seems to lead him to the conclusion that Paul meant that the Torah had completely lost its relevance—also for Jews—and that "obedient works are excluded from any role" (91). As I point out in my response to John Barclay in this book, Paul does nothing of the sort: rather, he expects non-Jews in Christ to conform to a certain Jewish moral standard as defined by the Torah. They are, for instance, to "refrain from idolatry" (φεύγετε ἀπὸ τῆς εἰδωλολατρίας, *pheugete apo tēs eidōlolatrias*) (1 Cor. 10:14), and they are "not to associate with sexually immoral persons" (μὴ συναναμίγνυσθαι πόρνοις, *mē synanamignysthai pornois*) (1 Cor. 5:9). Inappropriate behavior can even lead to some form of correction, penalty, or expulsion from the ἐκκλησία (*ekklēsia*), as is the case in 1 Corinthians 5:1–5, although it is not entirely clear what Paul

3. *PPJ*, 422.

4. See the essays in D. A. Carson, Peter T. O'Brien, and Mark A. Seifrid, eds., *Justification and Variegated Nomism*, vol. 1, *The Complexities of Second Temple Judaism*, WUNT 2/140 (Tübingen: Mohr Siebeck; Grand Rapids: Baker Academic, 2001).

has in mind.[5] It is nevertheless hard to sustain the idea that Paul attached no significance to "deeds."

I need to repeat my main argument from my presentation: in order to come close to the historical Paul, it is important, I believe, that we take seriously his self-definition to be the apostle to the gentiles. From this follows that his letters should be understood predominantly to deal with the problem of how to bring the nations into a covenantal relationship with Israel's god. Again, Paul's problem is not the salvation of the Jews but of the nations whose situation is described in Romans 1:18–32. Hence, I do not agree with Das that this passage also includes Jews.[6] But Das is obviously correct in assuming that Jews within the Jesus movement seem to have agreed that Jesus's death made the salvation of the nations possible. The discussions among various representatives of the Jesus movement concerned *how* this would be accomplished and *how* this new situation would influence the relations between Jews and members of the nations.

In general, I would say that Paul's view of the Torah is far more intricate than is usually assumed by representatives of a Traditional Protestant Perspective, and it is tempting to try to find a simple solution to the problem. The dichotomy between "deeds" and "faith" and the ensuing conclusion that Paul repudiated the Torah are such a simplification. As stated above, Paul is engaged in drawing pagans—that is, worshipers of pagan gods—into Judaism (Christianity is not an alternative, since it did not yet exist) *and* in preventing them from observing the Torah the way Jews commonly did. The simplest explanation, which I describe in detail in my essay, is that Paul encountered *non-Jews* who had wrongly come to the conclusion that Torah observance would make them righteous before the god of Israel. For various reasons, Paul was convinced, however, that the Jewish way of Torah observance was not an option for non-Jews. According to Paul, proper Torah observance was restricted to Jews only, which does not contradict the fact that Paul's halakah (to use an anachronistic term) for non-Jews is indeed Torah teaching.

This perspective explains why Paul seemingly downplays Abraham's obedience in Galatians and why he creates a dichotomy between "faith" and "works," which brings us back to the question of whether Paul's opponents embraced "a legalistic or works-based perspective" (85). I find it more likely

5. See Anthony C. Thiselton, *The First Epistle to the Corinthians: A Commentary on the Greek Text*, NIGTC (Grand Rapids: Eerdmans, 2000), 392–400.

6. See discussion in Magnus Zetterholm, "The Non-Jewish Interlocutor in Romans 2:17 and the Salvation of the Nations: Contextualizing Romans 1:18–32," in *The So-Called Jew in Paul's Letter to the Romans*, ed. Rafael Rodríguez and Matthew Thiessen (Minneapolis: Fortress, 2016), 39–58.

that Paul's non-Jewish audience had misunderstood the covenantal context of Torah observance than that his Jewish opponents advocated legalism. Given the ritualistic nature of Greco-Roman religion(s),[7] it is fully possible that the members of Paul's non-Jewish audience were the true legalists.

In Galatians 2:15–16 Paul seems to refer to an opinion representative for Jews in general: "*We ourselves are Jews by birth* and not Gentile sinners; yet *we know that a person is justified not by the works of the law* but through faith in Jesus Christ." Jews within the Jesus movement, it seems, all knew that the Torah, without trust in God's mercy, did not lead to "justification." The real question is this: Did members of the nations also know this?

---

7. As an example and with regard specifically to Roman religion, see Robert Turcan, *The Gods of Ancient Rome: Religion in Everyday Life from Archaic to Imperial Times*, trans. Antonia Nevill (New York: Routledge, 2000), 1–13.

Gift Perspective Response to Das

JOHN M. G. BARCLAY

Andrew Das offers an exegetical presentation of several features of a "Protestant" interpretation of Paul. The Protestant Reformers are not here referenced, but their views have been well summarized and analyzed elsewhere.[1] Key elements in Protestant readings are certainly present here: the centrality of grace, Christology, and faith; the broad definition of "works"; and the depth of the human plight. As Das indicates, his essay includes aspects also of the "New Perspective," with its emphasis on the inclusion of gentiles. But, as he rightly insists, what one needs to explain is not that Paul was an apostle to the gentiles but what constituted the theological foundation of this mission.

Readers will notice the prominence of grace in Das's essay: in Paul, there is "sheer grace exclusive of works" and "free grace" (83) in Romans 4:1–8, while Judaism is "a religion of grace" (84) with a "gracious framework" (85, 91) and "gracious election" (85, 93). For such a discussion we need a clear definition of "grace," what is meant when we call it "sheer" or "free," and how, as Das puts it, "Paul has reconceptualized God's grace in terms of Christ" (106). I have addressed this topic in *Paul and the Gift* (partially summarized in my essay in this volume), and I have offered there a reading that proposes solutions to many of the conundrums also addressed by Das. I have argued

---

1. See Stephen J. Chester, *Reading Paul with the Reformers: Reconciling Old and New Perspectives* (Grand Rapids: Eerdmans, 2018). I have summarized elements of the theologies of Luther and Calvin in *Paul and the Gift* (Grand Rapids: Eerdmans, 2015), 97–130. See also Stephen Westerholm, *Perspectives Old and New on Paul: The "Lutheran" Paul and His Critics* (Grand Rapids: Eerdmans, 2004).

that it is not adequate to define Judaism as "a religion of grace" unless we clarify the different ways in which grace was understood and perfected: in a tagline from that book, "grace is everywhere, but not everywhere the same." In particular, there was both diversity and debate among Second Temple Jews as to whether God's grace should be figured as a fitting gift to those who were (by one measure or another) worthy recipients of it, or whether it was wholly unconditioned by worth. My argument is that Paul has "perfected" grace as an *incongruous gift*, given without regard to worth, and that he has "reconceptualized God's grace" (Das, 106) by locating its definitive and final expression in the Christ-gift as an unconditioned gift. As we will see, this supports Das's claim that Paul's Christology shapes his theology of faith, grace, law, and work; but it also provides a fuller explanation for Paul's antithesis between "faith" and "works (of the law)."

I agree with Das that Abraham is often presented in Jewish sources as obedient and faithful to God, and that Paul is careful in both Galatians and Romans to present him otherwise.[2] But I find it both unhelpful and unnecessary to reintroduce the language of "legalism" (85) or "meritorious" works (101). The question is not whether Abraham *earned* his position before God, or justified himself by his works, but whether he was (or was not) a fitting recipient of divine favor or grace. Jewish exegetes of the Abraham story are responding to this question: Why would God graciously choose Abraham, at the beginning of the covenant? If there was nothing fitting or worthy about him, God's choice would look arbitrary and the whole covenant story would appear to be unfair. There were multiple grounds on which Abraham could be considered worthy of God's grace: his abandonment of idolatry, his embodiment of the law, his offering of Isaac, and so on. To highlight these aspects of the Abraham story was not a form of "legalism" but just the identification of the rationale for God's gracious election.[3]

For Paul, on the other hand, all that matters about Abraham is that he believed the promise of God. And here it is important to be clear what Paul means by "faith," a motif that he highlights in Galatians because of its connection with Christ (Gal. 1:23; 2:16, 20; 3:23–26). In Paul's discourse πίστις (*pistis*) is the correlate to divine promise and divine gift: to divine promise there corresponds human trust (that God will do what God has promised); to divine gift there corresponds human being-given-to, or receipt. In either case, faith has a *concave* shape: it is defined by what it receives or trusts. Its

---

2. Thus, following the verb πιστεύω (*pisteuō*) in Gal. 3:6, I would take the adjective πιστός (*pistos*) in 3:9 to mean not "faithful" but "believing" or "trusting."

3. I have spelled out this argument in full in *Paul and the Gift*, part 2.

focus is not on the human believer, but on the God who promises and gives.[4] If justification is by faith for both Jews and gentiles, this is not because it is simpler than works, or because it is ethnically nonspecific; it is because it sets no store on any human capacity or worth but places its hope wholly and entirely in the God who promises, and who confirms his promise in the death and resurrection of Christ. Faith is not an abstract principle of soteriology: it is defined completely by its object (God/Christ), who is also the subject of the gift or promise that has revolutionized the human condition.

In his reading of Galatians 3:10–14, Das is right to argue that there is an implied premise in 3:10: those whose worth depends on "the works of the law" cannot avoid the curse of the law, because of the pervasive human propensity to sin. This is spelled out much more fully in Romans, but it is already evident in Galatians with the claim that the present age is "evil" (1:4) and that "Scripture has shut up all things under sin" (3:22). Paul is by no means alone in this pessimistic view of the human condition: the Qumran hymns have an even more graphic description of this problem, and 4 Ezra laments that the "evil heart" has spoiled humanity, including Jewish humanity, from the time of Adam. The weight of this "curse" cannot be lifted except by a dramatic divine intervention, and, as Das notes, for Paul that intervention has been made, definitively, by Christ, who "gave himself for our sins to rescue us from the present evil age" (Gal. 1:4) and who took on himself the curse so that humanity can share in God's intended blessing (3:13–14). There is salvation in Christ and not via the law not because of some a priori assumption (if the one, not the other) but because Christ constitutes the divine saving gift (2:21), which resolves the human crisis as the law could not do. As Paul says, "If a law had been given that could *make alive*, then righteousness would truly be by the law" (3:21 AT). *Make alive*—that is what is needed, the creation of new life (cf. 6:15: "new creation"). What is required is not just "divine activity" in place of "human effort," but rather a power that refashions humanity, and re-creates human agency itself. That is possible, says Paul, only in Christ and through the Spirit, but it *is* possible there.

Also, as in the Abraham story, the possibility becomes reality through an unconditioned gift. I agree with Das that Romans 4 is a key text, and that the "New Perspective" has always struggled with the opening of this chapter. N. T. Wright, for instance, dubs Romans 4:4 "embroidery" that "carries no weight in this passage as a whole."[5] Like Das, I think that all of the elements

---

4. See the recent work by Jeanette Hagen Pifer, *Faith as Participation: An Exegetical Study of Some Key Pauline Texts*, WUNT 2/486 (Tübingen: Mohr Siebeck, 2019).

5. N. T. Wright, "Paul and the Patriarch," in *Pauline Perspectives: Essays on Paul, 1978–2013* (London: SPCK, 2013), 554–92, here 563.

of this chapter can be shown to fit together, and I have offered a new reading of it (better, I hope, than the one Das cites!) in *Paul and the Gift*.[6] There I have argued that the calling of both Jews and gentiles into the Abrahamic family is central to Paul's argument (4:9–15), not just an illustration of a general doctrine of justification by faith. But the *mode* of Abraham's relation to God (faith) and the *means* by which his seed has come into being (by creation *ex nihilo*) are also objects of central attention (4:1–8, 16–22). What integrates these concerns is the fact that the Abrahamic family is marked by a peculiar trait: from the beginning, it has been created by the grace and calling of God, which have never paid regard to the ethnic worth or the performance worth of their recipients. This incongruity is the unifying theme of Paul's argument: since neither ancestry nor achievement is of ultimate significance in God's eyes, the Abraham family is constituted without works, before circumcision, of both gentiles and Jews. In other words, the theological rationale for the inclusion of gentiles is the unconditioned grace of God.

I agree with Das that Romans 4:1–8 is significant in clarifying this matter and that "works" here and in some other places in Romans (e.g., 9:11–12; 11:5–6) have a wider reference than "works of the law" (whether narrowly or broadly defined). One might have interpreted the Abraham narrative as a story of "reward" or even "pay" (μισθός [*misthos*] can mean either). But Paul radicalizes the well-known distinction between "pay" and "gift" and insists that between God and Abraham it was a matter of gift without work, grace as an undeserved and incongruous gift. Paul finds in the Abraham story the "justification of the ungodly" (4:5), as a programmatic preenactment of the event of Christ, who "at the appropriate time died for the ungodly" (5:6). Abraham's faith thus marks not the fit but the *misfit* between Abraham and the righteousness accredited to him by God (4:3, citing Gen. 15:6), and this is the family trait that will mark the whole story of God's dealings with humanity. Drilling deep into the Abraham story, Paul rethinks the foundational narrative of the Jewish tradition in a form that relativizes (though it does not abolish) the difference between Jews and non-Jews. The rationale for this reading resides in the Christ-generated discovery that, from the beginning, the Abrahamic blessing was blind to every token of differential human worth.

Thus, like Das, I believe that we can get beyond Bassler's impasse: that the "New Perspective" has rightly highlighted the importance for Paul of the gentile mission but leaves some texts, on grace and works, largely unexplained (and more at home in the Protestant Perspective). Once we see what Paul means by grace, as an incongruous gift, without desert and without regard

---

6. Barclay, *Paul and the Gift*, 477–90.

for worth, and once we see this as the theological core of his interpretation of the Christ-event, we can see the "inclusion of gentiles" not as a sociological or merely ecclesial question but as the necessary expression of a gift that pays no regard to ancestral or ethnic worth ("neither Jew nor Greek" [Gal. 3:28]).

Paul insists, "I will not discount the grace of God" (Gal. 2:21 AT), and there is nothing arbitrary or a posteriori in his accompanying insistence that "if righteousness were by the law, Christ died in vain." God's unconditioned gift in Christ builds on no system of human worth and matches no differential ethnic distinctions. It extends to all humanity without distinction, sweeping those trapped "under sin" into a momentum of grace by which they are reconstituted as children of God, gifted with the Spirit of God's Son (Gal. 4:4–7). In comparison with that, to require gentiles to "Judaize" by taking on Jewish law practices ("works of the law") is not simply inadequate and unnecessary: it is to flout the gift given by God, the new creation that alone is competent to grant forgiveness, freedom, life, and a righteousness that counts before God.

Traditional Protestant Perspective
Reply to the Respondents

A. ANDREW DAS

Second Temple Jews, according to E. P. Sanders, understood the law's strict demand for obedience as embedded within a gracious framework of election, covenant, and sacrifice.[1] The gracious elements of that framework vary according to the particular Second Temple document in view, as John M. G. Barclay rightly nuances. One must, nevertheless, consider the possibility of pockets of legalistic thinking in Second Temple Judaism and that Paul, in places, may have had such thinking in view. One instance is the Second Temple extolling of Abraham.

Barclay questions whether Paul is objecting to a legalistic understanding of Abraham, but the traditions of Abraham's punctilious law observance are stubbornly insistent. Second Temple Jews were indeed praising Abraham's meritorious and, in many cases, *perfect* obedience of Moses's law. This was one of the grounds for God's choice of the patriarch. Recognition of genuinely legalistic strands in Second Temple Judaism serves to complement the other outstanding points in Barclay's response. God's gift in Christ eliminates any necessity to enjoy that favor by (failed) efforts to obey the law.

James D. G. Dunn, in response, attributes the Protestant position to a sixteenth-century (mis)reading of Paul.[2] Dunn pleads for placing the apostle

---

1. E. P. Sanders, *Paul and Palestinian Judaism: A Comparison of Patterns of Belief* (Minneapolis: Fortress, 1977). On the strict demand for obedience of the law in Second Temple Judaism, see A. Andrew Das, *Paul, the Law, and the Covenant* (Peabody, MA: Hendrickson, 2001), 1–44.
2. Ironically, Dunn's "New Perspective" was already championed by Erasmus and others. Luther was consciously responding to the relegation of Paul's critique of the law to its ceremonial

in his first-century social context.[3] "Works of the law" in Galatians 3:10 are, as Dunn describes it, "obligations prescribed by the law . . . [that] mark out . . . a member of the people of the law, the covenant people, the Jewish nation."[4] This is because "works of the law" in Galatians 3:10 must be understood in light of Galatians 2:16, where the phrase "most obviously refers back to the issues at the centre of the preceding controversies [cf. the Antioch incident in Gal. 2:11–14]—circumcision and food laws. That was what was at issue—whether to be justified by faith in Christ requires also observance of these 'works.'"[5] Alas, Dunn's first-century social context is unlikely: there is no evidence that food laws or circumcision were at issue in Antioch.[6] If Galatians 2:11–14 (or 2:16) is not about food laws or circumcision, then how can one refer to such a "context" for understanding Galatians 3:10's "works of the law"? In agreement with Dunn, an opposition to legalism would be a *consequence* of Paul's reaffirmation of the priority of faith in Christ and not an issue at Antioch.

Dunn emphasizes animal sacrifice; thus Paul describes Jesus's saving death in sacrificial images (e.g., Rom. 3:25). This is precisely the point: *Christ's* atoning sacrifice suffices, not the animals'. The gracious framework that Sanders describes has been reconceptualized in terms of Christ. Paul then contends in Romans 4 that Abraham's faith was always pointing forward to the fulfillment of the promises in Christ; that is, it was not just about circumcision but also about the promised Seed.[7] The emptying of animal sacrifice of any continuing relevance creates a problem for the embedded nomism. The law becomes an empty "to-do" list apart from that gracious framework and the provision for failure.[8]

Paul can modulate from "works of the law" to simply the law in Galatians 3:11–12, and the logic of those verses remains dependent on 3:10. To translate

---

aspects (e.g., circumcision). See A. Andrew Das, "Luther on the Scriptures in Galatians—and Its Readers," in *Semper Reformanda: The Enduring Value of Martin Luther's Insights for Biblical and Theological Studies*, ed. Channing Crisler and Robert Plummer (Bellingham, WA: Lexham Press, forthcoming).

3. James D. G. Dunn, "Works of the Law and the Curse of the Law (Gal. 3.10–14)"; reprinted with responses to critics in Dunn, *Jesus, Paul, and the Law: Studies in Mark and Galatians* (Louisville: Westminster John Knox, 1990), 215–41—a provocative essay that steered me into Pauline studies.

4. Dunn, "Works of the Law," 219–20.

5. Dunn, "Works of the Law," 220.

6. See, in more detail, my response to Dunn in A. Andrew Das, *Galatians,* ConcC (St. Louis: Concordia, 2014), 216–32.

7. As for the implications of Abraham in Rom. 4 for the inclusion of the gentiles, Dunn continues to misinterpret me as suggesting an "either-or," when Paul's generalized point about works and grace *supports* the inclusion of the gentiles, as my original essay maintained.

8. See Das, *Paul, the Law, and the Covenant,* 113–44, and the "newer perspective" reading of Gal. 2:11–14 in Das, *Galatians,* 196–232.

verse 11: "*Because* no one is justified before God by the law [building on 3:10], it is clear that 'the righteous one by faith will live.'" Dunn thinks that the traditional reading is "at cross purposes" with verses 11–12.[9] The best translation of verse 11, however, reaffirms the traditional view.[10] The missing premise in 3:10 (an *expected* feature in ancient enthymemes) would have been obvious to Paul's readers and proves crucial to his logic. The ultimate question is whether a denial of any saving value to Jewish ethnic identity is at the center of Paul's critique or is a *consequence* of it. If salvation is in Christ and not the law (or the law as misunderstood by Paul's peers), then why force the gentiles to become Jewish? Dunn's "New Perspective" reasoning continues to place the cart before the horse.

Brant Pitre rightly maintains in his response that "works of the law" refers to the *whole* Torah and not just to boundary markers. With Pitre, the "works" at issue in 4QMMT often were of a generally moral nature and not the boundary-marking aspects of this community's legal tradition—for example, slander, blasphemy, and fornication. There are implications for Pitre's approach: since "works of the law" encompasses the *entirety* of the law, Pitre cannot limit Paul's critique of "works of the law" to circumcision and boundary markers. Pitre maintains a justification by works, just not by the works of the law (boundary markers). However, for Paul, a person is not justified by works, period.

Pitre therefore appeals to Paul's *positive* discussions of works: "Although for Paul, initial justification is by faith apart from any good work, final judgment is so clearly according to works that Paul can even describe the eschatological reward as a 'wage' (*misthos*) earned for the 'work' (*ergon*) done in Christ" (112). Unfortunately, Pitre did not have the response to his essay in hand when he faulted my neglecting Paul's language of "wages" for the good works done in Christ. Pitre limited himself to the critique of the law in *Paul, the Law, and the Covenant* and overlooked the *positive* construal of the law in the subsequent *Paul and the Jews*.[11] Pitre appeals to Galatians 6:4–9 for the centrality of works in Paul but did not engage the exegesis of these verses.[12] The response to Pitre's essay thus sketches a more comprehensive response available elsewhere.

For final justification to be "*according* to works" is not at all inconsistent with its being "*by* faith" (apart from works). The reward is no less gracious and gifted since it depends on Christ's and his Spirit's activity. Christ

---

9. Dunn, "Works of the Law," 226.

10. Das, *Galatians*, 316–17.

11. A. Andrew Das, *Paul and the Jews*, LPS (Peabody, MA: Hendrickson, 2003), 166–86.

12. Das, *Galatians*, 612–23.

is creating in the lives of his saints the very works that vindicate a just (and gracious!) God. Paul's regular explication of justification as a gift as opposed to something earned—with no clear differentiation between initial and final justification—remains a stumbling block for Pitre's perspective.

For Magnus Zetterholm, hidden assumptions call the Protestant Perspective into question. No one would dispute Zetterholm's primary claim that Paul allows for Jews to continue Torah observance. The question is whether Paul ascribes any *salvific* value to that observance. For Zetterholm, Paul is writing about how *gentiles* are saved, not Jews. At the climactic, concluding point in his response Zetterholm cites Galatians 2:15–16: Jews by birth are already agreed that a person is not justified by the works of the law but through faith in Jesus Christ. Unfortunately, Zetterholm overlooked the deliberate ambiguity in the Greek. In 2:16 "but" (ἐὰν μή, *ean mē*) is actually better translated as "except": a person is not justified by the works of the law *except* through faith in Christ, and then one *is* justified by the works of the law. The ambiguity of the Jewish "shared ground" allows Paul's rivals to emphasize law observance as necessary for salvation.[13] The Jewish Christian rivals could therefore stress the necessity of rigorous obedience of God's law in Galatians 3:10 via Deuteronomy 27:26, a Torah verse pointed primarily toward God's own people of Israel. Leviticus 18:5 (Gal. 3:12), another proof text of the rivals, required doing the law for one to live—an exhortation for the Galatians to adopt law observance as necessary, but via a Torah passage originally pointed toward the Jews.[14] Zetterholm's assumption that these passages apply only to gentiles and not to Jews does not withstand critical scrutiny. As Paul writes of the Jew first and the Greek in Romans 1:16–17, it is no surprise that in Romans 1:23 the apostle draws on Jeremiah's (2:11) critique of *Jewish* idolatry, now *extended* to the gentiles.[15] One should not assume a reading of Paul but must demonstrate plausibility—a problem in Zetterholm's original essay.

Zetterholm stresses multiple translations of Galatians 6:16. If the "Israel of God" is a rephrasing of "those who will follow this rule" (118), then Paul is talking about the implications of his gospel for *his own* people, included in the church![16] The "Israel *of God*" adheres to Paul's gospel "rule." Even if

---

13. Argued at length in A. Andrew Das, "Another Look at ἐὰν μή in Galatians 2:16," *JBL* 119 (2000): 529–39; confirmed in Das, "The Ambiguous Common Ground of Galatians 2:16 Revisited," *BR* 58 (2013): 49–61.

14. A. Andrew Das, *Paul and the Stories of Israel: Grand Thematic Narratives in Galatians* (Minneapolis: Fortress, 2016), 23–26.

15. See the case in Das, *Paul, the Law, and the Covenant*, 171–77.

16. See Das, *Galatians*, 644–52.

"the Israel of God" is separate from "those who follow this rule," Paul still contrasts a Jerusalem above to the present Jerusalem, and the distinction revolves around law observance. In Galatians 4:25 "Mount Sinai in Arabia" corresponds to the "present Jerusalem," and "she [the Jewish Jerusalem] is in slavery *with* her [gentile?] children." Merely mentioning two translational options does not suffice when both appear inimical to Zetterholm's conclusion.

Zetterholm questions whether the Second Temple obsession with Abraham's obedience is representative.[17] Certainly, 4 Ezra conveys a reliance on works, but perfect obedience is a motif *all through* Second Temple literature. To repeat what has been argued elsewhere, consider the second-century-BCE Jubilees.[18] Jubilees affirms Israel as God's elect people (1.17–18, 25, 28; 16.17–18; 19.18; 22.11–12) and praises God's gracious provision of repentance (1.22–23; 23.26; 41.23–27) and the sacrificial system (6.14; 50.10–11; 34.18–19). God's elect could be "righteous" even when not perfectly obedient, and yet the Mosaic law demands strict, even perfect, obedience. Perfect conduct remains the ideal. Not only is Abraham extolled as perfect in his conduct (15.3; 23.10). "All of [God's] commands and his ordinances and all of his law" are to be carefully observed "without turning aside to the right or left" (23.16).[19] In 5.19, "[God] did not show partiality, except Noah alone, . . . because his heart was righteous in all of his ways just as it was commanded concerning him. And he did not transgress anything which was ordained for him." Noah, while the recipient of God's mercy (10.3), did "just as it was commanded" and was "righteous in all of his ways." "He did not transgress." Jacob was also "a perfect man" (27.17). Leah "was perfect and upright in all her ways," and Joseph "walked uprightly" (36.23; 40.8). While God granted mercy to the elect, the requirement of right conduct "in all things" (21.23) is still upheld and admonished through these exemplary models. The law must still be obeyed (1.23–24; 20.7). The author looked forward to the day Israel would be *perfectly* obedient (1.22–24; 5.12; 50.5). Sanders candidly conceded on the basis of these passages, "Perfect obedience is specified."[20] He adds, "As we have now come to expect, the emphasis on God's mercy is coupled with a strict demand to be obedient."[21] While God offered provision for sin and failure, the ideal remained strict and perfect obedience of the law.

17. See Das, *Paul and the Stories*, 93–124.
18. Das, *Paul, the Law, and the Covenant*, 13–17; Das, "Beyond Covenantal Nomism: Paul, Judaism, and Perfect Obedience," *ConcJ* 27 (2001): 235–36.
19. Translations from *OTP* 2:52–142.
20. *PPJ*, 381.
21. *PPJ*, 383.

The same proves true in Philo.[22] In *De praemiis et poenis* 79–83 it is not enough to hear or profess the precepts of God's law; one must actually do them. Individuals will be weighed in the scales (e.g., *Congr.* 164; *Her.* 46). In *Quod Deus sit immutabilis* 162 one must not deviate to the right or to the left from the path God has prepared for humanity in the law (*Abr.* 269; *Post.* 101–2; cf. *Leg.* 3.165; *Migr.* 146). Like Abraham (*Abr.* 192, 275–76; *Migr.* 127–30; *Her.* 6–9), Noah was "perfect" in virtue (*Deus* 117, 122, 140; *Abr.* 34, 47). Interestingly, Philo immediately qualifies the attribute of perfection for Noah (*Abr.* 36–39). Noah attained a perfection only relative to his generation; he was "not good absolutely." Philo then compares Noah's "perfection" with other sages who possessed an "unchallenged" and "unperverted" virtue. Noah therefore won the "second prize." Philo clearly commends the "first prize" of an unqualified virtue to his readers. Moses, for instance, attained that highest level as a model of perfection (*Mos.* 1.158–59, 162; 2.1, 8–11; *Leg.* 3.134, 140; *Ebr.* 94; *Sacr.* 8). Perfect obedience and sinlessness remain the ideal.

At the same time, God "ever prefers forgiveness to punishment" (*Praem.* 166)—thus atoning sacrifice (*Leg.* 1.235–41; 1.188–90; 1.235–39). God allows for repentance in view of the human tendency to sin (*Fug.* 99, 105; also *Abr.* 19; *Leg.* 1.187–88; *QG* 1.84; *Mut.* 124; *Somn.* 1.91). Those who repented, though, still bear the scars of their misdeeds (*Leg.* 1.103). While Philo affirms Israel's special status as recipients of God's mercy, and repentance as a means to remedy the situation caused by sin, he nevertheless commends those whose conduct is perfect. The sinless and unblemished are superior to those who repent and are healed of their illness (*Abr.* 26; *Virt.* 176).

The issue is when the gracious elements of Second Temple Judaism are reinterpreted in terms of Christ—the very point Zetterholm overlooks in his response. Sacrifice, repentance, and atonement are all expressed in *strictly christocentric* terms. The law's own demand for strict, even perfect, obedience is effectively stranded from God's grace in Paul's thought. Observing the law's commands becomes a matter of empty works and human merit. Zetterholm's analysis does not appreciate the implications of Paul's Christ-centered reasoning for law observance—whether the gentile's *or the Jew's*. The Protestant Perspective on the apostle remains the most satisfactory understanding. The contrast of works and grace, understood as law and gospel, is not a sixteenth-century misinterpretation but rather expresses Paul's own juxtaposition.

---

22. Das, *Paul, the Law, and the Covenant*, 23–31; Das, "Beyond Covenantal Nomism," 239–40.

3

The New Perspective on Paul

JAMES D. G. DUNN

I should begin by confessing that the invitation to contribute to this volume left me a little nonplussed. Had I not said all that I could say on the subject— first in the original 1983 article of my lecture,[1] then in the collection of my various essays on the same subject,[2] often including the same elements in the title, and finally in my contribution to and debate with other authors in *Justification*?[3] Perhaps I should mention also my *Jesus, Paul and the Law: Studies in Mark and Galatians*,[4] my commentary on Galatians,[5] and my

1. "The New Perspective on Paul," the Manson Memorial Lecture, November 4, 1982; article version, James D. G. Dunn, "Paul and the New Perspective," *BJRL* 65 (1983): 95–112; reprinted in *The New Perspective on Paul*, 99–120 (see the next note below).

2. James D. G. Dunn, *The New Perspective on Paul: Collected Essays*, WUNT 185 (Tübingen: Mohr Siebeck, 2005); rev. ed. published in 2008 (Grand Rapids: Eerdmans), with chap. 1 as an overview, "The New Perspective on Paul: Whence, What and Whither?," 1–97, and several others with "New Perspective" in the title. I gave specific attention to "The Incident at Antioch (Gal. 2:11–18)" in *JSNT* 18 (1983): 3–57; reprinted in Mark D. Nanos, ed., *The Galatians Debate: Contemporary Issues in Rhetorical and Historical Interpretation* (Peabody, MA: Hendrickson, 2002), 199–234.

3. James K. Beilby and Paul Rhodes Eddy, eds., *Justification: Five Views* (Downers Grove, IL: IVP Academic, 2011).

4. James D. G. Dunn, *Jesus, Paul and the Law: Studies in Mark and Galatians* (London: SPCK, 1990).

5. James D. G. Dunn, *A Commentary on the Epistle to the Galatians*, BNTC (London: A&C Black, 1993).

examination of the theology of Galatians.[6] Paul's Letter to the Galatians has indeed been one of the central foci of my interest in and fascination with Paul's ministry and theology. So, was there more I needed to say? Is there more that I need to say—again? Let us see.

Galatians 2:16 Yet Once More

Perhaps it would be best to begin with a restatement of the thesis of my "New Perspective" essay. The chief disquiet expressed in the 1982 lecture/essay was that the original context of Paul's argument in Galatians 2 had been lost to sight. In the buildup to the Reformation in the sixteenth century it was quite natural to read Paul's reference to "works of the law" as the "good works" disparaged by the Reformers as the ground for acceptance by God. One does not need to read Luther's commentary on Galatians for long to realize that he heard Galatians 2:16 speaking directly to his own situation: "Take thou the work of the law generally for that which is contrary to grace. Whatever is not grace is the law, whether it be judicial, ceremonial, or the ten commandments. . . . The work of the law then, according to Paul, signifieth the work of the whole law, whether it be judicial, ceremonial, or moral."[7] In other words, Galatians 2:16 spoke so directly to Luther because it seemed to speak so directly to the situation he was confronting. The assurance that one who heard a Mass or gave alms deserved grace, or that sins could be remitted through the purchase of an indulgence, sounded like the sixteenth-century equivalent of the promise of eternal life to those who wrought good works. So it was natural to read Paul's "works of the law" as referring to such "good works" and so as addressing Luther's situation directly and almost explicitly. And who can complain that Luther brought out the force of the passage for sixteenth-century Europe so effectively?

What was overlooked then, however, and all too often since then, was that the sixteenth-century Reformation situation and concerns were not the first-century situation and concerns of Paul. A key consideration was that Paul was writing as apostle to the gentiles; Luther was well aware of this, but he wanted to generalize to his own situation too quickly. Central to an adequate appreciation of this passage is the fact that here Paul gives the first clear statement of how he conceived his mission—and the mission of the new movement to

---

6. James D. G. Dunn, *The Theology of Paul's Letter to the Galatians*, NTT (Cambridge: Cambridge University Press, 1993).

7. Martin Luther, *A Commentary on St. Paul's Epistle to the Galatians* (London: James Clarke, 1953), 128.

be known as Christianity. Moreover, he was writing to resist those who saw the new movement as an extension of Judaism—the messianic Judaism of Jesus Christ, eschatological Judaism we might say, focused on Messiah Jesus, but Judaism in any case. So, naturally, for most of the first Christians—all of them Jewish Christians—proselytes, gentile converts, should be expected to become Jews and to live like Jews.

This is precisely the situation that confronted Paul.

However, before we go into more detail on the passage itself, we need to recall how unusual and exceptional was the conversion of Paul and its consequences. Paul himself makes clear, and in the same letter, how astonishing was his volte-face.

> You have heard, no doubt, of my earlier life in Judaism. I was violently perse-
> cuting the church of God and was trying to destroy it. I advanced in Judaism
> beyond many among my people of the same age, for I was far more zealous for
> the traditions of my ancestors. But when God . . . was pleased to reveal his Son
> [to/in] me, so that I might proclaim him among the Gentiles . . . (Gal. 1:13–16)

It was this summons to take the news of the Jewish Messiah to *gentiles* that was the most astonishing and astounding feature of his conversion, as Paul himself all too well realized. Luke underlined the same point in his own way, by rehearsing the story of Paul's conversion three times (Acts 9:1–19; 22:3–21; 26:4–23), each time bringing out ever more clearly the transformative effect of his commission—to bring the message of Jesus Messiah not only to Jews but also to gentiles, to whom the Lord Jesus explicitly sent him "to open their eyes so that they may turn from darkness to light and from the power of Satan to God, so that they may receive forgiveness of sins and a place among those who are sanctified by faith in me" (Acts 26:18).

It is no surprise, but its significance is too easily forgotten, that Paul is remembered precisely as "the apostle to the gentiles"—not that he alone preached openly to gentiles, but that without his mission it must be questionable whether Christianity would have emerged as a predominantly gentile religion. This is why the Letter to the Galatians is so important. For it is there, nowhere else as sharply and nowhere else as clearly, that Paul explains and defends his expansion of the mission of Messiah Jesus, to open it fully and immediately to gentiles—and without requiring them to become Jews in the process. It is precisely this transformation of a Jewish messianic sect into something much larger and more universal that is expressed and defended in Galatians. Luther's reaffirmation of the gospel preached by Paul in the face of papal neglect and corruption certainly has many echoes of Paul's concerns and emphases, but even the emergence of a reformed church has not the same epochal significance as the emergence of Christianity from first-century Judaism. And the crisis involved is nowhere so clearly outlined as in his Letter to the Galatians.

What again is too easily missed is that Galatians 2:16 is the climax of the history that Paul unfolds in Galatians 2. In 2:16 we have the summing up of what evidently had been a crucial sequence of events for Paul. When Paul affirms that "a person is justified not by the works of the law," he is summarizing what for him was the significance and conclusion of the events in Jerusalem and Antioch referred to and described in 2:1–15. The crucial issue in both cases was whether gentiles who came to faith in Christ should be regarded as proselytes—that is, proselytes to Judaism—and should therefore act accordingly. The issue, then, naturally focused on whether gentile converts should be circumcised and should be expected to observe the Jewish food laws. In a world rich in religions that were distinguished by the rituals they practiced, these, circumcision and food laws, were precisely the rituals that distinguished Judaism.[8] So it is hardly surprising that the buildup to Galatians 2:16 is Paul recalling how the issues of whether gentile converts should be circumcised and whether they should observe the distinctive Jewish food laws were resolved.

In Galatians 2:1–10, then, Paul begins by recalling, or reminding the Galatians, how the circumcision issue, whether gentile converts should be *circumcised*, was settled. Fourteen years after his first postconversion trip to Jerusalem, Paul and Barnabas had gone up to Jerusalem "in response to a revelation" (2:2). Paul does not say what the "revelation" was, or why it was given, though Acts 15:1–2 indicates that reports of what had been happening in Antioch had caused unease in Jerusalem. In consequence, some had come up from Jerusalem, insisting that "unless you [gentile converts] are circumcised according to the custom of Moses, you cannot be saved" (15:1).

To resolve the consequent dissension ("no small dissension"), Paul and Barnabas had gone up to Jerusalem to report on the success of their mission and to "discuss" the issue "with the apostles and the elders"—that is, the question of whether gentile believers in Messiah Jesus should be circumcised (15:2). Probably deliberately, Paul and Barnabas had been accompanied by the gentile Titus—that is, the uncircumcised gentile Titus. Inevitably, as Paul and Barnabas must have anticipated, some were present who insisted that

---

8. The other distinguishing feature of Judaism was observance of the Sabbath, which does not stand at the center of Paul's argument but is alluded to in Gal. 4:10.

Titus be circumcised; Paul even uses the language of being "compelled" to be circumcised (Gal. 2:3), presumably indicating the forcefulness of those who made the demand. Paul calls them "false brothers"—hardly a positive ecumenical attitude—presumably Jewish believers who regarded the Jesus movement as a form of eschatological Judaism. His further description of them as having "slipped in to spy on the freedom we have in Christ Jesus, so that they might enslave us" (Gal. 2:4) indicates something of the depth of tension within the Jerusalem community.

Paul's point, however, is that the attempt to insist that Titus be circumcised, and that in consequence all gentile believers be regarded and treated as proselytes to Judaism, was rejected. Paul and Barnabas "did not submit to them even for a moment," in defense of what he called "the truth of the gospel" (2:5). More important, indeed crucially important, Paul and Barnabas's stand was supported by the leadership of the new movement, James, Cephas (Peter), and John—though the somewhat dismissive words in 2:6 ("those who were supposed to be acknowledged leaders—what they actually were makes no difference to me") add a somewhat sour note. Nevertheless, the happy (?) result for Paul and Barnabas was that the Jerusalem leadership recognized the grace given to them and that they had been appointed as missionaries to the gentiles. The good result was an amicable (?) twofold mission: the Jerusalem leadership to the circumcised; Paul and Barnabas to the uncircumcised (2:7–9). According to Paul, the Jerusalem leadership asked of the latter only one thing, "that they should remember the poor," which Paul was eager to do (2:10)—a commitment, ironically, that resulted in his final arrest in Jerusalem and ultimate death (Acts 21–28).

However, what had been a positive outcome soon gave way to further tension. How soon we cannot say, but the fact that more and more serious confrontation took place this time not in Jerusalem, the conservative headquarters of the new movement, but in Antioch, where the door was first opened fully to gentiles, must have been particularly galling for Paul. Cephas (Peter)[9] had come to Antioch and had been happy to join the local Jewish Christians in their table fellowship with the local gentile believers. But when "certain people came from James, . . . [Cephas] drew back and kept himself separate for fear of the circumcision faction" (Gal. 2:12). Paul continues, the memory particularly painful for him: "And the other Jews joined him in this hypocrisy, so that even Barnabas was led astray by their hypocrisy" (2:13) (the reader can almost hear the sob in Paul's voice when he recalled the

---

9. Did Paul refer to Peter as "Cephas" in Gal. 2:9, 11–14 as a way of indicating his traditionalist outlook?

painful memory). Paul evidently was shocked at this. For him, the action of Peter, Barnabas, and the others was completely inconsistent with "the truth of the gospel" (2:14). James was going back on the agreement so hard won in Jerusalem!

Quite clearly, that the gospel was open to gentiles as gentiles, without requiring them to become proselytes, was for Paul the essence of the gospel message. This, somewhat surprisingly, was what had been revealed to him on the road to Damascus. This was what had been confirmed to him by the success of his preaching and ministry among gentiles. And this is what he thought had been agreed in Jerusalem. How could Peter, Barnabas, and the others fail to realize that by refusing to eat with the gentile believers they were going back on the agreement made in Jerusalem? "The truth of the gospel"— that is, the gospel itself—was at stake!

Paul's indignation and anger are clear in the way he responded. He had confronted Peter, not quietly in a private meeting, but publicly "before them all," and had protested forcefully: prior to the coming of the "people from James" Peter had been quite willing to maintain full fellowship with the gentile believers by eating with them, leaving aside the distinctive Jewish rules governing table fellowship. So how could Peter now withdraw from such fellowship and, in effect, make gentile acceptance and practice of these food rules the condition for the table fellowship of Jewish and gentile believers? After the agreement in Jerusalem, the agreement that mission to Jews and mission to gentiles were distinctive missions (2:7–9), how could Peter insist— Paul uses the more forceful word "compel"—even in Antioch, the center of the gentile mission, that gentile believers must/should conform to the norms of the mission to Jews (2:14)?

Then comes the forceful statement, the key statement in which Paul asserts "the truth of the gospel," that it did not insist or presuppose that gentiles who believed the gospel were thereby becoming proselytes to Judaism. "We ourselves are Jews by birth and not Gentile sinners; yet we know that a person is justified not by works of the law but through faith in Jesus Christ" (2:15–16a). And to make his point clear beyond dispute, he repeats it twice more: "And we have come to believe in Christ Jesus, so that we might be justified by faith in Christ, and not by doing the works of the law, because no one will be justified by the works of the law" (2:16bc).[10]

---

10. A quite popular alternative translation of the key phrase "by faith in Christ" as "by the faith of Christ" (NRSV margin) in effect distorts Paul's argument, where the key issue is whether belief alone, the commitment of faith in Christ and to Christ, is sufficient for gentile converts, as Paul insists, or must such converts also perform "the works of the law" before they can be recognized as Christians, as believers in Messiah Jesus.

What Paul meant by "works of the law" is obvious from the context. He was referring to the double attempt by traditionalist Jewish believers to require gentiles, gentiles who believed in and committed themselves to Jesus in baptism, both to be circumcised (2:1–10) and to observe the Jewish food laws (2:11–13). Those whom Paul was debating or arguing with clearly understood the new movement initiated by Jesus as a form of messianic Judaism—a Judaism drawing in gentiles as some prophets had foretold, but drawing them into what was still traditional Judaism. Paul's vision and his successful mission challenged that assumption. Quite why he was so adamant on the point is not entirely clear. Presumably, the memory of his own commitment to ensuring his own righteousness under the law and his zealous persecution of the believers in Jesus (Phil. 3:6) underlined for him the importance of maintaining that the gospel of Christ looked only for the response of faith, faith alone. The point was so important to him that any requirement for more than faith was in effect an attempt to construct one's own righteousness and to rely on that. As he said in continuing his argument, "If I build up again the very things that I once tore down, then I demonstrate that I am a transgressor. For through the law I died to the law, so that I might live to God" (Gal. 2:18–19).

So the issue confronting Paul was in effect whether gentile believers had to become proselytes to Judaism if they were to be saved, and this we should never forget or set to one side. But his formulation of his key point obviously had much wider relevance. For if circumcision and Jewish food laws should not be a necessary requirement for faith, neither should many other religious requirements and traditional practices, including so many that grew up in the history of Christianity. Luther saw Paul's point and made it central to his own restatement of Christian faith. But the Jew/gentile issue, and whether Christianity is nothing more than a form of Judaism, the issue that Paul brought to clarity for the first time and that is central to Christianity's self-definition, should never be forgotten—not least because it resulted in Paul's most distinctive teaching on justification by faith, by faith alone.

Luke Complicates the History

A large part of the responsibility for subsequent Christianity's loss of clarity and failure to maintain this crucial point lies at the feet of Luke. For Luke blurs the distinctiveness and indeed revolutionary impact of Paul on just this point. The reason is, presumably, that Luke was all too aware that a forceful restatement of Paul's position in Antioch (Gal. 2:11–16) might be disruptive or divisive for the new movement. But if so, the question inevitably arises, whether his presentation of Christianity's beginnings is adequate to maintain "the truth of the gospel," which Paul saw as so central to his message and mission.

Worth noting are three points in particular.

1. The first is that Luke seems to qualify Paul's proud claim to be the apostle to the gentiles, indeed the pioneer apostle to the gentiles. Why else did he insert the story of Peter's encounter with the Roman centurion Cornelius (Acts 10–11) prior to his account of Paul's first missionary journey (Acts 13)? Not only so, but he rehearses the story of Cornelius's conversion three times (Acts 10:1–48; 11:1–18; 15:7–11), just as he retold the story of Paul's conversion three times (Acts 9:1–19; 22:3–21; 26:4–23). The way he tells it underlines the degree to which he saw Peter's readiness to accept Cornelius as the real breakthrough of the gospel to gentiles. According to Acts, it took a revelatory dream or vision to win a change of mind in Peter.

> He saw the heaven opened and something like a large sheet coming down, being lowered to the ground by its four corners. In it were all kinds of four-footed creatures and reptiles and birds of the air. Then he heard a voice saying, "Get up, Peter; kill and eat." But Peter said, "By no means, Lord; for I have never eaten anything that is profane or unclean." The voice said to him again, a second time, "What God has made clean, you must not call profane." This happened three times, and the thing was suddenly taken up to heaven. (Acts 10:11–16)

This is altogether astonishing: Peter had "never eaten anything that is profane or unclean"! Had he not been with Jesus when Jesus gave clear teaching on the subject? In the Gospels of Matthew and Mark we read Jesus's explicit teaching, that "whatever goes into a man from outside cannot defile him, since it enters, not his heart but his stomach, and so passes on" (Mark 7:18–19 RSV). Mark adds what for him was the obvious corollary: "Thus he declared all foods clean" (7:19). That is, Mark took to be the clear corollary of Jesus's teaching that the laws or traditions of clean and unclean foods no longer applied to followers of Jesus. It is not what goes into a person, but what comes out, that defiles—evil thoughts, covetousness, and so on (7:20–23).

Interestingly, Matthew retains the key point, that it is what comes out of a person that defiles, not what the person eats (Matt. 15:16–20). But he omits Mark's addition; he does not draw Mark's inference or conclusion, that Jesus thereby declared all foods clean. This slight disagreement, if that is the best way to describe it, is easily explained if Mark was writing his Gospel with the gentile mission in view, whereas Matthew was writing with a view to the continuing mission among his fellow Jews.

But that leaves us quite unprepared for the fact that Luke has no parallel to the Mark 7 // Matthew 15 passage. The implication seems to be that he wanted to attribute the breakthrough of the gospel to the gentiles to Peter. For Luke, the implication and the issue were of course clear: the laws of clean and unclean were a major stumbling block for the mission to the gentiles. So rather than remind his readers that the fundamental issue had been resolved already during the mission of Jesus, and well before the possibility of mission to gentiles posed the issue in a sharp light, Luke evidently chose to ignore the tradition of Mark 7 and held back the issue till it was posed (afresh?) for Peter in the Cornelius episode.

As Luke tells the story in Acts 10–11, it is a wonderful breakthrough. Peter is convinced by the heavenly vision—interestingly, the voice that convinced him is not identified as the voice of Jesus (10:13)—and responds immediately to the appeal from Cornelius. His opening words to Cornelius indicate that he has clearly heard the heavenly message: "You yourselves know that it is unlawful for a Jew to associate with or to visit a Gentile; but God has shown me that I should not call anyone profane or unclean" (10:28). Luke may have omitted the Mark 7 tradition, but not that he might give Paul the whole credit for the breakthrough to a gentile mission. According to Luke, the credit for that is Peter's. The point in Luke's retelling of the story is that although Peter's vision came after Paul's conversion, it was Peter who was the first to spell out the fact that mission to gentiles involved a decisive breach with the Jewish clean/unclean tradition.

2. The second point worthy of note is the differences between Paul's recollection of the critical meeting in Jerusalem (Gal. 2:1–10) and Luke's account of the same meeting (Acts 15). Whether it was "the same meeting" that Luke recounts leaves many commentators nonplussed—so different are the accounts. But almost certainly the differences are not simply different memories of the same meeting but rather result from the same concern of Luke to avoid any impression of a fundamental disagreement between the leading figures of the Jesus movement.

According to Paul, he went up to Jerusalem "in response to a revelation" (Gal. 2:2). That account can be readily correlated with Luke's version in Acts 15:1–2. Likewise, Paul's reference to those who insisted that gentile believers should be circumcised as "false brothers" (Gal. 2:4) can be readily identified with those whom Luke refers to as "some believers who belonged to the sect of the Pharisees" (Acts 15:5). But thereafter the differences become rather striking.

As already noted, in Galatians 2 Paul recalls having to take a strong stand against those who wished to "enslave us" by insisting that believing gentiles must be circumcised. To them, Paul states firmly, "We did not submit even for a moment" (2:5). And he goes on to report the support he received "from those who were supposed to be acknowledged leaders"—a note of some distrust and disrespect, we would have to admit. Nevertheless, as we have already seen, the outcome was an agreed compromise: James, Cephas/Peter, and John to mission among the circumcised; Paul and Barnabas to the gentiles.

The Acts 15 account of the latter stage of what was most probably the same meeting is noticeably different. There is no indication of tension, far less of a tension as recalled by Paul in Galatians 2. Instead, the decisive contribution to the discussion is attributed to Peter, recalling, of course, his conversion of the Roman centurion Cornelius (Acts 15:7–11). Then, in a single sentence, Luke notes that Barnabas and Paul (note again the order) reported the success of their gentile mission (15:12). Finally, and again notably, it is James, who apparently was chairman of the meeting, who sums up the results of the meeting by concluding that it was evidently God's will for the good news of Jesus to be open to gentiles, citing particularly Amos 9:11–12 in support. The letter that James decides to send to the believing gentiles exempts them from the troublesome food laws (15:19–21). Thus Luke again draws something of a veil over what initially at least had been a tense and disruptive meeting. His point is evidently to make clear to his readers that the mission to gentiles as pioneered by Paul did not divide the leadership of the new movement but was supported by all with no little enthusiasm.

3. But then comes the most striking divergence between Paul's recollection of those early days and Luke's account. For, surprise, surprise, Luke gives absolutely no hint of the subsequent Antioch confrontation between Paul and Peter, recalled as such a troubled memory by Paul in Galatians 2:11–14. The reason, presumably, is that the Antioch incident showed all too clearly that the agreement in Jerusalem had not, after all, been final. It was "certain people from James" (2:12) who caused the crisis in the Antioch meeting of believers by insisting, once again, that Jews and gentiles should not eat together, all being believers in Jesus notwithstanding. But on Luke's account that could/should not have happened. Peter's breakthrough with Cornelius and the felicitous meeting in Jerusalem had resolved the issue. So, nothing more need be said. Here, it would appear, Luke the apologist has taken over from Luke the historian.

But if all this is so, we should not blame Luke too harshly. Certainly, he sets a more balanced picture than we can draw from Paul's correspondence. Paul is a protagonist, Luke a historian. But he leaves a somewhat troublesome question: By diminishing the degree of confrontation that Paul's mission and his advocacy of that mission seems to have caused, does he miss Paul's crucial point about the gospel? Alternatively, was Paul a little too extreme on the point? Luke evidently realized that there was a serious danger that the gentile mission might lead to schism, a movement split in two more or less from the first. His history of these early days, and of how that danger was averted, means that a schism was avoided, that Peter and Paul are remembered as partner missionaries on the same mission. The tension reemerged later, when Jewish Christianity became in effect separate from the growth of Christianity predominantly among gentiles. But the success of Luke is indicated by the formation of a New Testament, in which the letters of Paul are prominent, but also the Gospels of Matthew and Mark and a letter of James, held together by Luke-Acts.

Paul and/or Luke?

This disagreement and tension between Paul's recollection of the Antioch incident and Luke's account of Christianity's beginnings raises some important issues.

The key issue is whether Paul was right to insist on justification by faith (alone) at the cost of disagreement and confrontation with the rest of the first-century Christian leadership. Would it be fair to say that Luke's portrayal of a development of Christianity led by Peter, his avoidance of the confrontation between Paul and Peter regarding the truth of the gospel, his assumption that the Jerusalem leadership coped well with the tensions, and his portrayal of Paul's contentment with the outcome of the Jerusalem conference led directly to the subsequent form of Christianity dominated by a papal successor to Peter in Rome, with Paul in effect banished, or better, sidelined, to the outskirts of the same city? And was Luther's rediscovery of Galatians 2:16 in effect an outcome precisely of that confrontation, and a reaction to the course set by Luke in his history of Christianity's beginnings?

A further uncomfortable issue is whether a natural Christian desire for ecumenism may give way too readily to desires to soften the harder edges of the gospel, to avoid restatements of "the truth of the gospel" because the confrontation of modern-day Peters and Pauls is too challenging. The disagreement between Paul and Luke in their diverse portrayals of fundamental disagreements within early Christian leadership poses a question that should not and cannot be ignored: Which comes first—mutual ecumenical acceptance or "the truth of the gospel"? An inescapable corollary question, given that it was the ecclesial and theological developments that Luther saw to have obscured that truth, is whether developments since Luther have obscured that same truth yet again.

Another line of questioning emerges from the fact that the New Testament successfully combines Luke-Acts and Paul in the same canon. Its success in doing so is due partly at least to the close correlation between their portrayals of the Holy Spirit and the Spirit's crucial role in defining Christianity. Luke's emphasis on the defining Spirit well matches that of Paul. Consider, for example, Luke's introduction to his account of Christianity's beginnings by focusing on the promised Spirit baptism (Acts 1:5), his emphasis on the Pentecost experience as the energizing beginning of Christianity and its initial expansion (1:8; 2:1–47), on Peter's resolution of Philip's partial conversion of the Samaritans (8:4–17) and his central role in the conversion of the centurion Cornelius (10:1–11:18), and on Paul's resolution of the ambiguous status of "some disciples" converted by Apollos (18:24–19:7). Also, compare that with Paul's equivalent focus: in particular, the definition of a Christian in terms not of belief or baptism but of having the Spirit of Christ (Rom. 8:9–14); the understanding of church as the body of Christ empowered by the Spirit, of worship as enabled and led by the Spirit (1 Cor. 12; 14), and of life granted and growth energized by the Spirit, transforming believers into the image of Christ (2 Cor. 3); and his challenge to his Galatian converts to recall that they started by receiving the Spirit, not by doing works of the law, so why should they think that advancing in the Christian life was any different (Gal. 3:1–5)?[11]

It was the tie-in between justification by faith and the gift of the Spirit that was so clearly central in Paul's preaching and theology, and that is so clearly illustrated particularly in the sequence of Romans 5–8, and of Galatians 2:16–21 followed immediately by 3:1–14, which was rather sadly slackened by Luke in his history of Christianity's beginnings. In contrast, Luke, while certainly emphasizing the importance of the Spirit, makes no real effort to highlight the centrality of justification by faith in Paul's preaching. The point is clearly illustrated in Acts 13:38–39, the only two verses in which Luke refers to Paul's speaking of justification in his records of Paul's preaching. The problem—if that is the right word—is that his report is quite hard to match with what Paul himself says about justification in his letters.[12] Could it be that in trying to diminish the distinctiveness of Paul's ministry, and to

11. Perhaps I should mention here also my essay "Galatians," in Trevor J. Burke and Keith Warrington, eds., *A Biblical Theology of the Holy Spirit* (London: SPCK, 2014), 175–86.

12. For example, C. K. Barrett notes sadly, "We cannot ascribe these verses to Paul. On a central question of faith Luke shows his devotion to Paul but less than full understanding of his theology." *A Critical and Exegetical Commentary on the Acts of the Apostles*, 2 vols., ICC (Edinburgh: T&T Clark, 1994), 1:651. Modern translations tend deliberately to avoid using the word "justify" in their versions.

fit him more comfortably into a universal mission led from Jerusalem, Luke actually lost sight of the distinctiveness of the gospel as preached by Paul?

Is this the issue that Luke's handling of Paul's gospel poses—today as well as in the first and sixteenth centuries? Is there a tension between the understandably ecumenical motivation in Luke's portrayal of Christianity's beginnings and the challenge and demands of the gospel as preached by Paul? Do we have to choose between the sharp challenge of Paul's gospel and Luke's portrayal of a united church as led by Peter and his successors? The New Testament itself says no! They belong together, one gospel, one church. Peter's preeminence is well grounded in the New Testament but little reflected there in comparison with the major status given to Paul's Letters. Yet the diminution of Paul in comparison with Peter in the early centuries, and Luther's rediscovery of Paul in the sixteenth century, can hardly be ignored.

Conclusion

So I make no apology for concentrating on Galatians 2:11–16 to the extent that I have. There is a danger that we allow the ecumenical character of Luke's portrayal of Christianity's beginnings to obscure what was of central importance for Paul. The challenge of a gospel effective only through faith, through faith alone, was all too readily lost to sight in Luke's history and in the subsequent history that he in effect encouraged. As that history all too well documents, it is all too easy for the fundamental simplicity of the gospel as expressed in Galatians 2:16 to be forgotten and in effect hidden under the weight and solemnity of creedal statements, church order, ecclesial hierarchy, and the like. That was what Luther realized and why the Reformation protested as it did. If the truth of the gospel required Paul to confront Peter, it also required Luther to confront the pope. And should not that truth be restated today, even when it challenges us to ask whether there is much, indeed too much, in today's churches that obscures or ignores the gospel preached and proclaimed by Paul?

Roman Catholic Perspective Response to Dunn

BRANT PITRE

James Dunn begins by saying he was "a little nonplussed" when he received the invitation to contribute yet another essay on the New Perspective on Paul (133). I for one was thrilled. Over twenty years ago, when I was a poor graduate student, Dunn's *The Theology of Paul the Apostle* was the first book on Paul I ever purchased—and it was worth every penny.[1] I consider it a privilege to respond to his essay, and will begin by highlighting a few major points of agreement.

The Necessity of Contextualizing Paul: The "Apostle to the Gentiles"

First, I wholeheartedly agree with Dunn that the letters of Paul must always be interpreted first and foremost in light of the historical fact "that Paul was writing as apostle to the gentiles" (134) (cf. Gal. 1:16; 2:8–9; Rom. 11:13). When it comes to Galatians in particular, Dunn rightly insists, "The crucial issue . . . was whether gentiles who came to faith in Christ should be regarded as proselytes—that is, proselytes to Judaism—and should therefore act accordingly" (136). In other words, before all else, Paul's extremely consequential statements about "justification" through "faith" apart from "works of the law" (Gal. 2:15–21) have to be interpreted in their historical and literary

1. James D. G. Dunn, *The Theology of Paul the Apostle* (Grand Rapids: Eerdmans, 1998).

context. To my mind, this remains one of the lasting contributions of the New Perspective on Paul: *the first task of the exegete must be to interpret Paul on his own terms and in his own context*, whatever the theological implications may be. By its insistence on prioritizing the historical context of Paul's statements, I think that the New Perspective has done much to help disentangle Pauline exegesis from centuries-old post-Reformation debates that have, at times, exerted undue influence in both Catholic and Protestant circles. If the tsunami of publications on Paul and justification in the wake of the New Perspective on Paul is any indication, it has at the very least succeeded in stimulating fresh questions being asked of the text. We are all in Dunn's debt for the trailblazing he has done in placing Pauline soteriology at the center of a continuing conversation.

The Peril of Modernizing Paul: "Works of the Law" ≠ "Good Works" Done after Baptism

Along similar lines, from the first time I read Dunn's now famous 1982 lecture "The New Perspective on Paul," I was convinced by his basic argument, reiterated in his essay here, that it is anachronistic to identify the "works of the law" to which Paul refers in Galatians 2 with "the 'good works' disparaged by the Reformers as the ground for acceptance by God"—things such as hearing a Mass, giving alms, or the purchase of an indulgence.[2] Dunn rightly insists that "the sixteenth-century Reformation situation and concerns were not the first-century situation and concerns of Paul" (134). I also concur that, at least when it comes to Galatians 2, "what Paul meant by 'works of the law' is obvious from the context. He was referring to the double attempt by traditionalist Jewish believers to require gentiles . . . both to be circumcised (2:1–10) and to observe the Jewish food laws (2:11–13)" (139). Whatever else the expression "works of the law" might mean elsewhere in Paul's Letters, it seems incontrovertible to me that, in context, these two issues do indeed seem to be first and foremost in Paul's mind as he pens the opening sections of his angry letter to the Galatians, even if he does not mean to exclude other works of the law.[3]

2. For a recent reprint of this article, see James D. G. Dunn, *The New Perspective on Paul*, rev. ed. (Grand Rapids: Eerdmans, 2008), 99–120.

3. Over the years, Dunn has repeatedly clarified that his emphasis on circumcision and food laws does not exclude other works of the law or the Torah as a whole. Note, e.g., Dunn, *The New Perspective on Paul*, 23: "I have no doubt that 'works of the law' refers to what the law required, the conduct prescribed by the Torah"; and again: "I do not want to narrow 'the works of the law' to boundary issues" (28).

The "Essence of the Gospel Message" in Galatians = Justification by "Faith Alone"

Once this distinction between "works of the law" (e.g., circumcision, food laws) and "good works" done after baptism (e.g., participating in the Lord's Supper, giving alms to the poor) is clear, I even find myself able to agree with Dunn's description of the "essence" of the "gospel" in Galatians as "justification" by "faith alone" (when the latter is properly understood).[4] As Dunn puts it, "Quite clearly, that the gospel was open to gentiles as gentiles, without requiring them to become proselytes, was for Paul the essence of the gospel message" (138). In the context of Galatians, this seems to be correct, especially when we look at how Paul uses the expression "the gospel" at the opening of the letter: "I am astonished that you are so quickly deserting the one who called you in the grace of Christ and are turning to *a different gospel*—not that there is *another gospel*, but there are some who are confusing you and want to pervert *the gospel of Christ*. But even if we or an angel from heaven should proclaim to you *a gospel* contrary to what we proclaimed to you, let that one be accursed!" (Gal. 1:6–8).

In the context of Galatians, "the gospel" (τὸ εὐαγγέλιον, *to euangelion*) (Gal. 1:7; cf. 2:14) seems to be shorthand for the fact that "a person is justified not by the works of the law but through faith in Jesus Christ" (Gal. 2:16). Thus, despite the contemporary debate over whether justification by faith is the "center of Pauline theology," when it comes to Galatians, Dunn is right to point to it as the "essence" of what Paul means when he contrasts his "gospel" with the "different gospel" of his opponents (Gal. 1:6–7). As Dunn puts it later in his essay, it was "the Jew/gentile issue" that "resulted in Paul's most distinctive teaching on justification by faith, by faith alone" (139). If by this Dunn means that, when it came to entry into the body of Christ—that is, the initial act of justification by which a person becomes a member of Christ—"the gospel of Christ looked only for the response of faith, faith alone" (139), I concur.

With that said, I do have three questions about Dunn's essay.

How "New" Is the "New Perspective"?

First, I have always wondered: When Dunn coined the phrase "the New Perspective on Paul," was he aware that key elements of his view—such as its emphasis on circumcision and food laws—had been part of the Catholic exegetical tradition for centuries? Having searched through the indices of his many writings, I

4. See my essay herein on the patristic, medieval, and modern Catholic tradition of initial justification *sola fide*.

see little to no interaction with patristic and medieval Pauline interpreters such as John Chrysostom and Thomas Aquinas, both of whom wrote commentaries on all of Paul's Letters.[5] Is there a reason Dunn does not engage these giants of Pauline exegesis? As I mention in my essay, the view that Paul was referring *not* to good works done after baptism (the position that Dunn attributes to the Protestant Reformers) but rather primarily to Jewish "works of the law" is actually quite ancient. It was taught by the two towering Pauline exegetes of the first four centuries: Origen of Alexandria (d. AD 253) and Jerome of Stridon (d. AD 420):

> The works that Paul repudiates and frequently criticizes are *not the works of righteousness* that are commanded in the law, but . . . the *circumcision* of the flesh, the sacrificial rituals, the observance of Sabbaths or new moon festivals. (Origen, *Commentary on the Epistle to the Romans* 8.7.6)[6]

> I should ask about what is at hand [in Gal. 3:2]: whether it was *works of the law*, observance of *the Sabbath*, the superstition of *circumcision*, and new moons. . . . Let us consider carefully what [Paul] does *not* say, "I want to learn from you" whether you "receive the Spirit" by works, but instead "by the works of the law." (Jerome, *Commentary on Galatians*, 1.3.2)[7]

These are by no means the only patristic examples of such Pauline exegesis.[8] In light of such readings, would Dunn agree that we should perhaps qualify the "new" in "New Perspective"?[9]

Justification by "Faith Alone" ≠ "Faith without Love"

My second question is more exegetical. While I was grateful that Dunn spent time explaining how he understands "justification by faith" apart from "works

---

5. See, e.g., Thomas Aquinas, *Commentary on the Letter of Saint Paul to the Romans*, trans. F. R. Larcher, ed. J. Mortensen and E. Alarcón (Lander, WY: Aquinas Institute for the Study of Sacred Doctrine, 2012), 99, where Aquinas summarizes the centuries-old debate between some who interpret Paul's expression "works of the law" as referring to "the Mosaic law, as the observance of ceremonial precepts," such as circumcision and food laws, and others who think that "the Apostle intends to say that by no works of the Law, even those commanded by the moral precepts, is a man justified" (3.2.297; cf. 3.4.317).

6. Origen, *Commentary on the Epistle to the Romans*, trans. Thomas P. Scheck, 2 vols., FC 103, 104 (Washington, DC: Catholic University of America Press, 2001–2), 2:159 (emphasis added).

7. *St. Jerome's Commentaries on Galatians, Titus, and Philemon*, trans. Thomas P. Scheck (Notre Dame, IN: University of Notre Dame Press, 2010), 114 (emphasis added).

8. See further Matthew J. Thomas, *Paul's "Works of the Law" in the Perspective of Second Century Reception*, WUNT 2/468 (Tübingen: Mohr Siebeck, 2018).

9. See also Thomas P. Scheck, *Origen and the History of Justification: The Legacy of Origen's Commentary on Romans* (Notre Dame, IN: University of Notre Dame Press, 2008).

of the law" in the opening chapters of Galatians, I was hoping that he would say something about Paul's statements later in Galatians regarding the relationship between justification, "faith," and "love": "You who want to be justified by the law have cut yourselves off from Christ; you have fallen away from grace. For through the Spirit, by faith, we eagerly wait for the hope of righteousness. For in Christ Jesus neither circumcision nor uncircumcision counts for anything; *the only thing that counts is faith working through love*" (Gal. 5:4–6).

As I mention in my essay, from a Catholic perspective, the tradition of summarizing Paul's teaching as initial justification by "faith alone" (Latin *sola fide*) is unobjectionable, as long as one does not mean justification by "faith" (Greek πίστις, *pistis*; Latin *fides*) *apart from* "love" (Greek ἀγάπη, *agapē*; Latin *caritas*). One foundation for this insistence on keeping faith and charity together is Paul's statement that, when it comes to "righteousness," all that matters is "faith working through love" (πίστις δι' ἀγάπης ἐνεργουμένη, *pistis di' agapēs energoumenē*) (Gal. 5:6). Since, historically speaking, this was a point of division between some of the Protestant Reformers and the Catholic reading, I was hoping that Dunn would say something about it in his essay. Thankfully, Dunn addresses it in his 1993 commentary on Galatians. There he writes,

> This verse [Gal. 5:6] provides a basis for response to any criticism of Paul's view of justification by faith—that it encouraged a passive quietism, an inactivism, or even antinomianism (Rom. iii.8; vi.1). On the contrary, Paul understood "in Christ" as a new and living relationship active in well doing (see also vi.15). He understood justification as a sustained relationship with God through Christ (faith), which produced the righteousness looked for and acknowledged by God (love). *The phrase is almost a single concept, faith-through-love, love-energized-faith. This is the faith he was talking about; not faith as a beginning and love as an outcome, as though the two were separate* . . . , but faith coming to expression in and through love. *Such an understanding should not be seen as a threat* to the *sola fide*; for it is precisely that complete reliance on and openness to God's grace which comes to expression in love, love not as a requirement of faith, but as its natural expression. . . . But we should do Paul the justice of taking him seriously when he claimed that only through this dynamic relationship could the law be fulfilled as God wanted it fulfilled . . . ; "the *sola-fide* principle is indeed an exclusive but not a restricted principle" (Mussner 353). Here Paul comes as close as he ever does to James (James ii.18).[10]

10. James D. G. Dunn, *The Epistle to the Galatians*, BNTC (1993; reprint, Grand Rapids: Baker Academic, 2011), 272 (emphasis added). Dunn quotes from F. Mussner, *Der Galaterbrief*, HTKNT, 3rd ed. (Frieburg: Herder, 1977).

It is remarkable how well aspects of Dunn's exegesis here cohere with the patristic, medieval, and modern Catholic tradition of *sola fide*. As I show in my essay, in the Catholic tradition justification *sola fide* means initial justification by grace through "faith apart from works"—not "faith apart from love." In particular, Dunn's interpretation of Paul's words as a *"love-energized-faith"* that does not threaten justification *sola fide* comes very close to the Catholic perspective taught by the Council of Trent: "Faith without hope and charity neither unites a man perfectly with Christ nor makes him a living member of his body. Therefore it is rightly said that faith by itself, if it has no works, is dead and unprofitable (cf. James 2:17, 20) and that 'in Christ Jesus neither circumcision nor uncircumcision is of any avail, but faith working through love' (Gal. 5:6)" (Council of Trent, *Decree on Justification*, chap. 7).[11]

In light of this striking point of convergence, I wonder: Would Dunn agree with the Council of Trent's summary of Paul's teaching on justification: "initial justification" by "grace" through "faith apart from works" but not "faith apart from charity"? Does the patristic, medieval, and modern Catholic tradition of initial justification *sola fide* that I outline in my essay constitute a point of common ground on which we can agree?

When Was Paul's Doctrine Justification by "Faith Alone" Lost?

My final question is more ecumenical in character. Dunn brings his essay to a close with the following:

> The challenge of a gospel effective only through faith, through faith alone, was all too readily lost to sight in Luke's history and in the subsequent history that he in effect encouraged. As that history all too well documents, it is all too easy for the fundamental simplicity of the gospel as expressed in Galatians 2:16 to be forgotten and in effect hidden under the weight and solemnity of creedal statements, church order, ecclesial hierarchy, and the like. That was what Luther realized and why the Reformation protested as it did. If the truth of the gospel required Paul to confront Peter, it also required Luther to confront the pope. (145)

In the light of my essay, in the present volume, on the Roman Catholic perspective on Paul, I wonder if Dunn would consider nuancing such a sweeping claim about Catholicism. To be specific: if initial justification by "faith alone" (*sola fide*) was taught by patristic, medieval, and modern Catholic writers,

---

11. Heinrich Denzinger, *Compendium of Creeds, Definitions, and Declarations on Matters of Faith and Morals*, ed. Peter Hünermann, 43rd ed. (San Francisco: Ignatius, 2012), no. 1531.

including bishops such as Augustine, priests such as Aquinas, and popes such as Benedict XVI, is it fair to say that the gospel was "lost" or "hidden"?

In short, just as Pauline scholars need to continue work to be more precise in their description of first-century Judaism, I would humbly suggest that Protestant scholars seek to do the same when it comes to Catholicism. Just as first-century Jews did not perform good works in order to "get in" to the old covenant but rather to "stay in," so too medieval Catholics did not hear Mass, or give alms, or perform indulgences (examples that Dunn uses in his essay) in order to "get in" to the new covenant ("getting in" was done through infant baptism). Rather, they performed good works by grace in order to be conformed to Christ and to "stay in" the new covenant. Once this distinction is clear, it is not quite clear to me how Luther's insistence on justification *sola fide* applies in the way Dunn uses it, since I know of no medieval Catholic who rejected initial justification *sola fide*. At the very least, I do not think anything would be lost to the contemporary ecumenical movement by adding more nuance to how the doctrine of justification is discussed with reference to Catholic practice and belief. Indeed, when it comes to Pauline exegesis, it might actually bring into sharper focus where Catholics and Protestants really do agree.

Traditional Protestant Perspective
Response to Dunn

A. ANDREW DAS

Professor Dunn's essay advances two claims to supplement his immense body of scholarship. First, the conflict at Antioch in Galatians 2:11–14 concerned Jewish ethnic distinctives: food laws and circumcision. Second, Luke in Acts sought to minimize the conflict between Peter and Paul and identifies Peter as the key figure inaugurating the gentile mission. In arguing for Peter's central role, Dunn links Acts 15 with Galatians 2:1–10.[1] He explains discrepancies between the two accounts as a result of Luke's competing interests, but the discrepancies are quite severe, so much so as to jeopardize Dunn's identification. A more defensible position takes the Galatians 2:1–10 meeting as an event that took place during the famine-relief visit in Acts 11:27–30 // Acts 12:25.[2] Of greater significance, however, is Dunn's claim that the Antioch conflict revolved around food laws and circumcision.

How to understand the phrase "works of the law" in Galatians 2:16 has been a key difference between the traditional view and Dunn's "New Perspective." Galatians 2:16 is best interpreted in view of its immediate context, especially the conflict that took place at Antioch (2:11–14)—thus the importance of understanding that conflict aright. For Dunn, "works of the law" refers to all that the law requires, but those aspects of the law that serve as

1. See also James D. G. Dunn, *The Epistle to the Galatians*, BNTC (Peabody, MA: Hendrickson, 1993), 3–19.
2. A. Andrew Das, *Galatians*, ConcC (St. Louis: Concordia, 2014), 36–43.

ethnic distinctives are *primarily* in view; thus for Dunn, "works of the law" in 2:16 appears immediately after conflict over "whether gentile converts . . . should observe the distinctive Jewish food laws" (136) and be circumcised. "What Paul meant by 'works of the law' is obvious from the context. He was referring to the double attempt by traditionalist Jewish believers to require [Christ-believing] gentiles . . . both to be circumcised (2:1–10) and to observe the Jewish food laws (2:11–13)" (139). By withdrawing, Peter was making "gentile acceptance and practice of these food rules the condition for the table fellowship of Jewish and gentile believers" (138). The traditional view, on the other hand, recognizes that "works of the law" refers to the law as a whole, but *not necessarily* with those boundary markers in view. Depending on context, the phrase may simply refer to the law's works/requirements.

Peter, James, and John agreed that they would focus on the circumcised and Paul and Barnabas would focus on the uncircumcised (Gal. 2:7–9). Paul then narrates Peter's eating with gentiles at Antioch (2:11–14). "Certain men" from James arrived, and Peter withdrew from the table, followed by Barnabas and the rest of the Jews. Paul does not denigrate the arriving party as he does the "false brothers" in 2:4–5, and he is respectful of James in 1:19; 2:6–10. Were the arriving group not legitimately representing James's interests, they would not have carried weight with Peter, and Paul's case would be strengthened to expose their illegitimacy or to leave James out of the narration entirely. Without any such qualification, one may safely conclude that the concerns they represent are James's. What motivated the concerns?

Food Laws?

Avoiding unclean food was a defining feature of the Jewish faith, especially after the struggle to maintain these laws in the face of Antiochus IV Epiphanes's persecution in the second century BC.[3] Peter boasted in Acts 10:14, "I have never eaten anything that is profane or unclean." The Lord had to offer Peter an emphatic revelation before he would consider partaking of gentile food. Had the shared meals in Galatians 2:11–14 violated Mosaic stipulations, the Jewish Christians would have objected well before anyone arrived from Jerusalem.[4] Many Antiochene Jewish Christians, without the benefit of a

---

3. E.g., 1 Macc. 1:62–63; 4 Macc. 5–6; 8–12; cf. Lev. 11:1–47; Deut. 14:3–21; Philo, *Spec.* 4.100–118.

4. James D. G. Dunn, *Jesus, Paul, and the Law: Studies in Mark and Galatians* (Louisville: Westminster John Knox, 1990), 152: "It must be doubted whether so many Jewish believers at Antioch would have given up the law so unreservedly"; 137: "No one who cherished the memory of the Maccabees would even dream of eating unclean food."

special revelation, would have had similar reservations about eating unclean food, and the ensuing fuss would have left its mark on Paul's account. The Antiochene Jews had long been attracting gentiles to their customs.[5] The first gentile Christian converts likely came from the ranks of God-fearers, who had been accustomed to avoiding certain foods for the sake of their Jewish friends.[6] Gentile Christians could respect Jewish Christians' scruples by buying meat and wine from Antioch's Jewish vendors. The Jews would resort to vegetables and water, if necessary, to avoid objectionable sustenance.[7] Had the Jews been asking the gentiles to be respectful of their dining customs, Paul probably would have advocated yielding for the sake of weaker believers (Rom. 14:13–15:3; 1 Cor. 8:7–13).[8] He does not mention the food involved or Jewish Christian avoidance of menu options. That the Antiochene Jewish believers were abandoning Mosaic food laws in their meals with gentiles is unlikely.

Circumcision?

Perhaps the James party was requiring the gentiles to become proselytes and circumcised. Perhaps, under pressure from James's party, Peter shifted from a lenient position, "living like a gentile" (2:14), to a stricter one requiring conversion. Such scenarios are unlikely. In recognizing the ministry of Paul and Barnabas to the gentiles, Peter, James, and John had already agreed in 2:1–10 that the gentiles need not be circumcised.

James did not renege on the Jerusalem agreement under subsequent pressure from the non-Christ-believing Jews in Jerusalem. Paul never claims that James violated their agreement. Peter was not in Jerusalem at the time of James's supposed change of mind and was not subject to the same pressures at Antioch. Peter had already agreed that the gentiles need not be circumcised, despite the influence and tactics of the "false brothers" (2:4).[9] James would not have acted unilaterally, and Paul does not identify Peter's withdrawal as violating their prior agreement. Requiring the gentiles to become Jewish (ἰουδαΐζειν, *ioudaizein* [2:14]) appears to be the practical *result* of the

---

5. Josephus, *J.W.* 7.45.

6. Dunn, *Jesus, Paul, and the Law*, 152.

7. E.g., Josephus, *Ant.* 14.226, 259–61.

8. Dunn, *Jesus, Paul, and the Law*, 152–53; Peter J. Tomson, *Paul and the Jewish Law: Halakha in the Letters of the Apostle to the Gentiles*, CRINT 3/1 (Assen: van Gorcum; Minneapolis: Fortress, 1990), 228: "If Paul really would have violated the food laws and induced others to do so in the presence of Barnabas, Peter and the Antioch Jews, he would have made the agreement null and void and his own apostolate impossible."

9. Dunn, *Jesus, Paul, and the Law*, 153–54.

withdrawal and not what was being advocated in the first place. Other false leads include tithing or ritual purity concerns.[10]

A Broad Range of Jewish-Gentile Interactions

When Jews chose to participate in shared meals, they were known for avoiding sacrificed meat and the wine of libation.[11] Second Temple texts typically are silent on whether or not gentile foods violated Torah. Potential idolatry was the issue. Occasionally, Second Temple texts go beyond concerns about idolatry to express qualms about the gentiles *themselves*.[12]

The Jews practiced a broad range of social interactions with gentiles, from the stricter to the more lenient. The law-observant philosopher Philo went to the gymnasium, public baths, and theater and encouraged fellow Jews to participate in gentile social institutions and education. For other Jews, the stigma of potential idolatry lingered over meals with gentiles, and perhaps even over the gentiles themselves. Some Jews urged complete separation from abominable gentiles.[13] In Acts 10:28 Israelites are not to associate with (κολλᾶσθαι, *kollasthai*) or visit (προσέρχεσθαι, *proserchesthai*) common (κοινός, *koinos*) or unclean (ἀκάθαρτος, *akathartos*) gentiles (cf. m. 'Ohol. 18.7; m. Ḥul. 2.7). Thus, some Jews would avoid sharing the meat and wine of the gentiles; others would not ask about the provisions set before them; still others avoided gentiles as much as possible.

The rise of Jewish zealotry complicated interactions between Jew and gentile. The Roman governors of Judea in the 40s and 50s had on several occasions acted against nationalist movements and even the expression of the Jewish faith itself.[14] Diaspora Jews likewise experienced threats to their faith.[15] Claudius's edict in AD 41 affirming the rights of Antiochene Jews was similar

---

10. See the critiques in Das, *Galatians*, 219–23.

11. Dan. 1:3–20 [cf. Josephus, *Life* 13–14]; Jdt. 10–12, esp. 12:1–4, 19; Add. Esth. 14:17; Tob. 1:10–12; Jub. 22.16 (nothing on the foods involved); 3 Macc. 3:4–7; Jos. Asen. 7.1; 8.5; 21.14–15; Let. Aris. 142, 172–294; 4 Macc. 5:2; m. Demai 6.10; m. 'Abod. Zar. 5.3–7, R. Meir. Rabbi Shimon ben Elazar, Meir's student, took a stricter view: even with your own servants and food and drink, it is *still* idolatry (t. 'Abod. Zar. 4.6); see Tomson, *Paul and the Jewish Law*, 233–34. Shimon ben Elazar: eating at a gentile table causes exile for his children (b. Sanh. 104a).

On Jewish avoidance of idolatrous gentile meat and wine, see the texts compiled by Menahem Stern, ed. and trans., *Greek and Latin Authors on Jews and Judaism*, 2 vols. (Jerusalem: Israel Academy of Sciences and Humanities, 1974), 1:20–21, 26, 28, 148, 155, 156, 181–83, 332, 335–36, 338; 2:19, 26, 340–41.

12. Acts 10:11–16, 28, 47–48; 11:2–3, 5–12; 15:9—note: not the food, but the people involved.

13. E.g., Jub. 22.16; cf. 30.7, 14–17; Jos. Asen. 7.1.

14. Josephus, *Ant.* 19.279; 20.6, 97–99, 102, 112–24; also *J.W.* 2.223–27.

15. E.g., Philo, *Flacc.* 41–54; *Legat.* 132–37.

to the edict for the Alexandrian Jews and suggests that the Antiochene Jews had been similarly threatened, whether in the wake of riots or of Caligula's threat against the Jerusalem temple.[16]

The first Jewish believers in Jesus could not escape these pressures.[17] Jerusalem Jews slaughtered Stephen for his witness in the early or mid-30s even as Paul the "zealot" violently persecuted Christ-believers (ζηλωτής, zēlōtēs [Gal 1:14; Acts 22:3]). Agrippa slaughtered James the brother of John, which "pleased the Jews" and encouraged Agrippa to try to kill Peter (Acts 12:1–3 [AD 44]). Jewish Christians were advocating gentile circumcision (Gal. 2:4–5; Acts 11:2–3; 15:1–5). The pressure on the early Christian movement would have been palpable. For Jews to associate with gentiles would evoke suspicion by fellow Jews. Paul's visit to Jerusalem in Acts 21:20–21 (mid-50s or later) represented a perceived threat to the Jewish faith.[18] In 1 Thessalonians 2:14–16 Paul describes the early persecution of Christians in Judea.[19] Jews would not want to appear disloyal to their heritage.

The Antioch Situation

James does not send word to Barnabas or to the other Jewish Christians; he sends word *exclusively to Peter*. Peter "used to eat with the gentiles" (Gal. 2:12). The men from James likely accused Peter of "living like a gentile" even before Paul spoke of it (2:14). They probably introduced the pejorative language of "gentile sinners" (2:15). Why Peter?

When the Jerusalem pillars agreed that Paul and Barnabas would focus primarily on the non-Jews (ἡ ἀκροβυστία / τὰ ἔθνη, hē akrobystia / ta ethnē) (2:7–9), it is difficult to imagine that they had not also anticipated Jews and gentiles sharing bread, wine, and meals.[20] Peter, however, would take the message of Christ to the Jews (2:7–9). What would become of Peter's missionary labors were his association with gentiles to become known? In Acts 10 Peter had recognized with Cornelius that all foods and gentile persons are clean, but nationalist pressures were on the rise.[21] Although Jews could eat with

---

16. Josephus, *Ant.* 19.279. Likewise Dunn, *Jesus, Paul, and the Law*, 134.

17. Dunn, *Jesus, Paul, and the Law*, 154–55.

18. As Dunn (*Jesus, Paul, and the Law*, 135) concluded, "*Wherever this new Jewish sect's belief or practice was perceived to be a threat to Jewish institutions and traditions its members would almost certainly come under pressure from their fellow Jews to remain loyal to their unique Jewish heritage*" (emphasis original).

19. On the authenticity of this text, see A. Andrew Das, *Paul and the Jews*, LPS (Peabody, MA: Hendrickson, 2003), 129–38.

20. Dunn, *Jesus, Paul, and the Law*, 155.

21. Robert Jewett, "The Agitators and the Galatian Congregation," *NTS* 17 (1971): 198–212, underscoring the rise in violence.

gentiles under the right circumstances, shared meals would be perceived by some Jews as reeking of idolatry, if not also law violations.[22] In a time when zealots were acting against any perceived as disloyal to their Jewish heritage, Peter's witness to his fellow Jews was in jeopardy. James sent word to Peter: "*You* should not eat with the gentiles, Peter!"[23]

As a Jerusalem "pillar" and apostle, Peter would have no reason to fear "those of the circumcision" (τοὺς ἐκ περιτομῆς, *tous ek peritomēs*), were they Jewish Christians. His fear indicates that they were a *separate* group from the men from James and non-Christ-believing. The nearest antecedent for this group is in 2:7–9, where Peter is to evangelize the circumcised (ἡ περιτομή, *hē peritomē*).[24] Peter had not been afraid of human authorities (Acts 2:14–41; 3:17–26; 4:8–12; 5:29–32). The fear was not for his own well-being but for the potential persecution of the Jerusalem church by other Jews or for the damage to his credibility as a missionary to the circumcised.

James therefore advised Peter to withdraw from the meal. Peter recognized the wisdom of the advice. Of course, if Barnabas and other Jewish Christians at the meal still hoped to have an audience with non-Christ-believing Jews, they too would have felt compelled to withdraw. As Paul explained, Peter may not technically have been forcing gentiles to become law-observant, but he was doing so practically for the shared bread and cup (of the Lord [1 Cor. 11:27]). They would have to observe Torah. When Paul speaks of "works of the law" in Galatians 2:16, he has in mind the *entirety* of the Jewish law—an impossible demand (Gal. 3:10).[25] So Paul cites in Galatians 2:16, with "works of the law," a psalm that says nothing about ethnic boundary markers: *no one* is righteous before God (Ps. 143:2). God *alone* saves: "In *your* righteousness bring me out of trouble" (143:11).

---

22. E. P. Sanders, *Jewish Law from Jesus to the Mishnah: Five Studies* (Philadelphia: Trinity Press International, 1990), 284; Sanders, "Jewish Association with Gentiles and Galatians 2:11–14," in *The Conversation Continues: Studies in Paul and John in Honor of J. Louis Martyn*, ed. Robert T. Fortna and Beverly R. Gaventa (Nashville: Abingdon, 1990), 170–88, here 186; Philip F. Esler, *Galatians*, NTR (London: Routledge, 1998), 107; Tomson, *Paul and the Jewish Law*, 236; Dunn, *Jesus, Paul, and the Law*, 157: "To become known himself as a 'sinner' would at once cut him off from the bulk of faithful Jews."

23. Sanders, "Jewish Association," 186. Richard B. Hays, "The Letter to the Galatians," *NIB* 11:181–348, here 232; Charles B. Cousar, *Galatians*, IBC (Louisville: John Knox, 1982), 44: "What seems at issue in the text is not the menu of the meals but the guest list."

24. Paul regularly refers to non-Christ-believing Jews as "the circumcised" (Rom. 3:30; 4:9, 12; 15:8; Eph. 2:11; Col. 3:11; 4:11; Titus 1:10); see Richard N. Longenecker, *Galatians*, WBC 51 (Dallas: Word, 1990), 73.

25. A. Andrew Das, "Galatians 3:10: A 'Newer Perspective' on an Omitted Premise," in *Unity and Diversity in the Gospels and Paul: Essays in Honor of Frank J. Matera*, ed. Christopher W. Skinner and Kelly R. Iverson, SBLECL 7 (Atlanta: Society of Biblical Literature, 2012), 203–23.

Paul within Judaism Perspective
Response to Dunn

MAGNUS ZETTERHOLM

In his essay James Dunn returns to one of the most interesting—and debated—texts in the Pauline corpus: Paul's description of what happened during the so-called Antioch incident (Gal. 2:11–14), a description that culminated in the statement "We know that a person is justified not by the works of the law but through faith in Jesus Christ" (2:16). I will not fully repeat my argument regarding the incident itself[1] but will restrict myself to a few observations and alternative suggestions, which from my point of departure—a Paul within Judaism Perspective—make more sense. Dunn, naturally, bases his interpretation on a somewhat different set of assumptions: Dunn's Paul does not operate within Judaism anymore.

According to Dunn, Paul resists those who saw the new movement "as an extension of Judaism" (135), thereby implying that Paul did not. Whatever Paul represents, it is not a form of "eschatological Judaism," Dunn states, but something "much larger and more universal" (135). Paul's radical conversion, as referred to by himself (Gal. 1:13–16) and by Luke (Acts 9:1–19; 22:3–21; 26:4–23), made him realize that God had called him to be an apostle to the gentiles. I am in full agreement with Dunn that this is how Paul interpreted

---

1. For such treatments, see Magnus Zetterholm, *The Formation of Christianity in Antioch: A Social-Scientific Approach to the Separation between Judaism and Christianity* (London: Routledge, 2003); Zetterholm, "Purity and Anger: Gentiles and Idolatry in Antioch," *IJRR* 1 (2005): 1–24; Zetterholm, "The Antioch Incident Revisited," *JSPL* 6 (2016): 249–59.

his mystical experience, but the question is this: Does that necessarily entail a radical break with Judaism, as Dunn seems to contend, or is it possible to reconcile Paul's "conversion" with a view of him still being a Jew practicing Judaism?

As pointed out by Johannes Munck and Krister Stendahl many decades ago, it is quite possible to understand Paul's mystical experience in terms of a prophetic call *within* Judaism rather than as a conversion *from* Judaism to Christianity,[2] which, by the way, did not yet exist. Thus, when Paul speaks in Galatians 1:13 of his "former" lifestyle in Judaism (τὴν ἐμὴν ἀναστροφήν ποτε ἐν τῷ ᾽Ιουδαϊσμῷ, *tēn emēn anastrophēn en tō Ioudaismō*), it is feasible to understand this in relation to his *present* lifestyle *in Judaism*. Thus, instead of making a transition from Judaism to (nonexisting) "Christianity," it is more likely that Paul (and Luke) portray a reorientation within a Jewish matrix, a process called "intensification" by Lewis R. Rambo: "[Intensification] occurs when nominal members of a religious institution make their commitment a central focus of their lives, or when people deepen their involvement in a community of faith through profound religious experience and/or life transitions like marriage, childbirth, and approaching death."[3] Thus, due to a "profound religious experience," Paul the Pharisee becomes Paul the messianic Jew, with a special mission to carry out the task of being "a light to the nations" so that God's "salvation may reach to the end of the earth" (Isa. 49:6). The Greek also clearly supports such an interpretation.

Furthermore, while it is quite possible that Paul's "conversion" was "unusual" and "exceptional" (135), as Dunn states, it is also important to appreciate that Paul and the early Jesus movement were not alone in developing an interest in the eschatological destiny of the nations.[4] Thus, it is quite natural that Jews reflected upon and constantly negotiated the relations between Israel and members of the nations. Paul's particular solution may have been unusual, but the discourse as such seems to have been part of a much larger universal trend within first-century Judaism.

This brings us closer to the problem of Galatians 2:16. The meaning of the peculiar phrase "works of the law" is obvious from the context, Dunn argues, and Paul refers to the attempt by traditionalist Jewish Christ-believers to require Jesus-believing gentiles both to be circumcised and to observe the

---

2. Johannes Munck, *Paul and the Salvation of Mankind*, trans. Frank Clarke (Richmond: John Knox, 1959); Krister Stendahl, *Paul among Jews and Gentiles* (London: SCM, 1977), 7–23.

3. Lewis R. Rambo, *Understanding Religious Conversion* (New Haven: Yale University Press, 1993), 13.

4. See Terence L. Donaldson, *Judaism and the Gentiles: Patterns of Universalism (to 135 CE)* (Waco: Baylor University Press, 2007).

Jewish food laws. I am not so sure that the meaning is that obvious, and there are quite a few suggestions out there.[5] It is clear, even obvious, that Paul objected to male non-Jews being circumcised—that is, becoming Jews. There may be several reasons for this, but one possibility, which I find quite convincing, is that Paul simply did not believe that conversions were possible for genealogical reasons, as argued by Matthew Thiessen.[6]

So, Dunn is obviously right about the circumcision/conversion part, but is it correct to assume that Paul would have objected to non-Jews following Jewish food regulations? And is it correct that Jewish adherents to the Jesus movement had downplayed the importance of the Jewish food regulations by, for instance, accepting invitations from non-Jewish followers of Jesus "without asking too many questions" and that this was what the people from James reacted against?[7] Such a conclusion follows, I believe, from Dunn's overarching (and by now somewhat dated) "New Perspective on Paul," according to which Paul reacted against Jewish identity markers such as circumcision, food, and purity regulations.

In my view, it is more likely that the incident did not concern food at all, but commensality, and I do not think that the so-called apostolic decree of Acts "exempts [non-Jews] from the troublesome food laws" (142), as Dunn maintains in his essay. Quite the opposite. To some extent building on previous scholarship,[8] Holger Zellentin has recently, quite convincingly, argued that the apostolic decree echoes the so-called Holiness Code in Leviticus and in effect serves as a prohibition against consumption of blood, idol meat, and improperly slaughtered meat and against fornication (Lev. 17): "Acts, in its prohibition of the *pollutions* incurred through idol meat, through fornication, through things strangled and through blood, thus explicitly promulgates for

---

5. See, e.g., Donald Guthrie, *Galatians*, NCBC (Grand Rapids: Eerdmans, 1984), 87 ("observances of any legal code"); Ben Witherington III, *Grace in Galatia: A Commentary on St. Paul's Letter to the Galatians* (Edinburgh: T&T Clark, 1998), 177 ("actions performed in obedience to the Mosaic law"); Mark D. Nanos, "The Question of Conceptualization: Qualifying Paul's Position on Circumcision in Dialogue with Josephus's Advisors to King Izates," in *Paul within Judaism: Restoring the First-Century Context to the Apostle*, ed. Mark D. Nanos and Magnus Zetterholm (Minneapolis: Fortress, 2015), 105–52, esp. 139 ("circumcision").

6. Matthew Thiessen, *Contesting Conversion: Genealogy, Circumcision, and Identity in Ancient Judaism and Christianity* (Oxford: Oxford University Press, 2011). See also Paula Fredriksen, *Paul: The Pagans' Apostle* (New Haven: Yale University Press, 2017), 96–99.

7. James D. G. Dunn, *A Commentary on the Epistle to the Galatians*, BNTC (London: A&C Black, 1993), 121.

8. See Holger Zellentin, "Judaeo-Christian Legal Culture and the Qur'ān: The Case of Ritual Slaughter and the Consumption of Animal Blood," in *Jewish-Christianity and Origins of Islam: Papers Presented at the Colloquium Held in Washington DC, October 29–31, 2015 (8th ASMEA Conference)*, ed. Francisco del Río Sánchez, JAOC 13 (Turnhout, Belgium: Brepols, 2018), 117–60, esp. 118n1.

all gentile followers of Jesus four of the injunctions that the Hebrew Bible had already imposed on resident aliens."[9] Thus, Jewish food laws, or purity regulations, seem to have played a vital part in the early Jesus movement—and in early Christianity throughout late antiquity.[10]

Furthermore, I disagree with Dunn's interpretation of the Cornelius story in Acts (10:1–48; 11:1–18; 15:7–11). Dunn is right, of course, that Luke attributes the breakthrough of the mission to the gentiles to Peter, not to Paul. But does the revelation that Peter receives through his vision lead him to conclude that all aspects of Jewish purity regulations have become null and void, as Dunn argues? Dunn is surprised that Luke does not reveal any knowledge of Jesus having declared "all food clean" in Mark 7:19, which, according to Dunn, means that "the laws or traditions of clean and unclean foods no longer applied to followers of Jesus" (140), a conclusion that is highly questionable.[11] Interestingly enough, neither is it how Peter understands the vision. Rather, he concludes that God has now made clear to him that one should "not call anyone profane [κοινόν, koinon] or unclean [ἀκάθαρτον, akatharton]" (Acts 10:28 [cf. vv. 14–15]). Food is simply not on the table, while the profane and unclean status of non-Jews is,[12] which illustrates exactly what was the real and main problem within the early Jesus movement: how to relate to unclean and profane members of the nations during the period until "the Son himself will also be subjected to the one who put all things in subjection under him, so that God may be all in all" (1 Cor. 15:28). This important aspect gets completely lost if one concentrates on finding evidence of Paul rejecting Jewish "identity markers."

A final observation: Dunn finds that Paul and Luke portray the early development of the Jesus movement in different ways, Paul by expressing the simplicity of the gospel in Galatians 2:16 in an uncompromising way, Luke by harmonizing and smoothing over all conflicts. Dunn clearly prefers Paul over Luke: there is a danger, he states, of letting the ecumenical character of Luke's portrayal "obscure what was of central importance for Paul" (145). Paul had to confront Peter as Luther had to confront the pope, in essence, because of "the truth of the gospel."

Now, what Paul really meant by "the truth of the gospel" is not entirely clear. Historically, Christian groups have understood this in different ways,

9. Zellentin, "Judaeo-Christian Legal Culture," 131 (emphasis original). See also Isaac W. Oliver, *Torah Praxis after 70 CE: Reading Matthew and Luke-Acts as Jewish Texts*, WUNT 2/355 (Tübingen: Mohr Siebeck, 2013), 370–98.

10. Zellentin, "Judaeo-Christian Legal Culture," 132–48.

11. See, e.g., John van Maaren, "Does Mark's Jesus Abrogate Torah? Jesus' Purity Logion and Its Illustration in Mark 7:15–23," *JJMJS* 4 (2017): 21–41.

12. See Oliver, *Torah Praxis after 70 CE*, 320–64; Zetterholm, "Purity and Anger," 8–10.

often resulting in harsh conflicts, sometimes with rather destructive consequences. In my view—from a Paul within Judaism Perspective—if Paul has something to teach contemporary society, it is not dogmatic exclusivism. Rather, in a world becoming increasingly Trumpian, perhaps the lesson learned from Paul is his (admittedly failed) vision of accepting people's ethnic and cultural differences while striving for a new kind of unity, in his case ἐν Χριστῷ (en Christō). Or as the New York Times columnist David Brooks wrote, in a completely different context, "to take the diverse many and make them one."[13]

13. David Brooks, "Donald Trump Hates America: The Rest of Us Can Love America Well," New York Times, July 18, 2019.

Gift Perspective Response to Dunn

JOHN M. G. BARCLAY

Jimmy Dunn's stimulating essay raises for me a host of questions. I will leave to one side the section on Luke's reception of Paul, as I do not think that this is central to the New Perspective. Dunn's comments on Acts reflect the strong, subterranean influence of F. C. Baur, whose nineteenth-century reconstruction of early Christian history, channeled through the Bultmann school (e.g., Hans Conzelmann and Ernst Käsemann), contained all the ingredients evidenced here: Acts as the irenic "synthesis" that smoothed over the conflict between Paul and his Jewish Christian opponents; the early overshadowing of Paul; the trend toward features dubbed "early Catholicism," and so on. This reading of Acts and of early Christian development has come under heavy criticism in recent years, and it would take us too far afield to enter those debates.[1] Luke has, indeed, his own perspective on Paul, but it is not the task of this volume to analyze that.

I will also leave to one side Dunn's representation of Luther (though there is much that I would want to question).[2] But there is one significant weakness in the reading of Paul (and also of Luther) that I will focus upon, as it goes to the heart of my dissatisfaction with the New Perspective on Paul.

---

1. See, e.g., Benjamin L. White, *Remembering Paul: Ancient and Modern Contests over the Image of the Apostle* (Oxford: Oxford University Press, 2014).

2. For my own analysis of Luther's reading of Paul, see *Paul and the Gift* (Grand Rapids: Eerdmans, 2015), 97–116, 571–72, which has been affirmed by Luther experts. Once again, I recommend Stephen J. Chester, *Reading Paul with the Reformers: Reconciling Old and New Perspectives* (Grand Rapids: Eerdmans, 2017).

I consider the New Perspective to be quite right in taking the gentile mission as central to Paul's calling and theology, together with Paul's radical insistence that gentiles did not need to adopt Jewish "works of the law." One could quibble with some of the language Dunn uses to express this, but the basic point is sound, and I think now widely accepted.[3] But the question is this: On what basis did Paul insist that gentile converts did not need to become Jewish proselytes? Dunn is puzzled: "Quite why [Paul] was so adamant on the point is not entirely clear" (139). He points to Paul's own experience ("presumably, the memory of his own commitment . . . and his zealous persecution of the believers in Jesus" [139]), but I think that we can trace a *theological* rationale much deeper than that, and one that explains how Paul interpreted his experience. Dunn resorts time and again to the topic of faith ("The gospel of Christ looked only for the response of faith, faith alone" [139]; "a gospel effective only through faith, through faith alone" [145]), and he represents this as a single or simple thing, not to be encumbered with "traditions," either Jewish or ecclesial.

But something crucial is missing here: Faith in what or whom? Paul is not interested in faith as such. Everything depends on the object of faith, Jesus Christ, who is the subject of the "good news" and on whom the one who exercises faith (or trust) is radically and wholly dependent. Without this christological orientation, "faith" becomes an alternative human condition to be fulfilled, an easier hurdle, perhaps, than some others, but still a requirement for salvation on the same level as other forms of human capital.[4] And without this christological content, faith can be represented as a minimal requirement, expressing the "fundamental simplicity" of the gospel unburdened by "creedal statements, church order, ecclesial hierarchy, and the like" (145).[5]

---

3. Although Paul did not require his gentile converts to "live like Jews" (Gal. 2:14), he did require them to abandon idolatry, "to serve the true and living God" (1 Thess. 1:9–10). Paul considered this to be simply his converts' recognition of the truth (Gal. 4:8–10), but his contemporaries (like some today in the "Paul within Judaism" school) might have considered this a "Jewish" form of behavior.

4. It was in reaction to this thinned-down understanding of faith that those with theological antennae (Hays, Martyn, Campbell, et al.) propounded the alternative interpretation of πίστις Χριστοῦ (*pistis Christou*) as "the faithfulness of Christ." I do not think that that is necessary (or linguistically convincing), so long as one has a proper Pauline notion of faith as the receipt of gift—that is, as the acknowledgment that the only thing of worth is what God has achieved in Christ.

5. Does this model really fit Paul? For Paul, faith is expressed in a core creedal statement, "Jesus is Lord" (1 Cor. 12:3), which is unpacked in Phil. 2:6–11. How much of a "creedal statement" would be too "weighty" and too "solemn" (see 145)? Faith is also expressed in baptism (Gal. 3:26–28), and in the Lord's Supper (1 Cor. 10:16–17; 11:17–34), around which (as around spiritual gifts) Paul expects a certain "church order." Again, how much is too much? Are there

But with the Christ-event as the proper object of faith (the coming of faith is aligned with the coming of Christ [Gal. 3:24–25]), and when justification by faith is properly integrated with participation in Christ (Gal. 2:16–21), we can see that πίστις (*pistis*) for Paul means centrally faith *in Christ*. And what it expresses is not a positive achievement but a declaration of bankruptcy, a total renunciation of symbolic capital in recognition that the only capital that counts is the *gift* given by God in Christ.

What was at stake for Paul in Antioch that he could declare that Peter was "not walking straight in line with the truth of the good news" (Gal. 2:14)? Is it adequate to say, as Dunn does, that this concerns the gospel being "open to gentiles as gentiles, without requiring them to become proselytes"? What is it about the "good news" that carries this entailment? As I have argued, what was at stake here was something intrinsic to the "good news" (which is news, after all, *about Christ*): that both Jews and non-Jews are called by an incongruous grace that suspends every judgment of worth extrinsic to the Christ-event. Believers are therefore drawn into an association of mutual recognition that is blind to ethnic evaluations (though it does not erase ethnic difference), as to other evaluations of worth (Gal. 3:28). To reinstate a Jewish rule of sociality would be to condition this association by a differentiating norm that is not derivable from the good news. For Paul, the inclusion of gentiles without requiring them to "Judaize" arises from the radical incongruity of grace.[6]

In my view, a recurrent weakness in the New Perspective has been its inability to speak clearly of grace. At the roots of the New Perspective, Dunn and Wright were convinced by Sanders's unexamined understanding of "grace," such that Judaism could be defined, simplistically, as "a religion of grace." Dunn's statement is representative: "The Judaism of what Sanders christened as 'covenantal nomism' can now be seen to preach good Protestant doctrine: that grace is always prior; that human effort is ever the response to divine initiative; that good works are the fruit and not the root of salvation."[7] Like Sanders, this takes the "priority" of grace to be its main (or sole) defining characteristic, whereas for Paul (as for the Reformers) what was far more significant was whether grace was, or was not, incongruous.[8] Since, rightly, everyone wants to acknowledge the significance of grace in Second Temple

---

hints in Dunn's essay of a Protestant romanticism, longing for a return to a supposedly simple, uncluttered beginning?

6. See Barclay, *Paul and the Gift*, 365–70.

7. James D. G. Dunn, *The New Perspective on Paul: Collected Essays*, WUNT 185 (Tübingen: Mohr Siebeck, 2005), 193.

8. For the difference between these and other "perfections" of grace, see Barclay, *Paul and the Gift*, 66–78; that book also contains an analysis of Sanders (151–58) and of the New Perspective (159–65), indicating their weaknesses on this score.

Judaism, it has been felt that to emphasize this motif in Paul would be somehow to reinstate old caricatures of Judaism as works-based and grace-less. But if we think carefully about the different possible meanings of "grace," we can recognize its presence everywhere across Second Temple Judaism, but in very different forms; and at the same time, we can identify the special Pauline emphasis on the Christ-event as an incongruous gift. And then we can see that the theological rationale for the gentile mission is not because of the "simplicity" of "faith alone," nor is it grounded in protest against "nationalism" or "ethnocentrism." Rather, as a singular, particular, but unconditioned event, the Christ-gift is of universal import precisely because it is incongruous: it belongs to no subset of humanity, but is destined for all. Since no one is granted this gift on the grounds of ethnic worth, no one of any ethnicity is excluded from its reach.

That is the reason Paul finishes his description of the Antioch incident, and its accompanying discourse about justification by faith in Christ, by stating in categorical terms, "I do not reject the grace of God" (Gal. 2:21).

New Perspective Reply to the Respondents

JAMES D. G. DUNN

In Dialogue with John Barclay

I appreciate John's response and apologize that a sense of having overwritten on the subject prompted me to go off-piste into a study of Acts, which is less relevant to the issues raised by Galatians 2—perhaps to be discussed some other time.

I was surprised, however, at his principal critique: that my emphasis that Paul's gospel insisted on a "faith alone" response failed to emphasize that "the object of faith" is Christ, "faith *in Christ*" (166). This rather surprised me since all the initial references to "faith" in my essay are explicitly to faith in Christ—"faith in me" (Acts 26:18) (135), "faith in Christ" (136), quotations from Galatians 2:16 (e.g., 136), and a footnote on the key phrase (138n10). In focusing latterly on the faith issue I naturally assumed that this focus of faith in Christ would be understood. As John rightly notes, "Everything depends on the object of faith, Jesus Christ, who is the subject of the 'good news' and on whom the one who exercises faith (or trust) is radically and wholly dependent" (165).

A further critique might focus on Paul's insistence that faith was the (only) appropriate initial response to the good news, in order to express some puzzlement and surprise that the equivalent response to the *gift* is much less clear in John's emphasis on the gift of grace.

In Dialogue with Brant Pitre

Brant is very commendatory in his opening paragraphs, for which I am very grateful. I naturally concur with his emphasis on "faith alone," and I accept his criticism that I have neglected the testimony of the great fathers of Christian theology. Though given that the emphasis Paul gives did become clouded in the history of the church, perhaps Brant would accept a rewording of the subject of discussion as "the renewed perspective on Paul." And how could I disagree with Brant over the importance of love for Paul, especially when he quotes my Galatians commentary so effectively? On this point I would happily affirm my agreement with his quotation from the Council of Trent. It was only with his last point that I felt my Protestant hackles rising slightly. Does he imply that the Reformation/Reformers had no good grounds for its/ their protest? What was Luther objecting to? To Augustine or Aquinas? The history of Christianity does not consist solely of those we agree with, does it?

In Dialogue with Magnus Zetterholm

I must confess to some puzzlement at Magnus's determination to see "Paul within Judaism." Paul, of course, was a Jew who drew on his Jewish heritage deeply and constantly. He certainly was no anti-Semite! But did he think of himself as still "within Judaism"? He uses the phrase itself only twice, both of his past, preconversion experience (Gal. 1:13–14). And he uses the verb "Judaize" only once (2:14), to describe "Judaizers" who insisted that Paul's gentile converts should "Judaize"—that is, become Jews or live in accordance with distinctively Jewish practices, a policy that he strongly resisted. So, does the phrase "within Judaism" really express Paul's understanding as to his own postconversion position? I hardly think so. "Within Judaism" is *not* an accurate description of Paul's postconversion self-understanding. Of course Paul the Christian Jew did not operate "within Judaism." "Judaism" evidently was no longer the word Paul used when he wanted to refer to his own rich Jewish heritage. Is that not plain enough?

I admit that I have not been able to keep up with recent discussion, as footnoted by Magnus, but I also confess to some surprise at how often Paul's argument/exposition in Galatians 2:16 is divorced from the reminiscence of which it is the climax (2:1–16). The context surely makes clear enough that "the works of the law" in mind were particularly circumcision and the (Jewish) food laws, the attempts in effect to insist that gentile believers had to Judaize. And 2:14–16 surely makes clear enough that "the truth of the gospel" was summed up in Paul's insistence that justification is not by works of the law but through faith in Jesus Christ. It was the degree to which continued insistence on the Jewish food laws disrupted the fellowship of Jewish and gentile believers that upset Paul so much. Does Magnus recognize sufficiently that the distinctions between clean and unclean in regard to foods could so easily reflect or reinforce a distinction between clean and unclean people? This is the very thing that Paul, apostle to the gentiles, saw himself as called to resist!

In Dialogue with A. Andrew Das

I confess to some confusion over Andrew's reference to Paul's "famine-relief visit" to Jerusalem as documented by "Acts 11:27–30 // Acts 12:25." But my main questioning arises in reference to what appears to be his defense of James, when it seems pretty obvious to me that the arrival of "certain people . . . from James" resulted directly in Jewish believers, even Barnabas, being "led astray by their hypocrisy" (Gal. 2:11–13). Is it the case that having conceded that gentile believers need not be circumcised, James found the abandonment of the food laws to be a step too far for the new Jesus movement? I hardly think that requiring gentile believers to Judaize was only the *result* of the Jewish believers' withdrawal, when it is pretty clear that this must have been the motivation for the withdrawal—the unacceptability of uncircumcised gentile believers in Jewish Christian fellowship groups.

For the most part I follow the rest of Andrew's essay, noting that, ironically, the degree of flexibility in Jewish participation in gentile activities provides an interesting context for the Antioch incident. On that situation it is hardly clear, is it, that the word from James was "exclusively to Peter," though it is a fair inference to draw that Peter's less inhibited fellowship with gentile believers might have restricted his mission to his fellow Jews. And why Andrew's insistence that in speaking of the "works of the law" Paul had in mind "the *entirety* of the Jewish law" (158), when it is so clear from the context that Paul was thinking specifically of those laws (circumcision and food laws) that prevented Jewish and gentile believers from fellowshipping together?

4

The Paul within Judaism Perspective

MAGNUS ZETTERHOLM

Introduction

The so-called Paul within Judaism Perspective can generally be described as a natural development from E. P. Sanders's new interpretation of the nature of ancient Judaism in his now classic *Paul and Palestinian Judaism*.[1] It probably is fair to say that before the 1980s the dominant hermeneutical key for understanding Paul in general, and more specifically his relation to Judaism, was that of conflict. The post-Damascus Paul was understood as standing outside of and against Judaism: his encounter with the risen Christ had convinced him that the Torah had had its day (e.g., Galatians; cf. Rom. 10:4). According to most mainstream interpreters before Sanders (Munck, Dahl, and Stendahl being conspicuous exceptions), in terms of his religious commitments and sensibilities, Paul ceased being a Jew when he became a "Christian."

Although Paul presents himself as the apostle to the *gentiles* (e.g., Gal. 1:15–16; Rom. 1:5; 11:13), the principal problem that Paul was believed to have faced, according to traditional interpretations, concerned the salvation

---

I am very grateful to Paula Fredriksen for helpful comments on this text.

1. E. P. Sanders, *Paul and Palestinian Judaism: A Comparison of Patterns of Religion* (Minneapolis: Fortress, 1977).

of *all humankind*.[2] Paul's gospel, in this view, was directed both to Jews and to non-Jews. For this reason, many scholars concluded that Paul had abandoned Torah and thus a Jewish way of life. The conflicts within the early Jesus movement coded a clash between two opposing religious systems: one, conservative and Jerusalem-centered, characterized by "legalism"; the other, new and outward-looking, characterized by grace.[3] Paul's adversaries advocated precisely that religious system that Paul was thought to have left behind. They—often referred to as "Jewish Christians"—argued for the continued validity of the Torah, Paul for its abolition.

Read this way—if Paul for instance meant that every human being who relies on the works of the law is under a curse (Gal. 3:1), and if the Jewish people also are included among those over whom God's wrath is revealed (Rom. 1:18)—the traditional understanding of Paul is theologically extremely useful. As Stephen Westerholm has noted in connection with the idea of Judaism's supposed legalism, "A better foil for the Lutheran doctrine of justification could scarcely be conceived."[4]

But what if we read Paul from a different vantage point? It is a common mistake to assume that the historical Paul can be accessed only through the biblical text. Such a statement is not a concession to postmodern relativistic ideology, which I rather forcefully would oppose, but simply is the recognition of how textual interpretation works.[5] History is not just textual; it is also and necessarily *con*textual. Simply put, if we do not have relevant information concerning important data given in a text, we cannot understand it properly; and if we are wrong about the context, we will likely end up with strong misreadings and flawed interpretations. What Paul meant by the expression

---

2. "Pauline theology is not a speculative system. It deals with God not as He is in Himself but only with God as He is significant for man, for man's responsibility and man's salvation." Rudolf Bultmann, *Theology of the New Testament*, trans. Kendrick Grobel, 2 vols. (New York: Scribner, 1951–55), 1:190–91.

3. I am not convinced, as many seem to be, that terms like "religion" and related designations should be avoided in a first-century setting. I agree with Brent Nongbri that the concept of religion can be used, although with caution. See Nongbri, "The Concept of Religion and the Study of the Apostle Paul," *JJMJS* 2 (2015): 1–26. Nongbri's arguments are more thoroughly developed in *Before Religion: A History of a Modern Concept* (New Haven: Yale University Press, 2013).

4. Stephen Westerholm, *Perspectives Old and New on Paul: The "Lutheran" Paul and His Critics* (Grand Rapids: Eerdmans, 2004), 130.

5. Cf. Donald Hagner, who, referring to my *Approaches to Paul: A Student's Guide to Recent Scholarship* (Minneapolis: Fortress, 2009), 237, believes that what I argue reflects my "postmodern hermeneutical conviction," thus proving my point: it is sometimes hard to understand what people are trying to communicate. See Hagner, *How New Is the New Testament? First-Century Judaism and the Emergence of Christianity* (Grand Rapids: Baker Academic, 2018), 9n25.

ἔργα νόμου (*erga nomou*) (Rom. 3:20, 28; Gal. 2:16; 3:10),[6] or by stating that Christ is the τέλος (*telos*) of the law (Rom. 10:4),[7] or by referring to the person in Romans 2:17 as someone who calls himself a Jew[8] are but some examples where the scholar has to go outside the text in order to interpret it. Consequently, everyone, regardless of what scholarly tradition he or she belongs to, is compelled to start from certain assumptions and to (re)construct historical context.[9] Uncertainty is inevitable, but propositions and interpretations can be tested and ranked in terms of plausibility. In many cases we have to assume a posture of interpretative humility: we simply cannot know *with certainty*.[10]

Before Sanders most scholars worked from the assumption that Paul's theology contradicted common Jewish beliefs and behaviors, especially Torah observance. This general statement cannot be considered controversial. I have elsewhere described in detail how I understand the emergence of the anti-Jewish Paul.[11] The main argument is that an originally political conflict in the wake of the Jewish War rapidly turned into a theological schism. This eventually resulted in the rise of Christianity as a non-Jewish—and even an anti-Jewish—religion,[12] although various groups of Jesus-oriented Jews seem to have existed for several hundred years following the founding generation.[13]

During Roman late antiquity and the European Middle Ages, when theological debates focused on the conditions for the salvation of the individual,

6. See the discussion in James D. G. Dunn, "Yet Once More—'The Works of the Law': A Response," *JSNT* 46 (1992): 99–117.

7. See overview in Joseph A. Fitzmyer, *Romans: A New Translation with Introduction and Commentary*, AB 33 (New York: Doubleday, 1993), 584–85.

8. As suggested by Runar M. Thorsteinsson, *Paul's Interlocutor in Romans 2: Function and Identity in the Context of Ancient Epistolography*, ConBNT 40 (Stockholm: Almqvist & Wiksell, 2003) (reprinted in 2015). See also Runar M. Thorsteinsson, Matthew Thiessen, and Rafael Rodríguez, "Paul's Interlocutor in Romans: The Problem of Identification," in *The So-Called Jew in Paul's Letter to the Romans*, ed. Rafael Rodríguez and Matthew Thiessen (Minneapolis: Fortress, 2016), 1–37.

9. For another version of the same argument, see Magnus Zetterholm, "The Antioch Incident Revisited," *JSPL* 6 (2016): 249–59, esp. 249–50.

10. See John M. G. Barclay's quite apt description of the difficulties in understanding what was going on in the so-called Antioch incident, in *Paul and the Gift* (Grand Rapids: Eerdmans, 2015), 366–67.

11. Magnus Zetterholm, *Approaches to Paul: A Student's Guide to Recent Scholarship* (Minneapolis: Fortress, 2009). See also Pamela Eisenbaum, *Paul Was Not a Christian: The Original Message of a Misunderstood Apostle* (New York: HarperCollins, 2009), 32–54.

12. Magnus Zetterholm, *The Formation of Christianity in Antioch: A Social-Scientific Approach to the Separation between Judaism and Christianity* (London: Routledge, 2003); Zetterholm, "Paul within Judaism: The State of the Questions," in *Paul within Judaism: Restoring the First-Century Context to the Apostle*, ed. Mark D. Nanos and Magnus Zetterholm (Minneapolis: Fortress, 2015), 31–51, esp. 35–38.

13. Karin Hedner Zetterholm, "Alternate Visions of Judaism and Their Impact on the Formation of Rabbinic Judaism," *JJMJS* 1 (2014): 127–53.

Jewish Torah observance was increasingly understood as opposing the (gentile) Christian concept of grace. Such development culminated during the Reformation, creating a sharply polarized distinction between two opposing religious systems, Judaism and Christianity. Later, during the nineteenth century, we find that ideas based on normative theology found their way also into New Testament scholarship,[14] producing a fundamental orientation that exercised considerable influence over scholarship well into the twentieth century.[15] Judaism was Christianity's dark "Other." Emil Schürer's conclusion, in his infamous section "Life under the Law" in *A History of the Jewish People*, gives a classic example of this point of view:

> In all questions everything [in Judaism] depended only upon settling what was according to law, and that with the utmost possible care, that so the acting subject might have certain directions for every individual case. In a word: ethic and theology were swallowed up in jurisprudence. The evil results of this external view on practical matters are very evident. And such results were its necessary consequence. Even in that most favourable case of juristic casuistry moving on the whole in morally correct paths, it was in itself a poisoning of the moral principle, and could not but have a paralysing and benumbing effect upon the vigorous pulsation of the moral life. But this favourable case by no means occurred. When once the question was started: "What have I to do to fulfil the law?" the temptation was obvious, that a composition with the letter would be chiefly aimed at, at the cost of the real demands of morality, nay of the proper intention of the law itself.[16]

Sanders's new description of ancient Judaism thus changed the game,[17] challenging traditional Pauline scholarship by confronting it with a new context based on actually reading ancient Jewish texts, as opposed to resorting to Strack-Billerbeck.[18] The idea of Judaism as a religion of grace, where the individual did not strive for salvation by observing obsolete *mitzvot*, provided

---

14. On normative theology, see John T. Granrose, "Normative Theology and Meta-Theology," *HTR* 63 (1970): 449–51.

15. See, e.g., Anders Gerdmar, *Roots of Theological Anti-Semitism: German Biblical Interpretation and the Jews, from Herder and Semler to Kittel and Bultmann* (Leiden: Brill, 2009).

16. Emil Schürer, *A History of the Jewish People in the Time of Jesus Christ* (Edinburgh: T&T Clark, 1890), division 2, vol. 2, p. 120. Schürer and other subsequent scholars, such as Wilhelm Bousset, Paul Billerbeck, and Rudolf Bultmann, were heavily dependent on Ferdinand Weber's *System der altsynagogalen palästinischen Theologie aus Targum, Midrasch und Talmud* (Leipzig: Dörffling & Franke, 1880).

17. Admittedly, Sanders's investigation is limited to *Palestinian* Judaism, but it has in effect been understood in terms of describing Judaism in general.

18. Herman Strack and Paul Billerbeck, *Kommentar zum Neuen Testament aus Talmud und Midrasch*, 6 vols. (Munich: C. H. Beck, 1922–28).

scholars with an entirely new context for reading Paul. After Sanders, Paul had to be related not to Judaism as a legalistic religion but to a religious system where Torah observance functioned in a covenantal context—that is, what Sanders labeled *covenantal nomism*:

> The "pattern" or "structure" of covenantal nomism is this: (1) God has chosen Israel and (2) given the law. The law implies both (3) God's promise to maintain the election and (4) the requirement to obey. (5) God rewards obedience and punishes transgression. (6) The law provides for means of atonement, and atonement results in (7) maintenance or re-establishment of the covenantal relationship. (8) All those who are maintained in the covenant by obedience, atonement and God's mercy belong to the group which will be saved. An important interpretation of the first and last points is that election and ultimately salvation are considered to be by God's mercy rather than human achievement.[19]

Even though there has been a discussion on whether or not Sanders's concept of covenantal nomism adequately captures the nature of first-century Judaism, not least the relation between "grace" and "merit,"[20] the general idea of placing Torah observance within a covenantal framework was well received, even by scholars who maintained the idea that Paul in some way stood in opposition to Judaism.[21]

It probably is correct to state that while most scholars seem to have accepted Sanders's general view of Judaism as not being "legalistic" or characterized by "works righteousness," they were less convinced by his interpretation of Paul. As a result, Pauline scholars started looking for other ways of applying Sanders's reconstruction of ancient Judaism to a still-familiar Paul. Thus, beginning with Sanders's own interpretation of Paul and, more importantly, James Dunn's very influential article "The New Perspective on Paul,"[22] there has been a clear tendency of scholars being involved in the process of gradually bringing Paul closer to contemporary Judaism. The endpoint of such a process is, of course, to place the apostle firmly, completely, and comfortably within Judaism. It is precisely within this intellectual process that the Paul

---

19. *PPJ*, 422.

20. See, e.g., the various essays in D. A. Carson, Peter T. O'Brien, and Mark A. Seifrid, eds., *Justification and Variegated Nomism*, vol. 1, *The Complexities of Second Temple Judaism*, WUNT 2/140 (Tübingen: Mohr Siebeck; Grand Rapids: Baker Academic, 2001).

21. See, e.g., Heikki Räisänen, *Paul and the Law*, 2nd ed., WUNT 29 (Tübingen: Mohr Siebeck, 1987), 167–68; Frank Thielman, *From Plight to Solution: A Jewish Framework for Understanding Paul's View of the Law in Galatians and Romans*, NovTSup 61 (Leiden: Brill, 1989), 25; Westerholm, *Perspectives Old and New*, 350; N. T. Wright, *Paul and His Recent Interpreters: Some Contemporary Debates* (London: SPCK, 2015), 69–76.

22. James D. G. Dunn, "The New Perspective on Paul," *BJRL* 65 (1983): 95–122.

within Judaism position should be seen. It is one of many "perspectives" by which to see the historical Paul.[23]

In the following, I will present my understanding of the two most fundamental assumptions underlying the Paul within Judaism Perspective: first, Paul's continuing Jewish identity, and second, his focus on non-Jews. While I assume that all scholars who share this perspective on Paul agree with me on the importance of these fundamental assumptions, not everyone will accept all my specific proposals on how to reconstruct Paul from these assumptions. This is as it should be: Paul within Judaism scholars represent a historiographical movement, not a sect; and there is considerable variation within this scholarly commitment. "What we share," Pamela Eisenbaum states, "is the same basic orientation toward Paul."[24]

I approach this endeavor from a secular perspective, meaning that the implications of a Jewish Paul for normative theology lie outside the scope of this presentation. Although I have nothing against the idea that scholarship influences contemporary religion—or in the specific case of Pauline studies, for instance, enhances Jewish-Christian dialogue—I also believe that normative theology has negatively affected Pauline scholarship and prevented us from finding the historical Paul. Normative theology should simply be left out of the equation, since one of the most vital parts of academic freedom is autonomy from various interest groups.

Paul within Judaism: Two Fundamental Assumptions

Paul Was Jewish, Thus Torah Observant

The suggestion that Paul was Torah observant probably is the most difficult proposition to digest for traditionally oriented scholars, since it seemingly strikes at the heart of Lutheran theology, which, as we have seen, has been extremely influential when it comes to Pauline scholarship. The connection between normative theology and academic scholarship is quite complicated—and indeed problematic—and I do find it strange that it still should be a factor to reckon with. Put differently, that a Christian theologian from the sixteenth century should still exercise influence on the modern scholarly discussion on Paul is simply not good.

Be that as it may, the idea that Paul was Torah observant follows from the assumption that he was Jewish. Now, most scholars would of course accept

---

23. See also Karl Olav Sandnes's succinct history of the development of the study of Paul in *Paul Perceived: An Interactionist Perspective on Paul and the Law*, WUNT 412 (Tübingen: Mohr Siebeck, 2018), 8–15.

24. Eisenbaum, *Paul Was Not a Christian*, 250.

the statement that Paul was Jewish *ethnically* while insisting that this had little or no religious significance.[25] As pointed out by Mark Nanos, "[Paul] is treated as a Jew or Judean who no longer behaved Jewishly."[26] However, for scholars who work from a Paul within Judaism Perspective, Paul's Jewishness means that he also *practiced* Judaism. Even though there are examples of Jews who consciously tried to find ways to cease being Jewish—Philo's nephew Tiberius Julius Alexander, or Antiochus, the son of the chief magistrate of the Jews in Antioch, who sacrificed after the manner of the Greeks,[27] or the Jews who "removed the marks of circumcision [literally, "made foreskins"], and abandoned the holy covenant" in Jerusalem,[28] being the most notable examples—this was clearly not the case with Paul, who rather expresses his loyalty with the people of Israel and emphasizes his Jewishness (Gal. 1:13–14; 2:15; Rom. 9:3; 11:1).

Even the passage from Philippians below,[29] which often is taken as evidence of Paul's "conversion to Christianity"[30] and repudiation of Jewish traditions, could in fact be read to mean the opposite.

> Beware of the dogs [τοὺς κύνας, *tous kynas*], beware of the evil workers [τοὺς κακοὺς ἐργάτας, *tous kakous ergatas*], beware of the mutilation [τὴν κατατομήν, *tēn katatomēn*]![31] For it is we who are the circumcision, who worship in the Spirit of God and boast in Christ Jesus and have no confidence in the flesh—even though I, too, have reason for confidence in the flesh. If anyone else has reason to be confident in the flesh, I have more: circumcised on the eighth day, a member of the people of Israel, of the tribe of Benjamin, a Hebrew born of Hebrews; as to the law, a Pharisee; as to zeal, a persecutor of the *ekklēsia* [ἐκκλησία];[32] as

25. See, e.g., James D. G. Dunn, "Who Did Paul Think He Was? A Study of Jewish-Christian Identity," *NTS* 45 (1999): 174–93; Dunn, *Christianity in the Making*, vol. 2, *Beginning from Jerusalem* (Grand Rapids: Eerdmans, 2009). See also Pamela Eisenbaum, "Paul, Polemics, and the Problem of Essentialism," *BibInt* 13 (2005): 224–38, esp. 227–28, where she makes a distinction between scholars who understand Paul to be Jewish *kata sarka* but no longer religiously Jewish, and scholars who understand "Paul as Jewish—period, that is, without qualifiers" (228).

26. Mark D. Nanos, "Paul and Judaism: Why Not Paul's Judaism?," in *Paul Unbound: Other Perspectives on the Apostle*, ed. Mark D. Given (Peabody, MA: Hendrickson, 2010), esp. 119.

27. Josephus, *J.W.* 7.50.

28. 1 Macc. 1:11–15.

29. Translations are from the NRSV, sometimes with minor alterations.

30. Cf., however, Dunn, "Who Did Paul Think He Was?," 179, who rightly points to the fact that Paul hardly could have converted to "Christianity," "since the term 'Christianity' did not yet exist."

31. The NRSV's translation "those who mutilate the flesh" seems a trifle too eisegetical.

32. The NRSV's translation of ἐκκλησία with "church" is quite unfortunate. Paul never founded or visited a church, let alone persecuted one. This is but one example of how translations often reflect a certain theological position. On the importance of using nonbiased terminology, see Anders Runesson, "The Question of Terminology: The Architecture of Contemporary

to righteousness under the law, blameless. Yet whatever gains I had, these I have come to regard as loss because of Christ. More than that, I regard everything as loss because of the surpassing value of knowing Christ Jesus my Lord. For his sake I have suffered the loss of all things, and I regard them as rubbish [σκύβαλα, *skybala*] in order that I may gain Christ. (Phil. 3:2–8 NRSV adapted)

While most interpreters, taking the conflict paradigm as their point of departure, assume that Paul's opponents in Philippi were "Judaizers" (Jews, Jesus-oriented Jews, or even proselytes) trying to influence the Philippians to undertake circumcision and other expressions of Judaism,[33] Mark Nanos has offered an alternative interpretation.[34]

The antagonists whom Paul warns against in 3:2, "the dogs" (τοὺς κύνας) and "the evildoers" (τοὺς κακοὺς ἐργάτας), are commonly identified as "Jews" (or "Jewish Christians").[35] Paul's choice of the condescending epithet "dog" is believed to be a conscious reversal of Jewish slander of non-Jews, now applied to Jews.[36] Similarly, "the mutilation" (τὴν κατατομήν) is taken as a negative reference to circumcision.[37] Nanos, on the other hand, suggests that Paul's concern rather relates to a Greco-Roman cultural and religious context and that the problem concerns how, especially, non-Jewish followers of Jesus should live within Jesus-as-Messiah-based Judaism.[38] According to Nanos, the idea that the epithet "dog" would refer to Jews cannot be maintained, since there is no literary evidence to substantiate such a claim.[39] As for "the

---

Discussions on Paul," in Nanos and Zetterholm, *Paul within Judaism*, 53–77; Magnus Zetterholm, "Jews, Christians, and Gentiles: Rethinking the Categorization within the Early Jesus Movement," in *Reading Paul in Context: Explorations in Identity Formation; Essays in Honour of William S. Campbell*, ed. Kathy Ehrensperger and J. Brian Tucker, LNTS 428 (London: T&T Clark, 2010), 242–54.

33. For an overview, see D. K. Williams, *Enemies of the Cross of Christ: The Terminology of the Cross and Conflict in Philippians* (Sheffield: Sheffield Academic, 2002), 54–60; Jerry L. Sumney, "Studying Paul's Opponents: Advances and Challenges," *Paul and His Opponents*, ed. Stanley E. Porter, Pauline Studies 2 (Leiden: Brill, 2005), 7–58, here 25–29; and John J. Gunther, *St. Paul's Opponents and Their Background: A Study of Apocalyptic and Jewish Sectarian Teachings*, NovTSup 35 (Leiden: Brill, 1973).

34. Mark D. Nanos, "Paul's Polemic in Philippians 3 as Jewish-Subgroup Vilification of Local Non-Jewish Cultic and Philosophical Alternatives," *JSPL* 3 (2013): 47–91.

35. G. Walter Hansen, *The Letter to the Philippians*, PNTC (Grand Rapids: Eerdmans, 2009). For a recent example, see Dorothea Bertschmann, "Is There a Kenosis in This Text? Rereading Philippians 3:2–11 in the Light of the Christ Hymn," *JBL* 37 (2018): 235–54, esp. 236.

36. See, e.g., Gordon D. Fee, *Paul's Letter to the Philippians*, NICNT (Grand Rapids: Eerdmans, 1995), 295.

37. Fee, *Philippians*, 296.

38. Nanos, "Paul's Polemic in Philippians 3," 52–53.

39. Mark D. Nanos, "Paul's Reversal of Jews Calling Gentiles 'Dogs' (Philippians 3:2): 1600 Years of an Ideological Tale Wagging an Exegetical Dog?," *BibInt* 17 (2009): 448–82.

mutilation," Nanos argues that it is possible that Paul uses a generally negative reference to his opponents, perhaps influenced by the story of Elijah and
the prophets of Baal in 1 Kings 18–19, where it is explicitly stated that the
"false" prophets "cut themselves with swords and lances" (18:28), or that he
alludes to specific local cults or philosophical schools (like the Cynics) present
in Philippi. In short, according to Nanos, Paul lambastes pagan influences,
not Jewish ones.

From this perspective, Paul's appeal to his Jewish identity in 3:4–6 is not intended to denounce his "former" identity but rather to encourage his audience
to follow his example in not competing for honor or rank either on Jewish or
non-Jewish terms: "[Paul's] argument is predicated on his audience knowing
him to be a Jew who 'still' practices Judaism in exemplary fashion. Thus,
he wants to communicate that he does not let the social advantage normally
accompanying Jewish identity to come before his shared identity with them
'in Christ'; nor should they seek social advantage among themselves by the
various 'pagan' communal terms available to them."[40] Nanos has, in my view,
presented a credible alternative interpretation and shown that it is at least
possible to approach even "complicated" texts from a Paul within Judaism
Perspective. Note, too, that Paul speaks in the present tense: he "is" still blameless with respect to the law; he is still a Pharisee. He does not renounce these
identifications: he simply values them less than he does being "in Christ." But
he still values them, or he would not list them as reasons for confidence. The
assumption that Paul denounces his "former" life in Judaism in Philippians
3:4–6 can at least no longer be said to be carved in stone.

It is true, of course, that the proposition that Paul practiced Judaism seems
to be in conflict with his famous negative statements of the Jewish law. How
is it possible to reconcile the view of a Torah-observant Paul with statements
like the following?

> Christ redeemed us from the curse of the law. (Gal. 3:13)

> Now before faith came, we were imprisoned and guarded under the law until
> faith would be revealed. Therefore the law was our disciplinarian until Christ
> came, so that we might be justified by faith. (Gal. 3:23–24)

> While we were living in the flesh, our sinful passions, aroused by the law, were
> at work in our members to bear fruit for death. But now we are discharged from
> the law, dead to that which held us captive, so that we are slaves not under the
> old written code but in the new life of the Spirit. (Rom. 7:5–6)

40. Nanos, "Paul's Polemic in Philippians 3," 89–90.

The answer to this is partly connected to the question of Paul's audience, a problem to which we will return below. Suffice to say, for the moment, that Paul's view of the Torah cannot be said to be entirely negative. For instance, in Romans 3:31 he asks, "Do we then overthrow the law by this faith?" and answers, "By no means! On the contrary, we uphold the law." In Romans 7:7 he asks, "What then should we say? That the law is sin?" and answers, "By no means!" In Romans 7:12 he claims, "The law is holy, and the commandment is holy and just and good." Thus, Paul seems to speak both negatively and positively about the Torah.

From a general perspective, the idea that Paul would have advocated a "law-free" gospel is itself not without problems. The notion that the relation between the human and the divine was governed by certain rules, regulations, and rituals was not confined to Judaism; it was shared among the ancient religions and connected to ethnicity.[41] In the words of Robert Turcan, "True devotion, the Roman sense of the sacred (*sanctitas*), is 'the knowledge of the regard and consideration due to the gods' ([Cicero, *De natura deorum*], 1, 116), advisedly and keeping to the rules."[42]

Furthermore, it is not entirely clear what we mean when stating that someone was or was not "observing the Torah." However, Christian scholars are, bluntly put, often quite confident in determining exactly how Torah observance functioned during the first century—how it was supposed to be observed and when it was violated. Heikki Räisänen, for instance, believes that "Paul strongly encouraged Jewish and Gentile believers to live together, sharing meals without regard to dietary laws,"[43] assuming that this was part of the problem in the so-called Antioch incident (Gal. 2:11–14 [or 2:11–21]).[44] Similarly, Scot McKnight, after having listed five potential explanations for what the conflict concerned, suggests that the problem most likely involved Peter eating foods that were "expressly prohibited in Leviticus or Deuteronomy."[45]

Paul's call to the Corinthians "to eat whatever is sold in the market [μάκελλον, *makellon*]" (1 Cor. 10:25) is another classic text from which many scholars conclude that Paul violates the Torah and drops Jewish food practices. For instance, C. K. Barrett believes that Paul here "makes a clean break with

41. Paula Fredriksen, "Judaizing the Nations: The Ritual Demands of Paul's Gospel," *NTS* 56 (2010): 232–52, esp. 234.

42. Robert Turcan, *The Gods of Ancient Rome: Religion in Everyday Life from Archaic to Imperial Times* (New York: Routledge, 2000), 2.

43. Heikki Räisänen, *The Rise of Christian Beliefs: The Thought World of Early Christians* (Minneapolis: Fortress, 2010), 257.

44. Räisänen, *Rise of Christian Beliefs*, 258.

45. Scot McKnight, *Galatians: From Biblical Text to Contemporary Life*, NIVAC (Grand Rapids: Zondervan, 1995), 103.

Judaism,"[46] and Gordon Fee states that "it is hard to imagine anything more
un-Jewish in the apostle than this."[47]

However, in all discussions on Torah observance or assumed violations of
the Torah, it is wise to bear in mind that the idea of someone "observing" or
"violating" a legal code, such as the Jewish law, is to a large degree in the eye
of the beholder. It probably is true that most Jews honored their ancestral
traditions, one way or another,[48] which does not mean that everybody observed
the Torah in the same way, but only that there existed "a standard by which
loyalty to Israel and to the God of Israel was measured."[49]

Karin Hedner Zetterholm has pointed out that Torah observance means
different things for different groups and individuals, which is partly explained
by the nature of the Jewish law.[50] It is a fact that many individual commandments are vaguely formulated in the Torah and in need of clarification. Hedner Zetterholm takes the Sabbath commandment (Exod. 20:8–11; 31:13–17;
35:1–3) as an example. The biblical text states only that the Israelites, their
slaves, livestock, and alien residents are to abstain from "work," and that it
is forbidden to light a fire. As a result, the rabbis had to decide what activities were implied by the word "work," something that can be found in the
Mishnah in Šabbat 7.2.[51] As is implied by Mark 2:23–24, there seem to have
existed different opinions on what was "lawful" to do on the Sabbath already
during the first century: Jesus and his disciples seem to have no problem with
plucking grain on the Sabbath, while the Pharisees did. This scene may indicate no more than that Mark's Pharisees represent in the late first century
the view later codified in the Mishnah ("reaping" is explicitly forbidden in
Šabbat 7.2). Thus, the fact that many of the *mitzvot* in the Torah are in need
of interpretation or clarification naturally led to a hermeneutically diverse
process—that is, the emergence of different halakic systems. Different groups

46. C. K. Barrett, *A Commentary on the First Epistle to the Corinthians*, 2nd ed., BNTC
(London: A&C Black, 1971), 240.

47. Gordon D. Fee, *The First Epistle to the Corinthians*, NICNT (Grand Rapids: Eerdmans,
1987), 482. See also Wendell Lee Willis, *Idol Meat in Corinth: The Pauline Argument in 1 Corinthians 8 and 10*, SBLDS 68 (Chico, CA: Scholars Press, 1985), 230–31; Ben Witherington III,
Conflict and Community in Corinth: A Socio-Rhetorical Commentary on 1 and 2 Corinthians
(Grand Rapids: Eerdmans, 1995), 226–27.

48. Sanders's definition of "common Judaism" as what the priests and the people agreed
upon makes a good deal of sense. See Sanders, *Judaism: Practice and Belief, 63 BCE–66 CE*
(London: SCM; Philadelphia: Trinity Press International, 1992), 47. See also Sandnes, *Paul
Perceived*, 24–25.

49. Sanders, *Judaism: Practice and Belief*, 47.

50. Karin Hedner Zetterholm, "The Question of Assumptions: Torah Observance in the
First Century," in Nanos and Zetterholm, *Paul within Judaism*, 79–103.

51. Hedner Zetterholm, "The Question of Assumptions," 81.

developed different interpretations, and even within a certain group like the Pharisees there was not always agreement in matters concerning halakah, which the famous disputes between Hillel and Shammai show (m. Ber. 8.1–8), as indeed the existence of the whole Oral Torah.

From this it follows that one Jew could see a certain way of life as in accordance with the Torah, while another Jew, with a different interpretation of halakah, would see violation. Even certain adaptability, for instance in social interaction with non-Jews, fits into this category. Hedner Zetterholm uses the modern context and shows that even a quite orthodox person very well could eat (permissible food) in the home of non-Jews on plates that according to his or her halakah would be a kind of violation of the Torah. However, as is the case in every religious tradition (even Christianity!) there usually exists a hierarchy of ethical principles. The orthodox idea of using separate sets of plates for milk and meat, presented as an interpretation of Exodus 23:19; 34:26; Deuteronomy 14:21, could in a specific situation be perceived to be in conflict with principles considered to be of higher value, such as that of not offending people or of accepting hospitality from non-Jews. Thus, even though someone even more orthodox perhaps would consider this a violation of the Torah, many orthodox Jews are fully capable of eating in the homes of non-Jews and regard this as fully compatible with being Torah observant.[52]

This normal variation is highly relevant with regard to the texts mentioned above (Gal. 2:11–14; 1 Cor. 10:25). In the case of the so-called Antioch incident, it is fully possible that different opinions about how Jews should socially interact with non-Jews were at issue. That is, the problem concerned not the food, but commensality. I have argued elsewhere that the people from James perhaps represented a more stringent interpretation of Jewish law with regard to social contacts with non-Jews than did diaspora Jews, and that they reacted against what they perceived to be too close a social interaction in connection to common meals.[53] Or perhaps the community in Antioch did not observe "normal" Jewish conventions regarding seating or the distribution of food at communal meals.[54] If so, the real problem concerned the assumed moral impurity of the non-Jews and fear that this would negatively affect the Jewish followers of Jesus.[55] I believe that Paul's vision that Jews and non-Jews in Christ had the

52. Hedner Zetterholm, "The Question of Assumptions," 81.
53. Zetterholm, *The Formation of Christianity*, 129–64; Zetterholm, "The Antioch Incident Revisited."
54. Mark D. Nanos, "What Was at Stake in Peter's 'Eating with Gentiles' at Antioch?," in *The Galatians Debate: Contemporary Issues in Rhetorical and Historical Interpretation*, ed. Mark D. Nanos (Peabody, MA: Hendrickson, 2002), 282–318.
55. So also Douglas J. Moo, *Galatians*, BECNT (Grand Rapids: Baker Academic, 2013), 142–43.

same status before the god of Israel made him regard the non-Jews, who had turned to Christ, as holy and pure as Israel. Therefore, they could be trusted as they had been "washed" (ἀπελούσασθε, *apelousasthe*), "sanctified" (ἡγιάσθητε, *hēgiasthēte*), and "justified" (ἐδικαιώθητε, *edikaiōthēte*) in the name of the Lord Jesus Christ (1 Cor. 6:11). The "ones from James" simply took a different view, and argued that the non-Jews in the community should achieve the status as pure and holy the normal way—by conversion to Judaism—thereby solving the problem with moral impurity and social relations between Jews and non-Jews in the community. In my view, it is fully possible to read Galatians 2:11–14 from the assumption that Paul did not reject the Torah. It reads as an example of a clash between two different views of halakic obligations representing two different ways of interpreting the Torah.[56]

The same is true with regard to 1 Corinthians 10:25. Does Paul violate the Torah when he exhorts the Corinthians "to eat whatever is sold in the market," or could his statement also be compatible with being a Torah-observant Jew? The answer probably depended on which Jew you asked. Drawing conclusions from (admittedly later) rabbinic sources, Peter Tomson has proposed that Paul defines what is idol food in doubtful cases in 1 Corinthians 10:25–29. While the problem is introduced in 1 Corinthians 8, Paul then deals with food known to be consecrated to idols in 1 Corinthians 10:1–22, and then moves on to "food of unspecified nature in a pagan setting," according to Tomson.[57] The fact that in 10:14 Paul has urged the Corinthians to "flee from the worship of idols" makes it reasonable to assume that the issue of "idol food" is still on the table.[58]

Moreover, Tomson argues that συνείδησις (*syneidēsis*) in the context of 10:25, which usually is translated as "conscience," rather should be understood as "someone's 'consciousness' or 'intention,'" which is either directed toward idols or toward the Creator."[59] From rabbinic literature it is clear, Tomson claims, that the rabbis' view of idolatry was not "so much concerned with material objects or actions as with the spiritual attitude with which these are approached by the gentiles."[60] For instance, if a non-Jew wanted to buy a white cock from

---

56. For other Paul within Judaism views on what was at stake in the Antioch incident, see Paula Fredriksen, *Paul: The Pagans' Apostle* (New Haven: Yale University Press, 2017), 94–100; Mark D. Nanos, "How Could Paul Accuse Peter of Living 'Ethnē-ishly' in Antioch (Gal 2:11–21) If Peter Was Eating according to Jewish Dietary Norms?," *JSPL* 6 (2016): 199–223.

57. Peter J. Tomson, *Paul and the Jewish Law: Halakha in the Letters of the Apostle to the Gentiles*, CRINT 3/1 (Assen: van Gorcum; Minneapolis: Fortress, 1990), 208.

58. John Fotopoulos, *Food Offered to Idols in Roman Corinth: A Social-Rhetorical Reconsideration of 1 Corinthians 8:1–11:1*, WUNT 2/151 (Tübingen: Mohr Siebeck, 2003), 237.

59. Tomson, *Paul and the Jewish Law*, 214.

60. Tomson, *Paul and the Jewish Law*, 214.

a Jew, there is a high probability that the cock would be used in a ceremonial setting. In this case, selling the cock would be forbidden. However, if the non-Jew wanted to buy *any* cock, thus signaling that a sacrificial purpose was not intended, selling even a white one would be permitted. The famous story in the Mishnah ('Abod. Zar. 3.4) about Rabban Gamaliel, who considered the statue of Aphrodite in a pagan bathhouse merely as an ornament rather than as an "idol," reveals the same attitude: what is not treated as a god is permitted.[61]

It is true that one should be cautious when using later rabbinic sources for interpreting Jewish texts from the first century AD. However, given that Jews for many centuries had been forced to develop strategies for negotiating the shared space with non-Jews in a pagan diaspora environment, it does not seem overly daring to assume that a halakic system, similar to what we find in later rabbinic literature, was operative during Paul's lifetime. The opposite would be quite remarkable. Hedner Zetterholm concludes, "Far from declaring Jewish law null and void, Paul is engaged either in *establishing* a halakah concerning idol food for Jesus-oriented gentiles, or *teaching them an existing* local Corinthian Jewish halakah. In light of the rabbinic parallels, it is not unconceivable that he draws from a local Jewish halakah concerning food bought at the market in Corinth."[62] Thus, it is fully possible to read 1 Corinthians 10:25 to mean that Paul does not break with Judaism but rather acts in accordance with local Jewish halakic principles.

Finally, the idea that Paul was faithful to his religious heritage is indeed supported by Acts, which at least shows that such ideas were in circulation quite some time after Paul's death.[63] In Luke's narrative, Paul's arrival in Jerusalem introduces a sequence of incidents that eventually lead to the apostle's captivity in Rome (Acts 21–28). Faced with serious accusations, basically of having led Jews astray and abandoned a Jewish way of life, Paul delivers forceful apologies or performs actions expressing his loyalty to the Torah and Jewish traditions.

In Acts 21:17–26 Luke reports that thousands of Jewish believers, who "are all zealous for the law" (πάντες ζηλωταὶ τοῦ νόμου ὑπάρχουσιν, *pantes zēlōtai tou nomou hyparchousin*) (v. 20), have been told that Paul teaches Jews to abandon Jewish traditions. The fact that Jewish followers of Jesus apparently are Torah observant is not presented as an anomaly by Luke. In order

---

61. For an extensive discussion on συνείδησις and for several more examples on rabbinic views on "intention" in relation to "idolatry," see Tomson, *Paul and the Jewish Law*, 208–16. The discussion is also summarized in Hedner Zetterholm, "The Question of Assumptions," 91–103.

62. Hedner Zetterholm, "The Question of Assumptions," 99 (emphasis original).

63. What is meant by "quite some time" is, of course, dependent on the dating of Acts. For an overview, see Joseph A. Fitzmyer, *The Acts of the Apostles: A New Translation with Introduction and Commentary*, AB 31 (New York: Doubleday, 1998), 51–55.

to eliminate all doubts of his fidelity, Paul joins four men under a vow and undertakes a ritual that includes purification and a sacrifice in the temple.[64]

In Caesarea Paul is again accused, now of being an agitator and of having profaned the temple, among other things. Brought before the Roman governor, Felix, he declares himself innocent, stating, "I worship the God of our ancestors, believing everything laid down according to the law or written in the prophets" (Acts 24:14). This pattern is repeated in Acts 25:6–12, when Paul, now before Felix's successor, Festus, declares, "I have in no way committed an offense against the law of the Jews [εἰς τὸν νόμον τῶν Ἰουδαίων, *eis ton nomon Ioudaiōn*] or against the temple, or against the emperor" (v. 8). Finally, after having arrived in Rome, Paul declares before "the local leaders of the Jews" that he has done nothing wrong "against our people or the customs of our ancestors" (Acts 28:17).

Luke clearly intends to present Paul as a Torah-observant Jew, meeting fierce opposition from various Jewish groups, Jewish followers of Jesus included. This, of course, constitutes a conundrum for scholars working from more traditional points of departure. One solution is the one suggested by Ben Witherington, who argues that since Paul was indifferent to the Torah, he could "either observe it or not so long as it was understood that either way it had no soteriological significance."[65] Reidar Hvalvik argues along the same lines: Paul was raised as a law-observant Jew, which "makes it reasonable to assume that he often observed Jewish customs in his daily life—as long as they did not blur the gospel."[66] The bottom line seems to be this: even if Paul did observe the Torah, he did not mean anything by it.

Karl Olav Sandnes recently has dealt with Paul and the law in Acts, and much is to be commended in his presentation. He readily admits that Luke indeed presents Paul as loyal to Jewish traditions including the Torah, and even acknowledges that Paul within Judaism scholars, to some extent, "may consider Luke as substantiating evidence for their reading of the epistolary Paul."[67] Sandnes is also correct, of course, in stating that "Luke's portrayal is entangled in a *debate* on Paul's relationship with the Torah."[68]

However, in spite of what seems to be a rather univocal presentation by Luke, Sandnes concludes that Luke conveys an ambiguous picture of Paul's

---

64. There has been an extensive debate over exactly what kind of ritual Luke has in mind. See Ben Witherington III, *The Acts of the Apostles: A Socio-Rhetorical Commentary* (Grand Rapids: Eerdmans, 1998), 649.

65. Witherington, *Acts of the Apostles*, 648.

66. Reidar Hvalvik, "Paul as a Jewish Believer—According to the Book of Acts," in *Jewish Believers in Jesus: The Early Centuries*, ed. Oskar Skarsaune and Reidar Hvalvik (Peabody, MA: Hendrickson, 2007), 121–53, here 153.

67. Sandnes, *Paul Perceived*, 198.

68. Sandnes, *Paul Perceived*, 183 (emphasis original).

relation to the Torah. For instance, discussing Acts 18:12–17, where Paul is accused of "persuading people to worship God in ways that are contrary to the law" (v. 13), Sandnes argues that since the allegations take the Torah as the standard for worship, Paul is seen as undermining precisely that, mainly by introducing baptism (18:8). Paul creates "a growing distance towards the law and the fellowship upholding it."[69] The problem with Sandnes's interpretation is that it presumes an essentialist view of the Torah, which is precisely what we should beware of. Taking the discussion on the diversity of Torah observance above into consideration, we see that it is quite problematic to speak of the Torah as constituting a fixed standard for almost anything. Despite the fact that we do not know that much about the details of the synagogue service during the Second Temple period, there seems to have been a considerable difference in liturgy between the diaspora and Judea and probably also local variations.[70]

I find no reason to doubt that Paul met Jews who forcefully accused him of having violated the Torah according to their interpretation. But this sort of internal argument is Jewish business as usual. This, as we have seen, does not necessarily have to lead to the conclusion that Paul was not as Jewish or as Torah observant as any other Jew in the diaspora, which I firmly believe he was. Does the fact that sixty-two conservative clergy and lay scholars from twenty countries have signed a letter accusing Pope Francis of heresy, *by referring to church law*, mean that the pope is no longer Catholic?[71] In the eyes of some, perhaps, but I doubt that the Holy Father concurs (or loses any sleep over the accusation). In the ultraorthodox area of Mea Shearim, in Jerusalem, I noticed a banner in the fall of 2018 stating, "True Jewry always opposed Zionism and the State of Israel," implying that those who do not oppose Zionism and the State of Israel are not part of "true Jewry." My orthodox Jewish friends strongly disagree.

Some of the allegations against Paul seem to have been pure misconceptions. I find it unlikely that he ever instructed Jews to forsake Moses or told them not to circumcise their children, since in 1 Corinthians 7:18 he distinctly argues that Jews should not abandon their Jewish identity. The center of the Jewish critique of Paul, I would assume, is rather his theologically motivated close relations to non-Jews, which indeed could be perceived to constitute a threat to Jewish identity. Paul's insistence that Jews and non-Jews "in Christ"

69. Sandnes, *Paul Perceived*, 197.
70. Lee I. Levine, *The Ancient Synagogue: The First Thousand Years*, 2nd ed. (New Haven: Yale University Press, 2005), 171.
71. See *Correctio Filialis De Haeresibus Propagatis*, accessed March 5, 2020, http://www.correctiofilialis.org. Admittedly, the signatories "profess their loyalty to the holy Roman Church, assure the pope of their prayers, and ask for his apostolic blessing."

had the same status before the god of Israel is indeed a new interpretation of the Torah, motivated by the Christ-event and the firm belief that the world was about to end. Surely, such ideas were not met with unanimous acclamation.

That it was Paul's relation to non-Jews that was the major problem is hinted at in Acts 21:27–28, where Paul is accused of having brought "Greeks" into the temple. It also was, in my view, what underlies the Antioch incident. This complex of problems is intimately connected to the second main assumption of the Paul within Judaism Perspective, to which we now turn.

Paul—Apostle to the Nations

The second fundamental assumption on which the Paul within Judaism Perspective rests concerns Paul's self-definition as apostle to the nations (Rom. 1:5; 11:13; Gal. 2:8). For Paul within Judaism scholars, this means that Paul mainly, but not exclusively, deals with issues pertinent to the salvation of the nations. This is often framed in terms of the identity of Paul's addressees,[72] which to me seems to be beside the point. The important thing is that Paul deals with "the gentile problem," regardless of the target audience, of which we can speculate until the Messiah arrives (or returns). For the Paul within Judaism Perspective this is imperative: if Paul's gospel concerns the whole of humanity, this perspective is simply incorrect.

Thus, according to Paul within Judaism scholars, the problem that Paul faces is not *predominantly* related to how Israel is going to be saved, although he sometimes touches upon that problem too, as he occasionally deals with the new relation between Israel and the nations. This view is to be contrasted with the more traditional understanding, that Paul's gospel is universal and that his concern is the salvation of humankind, meaning that everything Paul says, for instance, about the Torah, also applies to Jews.[73]

Having said that, I think it is important to acknowledge that Paul indeed sees himself as being involved in events that will lead to the salvation of the whole world. But again, Paul's problem is not the Jews, but rather the nations (τὰ ἔθνη, *ta ethnē*)—or, to translate the same word in its religious rather than ethnic inflection, the pagans. Paul seems, in my view, to argue, especially in Romans

---

72. Eisenbaum, *Paul Was Not a Christian*, 217; John G. Gager, *Reinventing Paul* (Oxford: Oxford University Press, 2000), 51; Lloyd Gaston, *Paul and the Torah* (Vancouver: University of British Columbia Press, 1990), 7; Johannes Munck, *Paul and the Salvation of Mankind*, trans. Frank Clarke (Atlanta: John Knox, 1959), 196. Compare, however, Tomson, *Paul and the Jewish Law*, 59–61, who argues for a more complex picture for Romans.

73. For a summary of that position, including a critique of a Paul within Judaism Perspective, see Räisänen, *Rise of Christian Beliefs*, 256–64.

9–11, that the fate of Israel is in the hands of Israel's god;[74] and even if it does not look that way, Israel plays a leading part in that grand eschatological drama orchestrated by God, which will culminate in the coming of the new αἰών (*aiōn*), a new heaven and a new earth, as Revelation puts it (21:1). All Israel will eventually be saved—the gifts and the calling of God are irrevocable (Rom. 11:26, 29).

I find it hard to imagine that Jesus, as God's messianic agent, is not in some way involved in that process, even though Paul does not explicitly state how. This state of affairs has given rise to an extensive discussion of whether or not Paul advocates a "two-way solution"—that is, one path for the salvation of the Jews, through the Torah, and one for the nations, through Christ.[75] Many scholars who are involved in criticizing the traditional paradigm seem reluctant to admit that Christ would have any relevance for the salvation of Jews. Pamela Eisenbaum, for instance, denies that anything Paul writes implies that Jews "must convert to Christianity to be saved."[76] In the same vein, John Gager states that Paul "in maintaining the validity of the law . . . does not envisage an End-time conversion of Israel to Christ."[77] With more traditionally oriented scholars, there seems to be almost an obsession that Jews and non-Jews *must* be saved in the same way—through faith alone.[78]

To me, the whole problem seems to be heavily influenced by the tragic history of the European Christian use of coercive force against populations of European Jews, and a fair amount of normative ideology on behalf of both Jewish and Christian representatives in the debate. The issue at stake is, of course, not whether or not Paul expects Jews to "convert to Christianity" but rather if Christ is of any relevance for Israel in Paul's mind, which I tend to believe is so. It is not unlikely that Paul envisaged that Israel in the end would *turn* to Christ, and, as Paula Fredriksen has pointed out, "turning" is not "conversion."[79] However, given the limited information we have at hand, I cannot see how anyone can reach a clear answer to this question. Maybe Paul had not worked this out for himself and therefore describes the eschatological grand finale as a "mystery" (μυστήριον, *mystērion*) in Romans 11:25. Perhaps

74. Fredriksen, *Paul: The Pagans' Apostle*, 162.

75. A more or less fully developed "two-way solution" is first found in the Pseudo-Clementine Homilies 8.5–7; see Annette Yoshiko Reed, "'Jewish-Christianity' after the 'Parting of the Ways': Approaches to Historiography and Self-Definition in the Pesudo-Clementines," in *The Ways That Never Parted: Jews and Christians in Late Antiquity and the Early Middle Ages*, ed. Adam H. Becker and Annette Yoshiko Reed (Minneapolis: Fortress, 2007), 189–221, esp. 213–17.

76. Eisenbaum, *Paul Was Not a Christian*, 255.

77. Gager, *Reinventing Paul*, 146.

78. See, e.g., Sandnes's critique of Eisenbaum in *Paul Perceived*, 199.

79. Admittedly, with regard to non-Jews turning to Christ, see Fredriksen, *Paul: The Pagans' Apostle*, 75–76.

we have to settle with Stanley Stowers's rather cautious statement (in a discussion of Rom. 3–4) that "Paul's language shows him assuming that Jews and gentiles have similar but different relations to Christ, Abraham, and the law."[80]

The focus on the salvation of the Jews risks, however, making us overlook Paul's real concern. John Gager has formulated this fittingly: "As to the question of whether we can speak of Paul's *Sonderweg* or special path to salvation, I am rather of the view that it is the other way around. For Paul, Israel's salvation was never in doubt. What he taught and preached was instead a special path, a *Sonderweg*, for Gentiles."[81] This statement captures Paul's mission perfectly. Jewish attitudes toward the nations are somewhat conflicting: according to some traditions, the nations are to be destroyed by God or subjected to Israel, but according to other strata, non-Jews have a place in the world to come.[82] Paul makes use of both. On the one hand, he connects to what seem to be common, negative Jewish stereotypes of the non-Jewish pagan world as found, for instance, in Wisdom 11–15, *Sibylline Oracles* 3.8–45, and Jubilees 22.16–17. In Romans 1:18–32, which is strikingly similar to Wisdom 13–14, he describes the fate of the non-Jewish pagan nations,[83] over which God's wrath is revealed from heaven (1:18) and who deserve to die (1:32). On the other hand, Paul combines this negative view of the nations with currents found in the Hebrew Bible and other Jewish literature that predict the future salvation of the non-Jewish nations once they turn to Israel's god, as in Tobit 13:11: "A bright light will shine to all the ends of the earth; many nations will come to you from far away, the inhabitants of the remotest parts of the earth to your holy name, bearing gifts in their hands for the King of heaven. Generation after generation will give joyful praise in you; the name of the chosen city will endure forever."

According to Terence Donaldson, it is not always clear if non-Jews become Jews in this eschatological pilgrimage, or if they are included as non-Jews.[84]

---

80. Stanley K. Stowers, *A Rereading of Romans: Justice, Jews, and Gentiles* (New Haven: Yale University Press, 1994), 237.

81. Gager, *Reinventing Paul*, 146 (emphasis original).

82. Fredriksen, *Paul: The Pagans' Apostle*, 28–29; Matthew Thiessen, *Paul and the Gentile Problem* (New York: Oxford University Press, 2016), 20–26; Zetterholm, *The Formation of Christianity*, 136–40. On Jewish attitudes specifically in apocalyptic literature, see Michael P. Theophilus, "The Portrayal of Gentiles in Jewish Apocalyptic Literature," in *Attitudes to Gentiles in Ancient Judaism and Early Christianity*, ed. David C. Sim and James S. McLaren, LNTS 499 (London: Bloomsbury T&T Clark, 2013), 72–91.

83. On the identification of those referred to in Rom. 1:18–32 as non-Jews, see Thiessen, *Paul and the Gentile Problem*, 47–52; Magnus Zetterholm, "The Non-Jewish Interlocutor in Romans 2:17 and the Salvation of the Nations: Contextualizing Romans 1:18–32," in Rodríguez and Thiessen, *The So-Called Jew*, 39–58.

84. Terence L. Donaldson, *Judaism and the Gentiles: Patterns of Universalism (to 135 CE)* (Waco: Baylor University Press, 2007), 499–505. Compare, however, J. Ross Wagner, *Heralds*

Donaldson argues that only a few passages (e.g., Pss. Sol. 17.28) clearly envisage a continued existence of non-Jews as non-Jews.[85] It seems evident, however, that within "this strand of Jewish thinking, the inclusion of the Gentiles in the final consummation was an essential part of Israel's expectations and self-understanding."[86]

According to Paul within Judaism scholars, Paul firmly believed that non-Jews were to be included in the final salvation without giving up their ethnicity; that is, they were not to become Jews (nor should Jews abandon their Jewish identity, which seems evident from 1 Cor. 7:17–24).[87] Scholars have suggested different reasons for this. Mark Nanos has proposed that God's oneness would be compromised if non-Jews had to become Jews, since the god of Israel is not only the god of the Jews but also of the nations.[88] More recently, Matthew Thiessen has argued that Paul believed that there existed a divinely instituted genealogical divide between Israel and the nations, making it impossible for non-Jews to become Jews.[89]

This constitutes an important hermeneutical key for understanding Paul's view of the Torah, according to Paul within Judaism scholars. Paul argued that the ethnic division between Jews and the nations should remain, and this leads to the conclusion that non-Jews should not observe the Torah, at least not in the same way as Jews do, and definitely not for the same reasons.

Considering the various attitudes toward non-Jews within Second Temple Judaism, this was obviously not the only possible position. As Terence Donaldson has shown, some Jews had nothing against non-Jews who were involved in "Judaizing"—that is, adopting certain Jewish customs that in reality meant observing parts of the Torah.[90] This phenomenon can be observed also in later Jewish tradition. Marc Hirshman has argued that a similar universalistic trend can be found in the Tannaitic midrashim—for instance, the Mekilta de Rabbi Yishmael (Bahodesh 1), in an interpretation of Exodus 19:2, where it is stated that the Torah was given openly in a free place so that "everyone wishing to accept it could come and accept it." Similarly, in Sipra on Leviticus 18:1–5, a non-Jew "doing" Torah is compared to the high priest. According

---

of the Good News: Isaiah and Paul in Concert in the Letter to the Romans (Leiden: Brill, 2003).
85. Donaldson, *Judaism and the Gentiles*, 504.
86. Donaldson, *Judaism and the Gentiles*, 505.
87. See, e.g., J. Brian Tucker, *"Remain in Your Calling": Paul and the Continuation of Social Identities in 1 Corinthians* (Eugene, OR: Pickwick, 2011). See also Rom. 11:25–26; 15:9–12.
88. Mark D. Nanos, *The Mystery of Romans: The Jewish Context of Paul's Letter* (Minneapolis: Fortress, 1996), 9–10.
89. Thiessen, *Paul and the Gentile Problem*.
90. Donaldson, *Judaism and the Gentiles*, 469–82.

to Hirshman, nothing in these and related texts from the same tradition suggests that non-Jews should convert to Judaism; rather, they are "inviting the Gentile to observe Torah without becoming a full-fledged Jew."[91]

This universalistic position did not, however, stand unchallenged. In other texts, associated with the so-called school of Rabbi Akiba, it is evident that the Torah is considered the sole possession of Israel. In Sipre to Deuteronomy (§345), non-Jewish involvement in the Torah is even compared to adultery: "The Torah is betrothed to Israel and is like a married woman with respect to the nations of the world. And so it says, 'Can a man rake embers into his bosom without burning his clothes? Can a man walk on live coals without scorching his feet?' It is the same with one who sleeps with his fellow's wife; none who touches her will go unpunished."[92]

The existence of a similar ideology during the first century is not inconceivable, and Paul can very well be seen as an early representative of such a position. Another, or additional, solution that should be taken into consideration is Christine Hayes's recent suggestion that Paul's discourse on the Torah is a rhetorical strategy that makes use of the ancient dichotomy between divine law and human law. Divine or natural law, Hayes argues, was in Greek thought commonly depicted as unwritten, rational, universal, corresponding to truth, beneficial for virtue, static and unchanging, whereas human law was characterized as a set of rules that can be set in writing. Human law does not necessarily possess any of the characteristics of divine law: "It will contain arbitrary elements, that do not correspond with truth, and it must be enforced coercively; it is particular and subject to variation, and its ability to produce virtue is a matter of considerable debate."[93] Thus, many of the characteristics of the biblical, divine law fit very well into Greek ideas of human law, but very few into the concept of divine law.

Whereas, for instance, Philo, in an effort to make the Jewish law attractive, identified it with divine law,[94] thereby resolving the cognitive dissonance between Greco-Roman and biblical notions of divine law, Paul did the opposite, Hayes argues. To present to non-Jews the Jewish law as a privilege of that very group they could never join—Jews—would have been counterproductive. Instead, "Paul had to inspire Gentiles to worship the god of Israel without creating in them a further desire to enter into the privileged ranks of the

91. Marc Hirshman, "Rabbinic Universalism in the Second and Third Centuries," *HTR* 93 (2000): 101–15, here 109.

92. Cited from Steven D. Fraade, *From Tradition to Commentary: Torah and Its Interpretation in the Midrash Sifre to Deuteronomy* (Albany: State University of New York Press, 1991), 57.

93. Christine E. Hayes, *What's Divine about Divine Law? Early Perspectives* (Princeton: Princeton University Press, 2015), 4.

94. Hayes, *What's Divine about Divine Law?*, 111–24.

Torah-observant seed of Isaac."[95] Thus, by presenting the Torah as human law, *as it would appear to his Hellenized audience*, Paul was able to emphasize its temporary, enslaving, and lifeless nature, thereby making it the second-best option for non-Jews. Hayes concludes,

> To be sure, the Law was given by a good god to achieve an important end, and here Paul introduces a narrative that makes sense of his ambivalent assessment of the Law as good but not good enough: the Law was given to a fallen people in order to restrain and guard them until such time as faith—the true path to salvation—would be revealed (Gal 3:22–23), until in the fullness of time God would send his son for redemption (Gal 4:4), and until the Gentiles could be brought to a recognition of Yahweh (Rom 11:25).[96]

On the assumption that Paul's solution of presenting the Torah as human law was a minority position, this could very well be part of an explanation for the rise of negative reactions from other Jews, as reported by Acts.

These suggestions, or a combination of them—nomistic exclusivism, an unbridgeable genealogical divide, and the presentation of the Torah as human law—constitute a potential ideological background to Paul's discourse on Torah observance for non-Jews and a credible alternative to more traditional perspectives.

There is, however, a final piece of the puzzle that we need to give account of. The sources strongly indicate that there was an extensive interest in Judaism on the part of non-Jews.[97] Josephus's statements are well known: in *Against Apion* 2.282 he claims that Jewish customs have spread all over the world, and in *Jewish War* 7.45 he states that a multitude of Greeks in Antioch were attracted to the religious services (θρησκεία, *thrēskeia*) of the Jews. This picture is confirmed also by Roman sources.[98] As pointed out by Paula Fredriksen, "Where there were synagogues, there also seem to have been pagans."[99] This corresponds well to the universalistic patterns as outlined by Donaldson.[100] Thus, non-Jews sympathized and interacted with Jews, presumably in the context of the synagogue, and adopted some Jewish traditions encouraged

---

95. Hayes, *What's Divine about Divine Law?*, 152.

96. Hayes, *What's Divine about Divine Law?*, 163.

97. See, e.g., Michele Murray, *Playing a Jewish Game: Gentile Christian Judaizing in the First and Second Centuries CE* (Waterloo, ON: Wilfred Laurier University Press, 2004), 11–27.

98. See, e.g., Seneca, *Ep.* 108.22; Seneca in Augustine, *Civ.* 6.11; Dio Cassius, *Hist. rom.* 67.14.1–2. See also Donaldson, *Judaism and the Gentiles*, 471.

99. Fredriksen, "Judaizing the Nations," 238.

100. Donaldson, *Judaism and the Gentiles*. See also Shaye J. D. Cohen, *The Beginnings of Jewishness: Boundaries, Varieties, Uncertainties* (Berkeley: University of California Press, 1999), 140–74.

by Jews who shared a form of universalistic outlook. To some extent, we must conclude that these members of the nations were in varying degrees Torah observant.

From sociological points of view, there can be little doubt that the vast majority of non-Jews who were attracted by Paul's gospel had previously been in contact with Jews.[101] They most certainly had been taught that they were fulfilling their religious obligations by observing the Torah to various degrees and therefore were acceptable to Israel's god. Paul thus faces Judaizing non-Jews—that is, people interested in Judaism and positively inclined toward Jewish law, presumably presented as divine, being under the impression that their behavior was in accordance with the will of Israel's god. Paul, however, had excluded the possibility of non-Jews becoming Jews, and being convinced that the Torah is God's most precious gift to the *Jewish* people, he endeavored in the project of creating *a form of Judaism for non-Jews*, apart from the Torah *in a technical sense*, but emphasizing the need for non-Jews to turn to Israel's god *exclusively* and flee from all forms of idolatry. This appears to be, as Paula Fredriksen has pointed out, "a much more radical form of Judaizing than diaspora synagogues ever requested, much less required."[102]

Conclusion

Paul's competitive advantage consisted of offering non-Jews a well-defined position in the economy of salvation—the same eschatological status as Jews before the god of Israel—and as a result of this, he enacted closer social relations than was common among Jews. This aspect—the relations between Jews and non-Jews in Christ—is perhaps where Paul appears most radical. Still, while non-Jewish followers of Jesus could expect to join with Israel in the eschatological consummation, they could never be part of Israel, which created that strange paradox that, as time continued, eventually created the split between "Judaism" and "Christianity." As for Paul himself, nothing compels us, in my view, to reach the conclusion that he himself broke with Judaism. The Paul within Judaism Perspective is new, arguably only a decade or so old; undeniably, further work is needed. But my firm belief is that, in the end, it will win the day.

101. Meredith B. McGuire, *Religion: The Social Context*, 3rd ed. (Belmont, CA: Wadsworth, 1992), 91.
102. Fredriksen, *Paul: The Pagans' Apostle*, 111.

Roman Catholic Perspective
Response to Zetterholm

BRANT PITRE

I would like to sincerely thank Magnus Zetterholm for his rich and wide-ranging essay on the "Paul within Judaism Perspective." In my opinion, this approach to Paul represents one of the most significant developments in Pauline scholarship in recent years. With this in mind, I want to highlight several major points of agreement with Zetterholm.

Paul "within" Judaism—His Continuing Jewish Identity

First, I wholeheartedly agree with Zetterholm's claim that one principal result of the work of E. P. Sanders, James Dunn, and the New Perspective on Paul is "to place the apostle firmly, completely, and comfortably within Judaism" (175). Indeed, whenever Paul does wax autobiographical in his letters, he always refers to himself as a Jew, a Hebrew, or an Israelite:

> *We ourselves are Jews by birth* and not Gentile sinners. (Gal. 2:15)

> If anyone else has reason to be confident in the flesh, I have more: *circumcised on the eighth day, a member of the people of Israel, of the tribe of Benjamin, a Hebrew born of Hebrews*; as to the law, a Pharisee; as to zeal, a persecutor of the church; as to righteousness under the law, blameless. (Phil. 3:4–6)

For I could wish that I myself were accursed and cut off from Christ for the sake of *my own people, my kindred according to the flesh. They are Israelites.* (Rom. 9:3–4)

Notice the string of terms Paul uses to describe himself: he is a "Jew" (Ἰουδαῖος, *Ioudaios*) by "birth" or, more literally, by "nature" (φύσις, *physis*) (Gal. 2:15). Paul counts himself among the "Israelites" (Ἰσραηλῖται, *Israēlitai*) (Rom. 9:4). He is a "Hebrew [born] of Hebrews" (Ἑβραῖος ἐξ Ἑβραίων, *Hebraios ex Hebraiōn*) (Phil. 3:5). In light of such language, Zetterholm is correct to insist on Paul's continuing Jewish identity as a starting point.[1]

Paul Does Not Call for Jews to "Abandon" Their "Jewish Identity"

Second, I also think Zetterholm makes an extremely important point when he writes, "Paul firmly believed that non-Jews were to be included in the final salvation without giving up their ethnicity; that is, they were not to become Jews (nor should Jews abandon their Jewish identity)" (190). In support of this, Zetterholm rightly points to a crucial but often ignored passage in 1 Corinthians:

Was anyone at the time of his call already circumcised? *Let him not seek to remove the marks of circumcision.* Was anyone at the time of his call uncircumcised? *Let him not seek circumcision.* Circumcision is nothing, and uncircumcision is nothing; but obeying the commandments of God is everything. *Let each of you remain in the condition in which you were called.* (1 Cor. 7:18–20)

It seems to me incontrovertible from this passage that Zetterholm is right to insist that Paul's view is not simply that "non-Jews should not observe the Torah, at least not in the same way as Jews do" (190). Contrary to what some interpretations might suggest, Paul had no desire for Jews to abandon their Jewish identity. When it came to the marks of circumcision, Paul's modus operandi was for everyone, Jew or gentile, to "remain" (μένω, *menō*) in the state in which they were called (1 Cor. 7:20).

Paul and the Jewish Torah—No "Law-Free" Gospel

Third and finally, I also agree with Zetterholm's criticism of the tendency of some Protestant exegetes to speak of Paul's supposedly "law-free" gospel. For

---

1. See Brant Pitre, Michael P. Barber, and John Kincaid, *Paul, A New Covenant Jew: Rethinking Pauline Theology* (Grand Rapids: Eerdmans, 2019), 11–62.

one thing, as Zetterholm rightly points out, we should not assume that "everybody observed the Torah in the same way" in first-century Judaism (181). In addition, talk of a "law-free" gospel cannot be reconciled with Paul's own insistence that those who are in Christ must obey the law of Christ:

> Bear one another's burdens, and in this way you will fulfill *the law of Christ*. (Gal. 6:2)

> To those outside the law I became as one outside the law (though I am not free from God's law but am *under Christ's law*) so that I might win those outside the law. (1 Cor. 9:21).

Note well that Paul explicitly speaks both of fulfilling "the law of Christ" (ὁ νόμος τοῦ Χριστοῦ, *ho nomos tou Christou*) (Gal. 6:2) and even of being "under/in Christ's law" (ἔννομος Χριστοῦ, *ennomos Christou*) (1 Cor. 9:21). Finally, as Paula Fredriksen has ably shown, to speak of a "law-free" gospel completely ignores the fact that Paul continues to insist that his gentile readers comply with certain laws taken straight from the Jewish Torah: "Paul's core message to his gentiles about their behavior was not 'Do not circumcise!' It was 'No more *latreia* to lower gods!' His pagans were to worship strictly and only the Jewish god. They were to conform their new religious behavior precisely to the mandates of Jewish worship, *the first table of the Jewish Law, the first two of Sinai's Ten Commandments: no other gods, and no idols* (Exod. 20.1; Deut. 5:6)."[2] In other words, the only way to claim that Paul's gospel was "law-free" per se is to ignore that the Ten Commandments themselves were part and parcel of the Jewish Torah. The Paul within Judaism approach rightly insists that Paul was no antinomian, and it is quite misleading to describe his message as a "law-free" gospel.

With that said, I do have several questions about aspects of Zetterholm's essay.

Is Paul's "Mission" Exclusively to Gentiles?

My first question regards Zetterholm's description of the "mission" of Paul as exclusively focused on the salvation of gentiles. Zetterholm begins his essay with a critique of "traditional interpretations" that hold that Paul's gospel "was directed both to Jews and to non-Jews" (172). Later on, he contrasts this

---

2. Paula Fredriksen, *Paul: The Pagans' Apostle* (New Haven: Yale University Press, 2017), 108–22, here 112 (emphasis altered).

traditional view with the Paul within Judaism Perspective: "The focus on the salvation of the Jews risks, however, making us overlook Paul's real concern. John Gager has formulated this fittingly: 'As to the question of whether we can speak of Paul's *Sonderweg* or special path to salvation [for the Jews], I am rather of the view that it is the other way around. For Paul, Israel's salvation was never in doubt. What he taught and preached was instead a special path, a *Sonderweg*, for Gentiles.' This statement captures Paul's mission perfectly" (189).[3]

I completely agree that Paul sees himself as "apostle to the Gentiles" (Rom. 11:13; cf. Gal. 1:15–16). But where does Paul ever say that his mission is *not* to Jews? To the contrary, when Paul gives programmatic descriptions of his gospel and his mission, he always puts Jews first. Consider the following:

I am not ashamed of *the gospel*; it is the power of God for *salvation* to everyone who has faith, *to the Jew first* and also to the Greek. For in it the righteousness of God is revealed through faith for faith; as it is written, "The one who is righteous will live by faith." (Rom. 1:16–17)

To the Jews I became as a Jew, *in order to win Jews*. To those under the law I became as one under the law (though I myself am not under the law) *so that I might win those under the law*. To those outside the law I became as one outside the law (though I am not free from God's law but am under Christ's law) so *that I might win those outside the law*. To the weak I became weak, so that I might win the weak. I have become all things to all people, *that I might by all means save some*. (1 Cor. 9:20–22)

Note well that in Romans Paul is not just speaking about "salvation" in general but about "the gospel" (τὸ εὐαγγέλιον, *to euangelion*) in particular being "to the Jew first" (Ἰουδαίῳ τε πρῶτον, *Ioudaiō te prōton*) (Rom. 1:16). Do not these verses suggest that Paul's mission of evangelization gives priority to his fellow Jews and that Paul sees the "salvation" of Jews as taking place in the same way as of gentiles: through "faith" in the "gospel" (Rom. 1:17)? As for the passage from 1 Corinthians, I am not sure that one could ask for a clearer and more explicit statement of the fact that Paul sees his mission as inclusive of Jews and gentiles. What else might Paul mean when he says he strives "to win Jews" (ἵνα Ἰουδαίους κερδήσω, *hina Ioudaious kerdēsō*) (1 Cor. 9:20)? Note well here the linguistic parallel between his mission to "win" (*kerdēsō*) Jews ("those under the law" [1 Cor. 9:20]) with his mission

3. Here Zetterholm is quoting John G. Gager, *Reinventing Paul* (Oxford: Oxford University Press, 2000), 146.

to "win" (*kerdēsō*) gentiles ("those outside the law" [1 Cor. 9:21]). In context, his "winning" both Jews and gentiles is his desire for their *salvation*: that he might "by all means save [σώσω, *sōsō*] some" (1 Cor. 9:22). In light of such passages, would Zetterholm agree that Paul *himself* describes his mission as focused on both Jews and gentiles? If not, what does Zetterholm think Paul means when he speaks of "winning" and "saving" both Jews and gentiles?

Paul Himself Says That He Is "Not under the Torah"

My second question regards Zetterholm's assertion that "Paul was Torah observant" (176). Zetterholm argues that this aspect of the Paul within Judaism Perspective is the "most difficult proposition to digest for traditionally oriented scholars, since it seemingly strikes at the heart of Lutheran theology" (176). I was surprised when I read this, since it is certainly not a commitment to "Lutheran theology" that makes *me* wonder about this formulation. Rather, it is the words of Paul himself:

> To those under the law I became as one under the law (though I *myself am not under the law*) so that I might win those under the law. To those outside the law I became as one outside the law (though I am not free from God's law but am under Christ's law) so that I might win those outside the law. (1 Cor. 9:20–21)

> For sin will have no dominion over you, since you are *not under law* but under grace. What then? Should we sin because *we are not under law* but under grace? By no means! (Rom. 6:14–15)

In context, Paul's striking declaration "I myself am not under the law" (μὴ ὢν αὐτὸς ὑπὸ νόμον, *mē ōn autos hypo nomon*) (1 Cor. 9:20) is undoubtedly a reference to "Mosaic law."[4] Taken at face value, this statement suggests that Paul does not consider himself personally subject to the Torah of Moses. Instead, Paul is subject to the Torah of the Messiah: he is "under the law of Christ" (ἔννομος Χριστοῦ, *ennomos Christou*) (1 Cor. 9:21). Although some may contend that Paul is simply waxing rhetorical here, in context, this is not convincing. For one thing, Paul uses the same language elsewhere when he (twice) says that he and his readers are "not under law" (οὐ ὑπὸ νόμον, *ou hypo nomon*) but "under grace" (ὑπὸ χάριν, *hypo charin*) (Rom. 6:14–15). Finally, Paul says elsewhere that when he was "crucified with Christ" (presumably in

---

4. See, e.g., Shira L. Lander, "1 Corinthians," in *The Jewish Annotated New Testament: New Revised Standard Version Bible Translation*, ed. Amy-Jill Levine and Mark Zvi Brettler, 2nd ed. (Oxford: Oxford University Press, 2017), 338.

baptism; cf. Rom. 6:1–4), he "died to the law" (Gal. 2:19). Is this merely rhetorical? I think not. In any event, while Second Temple Judaism was extremely diverse, a solid case can be made that one thing that virtually all Jews held in common was the belief that they were bound to obey the law of Moses. Let me be specific: Can Zetterholm give examples of other Second Temple Jews who describe themselves as "not under the law"? I for one can think of none. Perhaps that is why many scholars of the Paul within Judaism Perspective simply ignore Paul's statement that he is not "under the law" (1 Cor. 9:20).[5] So, my question for Zetterholm is this: How would he interpret Paul's statement "I myself am not under the law" (1 Cor. 9:20 [cf. Rom. 6:14–15])? Does not this passage suggest that there is something fundamentally different about the way Paul sees his relationship to the Mosaic law from the way most Second Temple Jews did?

What about the "New Covenant" and the Lord's Supper?

Last, but not least, I wonder how to reconcile Zetterholm's conclusion that Paul's project was that of "creating *a form of Judaism for non-Jews*" (193) with Paul's statements about being a "minister" of the "new covenant" made in the "blood" of Jesus. Consider the following:

> [God] has made us competent to be *ministers of a new covenant*, not of letter but of spirit; for the letter kills, but the Spirit gives life. (2 Cor. 3:6)

> For I received from the Lord what I also handed on to you, that the Lord Jesus on the night when he was betrayed took a loaf of bread, and when he had given thanks, he broke it and said, "This is my body that is for you. Do this in remembrance of me." In the same way he took the cup also, after supper, saying, "*This cup is the new covenant in my blood.* Do this, as often as you drink it, in remembrance of me." (1 Cor. 11:23–25)

5. For example, Paul's declaration that he is "not under the law" (1 Cor. 9:20) is never even quoted in the collection of essays edited by Mark Nanos and Magnus Zetterholm, *Paul within Judaism: Restoring the First-Century Context to the Apostle* (Minneapolis: Fortress, 2015). Likewise, although Paula Fredriksen, *Paul: The Pagans' Apostle*, 165, 222n38, mentions 1 Cor. 9:20 in passing, she never explains what Paul means when he says that he himself is *not* "under the law." Finally, the one time that 1 Cor. 9:20 is quoted in John G. Gager, *Reinventing Paul* (Oxford: Oxford University Press, 2000), 147, he eliminates Paul's statement about not being "under the law" from the verse by means of ellipsis! By contrast, Mark D. Nanos, *Collected Essays of Mark D. Nanos*, vol. 4, *Reading Corinthians and Philippians within Judaism* (Eugene, OR: Cascade, 2017), 52–108, engages in an extensive analysis of this passage. In my view, however, Nanos's argument that Paul is merely being rhetorical is exegetically unconvincing. For more on this, see our evaluation in Pitre, Barber, and Kincaid, *Paul, A New Covenant Jew*, 30–62.

Notice here that Paul cannot simply be speaking of a renewed *Mosaic* covenant. As any first-century Jew would have known, the Mosaic covenant was inaugurated and renewed through the blood of *animals*—not the blood of a *human being* such as Jesus of Nazareth (cf. Exod. 24:1–8). Moreover, as is widely recognized, Paul is alluding here to the book of Jeremiah, which explicitly states that the "new covenant" will "*not be like* the covenant" made with Moses at Mount Sinai (Jer. 31:31–32). In light of such passages, when Zetterholm claims that "Paul's Jewishness means that he also *practiced* Judaism" (177), more nuance is needed. Were there any other Second Temple Jews who celebrated "new covenant" meals in which the elements were identified with the "body" and "blood" of a human being? If not, then does this not constitute a fundamental cultic and covenantal difference between the "Judaism" practiced by Paul and the Judaism practiced by most other Jews in the first century?[6]

In sum, my hope is that future work by scholars writing from the Paul within Judaism Perspective will pay more attention to passages in Paul's writings that speak of a mission to Jews (1 Cor. 9:20–22; Rom. 1:16–17), of Paul not being under the law of Moses (1 Cor. 9:20; Rom. 6:14–15), and of the significance of Paul's self-identification as a "minister" of a "new covenant" (2 Cor. 3:6) made in Jesus's "blood" and celebrated in the Lord's Supper (1 Cor. 11:23–25). Otherwise, they may risk swinging the pendulum too far in the other direction and painting a portrait of Paul that does not do justice to how he saw his ministry and his mission and that minimizes fundamental differences between Paul and most of his Jewish contemporaries.

---

6. See further Pitre, Barber, and Kincaid, *Paul, A New Covenant Jew*, 38–61, 211–50.

Traditional Protestant Perspective Response to Zetterholm

A. ANDREW DAS

For "Paul within Judaism" interpreters, Paul would encourage Jews to remain law-observant (1 Cor. 7:18). To advance the discussion: (1) Paul within Judaism proponents have offered alternative, *possible* readings of individual letters and passages, but how plausible are they? (2) One must ask whether Paul grants that Jews enjoy God's salvation within the realm of the law. The negative statements about the law must be weighed properly. (3) Professor Zetterholm points to the positive statements about the law, but each of these statements includes crucial qualifications. (4) One must identify the intended beneficiaries of Paul's gospel. Ultimately, one must ask what *weight* Paul gives to being "in Christ" versus "in Judaism."

1. Professor Zetterholm offers an example of a Paul within Judaism alternative reading: the James party in Galatians 2:11–14 was alarmed by Jewish Christ-believers' meals with gentiles as being too close an association with the morally impure. The non-Jews, to remain at a shared table, would need to *convert to Judaism*. In response, I maintain that James's party was *not* advocating for the non-Jews to convert; they were focused on *Peter*.[1]

---

1. A. Andrew Das, *Galatians*, ConcC (St. Louis: Concordia, 2014), 196–232 (summarized in my response to Dunn in this volume). For detailed critiques of other Paul within Judaism readings, see Das, *Solving the Romans Debate* (Minneapolis: Fortress, 2007), 115–48, against Nanos's reconstruction of the Romans situation; Das, *Galatians*, 10–14, against Nanos's alternative reading of Galatians.

Paul Holloway responded to Nanos's reading of Philippians 3:2. "Mutilation" naturally pairs with "circumcision" in the following verse and identifies *Jewish* influence and not pagan: "It is not the physical circumcision but spirit possession that marks the people of God. . . . This, in turn, makes placing 'confidence in the flesh'—understood as Torah observance, including circumcision ('mutilation')—irrational if not impossible."[2]

2. Paul's negative statements about Moses's law pose a significant challenge. Paul says in Romans 3:20, "For 'no human being will be justified in his sight' by deeds prescribed by the law, for through the law comes the knowledge of sin"— a categorical denial that the law offers a path to salvation. John Gager, a Paul within Judaism interpreter, would limit this statement to gentiles.[3] But note the universal language: in 2:12–13 all people are included among those in the law and those without the law. Romans 3:20's "no human being" (πᾶσα σάρξ, *pasa sarx*) is matched in the immediate context by "for all who believe" (3:22) and "all have sinned" (3:23). A limitation to gentiles may be safely eliminated.

For Paul, the law is a cosmic power that stands over *all* descendants of Adam and not just gentiles (Rom. 5:12–21). Romans 7:7–25 laments the problem posed by sin for the law. In 7:18 the "I" is simply unable to do the good. Paul asks about the law itself, "Is the law sin?" (7:7)—a question hardly limited to gentiles under the law.

In Galatians 3:10 the law pronounces a curse upon those identified by its works (ὅσοι ἐξ ἔργων νόμου εἰσιν, *hosoi ex ergōn nomou eisin*). The expression refers to those characterized by a Torah-observant (Jewish) way of life.[4] Gager explains that Galatians 3:1–14 focuses exclusively on gentiles, and he disregards the consensus among Galatians interpreters that the curse in Galatians 3:10 is upon those associated with the law.[5] Gager regularly adds wording to Paul's text—for example, "the law was added—*to Gentiles*—because of their transgressions" (Gal. 3:19).[6] In the immediate context, however, Paul is explaining why the law "was added" 430 years after the Abrahamic promise (Gal. 3:17)— that is, from the point of view of its historic origin with the people *of Israel*.

---

2. Paul A. Holloway, *Philippians: A Commentary*, Hermeneia (Minneapolis: Fortress, 2017), 153–54, here 154.

3. John G. Gager, *Reinventing Paul* (Oxford: Oxford University Press, 2000), 121–22. See my fuller response to Gager in A. Andrew Das, *Paul and the Jews*, LPS (Peabody, MA: Hendrickson, 2003), 96–106.

4. E.g., Hans Dieter Betz, *Galatians: A Commentary on Paul's Letter to the Churches in Galatia*, Hermeneia (Philadelphia: Fortress, 1979), 144; the very detailed case by Joseph B. Tyson, "'Works of Law' in Galatians," *JBL* 92 (1973): 423–31.

5. Gager, *Reinventing Paul*, 87–88, simply assuming Lloyd Gaston's dissent: *Paul and the Torah* (Vancouver: University of British Columbia Press, 1987), 29.

6. Gager, *Reinventing Paul*, 89 (emphasis added).

Second Corinthians 3:13–14 discusses the hardening of the Israelites' minds at the reading of the old covenant. After all, "the letter kills" (2 Cor. 3:6). Paul considers his Jewish prerogatives "rubbish," or better, "dung" in relation to what he enjoys in Christ (Phil. 3:8).

3. Zetterholm draws attention instead to positive statements about Moses's law but does not mention the repeated, crucial qualifications for the law to function positively. In Galatians 6:2 the law is *in the hands of Christ*! In Romans 8:2 the law results in death when grabbed hold of by the cosmic power of sin; grabbed hold of by the *Spirit*, the law results in life *in Christ Jesus*. The law is upheld as a witness to faith (Rom. 3:31), even as Abraham believed in promises fulfilled in Christ (Rom. 4:1–9, 23–25). In other words, Paul's positive comments about the law are always within the context of what God is doing in Christ and the Spirit.

For Gager, Abraham's "faith(fulness)" in Romans 4 is his faith/belief in a promise that the gentiles would be included in God's plan; Christ is not mentioned.[7] Certainly Abraham's faith rested in God's promises of what was still to come (Rom. 4:13), but Paul is careful to note, contra Gager, that Abrahamic faith must now include recognition of God's action *in Christ*— for uncircumcised gentile *and* circumcised Jew (Rom. 3:21, 30; 4:23–25).

4. As for the beneficiaries of the gospel of Jesus Christ, the problem of sin is universal ("all have sinned" [Rom. 3:23]). The law saves no one ("no human being": πᾶσα σάρξ, *pasa sarx* [3:20]). "All" people must appropriate Christ's redemptive work by "believing" ("for all who believe" [3:21–25, esp. 3:22]). Abraham's faith is why he is the father of both the circumcised and the uncircumcised who believe (4:11–12). The universal language precludes any limitation.

Scholars have long grappled with the sudden, powerful reversal in Paul's argument in Romans 11:26 when he proclaims, "All Israel will be saved." Most Paul within Judaism interpreters affirm that the verse refers to a separate "covenant" availing to the Jews' salvation. The Jew may have resisted what God was doing for gentiles in Christ, but this is not an unforgiveable sin. Nevertheless, Paul expresses genuine anguish in 9:1–5 about his fellow Jews for their failure to recognize their own Messiah. He wishes himself to be "cursed" (ἀνάθεμα, *anathema*) and cut off from Christ (ἀπὸ τοῦ Χριστοῦ, *apo tou Christou*)—that is, to exchange places with them to bear their "curse" and being "cut off."[8] His people face a far more severe predicament than merely failing to recognize God's plan for gentiles in Christ.

7. Gager, *Reinventing Paul*, 124–25.
8. Heikki Räisänen writes, "Why the *deep sorrow* expressed by Paul in 9:1–2; 10:1? A lot of Paul's statements make little sense if it was not Israel's failure to *believe in Jesus as the Christ* that was his problem." Räisänen, "Paul, God, and Israel: Romans 9–11 in Recent Research," in

In preparing for Romans 11, Paul in 10:11 adds the word "everyone" to his quotation of Isaiah 28:16 (cf. Rom. 9:33) and is clear in 10:12–13 that there is no difference between Jews and gentiles with respect to salvation. Both have the same Lord (10:12), the Lord Jesus Christ (10:9).[9] "*All* Israel . . . saved" in Romans 11:26 hearkens to the repeated use of "all" in Romans 10:8–13 to explain that one is saved, whether Jew or gentile, by believing in Jesus Christ.[10] Romans 11 must not be divorced from the strong statements about God's plan in Christ for all people in the prior chapters, including especially Romans 10. The most natural understanding of the Jews' "disobedience" (Rom. 11:11–12, 19, 28a) and "unbelief" or "unfaithfulness" (ἀπιστία, *apistia* in 11:20–23) is with reference to the faith in Christ spoken of throughout the letter. Israel will be restored "if they do not persist in unbelief." "By the time one arrives at chapter 11, then, Paul has established a christocentric semantic range for the key vocabulary of this seemingly nonchristological discourse."[11]

Worship of the Jewish God is necessarily christocentric. Paul praises Christ as God in Romans 9:5.[12] High Christology is also clear in Philippians 2:6–11 as Paul applies to Christ, who is in the form of God and equal with God, the worship strictly limited to Yahweh in Isaiah 45:23.[13] As many have observed, in 1 Corinthians 8:6 the apostle redefines the Shema to include reference to Jesus Christ alongside God the Father.[14]

Rather than a "separate way," the gospel of Jesus Christ is the power of salvation to *all* who believe, whether *Jew* or gentile (Rom. 1:16). The other Pauline letters corroborate the one salvation in Jesus Christ. Paul grants the genuine glory of the Mosaic covenant (2 Cor. 3), but the old covenant condemned people to death. Only the new covenant in Jesus Christ offers life, not Moses.[15] When 2 Corinthians 3:13–14 discusses the hardening of the Israelites'

The Social World of Formative Christianity and Judaism: Essays in Tribute to Howard Clark Kee, ed. Jacob Neusner et al. (Philadelphia: Fortress, 1988), 178–206, here 190; see also 180.

9. On Paul's christological adaptation of Joel 2:32 (Heb. 3:5) here, see C. Kavin Rowe, "Romans 10:13: What Is the Name of the Lord?," *HBT* 22 (2000): 135–73.

10. "There is no question for Paul that Jews need Jesus as their savior as much as Gentiles do (10:13)." Günter Wasserberg, "Romans 9–11 and Jewish-Christian Dialogue," in *Reading Israel in Romans: Legitimacy and Plausibility of Divergent Interpretations*, ed. Cristina Grenholm and Daniel Patte, RHCS (Harrisburg, PA: Trinity Press International, 2000), 174–86, here 182.

11. Terence L. Donaldson, *Paul and the Gentiles: Remapping the Apostle's Convictional World* (Minneapolis: Fortress, 1997), 233.

12. See the evidence discussed in Das, *Paul and the Jews*, 84–85.

13. Das, *Paul and the Jews*, 85.

14. N. T. Wright, *Climax of the Covenant: Christ and the Law in Pauline Theology* (Minneapolis: Fortress, 1991), with chapters on Phil. 2:5–11 and 1 Cor. 8.

15. Sigurd Grindheim, "The Law Kills but the Gospel Gives Life: The Letter-Spirit Dualism in 2 Corinthians 3.5–18," *JSNT* 84 (2001): 97–115.

minds at the reading of the old covenant, the veil is removed only in Christ; "the Spirit gives life" (2 Cor. 3:6).

In Galatians 2:7 the apostles agree: Peter will take the gospel message to the circumcised, Paul to the uncircumcised.[16] In Galatians 3:10 the Mosaic law places its adherents under God's "curse," a powerfully negative predicament resolved only by Christ's suffering the curse on their behalf (Gal. 3:13). Abraham's Seed is thus not the collective Israel, as one would expect from Genesis, but rather Christ (3:15–18) and those "in Christ" (3:28–29).[17]

In Galatians 2:15–16 faith in/of Christ must be understood alongside the necessity for Jews to believe in Christ Jesus: "We ourselves are Jews by birth and not Gentile sinners; yet we know that a person is not justified by the works of the law but through [the faithfulness of Jesus Christ / faith in Jesus Christ]. And we [emphatic: "*even we* (Jews)"] have come to believe in Christ Jesus."[18] The meaning of the "faith(fulness) of Christ" cannot be limited to God's inclusion of gentiles. The two-covenant reading does not withstand scrutiny. Zetterholm's tentativeness with respect to the necessity of Jewish faith in Christ is unwarranted. Far from being a Reformation vestige, the emphasis on the salvation of both Jews and gentiles in Christ is *Paul's own*.

As Terence Donaldson stressed, the first Christians whom Paul the Jew persecuted were themselves *Jewish*. What, then, drew Paul's ire? Had they adopted a lax approach to Torah? In that case, Paul might have, before or after his conversion, encouraged a more rigorously law-observant form of Christianity (cf. Acts 21:20–21). No, in terms of salvation, the pre-Christian Paul had come to view faith in Christ in fundamental opposition to Torah observance. What rendered Jewish Christians distinct were their claims regarding Christ and their worship of him. The first Christians bestowed saving significance upon the person of Jesus Christ, but this belief would, if consistently applied, jeopardize the saving efficacy of the law for the Jewish people. If Paul viewed the law and Christ as mutually exclusive means of salvation prior to his conversion, as appears to be the case, then his position has remained consistent after his conversion. A zealot for the law would not easily abandon his zeal. He simply found himself face-to-face with the very One he had denied. Paul recognized that if the law was not God's instrument

---

16. Bradley H. McLean, "Galatians 2.7–9 and the Recognition of Paul's Apostolic Status at the Jerusalem Conference: A Critique of G. Luedemann's Solution," *NTS* 37 (1991): 67–76. Gager, *Reinventing Paul*, 147, distinguishes Peter's "gospel" from Paul's, but Gal. 2:7 employs "gospel" only once for what *both* Peter and Paul are proclaiming to their respective audiences.

17. Gager, *Reinventing Paul*, 88–89, incomprehensibly ignores this line of reasoning in the apostle's thought. Is there a degree of ironic truth in his book's title?

18. See the discussion of this verse in Das, *Galatians,* 237–57; Das, "The Ambiguous Common Ground of Galatians 2:16 Revisited," *BR* 58 (2013): 49–61.

of salvation, then the works it required, apart from Christ, were mere, empty human activities that could not merit God's favor.[19]

Recognizing the significance of Jesus Christ thus represented a reversal in Paul's valuation before Christ and after Christ of his Jewish heritage. In Galatians 1:13–14 Paul uses the term "Judaism" ('Ιουδαϊσμός, *Ioudaismos*) twice, which doubly emphasizes his affiliation. Although he recognizes his kinsfolk "according to the flesh" (cf. 1:14; 2:15), he speaks of "Judaism" in relation to his *former* life.

Formerly	Now
1:13: violently persecuting the *church* of God	1:22: still unknown by sight to the *churches* of Judea
1:13: you have *heard* of my earlier life	1:23: they only *heard* it said
1:13: *in* Judaism	1:22: *in* Christ
1:13: I was violently *persecuting*	1:23: the one who was formerly *persecuting* us
1:13: I was trying to *destroy* it	1:23: now proclaiming the faith he once tried to *destroy*

Source: Modified from Beverly R. Gaventa, "Galatians 1 and 2: Autobiography as Paradigm," *NovT* 28 (1986): 309–26, here 316.

"In Judaism" (1:13–14) stands in contrast to being, by faith, "in Christ" (ἐν Χριστῷ, *en Christō*) (1:22; cf. 2:4, 17; 3:14, 26, 28; 5:6, 10). A decisive social and religious reversal has taken place.[20] God's people are not saved by birth, ethnic identity, or Torah obedience. Jew and gentile are brought together in the assembly of God through the same faith in the Messiah Jesus. As Professor Zetterholm conceded, Paul "values [his Jewish identity] less than he does being 'in Christ'" (179).

19. Terence L. Donaldson, "Zealot and Convert: The Origin of Paul's Christ-Torah Antithesis," *CBQ* 51 (1989): 655–82, here 656, 662.

20. Ben Witherington III, *Grace in Galatia: A Commentary on Paul's Letter to the Galatians* (Grand Rapids: Eerdmans, 1998), 98; Markus Cromhout, "Paul's 'Former Conduct in the Judean Way of Life' (Gal 1:13) . . . or Not?," *HTSTS* 65 (2009): 1–12.

New Perspective
Response to Zetterholm

JAMES D. G. DUNN

I am very grateful for Magnus Zetterholm's essay, even though, sad to confess, his many footnotes brought home to me how much I am now behind the curve of the current debate. I was particularly impressed by his insistence on setting and seeing Paul "within Judaism." That must be right, at least to some extent, since there was no "Christianity" as such in Paul's day—though there were followers of Jesus, of course. But did these first followers see themselves as becoming members of a new religion, distinct from Judaism? And that is precisely the point in the recovery of a first-century perspective as distinct from a sixteenth-century perspective. The issue is precisely this: What is it in the inheritance from biblical Judaism that is fundamental also to emerging Christianity? And what was it in first-century Judaism to which Paul objected? The answer to the latter question has to be, as Paul saw it, in terms of the limitation of the grace of God to Jews, not simply to ethnic Jews as such but also to those who became Jews/proselytes. The great thing about Paul's theology on this point is that he was able to argue for the direct continuity from Israel's own experience of grace, Abraham providing the classic example, to his gospel for all, gentiles as well as Jews, and without requiring gentiles to become Jews.

It was this that was at the heart of the Antioch incident. One of my disappointments was that Magnus broadened out his discussion of "Paul within Judaism" so quickly from that crucial Galatians 2 context. Valuable as that discussion is, it is in danger of missing what Paul judged to be central to a correct understanding of the gospel. Here not least it is of crucial importance to read Paul's first great exposition of justification by faith (alone) in its context—Galatians 2 from the beginning and not just 2:16. Even to note the continuity in what Paul says from 2:15 should be enough to remind us that the Jew/gentile issue was at the heart of Paul's teaching on the point. It is fine when reflecting theologically about Galatians 2:16 to bring into the discussion the question of how the passage was understood later and the role it played in subsequent debate. But if we are concerned with historical exegesis, how the passage related to the issues of its time, then the primary question has to be how Paul intended the passage to be understood. And in that context I have to insist that this was Paul's first literary attempt (so far as we know) to argue that his gospel (for gentiles) was not simply an invitation for gentiles to become Jews. The gospel's effectiveness did *not* depend on gentiles becoming proselytes, and to insist in effect that it did was to undermine the crucial point for Paul that the decisive initial response to the gospel is faith, faith in the Christ proclaimed in the gospel, faith alone.

So "Paul within Judaism" is a potentially misleading title since the predominant self-understanding of Judaism that then prevailed was precisely what Paul called into question. That is the "Judaism" we are talking about in this context. And it was precisely because conversion to Judaism, as effectively demanded by Peter and the other senior Jewish believers, so undermined Paul's emphasis on faith alone that another term other than "Judaism" had to emerge as the crucial identity for believers in Jesus. Which is why "Christianity" (in this context = "not Judaism") had to emerge—a term that because of that distinction conveyed the message that what gentile believers in Jesus were converting to was not Judaism.

Of course, Paul was not abandoning or denying his Jewish heritage—not at all! Magnus refers to the view (which he attributes to most mainstream interpreters before Sanders) that "Paul ceased being a Jew when he became a 'Christian'" (171). This view of Paul is simply ridiculous. He was simply reminding his fellow believers, Jews as well as gentiles, that grace, grace through faith alone, was at the heart of Israel's own history and religion, as demonstrated not least by father Abraham. However important and distinctive of that history and religion were circumcision, food laws, and so on, they did not provide the heart of that religion. It is hard to define "within Judaism" without including observation of the law, the very thing that Paul's gospel called into question. So, however justified it is to describe Paul's gospel and theology as "within Judaism," at this precise point, on Paul's gospel for gentiles as expressed and explained in Galatians 2, Paul can surely *not* be described in that way. Paul's gospel and theology cannot be adequately understood other than within his Jewish heritage, but to characterize it as "within Judaism" is to call into question the very point on which he was ready to rebuke Barnabas and Peter at Antioch. So "Paul the Jew" and "Paul's Jewish heritage," *yes*! But "Paul within Judaism," *no*!

Gift Perspective
Response to Zetterholm

JOHN M. G. BARCLAY

Magnus Zetterholm sets out clearly "the two most fundamental assumptions underlying the Paul within Judaism Perspective: first, Paul's continuing Jewish identity, and second, his focus on non-Jews" (176). From one point of view, there is nothing contentious here. Almost everyone acknowledges that Paul considered himself a Jew or "Israelite" (Gal. 2:15; Rom. 11:1; 2 Cor. 11:22), and no one denies that he was always conscious of being called as an apostle to non-Jews. What matters, then, is what is packed into those assumptions, and what, in particular, they are understood to deny. I will take each in turn.

1. Like many in the Paul within Judaism coalition, Zetterholm sets up a binary opposition that is clear but, in my opinion, far too simplistic. On the one hand, there is what Zetterholm calls the "conflict paradigm," according to which Paul "broke" with Judaism, stood "in opposition to" Judaism, declared the Jewish law "null and void," and, in general, engaged in a "repudiation of Jewish traditions" and "contradicted common Jewish beliefs and behaviors, especially Torah observance" (173). On the other hand, as its polar opposite, there is the Paul within Judaism view that Paul was Jewish and thus Torah observant: Paul "emphasizes his Jewishness," which "means that he also *practiced* Judaism" (177); he was "faithful to his [Jewish] religious heritage" (184) and was "as Jewish" and "as Torah observant as any other Jew in the diaspora" (186). These two positions stand in straightforward opposition to one another, and it is the task of Paul within Judaism scholars to foster the

"intellectual process" of "gradually bringing Paul closer to contemporary Judaism," with "the endpoint" of this process being "of course, to place the apostle firmly, completely, and comfortably within Judaism" (175).

There are two reasons why I think this model is flawed. One concerns the difficulty of measuring any ancient Jew's stance on a scale of proximity to or distance from "Judaism." The other concerns the complexity of Paul, who defies categorization on the terms of Zetterholm's polarity.

On the binary model, in which one can plot someone's stance by relative proximity ("closer") to Judaism, and can hope to show that they are "firmly" "within" it, one must be able to measure proximity and to define the boundary that determines whether someone stands "within" or "outside" Judaism. But, as Zetterholm himself makes clear, these are not neutral, objective, or measurable phenomena, because judgments in this matter are (in his words) "to a large degree in the eye of the beholder" (181). In ancient Judaism, as today, there was considerable flexibility in the interpretation and application of the law. On many matters what one Jew considered loyalty to the law, another might consider its flagrant denial; what one person considered an appropriate expression of Judaism, another might consider apostasy.[1] On this principle, scholars cannot declare that Paul was "within Judaism" or "not within Judaism," as if this was a matter of clear, objectively determined evidence. Paul might have claimed himself to be within Judaism, but his opponents might have disagreed. Who was right? Or Paul might have claimed to have distanced himself from his "former life in Judaism," but we might still view him as within it. Who decides? Zetterholm himself seems unsure how far to push this principle of relativity. At one point he indicates that "it is quite problematic to speak of the Torah as constituting a fixed standard for almost anything" (186). (What is in that "almost"? Are there some exceptions, and if so, what are they?) At another (181), he quotes Sanders's claim that there existed "a standard by which loyalty to Israel and to the God of Israel was measured."[2] Was there a fixed standard, or was there not? Who fixed it, and how?

The process of bringing Paul "closer" to Judaism requires that one can measure what lies near and what lies far. Paul was a Jew who said, "Through the law I died to the law" (Gal. 2:19). Can that be plotted on a scale, and if so, where? He was an Israelite who said, "I know and am persuaded in the Lord

1. I have applied this principle (the relative judgment of deviance) to ancient Judaism and early Christianity in two essays ("Deviance and Apostasy" and "Who Was Considered an Apostate in the Jewish Diaspora?"), reprinted in my *Pauline Churches and Diaspora Jews*, WUNT 275 (Tübingen: Mohr Siebeck, 2001), 123–55.

2. E. P. Sanders, *Judaism: Practice and Belief, 63 BCE–66 CE* (London: SCM; Philadelphia: Trinity Press International, 1992), 47.

Jesus that nothing is unclean in itself" (Rom. 14:14). Is that comfortably within Judaism? I am not pressing here for a decision one way or another, because I do not think the matter is anything that simple. I am just asking for clarity as to what we mean by "within Judaism," and by what criteria we would determine (objectively?) where a Jew in antiquity stood in this regard. If the relativity to which Zetterholm points goes all the way down, it becomes meaningless for *us* to judge whether someone was or was not "within Judaism." If it does not, where do we find the objective criteria to measure this matter?

The second reason I consider the binary model of Paul within Judaism to be flawed is that Paul is too complex to be plotted along some scale from one polarity to another. Clearly Paul self-identified as a Jew, but as a Jew "in Christ," and that qualifier added complexity to his identity, defining his prior loyalty and his highest value as "being found in Christ" (Phil. 3:9).[3] This does not distance Paul from his Jewish heritage or empty his Jewishness of "religious" significance; but it relativizes and reorients his Jewish identity and behavior such that they are always subordinate to, and challengeable by, his ultimate loyalty to Christ. One cannot place this on a scale of "near" or "far": it is a matter of living out his calling in Christ such that he can observe the Torah *for Christ*, or disregard the Torah *for Christ*, depending on the higher demands of "the good news." I will give just three examples.

(A) In the Antioch dispute, whatever exactly was being practiced or not practiced, Paul commends Peter for living "in a gentile and not in a Jewish fashion" (ἐθνικῶς καὶ οὐχὶ Ἰουδαϊκῶς, *ethnikōs kai ouchi Ioudaikōs*) for the sake of "the truth of the good news" (Gal. 2:14). Whatever Peter was doing in eating with gentiles, Paul regarded it as "not Jewish," and he thought that Peter was right to adopt that policy. That chimes with what Paul says about not being justified "by works of the law" (i.e., Torah observance), and about himself (note: *himself as a Jew* [2:15]) having "died to the law in order to live to God" (2:19).[4] We need to discuss further why Paul could commend Jews for living "not in a Jewish fashion" while beholden to "the truth of the good news."

(B) In Philippians 3:2–11 the key issue is not Paul's rhetorical target (pagan or Jewish) but rather how he can classify his Jewish pride as pride "in the

---

3. Zetterholm cites Pamela Eisenbaum's claim to take Paul "as Jewish—period, that is, without qualifiers." Eisenbaum, "Paul, Polemics, and the Problem of Essentialism," *BibInt* 13 (2005): 28. This claim falls prey to an essentialism that is belied by the historical facts: there were many kinds of Jews in antiquity, and Paul's was one variant among many.

4. Romans 7:4–6 is equally clear on this point, where the "we" who have been "deactivated" from the law (7:6) includes both the "I" who speaks (7:1) and the "you" who are the audience to whom he speaks (7:4).

flesh" and why he can consider those tokens of his symbolic capital, along with all other tokens of worth, "rubbish" (σκύβαλα, *skybala*), in comparison with knowing Christ and being found in him. This need not mean that Paul "renounces" or "repudiates" his Jewish heritage, but neither does he simply affirm it. However Paul now values his Jewishness, it is not his *ultimate* value: he might consider Torah observance in many circumstances valuable in his service of Christ, but apparently it is valuable *only in that frame*. However "blameless" (3:6) he might be by the law's standard, his ultimate value is not righteousness in the terms of the law (3:9: "not having my own righteousness, derived from the law, but that which comes through faith in Christ"). We need to discuss further what is meant by this hierarchy of worth.

(C) Paul says elsewhere that he can live "under the law" in service of the good news, but he does not consider himself ultimately beholden to the law (μὴ ὢν αὐτὸς ὑπὸ νόμον, *mē ōn autos hypo nomon*) because his highest loyalty is to Christ (ἔννομος Χριστοῦ, *ennomos Chistou*) (1 Cor. 9:20–21). Paul and other Jews should remain circumcised, on the principle that everyone, by preference, should remain in the state in which they were called (1 Cor. 7:17–24). Torah observance can, indeed, be a way to serve the Lord (Rom. 14:5–9), and it is "religiously significant" within that frame. But since Paul has rethought his own identity (as well as that of his gentile converts) in the wake of the Christ-gift, everything is now reoriented by the spread of "the good news" (1 Cor. 9:22–23). We need to discuss this text further.

One can no more say of Paul that he is "for" or "against" Torah observance than one can say of a Stoic that he is "for" or "against" health. For a Stoic, if good health serves the purposes of the good, by all means embrace it: if the good can be served only by forfeiting one's health (or life), health must be subordinated to the good. Until we are able to analyze Paul with the sort of subtlety evident in his letters, and familiar to ancient thought about value, worth, and the *telos* of life, we will remain stuck in false antitheses and sterile debates.[5]

2. What about Zetterholm's second fundamental assumption, that Paul's focus was on non-Jews. We can all agree that Paul was called as an apostle to the gentiles; the question is whether he also talks about the situation of Jews in the wake of the coming of Christ. I agree with Zetterholm that the question of Paul's *audience* is largely irrelevant to this question: the issue is what

---

5. I am puzzled by Zetterholm's use of Acts in supporting his thesis. We should surely first discuss Luke's agenda and why he might present Paul as he does. From a historical perspective, that a Christian apologist from the first century, with an evident agenda, should still exercise influence on the modern scholarly discussion of Paul is a sign of how much we are all beholden, one way or another, to the history of reception of Paul.

Paul is *talking about*, not whom he is *talking to*.[6] Zetterholm acknowledges that Paul does not talk *exclusively* about non-Jews, but he raises the stakes high with this claim: "If Paul's gospel concerns the whole of humanity, this [Paul within Judaism] perspective is simply incorrect" (187).

So does Paul's gospel concern the whole of humanity? Let us hear him speak on this matter (my translations): "For I am not ashamed of the good news, for it is the power of God for salvation for everyone who believes, for both the Jew first and the Greek" (Rom. 1:16); "for we have charged already that both Jews and Greeks—all—are under sin" (Rom. 3:9); "for all have sinned and fall short of the glory of God, being justified, as a gift, by his grace, through the redemption which is in Christ Jesus" (Rom. 3:23–24); "for there is no distinction between Jew and Greek; for the same Lord is Lord of all, who is rich towards all who call upon him" (Rom. 10:12); "for God has shut up all people into disobedience, in order that he might have mercy on all" (Rom. 11:32); "we preach Christ crucified, to the Jews a stumbling-block, to the gentiles foolishness" (1 Cor. 1:23). It is, I think, incontestable, that when Paul says "Jews and Greeks" or "Jews and gentiles," he means all people. He clearly regards the gospel as applicable to the whole of humanity. We may accept Zetterholm's invitation and draw the necessary conclusion concerning the correctness of the Paul within Judaism Perspective.

Of course, we must then add some nuance. Paul knows that the gospel is being preached both to non-Jews and to Jews. He (and Barnabas) is entrusted with the gentile mission; Cephas and others are given the mission to Jews—of which he wholeheartedly approved (Gal. 2:6–9). Paul hopes that even his mission to gentiles will rebound on Jews, that he might somehow provoke them to jealousy and "save some of them" (Rom. 11:14). As Zetterholm says, it is not likely that Paul considered the salvation of Israel to be unconnected to Israel's own Messiah. The references in Romans 11 to the current "unbelief" of some (which can only mean unbelief in Christ) (11:20) and Paul's hope for "the Redeemer from Zion" (11:26) make me wonder why Zetterholm considers Paul unclear on this matter. If Christ (the Messiah) was "the servant of the circumcision" (Rom. 15:8), their destiny is clearly bound up with his.

Let me be clear: Israel never loses its special status for Paul. Although both Jews and non-Jews are under sin and in need of rescue, the calling and the gifts of God to Israel are irrevocable (Rom. 11:29), and Paul is confident that God will find a way to save "all Israel."[7] It is for this reason that Paul cares

6. I take Zetterholm here to distance himself somewhat from the work of Matthew Thiessen, notably his *Paul and the Gentile Problem* (Oxford: Oxford University Press, 2016).
7. For my reading of Romans 9–11, see my *Paul and the Gift* (Grand Rapids: Eerdmans, 2015), 520–61.

so much, and grieves so much, about Israel's present unbelief (Rom. 9:1–3; 10:1): Israel is precisely the people who should be responding to the definitive expression of the divine mercy by which Israel first came into being and is perpetually sustained. The fact that Paul is an Israelite remains hugely significant for him "religiously" (Rom. 11:1–2), and it is precisely for this reason that, although he is an apostle to the gentiles, he cannot ignore what God is doing and will do for Israel. To suggest that Paul focused only, or predominantly, on non-Jews is, in fact, to play down *how theologically significant* his Jewish identity was for him. One would expect a Paul within Judaism Perspective to show, in fact, how essential it was for Paul to think through all of history, including his mission to the gentiles, from the perspective of the centrality of Israel to God's dealings with the world. Paul could not make sense of God, of his Scriptures, of the Christ-event, of his own experience, and of his mission without placing God's purposes for Israel at the center of each strand of his thought. That is why Romans 9–11 matters so much for the argument of Romans. There seems, indeed, something oddly gentile in a perspective on Paul that makes this aspect of his theology of such limited significance—to Paul the Jew!

Paul within Judaism Perspective
Reply to the Respondents

MAGNUS ZETTERHOLM

Critical discussions drive scholarship forward; so first of all, I would like to express my sincere gratitude to my colleagues for their stimulating and insightful comments on my view of Paul. Most, if not all, perspectives on Paul have their weaknesses, and it is only in dialogue with those who disagree that these things come to the fore. Points have indeed been made—but differences will remain.

For instance, it could be that James Dunn is correct in his reading of the so-called Antioch incident, but I tend to believe that he is not, which only has to do with, again, assumptions. Let us start with what we agree on. Dunn is undeniably right in stating that the Jew/gentile issue was Paul's main focus, and, of course, Paul vehemently opposed conversions to Judaism. I also agree that Paul made use of traditions already prevalent in Judaism. As mentioned elsewhere in this volume, there seems to have existed a fairly widespread, but multifaceted, universalistic tendency within first-century Judaism. Thus, Paul was not unique in arguing for a place for the non-Jew in the Jewish economy of salvation. What created tensions within the Jesus movement was less of a grand theological dispute involving the role of the Torah in a Jewish setting, but rather practical questions: how to relate to non-Jews in Christ on an everyday basis. This, I believe, is what the Antioch incident was really about: Can members of the nations be trusted, can they be considered holy and pure, or do they have to become Jews in order to socialize with Jews on equal terms

216

(because of purity concerns)? Paul's position was indeed the result of a grand theological (Jewish) idea, but the clash at Antioch initially involved practicalities. Nothing in this prevents us from placing Paul firmly *within Judaism*.

John Barclay calls for more objectivity with regard to defining Paul's Jewishness. I so wish I could help him with that, but this would require the discovery of several more authentic Pauline letters. Barclay certainly puts his finger on a problematic issue: How can we know anything about Paul's degree of practicing Judaism and thus place him within or outside Judaism? But even as I fully agree with Barclay in his critique, I also think he somewhat misses the point. It is not as though Paul was discovered yesterday, but all Pauline scholars have to relate to a two-thousand-year-long interpretative tradition, which mainly has defined Paul as outside Judaism. An hour spent with some of the standard commentaries would confirm this. The goal of placing Paul within Judaism is not to figure out precisely how he practiced Judaism, which is a lost cause from the very beginning; rather, the goal is to use a "within" perspective as a heuristic tool in order to see if it is possible to make sense of the pagans' apostle, *assuming* that he did not break with Judaism. As Barclay, interestingly enough, also aims at positioning Paul *within Judaism*, I cannot see that there is an abyss of disagreement between us.

Andrew Das offers a wide range of examples that are meant to undermine the Paul within Judaism Perspective. He is right, of course, in stating that not all possible readings are equally plausible, but plausibility is a tricky thing to determine in Pauline studies. Again, it depends on the fundamental assumptions. As I have pointed out several times in this volume, I find it implausible that the suppositions used in traditional Pauline scholarship are helpful. For example, Das states, "Ultimately, one must ask what *weight* Paul gives being 'in Christ' versus 'in Judaism.'" To me, it seems that there is no contradiction here. Being "in Christ" and being "in Judaism" are not opposites but different sides of the same coin. The idea of a messianic figure is, of course, a Jewish invention, and belief in such a figure was in antiquity fully compatible with being "in Judaism," regardless of whether a person considered other (former) ways of being Jewish less important in relation to being messianic. It is only when we apply the traditional dichotomy between Judaism and Christianity that "belief in Christ" and "being Jewish" appear incongruous, although the recent reemergence of messianic Judaism perhaps will change that.

I am, of course, happy to notice that Brant Pitre considers the Paul within Judaism Perspective "one of the most significant developments in Pauline scholarship in recent years" (194). I tend to agree. However, Pitre is having problems with the idea that Paul's mission is exclusively focused on the salvation of gentiles. Since John Barclay also found this problematic, it may be worthwhile to clarify. This perspective, too, has to be understood in relation to previous (traditional) scholarship according to which Paul aimed at creating a third race of sorts, "the Christians," meaning that Jews had given up Torah observance and Jewish identity markers, such as circumcision and dietary customs. In reality, Paul upholds the ethnic differences between Jews and members of the nations: Jews observe the Torah as they did before becoming followers of Christ, and non-Jews should refrain from such Torah observance while adopting a lifestyle suitable for ex-pagan gentiles (to borrow Paula Fredriksen's terminology). Still, both groups belong together: they are one in Christ. However, Paul's *main problem* is how to bring non-Jews into a covenantal relationship with the god of Israel, without them becoming Jews or observing the Torah (as Jews did). This mission to the nations is indeed part of the magnificent apocalyptic drama that eventually will culminate in the salvation of the whole world—Israel and the nations. Thus, Paul is by all means concerned with the salvation of Jews since the salvation of both groups is deeply interconnected, while at the same time he seems convinced that the fate of the Jewish people is in the hands of God, who has not rejected his people (Rom. 11:1). Their present unbelief is actually part of the divine plan to bring the world to its final consummation, which will take place through God's messianic instrument: Christ. There is no salvation for humankind except through Christ, but the roads leading to him are not identical.

5

The Gift Perspective on Paul

JOHN M. G. BARCLAY

The "Gift Perspective" on Paul derives its name—coined for this volume!—from analyses of Paul's theology that take as their starting point his theology of gift or grace. The basis of this perspective is exegesis, tracing the ways in which Paul's language of gift and the incongruity of the Christ-gift shape Paul's soteriology, his scriptural hermeneutics, his ecclesiology, his ethics, and much else besides. It is founded on historical and anthropological analysis of the social operations of gift (broadly defined), and it has come to expression not only in my book *Paul and the Gift* but also in a number of recent explorations of Pauline theology, by Jonathan Linebaugh, Orrey McFarland, Kyle Wells, Susan Eastman, Stephen Chester, and others.[1] These form a loose constellation of viewpoints rather than a well-defined "school," and I write

---

1. John M. G. Barclay, *Paul and the Gift* (Grand Rapids: Eerdmans, 2015); Jonathan A. Linebaugh, *God, Grace, and Righteousness in Wisdom of Solomon and Paul's Letter to the Romans: Texts in Conversation*, NovTSup 152 (Leiden: Brill, 2013); Orrey McFarland, *God and Grace in Philo and Paul*, NovTSup 164 (Leiden: Brill, 2015); Kyle B. Wells, *Grace and Agency in Paul and Second Temple Judaism: Interpreting the Transformation of the Heart*, NovTSup 157 (Leiden: Brill, 2014); Susan Grove Eastman, *Paul and the Person: Reframing Paul's Anthropology* (Grand Rapids: Eerdmans, 2017); Stephen Chester, *Reading Paul with the Reformers: Reconciling Old and New Perspectives* (Grand Rapids: Eerdmans, 2017). There are some points of affinity (alongside differences of emphasis) with so-called apocalyptic readings of Paul, notably those by J. Louis Martyn, Martinus de Boer, and Beverly Roberts Gaventa.

here on behalf of myself rather than these others. But they are bound together in at least five respects: (1) they are particularly drawn toward Paul's theology of gift/grace, as the shape or pattern of the whole of Pauline theology; (2) they seek to position Paul within Judaism in a way that goes beyond Sanders's *Paul and Palestinian Judaism*, while building on Sanders's determination to refute Christian caricatures of ancient or modern Judaism; (3) they draw on elements of the "New Perspective" on Paul, but offer readings of Paul beyond the standoff between "Old" and "New" Perspectives, and attempt to repair the weaknesses in each; (4) while retaining an independent, critical stance, they are sensitive to the history of reception of Paul, which, from Ephesians and the Pastoral Epistles onwards, has been especially attuned to Paul's theology of grace; (5) they are alert to the contemporary implications of Paul's theology and are not averse to making Paul's voice audible in social, political, and ecclesial domains.

It is important to be clear at the outset that the "Gift Perspective" operates at two levels in respect to the notion of gift. At one level, it traces the multiple vocabularies of gift, which are threaded through Paul's theology and ethics, and are closely linked to contiguous lexemes (e.g., mercy and love). But at another level, it traces in Paul's theology the structuring role of the Christ-event *as an incongruous gift*, a patterning sometimes signaled by gift-language (e.g., χάρις, *charis*), but sometimes not. Let me clarify these two levels before we proceed.

1. *Gift as a semantic domain.* It would be hard to ignore how often, and in what strategic roles, Paul uses the language of gift, sometimes through the term χάρις (*charis*) and its cognates, sometimes through variants of the verb δίδωμι (*didōmi*) and its cognate nouns. Just as his calling and the calling of his converts came about through the χάρις of God (Gal. 1:6, 15; 1 Cor. 1:4; 15:10), so he celebrates the enrichment of his churches in every gift (1 Cor. 1:5–7) and warns them not to reject the grace/favor of God (Gal. 2:21; 5:4). The whole Christ-event can be summarized as the advent of God's gift (Rom. 5:15–21, with multiple gift-terms), or as the self-giving of Christ (Gal. 2:20): "you know the χάρις of our Lord Jesus Christ" (2 Cor. 8:9), the inexpressible gift (δωρεά, *dōrea*) of God (2 Cor. 9:15). The generosity that binds believers together, even across distances, is similarly understood in gift-terms (2 Cor. 8–9; Phil. 4:10–20), since it is the gifts of the Spirit that constitute the body of Christ (1 Cor. 12:12–31; Rom. 12:3–8). This vocabulary of gift often overlaps with other core Pauline terminology, such as "love" (Gal. 2:20), "mercy" (Rom. 11:28–32), "promise" (Gal. 3:18), "calling" (Gal. 1:6), and "election" (Rom. 11:5–6), such that an analysis of the gift-language in Paul opens up to a study of the core features of his soteriology.

2. *Incongruous gift as a structuring grammar.*[2] As we will see, what is most distinctive about Paul's theology of gift is that it is chiefly identified with the Christ-event and is "perfected" (see below) as an incongruous, or unconditioned, gift—a gift that operates without regard to worth and in the absence of worth, that creates out of nothing or out of its opposite. The shape of this gift—life from death, strength in weakness, the justification of the ungodly, the reconciliation of enemies—patterns Paul's use of soteriological metaphors and structures the way he reads the Scriptures and narrates the stories regarding himself, his converts, Israel, and the cosmos. Sometimes this incongruity is signaled by the use of the term χάρις (e.g., Gal. 2:19–21; 2 Cor. 12:9–10; Rom. 3:24; 4:5–6; 11:5–6), and sometimes not (e.g., Rom. 5:6–11). But even where gift-lexemes are absent, Paul's theology is shaped by the incongruities of resurrection out of death, wisdom in folly, mercy on the disobedient, power in weakness—all of which are manifestations of the grace by which God's life-giving righteousness is at work amid sin and death (Rom. 5:12–21). As we will see, the incongruity of grace gives rise to much of the creativity in Paul's theology, and to his frequent use of antithesis and paradox. Thus, the "Gift Perspective" is concerned not just to follow a single thread in Paul's theology, or to trace only one of its many motifs, but rather to disclose the patterns that give to the whole of Paul's theology its highly distinctive shape.

What Do We Mean by "Gift"?

It is no surprise that Paul so frequently employs the language of gift, since gifts were a constituent element of ancient society right across the social scale, and often they were used as metaphors for divine activity, both in Jewish and in non-Jewish traditions. Indeed, one could fairly claim to be able to trace the structure of a society by its practices and ideologies of gift, and as anthropology since Marcel Mauss has shown, gifts tie societies together, but in culturally specific ways that change over time.[3] Thus we should not assume that gifts mean the same things, or operate in the same ways in different cultures and across different time periods, and we should be careful not to retroject onto antiquity the specific ways in which gifts have evolved, in practice and

---

2. For the notion of the "grammar" of Pauline theology, see Jonathan A. Linebaugh, "The Grammar of the Gospel: Justification as a Theological Criterion in the Reformation and in Galatians," *SJT* 71 (2018): 287–307.

3. Marcel Mauss, *The Gift: The Form and Reason for Exchange in Archaic Societies*, trans. W. D. Halls (London: Routledge, 1990); originally published as *Essai sur le don: Forme et raison de l'échange dans les sociétés archaïques* (1925); see further Barclay, *Paul and the Gift*, 11–65.

conceptuality, in the modern West. In this respect, even dictionary definitions of "gift" are hazardous, since they are bound to reflect the assumptions and practices of their time.

Taking together the evidence of Greco-Roman antiquity (which includes, for these purposes, Judaism as well), we may say that gift "denotes the sphere of voluntary, personal relations, characterized by goodwill in the giving of the benefit or favor, and eliciting some form of reciprocal return that is both voluntary and necessary for the continuation of the relationship."[4] Working by this definition, we note that gifts are distinct from wages, from market-place transactions, and from legally contracted loans, even if there might be some overlap in practice (e.g., favorable terms in a loan between friends). Neither gifts nor the expected returns can be compelled (by law or force) without ceasing to be gifts, but they do carry expectations of reciprocity and usually are surrounded by moral sanctions (e.g., social disapproval of the ungrateful recipient). Gifts can operate in both equal and unequal rela-tionships, both among the poor (e.g., food and services exchanged by those living at subsistence level) and between the powerful and their clients (e.g., public benefactions to citizens). But even in the latter case, some "return" is expected—not in material terms, but in honor or public praise. In fact, the circulation of benefits and counterbenefits was generally regarded as the glue that kept ancient societies together, both at microlevels and at the level of the state.

Such are the normal practices of gift. But it was also possible to develop practices or ideologies of gift to an extreme, to draw them out to an end-of-the-line absolute—in other words, to "perfect" them in one respect or another.[5] This was not infrequently the case, in antiquity as today, in relation to the giving of God, which is often presumed to be perfect in one respect or another. It is important to note, however, that gifts can be perfected in more than one way, and that these do not constitute a "package." One can identify, for instance, among the possible perfections of gift at least the following six:

1. *Superabundance*: the supreme scale, lavishness, or permanence of the gift

2. *Priority*: the timing of the gift, before the initiative of the recipient

3. *Singularity*: the giver's attitude marked solely by benevolence (not mixed with judgment or anger)

4. *Efficacy*: the impact of the gift, achieving what it was designed to do

4. Barclay, *Paul and the Gift*, 575.
5. For the notion of "perfections" of gift, see Barclay, *Paul and the Gift*, 66–78.

5. *Incongruity*: the distribution of the gift without regard to the worth of the recipient

6. *Noncircularity*: the escape of the gift from an ongoing cycle of reciprocity

Since these six possible perfections are independent of one another, a gift may be superabundant but not incongruous; that is, it might be lavish but nonetheless given with regard to the proper worth of the recipient. Alternatively, it may be prior but not efficacious; that is, it may be given first but still require a lot of effort on the part of the recipient to achieve its purpose. Most importantly for our purposes, a gift may be incongruous (given without regard to worth) but not noncircular: that is, it may be a "pure gift" in the sense of being unconditioned, but not in the sense that it carries no expectations and has "no strings attached." Of course, these perfections may be combined in various forms, and the history of reception shows the different ways in which Paul's language of grace has been perfected, from Marcion's emphasis on singularity (God is benevolent, and only benevolent, exercising no punishment) to modern forms of "cheap grace" (that carries no expectations or costs).[6] In fact, phrases like "pure gift," "sheer grace," and "by grace alone" require careful scrutiny to identify which, if any, of these perfections are being applied. By disaggregating them, we get a better sense of what is being claimed and contested, and it becomes clear that many theological disputes on this topic result not from greater or less emphasis on grace but from different perfections. That is important for understanding the history of interpretation of Paul but also, as we will now see, for appreciating how Paul stands within Second Temple Judaism.

Paul, Sanders, and Second Temple Judaism

According to a long-standing tradition of Christian interpretation, foregrounded in Lutheran readings of Paul, the grace of God in Christ can be contrasted with the religious character of Judaism (or at least the Judaism of the New Testament era): the latter, as a religion of "works" and thus of self-achieved salvation, knows nothing of grace (properly conceived) as gift to the undeserving. Sanders's achievement was to overturn this caricature, and his landmark *Paul and Palestinian Judaism* represented ancient Judaism as a "religion of grace" in the form of "covenantal nomism." Sanders analyzed the

6. See Barclay, *Paul and the Gift*, 79–188. In many popular theologies God is configured as a kind of Santa Claus who gives gifts in accordance with desert but expects nothing in return. As we will see, Paul's God is the exact inverse of this image.

structure of religion as a matter of sequence (first "getting in," then "staying in"), and put emphasis on the gift of the covenant as the foundation of Israel's law observance in (nearly) all the Second Temple texts he examined. Such texts, he insisted, were always clear on the *priority* of grace. However, as we have just noted, priority is only one of the possible perfections of grace, and this still tells us nothing about, for instance, whether God's grace is given to the deserving or the undeserving. Sanders assumed that if it was grace, it was given to the undeserving, but he noted that some texts that speak of grace nonetheless emphasize the fit between the gift and the worth of the recipient. He concludes that these were just unsystematic or unclear, but this awkwardness exposes a difficulty.[7] Is there a hidden assumption that any grace worth its salt must be incongruous? And is that assumption correct? In fact, there are plenty of reasons why one might *not* want to perfect grace in this form. If God gives salvation indiscriminately and without regard to worth, would that not flout justice? Surely we can expect God to uphold the moral order of the cosmos and to give gifts lavishly but discriminately to those who, by one criterion or another, are fit and worthy to receive them!

If we are conscious of the different ways in which grace can be perfected, closer scrutiny of Second Temple Jewish texts reveals, in fact, a diversity of views on this matter, and vigorous debate. The grace or mercy of God can be located in various forms (in creation, in the history of Israel, in the salvation of members of a sect), but it can also be perfected in diverse ways, as prior, as singular, as incongruous, and so on.[8] In 4 Ezra we find a fascinating debate between Uriel's hard-line, justice-oriented conviction that, at the end of the day, there can be no mercy on the undeserving and Ezra's pleas for a grace that supersedes justice and worth. Grace, in other words, is not a simple or singular concept, and if Judaism, like Christianity, is "a religion of grace," that says too little about the variety of ways in which this motif can be interpreted and applied. Grace is everywhere in Second Temple Judaism, but not everywhere the same. At this crucial point Sanders's "covenantal nomism" has offered a homogenized version of Jewish theology, without the analytical clarity necessary to see its inner diversity. Since most representatives of the "New Perspective" have assumed Sanders's work, and have taken it for granted that on the subject of grace Paul does not differ from any of his fellow Jews, they have built on a shaky foundation.

7. For more detailed analysis, see Barclay, *Paul and the Gift*, 151–58.

8. See in Barclay, *Paul and the Gift*, 194–328, the discussion of five representative texts/corpora: Wisdom of Solomon, Philo of Alexandria, the Qumran Hodayot, Pseudo-Philo's *Liber antiquitatum biblicarum*, 4 Ezra. For discussion of the first two in much greater detail, see Linebaugh, *God, Grace, and Righteousness*; McFarland, *God and Grace*.

If grace is a multifaceted concept, capable of perfection in a variety of ways, the question is not whether Paul and his fellow Jews "believed in" grace, but rather what they took it to mean. And when we start to see the diversity of views within Second Temple Judaism, Paul emerges as not just *the same as* all his fellow Jews on this matter, nor as standing alone *in contrast to* them all: he agreed with some on the incongruity of divine grace and disagreed with others.[9] In other words, Paul stands *within the diversity of Second Temple Judaism*. Paul was not alone in thinking that God's grace had been manifested in a form that was incongruous with the worth of its recipients: some fellow Jews thought that to be both possible and real, but not all. What makes Paul distinctive is not that he believed in grace, or even that he thought that God's grace could be unconditioned, but that he identified the Christ-event as the definitive, ultimate, incongruous gift, and expressed that conviction in a radical mission to non-Jews. Paul was not alone in perfecting the incongruity of grace; we should not lift him out as unique in that respect. But not all Jews would have welcomed that configuration of grace, and this emphasis could challenge some other understandings of the Jewish tradition. What is more, this incongruity, effected in the Christ-gift, emerges as the hallmark of Paul's theology, as we will now begin to trace.

The Incongruous Gift and the Gentile Mission

Paul's Letter to the Galatians helps us see most clearly how the gift of God in Christ shaped his theology and practice.[10] Here he perceives "the truth of the good news" to be at stake (Gal. 2:5, 14), and he sums this up in the phrase "the grace of God" (2:21; cf. 5:4). The contrary opinion (the "other gospel") that Paul faced in Galatia also believed that God was fulfilling his promises to Abraham in the blessing of all the nations. The issue was not whether there should be a gentile mission but rather the terms on which it should take place. Paul's opponents probably believed, like him, that Christ was the Messiah, sent to redeem the world; but they saw no reason to doubt that gentiles who believed in Christ should "Judaize" (2:14) by adopting the customs and traditions of the Jewish people. If they were children of Abraham, why should they not adopt the mark of the Abrahamic covenant in male circumcision? If they were blessed with the Spirit, why should the Spirit not lead them to observe the law, given through Moses to the people of God?

---

9. Compare the triangulation of Paul's interpretations of Scripture with those of various Second Temple texts in Francis Watson, *Paul and the Hermeneutics of Faith* (London: T&T Clark, 2004).

10. For further detail, see Barclay, *Paul and the Gift*, 331–446.

Paul rules these options out of court: if you take on circumcision, and thereby the whole law, you have fallen from grace (5:4); if you are led by the Spirit, you are not under the law (5:18). Why so? What is the logic in Paul's exclusions? The Letter to the Galatians is full of antitheses: slavery or freedom (2:4; 4:21–31), justification through faith in Christ or through works of the law (2:16; 3:2–5), curse or blessing (3:10–14), the present evil age or the new creation (1:4; 6:15), pleasing humans or pleasing God (1:10–11). How should we align and interpret these antithetical formulations? In what sense, and for what reason, has the Christ-event created these antithetical options?

The best answer lies in the way that the Christ-event is interpreted as an unconditioned gift. The good news concerns the Christ who "gave himself for our sins" (1:4), "the Son of God who loved me and gave himself for me" (2:20). To adopt the "other gospel" would be to reject the grace of God (2:21), to become disengaged from Christ and to fall from grace (5:4). Paul's converts have been called "in grace" (1:6), as was Paul himself in his calling before he was even born (1:15–16). Paul's retelling of his life history gives us a sense of the radical effects of this grace. In 1:13–17 he outlines his "advance" in Judaism, his faithful allegiance to the traditions of his ancestors, and his exceptional zeal, including his persecution of the church of God (cf. Phil. 3:4–6). Despite all this positive symbolic capital within the traditions of Judaism, it was not because of this worth that he was chosen and called, for that, he says, took place before he was born; and despite what he now realizes was his terrible mistake (persecuting "the church of God"), he was not beyond the reach of God's grace. Whichever way you looked at it—whether his positive or his negative worth—there was nothing in his life that made him a fitting recipient of the grace of God. The same unnerving truth applies to his gentile converts: despite their "inferior" ethnicity, their sinful background (2:15), and their idolatrous ignorance of God (4:8–9), they too have been "called in grace" (1:6), before and without circumcision, before adopting Jewish practices ("works of the law"), before "Judaizing" in any sense.

The grace that has reached gentiles in Christ, and was experienced in the gift and power of the Spirit (3:1–5), was given without regard for any previous criteria of worth: in Christ there is neither Jew nor Greek, neither slave nor free, no male and female (3:28). These previous marks of identity and status are not erased, but they are no longer what counts, what gives value: "In Christ neither circumcision counts for anything, nor uncircumcision, but faith working through love" (5:6). What has remapped reality and recalibrated all systems of worth is an event, the Christ-event, which is given and received as an incongruous gift. It "belongs" to no one and therefore goes to all, gentile as well as Jew. It does not accord with human norms (1:11) and therefore subverts preconstituted criteria of worth. As a result of this grace, there is a "good news of the uncircumcision" as well as a "good news of the circumcision" (2:8–10), because both the mark of Jewish specialness (circumcision) and a symbol of Greek pride (the "unmutilated" male body) are relativized by a gift that is the only thing of ultimate value. If Peter requires gentile believers to live in accordance with Jewish meal regulations, he is repackaging this gift within the criteria of a particular identity ("forcing them to Judaize" [2:14]) and thus rendering the unconditioned gift conditioned. That would be to walk out of line with "the truth of the good news" (2:14), which stands or falls on its announcement of the incongruous gift of God in Christ (2:21).

Paul's discussion of "justification by faith, not by works of the law" follows the account of the Antioch dispute (2:11–14) and builds upon it (2:15–21). What Peter and Paul agree upon (despite Peter's "hypocritical" behavior at Antioch) is that God justifies (i.e., considers to be "in the right") those who trust in Christ. Despite arguments to the contrary, I continue to interpret πίστις Χριστοῦ (*pistis Christou*) in 2:16 and elsewhere as meaning "trust in Christ."[11] What this trust represents is a declaration of bankruptcy and a recognition that the only source of worth, but the worth that counts for everything, is the death and resurrection of Christ, in which the believer is reconstituted and remade (2:19–20; 6:15). This gift is not conditioned by previous criteria of worth, ethnic, social, or moral: it starts, as it were, *de novo* (as "new creation" [6:15]), and this radicality extends even to the law. Jewish practices (the "works of the law") are by no means wrong or misguided, but they are not the criteria of worth in the Christ-economy. A person is not reckoned "in the right" before God on that ground, and in this sense Paul, as a representative Jewish believer, has "died to the law" (2:19); it is no longer what gives him his worth, and no longer the ultimate criterion of right and wrong. Like a Stoic "indistinguishable" (*adiaphoron*), it is inherent neither to the good nor to evil; in some circumstances, law observance might be the preferred practice, and in other circumstances not (cf. 1 Cor. 9:19–23), because the sole and ultimate criterion of good is to live in and for Christ (2:19–20). It is by this "canon" (6:15) that all the normal criteria have been brought into question ("The world has been crucified to me, and I to the world" [6:14]).

As we can now see, the incongruous gift matches the shape of the death-and-resurrection of Christ (2:20–21). The incongruity subverts the expected criteria of fit between the beneficence of God and the worth of the recipient,

---

11. See Barclay, *Paul and the Gift*, 378–84, though I would now prefer the term "trust" to "faith." See Teresa Morgan, *Roman Faith and Christian Faith: Pistis and Fides in the Early Roman Empire and Early Churches* (Oxford: Oxford University Press, 2015).

just as there emerges from the gift and the life of Christ the death of the old self and the emergence of a new. This disjunction explains why Paul describes the patterns of salvation in Galatians in such unusual forms. The promises to Abraham indicate God's long-held plans for the blessing of the nations through the Abrahamic "seed" and in the gift of the Spirit (3:6–16), but there is no linear progression in Israel's history. All things were "under sin," and even the law was unable to provide life (3:21–22): the Christ-event represents not the climax of a human progression but the redemption of slaves and their adoption as children (4:1–7). What happens in Christ is the birth of the impossible (like Isaac from the barrenness of Sarah [4:21–31]), the arrival of the miracle-working Spirit (3:2–5), the formation of a new regime (Spirit, not flesh), and the emergence of a new community who march in a different direction (5:25). We will return below to the ethical and social implications of this "new creation," but already we can sense that what patterns Paul's theology is not just the language of "grace" but the structure of an incongruous gift that gives a distinctive shape to the way Paul configures his soteriology and its constitutive metaphors.

The Grammar of Incongruity

As I noted in the introduction, the "Gift Perspective" is focused not just on the vocabularies of gift (Paul's use of terms from the semantic domain of "gift"), but also on the distinctive patterns of incongruity that shape the way Paul speaks about salvation. The shape we find there might also be called the "grammar" of Pauline language—the structuring rules by which the terms, phrases, and metaphors are combined to create theological sense. Sometimes these shapes are associated with χάρις (*charis*) or other gift-language, but not always; what matters is less the vocabulary than the common pattern of Pauline soteriology.

It is characteristic of Paul, for instance, that salvation is marked by death and resurrection—patterned after the crucifixion and resurrection of Jesus. The Pauline "I" does not progress or evolve into an enhanced state in Christ: it is "crucified" (Gal. 2:19; 5:24; 6:14) and brought to nothing in the death of Christ (Rom. 6:3–6; 7:4–6), so that it may be refounded and remade in resurrection life from the dead. Paul associates this radical transition with grace (Gal. 2:19–21; Rom. 5:12–21; 6:14), but it is stamped all over his theology even where this particular term does not occur. In Romans 6 he interprets baptism as "co-crucifixion" with Christ (6:6) such that the "newness of life" that believers enjoy is possible only through the resurrection of Christ. The whole of Christian existence is "carrying in the body the death of Jesus, so that the life of Jesus may also be made visible in our bodies" (2 Cor. 4:10; cf. 4:15 for the link with χάρις). Accordingly, the Christian faith that Paul sees adumbrated by Abraham is described as faith in the God "who gives life to the dead and calls into existence the things that do not exist" (Rom. 4:17). Life in Christ is a "new creation," marked by the passing away of the old, not by its improvement (2 Cor. 5:17; Gal. 6:15).

It is this incongruity—life from death, something from nothing—that gives Pauline theology its creative capacity to remap reality. The usual antitheses of ethnicity, gender, or social status are no longer what counts: the standard opposites and the norms they enshrine no longer apply.[12] The gift given without regard to male circumcision relativizes this fundamental mark of difference (Gal. 5:6; 6:15; 1 Cor. 7:19), because what matters now is the "calling" of Christ, a calling in grace (1 Cor. 7:17–24; Gal. 1:6). The baptismal formula of Galatians 3:28 and 1 Corinthians 12:13 (cf. Col. 3:11) is the most famous example of this remapping of society, but we find the same dynamic right across Paul's configuration of Christian community, where "the good" that believers share in Christ reframes even the relationship between a master and his formerly "useless" slave (Philem. 6, 15–19). Cultural differences within the community can be accommodated because they are no longer the most important features of the believers' identities, who serve their common Lord in divergent cultural forms (Rom. 14:1–11). What unites them is that they are equally "welcomed" in Christ (Rom. 15:7) by a "mercy" that disregards their differences (Rom. 11:28–32; 15:7–9).

This incongruous grammar of grace shapes all Paul's soteriological metaphors, creating surprising turns of thought and antithetical expressions. We would expect "sons" to develop into their maturity, but they are relabeled as slaves who require to be both liberated and adopted (Gal. 4:1–7). We would expect God to consider in the right ("justify") those who are righteous or noble, by one criterion or another, but he justifies "the ungodly" by a grace that matches no merit (Rom. 4:1–6). We would *not* expect God to choose the weak, the ignoble, and the uneducated or foolish, but that is precisely what God has done, choosing the despised and "the things that are not, to reduce to nothing the things that are" (1 Cor. 1:28). In all these ways, Paul highlights the mismatch between the saving power of God and the condition of its recipients. Christ died not for the good but for sinners (Rom. 5:7–8); through him God reconciles enemies (Rom. 5:10) and justifies, without distinction, the sinful,

---

12. See J. Louis Martyn, "Apocalyptic Antinomies in Paul's Letter to the Galatians," *NTS* 31 (1985): 410–24.

who have fallen short of the glory of God (Rom. 3:21–26). "Not by works of the law, but by trust in Christ" (Gal. 2:16); "not the children of the flesh but the children of the promise" (Rom. 9:8); "so it depends not on human will or exertion, but on the God who shows mercy" (Rom. 9:16); "those who were not my people I will call my people" (Rom. 9:25, citing Hosea)—through these and many other antitheses, Paul underlines the incongruity of grace, its disregard of human canons of possibility, reason, and justice.

Another product of this peculiar grammar is Paul's use of paradox. There is wealth only through the poverty of Christ (2 Cor. 8:9); the power and wisdom of God are displayed only in the weakness and folly of the cross (1 Cor. 1:18–25); there is life and fruitfulness for God only through death (Gal. 2:19–20; Rom. 7:4–6). As an apostolic representative of this paradoxical good news, Paul's own life is shot through with these anomalies: by the grace of God, it is when Paul is weak that he is strong (2 Cor. 12:8–10); he appears to be dying and sorrowful, but he is alive and happy; he appears poor and penniless, but he possesses everything and makes others rich (2 Cor. 6:9–10). Paul luxuriates in these paradoxes not from love of verbal dexterity but because they reflect the coincidence of opposites that mark "the grace of our Lord Jesus Christ" (2 Cor. 8:9)—life in death, wealth in poverty. Even in the absence of specific "gift" terminology we find the structuring role of grace across the landscape of Paul's theology. Narratives are here twisted into a particular shape and language reformulated by a peculiar grammar. To identify and connect these phenomena requires appreciation of the incongruity of grace.

Israel and the Mercy of God

One of the benefits of the "Gift Perspective" is its capacity to read Romans 9–11, and Paul's theology of Israel, in a way that unites his Christology with his conviction that "all Israel will be saved" (Rom. 11:26). It is not necessary either to adopt a *Sonderweg* ("special way") reading of Romans 11 (that Israel will be saved without trust in Christ) or to deny that "all Israel" in 11:26 refers to ethnic Israel. Neither is it necessary to hold that Paul changed his mind dramatically while writing Romans 11. To the contrary, these chapters make consistent sense if we follow their argument that Israel has been constituted, from the beginning, as the product of God's mercy or grace, which has now reached its ultimate and definitive expression in Christ.[13]

13. See Barclay, *Paul and the Gift*, 520–61; cf. Jonathan A. Linebaugh, "Not the End: The History and Hope of the Unfailing Word of God in Romans 9–11," in *God and Israel: Providence and Purpose in Romans 9–11*, ed. Todd Still (Waco: Baylor University Press, 2017), 141–63.

The crisis that faces Paul is that Israel's Messiah has not been accepted by the majority in Israel, such that it seems that God's word or promise has failed (Rom. 9:1–6). His answer might have been that only a few were ever intended to be saved, and that God does not care about the rest. But the opening stages of his argument in Romans 9:6–18 are better read as indicating that Israel has, from the start, been constituted by the elective grace of God and is sustained, in the past, present, and future, by that thread alone. Israel is not constituted by birth alone, but by the promise (9:6–9); not by moral achievement, but by election or call (9:10–13); not by human will or exertion, but by the mercy of God (9:14–18). God defines the character of Israel by declaring that "I will have mercy on whom I have mercy" (9:15, citing Exod. 33:19), which takes Israel's future out of its own hands and into the hands of God. As the rest of Romans 9 indicates, the operations of this mercy can be limiting or surprisingly expansive, but the fact that Israel has continued at all is due to the mercy of God, which is not limited by the conditions of merit. In Romans 10 the Christ-event is discussed as the ultimate expression of the righteousness and richness of God, and the current trauma of Israel's "disobedience" is faced. But we already know that God's mercy is not limited or conditioned by that disobedience, and in Romans 11 Paul indicates that God's mercy on the disobedient will be as effective in regrafting the natural olive branches as it has been in grafting in branches from a wild olive stock (gentile believers). The "root of richness" that sustains both, and into which they are grafted (11:17–24), is not the people of Israel as such, or even the patriarchs, but the mercy promised and enacted from the beginning, and now definitively displayed in the Messiah.

Romans 9–11 displays a complex dialectic between the Christ-event and the scriptural story of Israel. On the one hand, it is clear that Christ cannot be understood without the frame of the Scriptures and their narrative of Israel. On the other hand, Paul selects and interprets those Scriptures that match the peculiar shape of the Christ-event, and what makes his reading of Israel's history different is the christological shape of incongruous grace. Romans 9–11 is not a normal or natural reading of the Scriptures, just as Romans 4 is not a standard interpretation of the Abraham story; nonetheless, it is crucial for Paul that what is announced in the good news is the completion of the gracious purposes of God woven right through the scriptural account. In this sense, the Christ-event is "according to the Scriptures" (1 Cor. 15:3–5), inasmuch as Paul finds in the Scriptures echoes of the good news, pre-preached there (Gal. 3:8). What fuses them is not just that the story needs an ending, but a narrative shape that keeps redirecting attention back to the God who gives life to the dead and has mercy on the disobedient.

In this sense, the Christ-event clarifies also the very identity of God. Just as Exodus 33:19 ("I will have mercy on whom I have mercy") echoes and clarifies Exodus 3:14 ("I am who I am"), so Paul's citation of Exodus 33:19, which reverberates right through Romans 9–11, indicates that whatever may be said about God, mercy and grace are at the center of that truth. If Christ became poor precisely because he was "rich" (2 Cor. 8:9), and if that "richness" in generosity is what it means to be "in the form of God," demonstrated in self-giving, not taking (Phil. 2:6–8), then the overflowing and incongruous grace of God in Christ demonstrates that "the God-Who-Is" is "the God-Who-Is-In-Giving."[14] In this sense, the "Gift Perspective" on Paul helps us understand better not only Paul's Christology and soteriology but also his *theo*logy: gift becomes the lens through which God, and thus the whole of reality, is properly to be viewed.

Gift and Pauline Ethics

The "Gift Perspective" is well able to explain both the contents and the structure of obligation in Paul's ethics. We may recall (see above, "What Do We Mean by 'Gift'?") that to speak of "grace alone" in the sense of an incongruous, undeserved gift does *not* entail that the gift carries no obligations or expectations of response; incongruity is different from noncircularity. Although in the modern West we have perfected notions of gift without obligation ("with no strings attached"), and have idealized the unilateral gift, this was not a natural understanding of gift in antiquity (or, at present, in most parts of the world); gifts normally are understood to create and cement social ties, and reciprocity is integral to their purpose. In the case of Paul, it is clear that the gift/mercy of God is designed to elicit a response: "I appeal to you by the mercies of God to present your bodies as a living sacrifice" (Rom. 12:1). For Paul, believers are "under grace" (Rom. 6:14–15) and are brought through baptism into a new obedience, even slavery (Rom. 6:15–25). In fact, Romans 6:1–2 (cf. 3:8) seems specifically designed to ward off the notion of a "cheap grace" (see Dietrich Bonhoeffer, *The Cost of Discipleship*) that gives without expectation of response. In this sense, grace, for Paul, is unconditioned, but not unconditional.

We can well appreciate why the transformation of believers' lives is integral to salvation. Christ died for the ungodly, but they are not intended to stay that

---

14. For this reading of 2 Cor. 8:9, see John M. G. Barclay, "'Because He Was Rich He Became Poor': Translation, Exegesis, and Hermeneutics in the Reading of 2 Cor. 8.9," in *Theologizing in the Corinthian Conflict: Studies in the Exegesis and Theology of 2 Corinthians*, ed. Reimund Bieringer et al., BTS 16 (Leuven: Peeters, 2013), 331–44.

way: rather, by being brought into union with Christ, their lives are reshaped, through the Spirit, into new patterns of existence that match the gift that they have (undeservedly) received. All of Paul's Letters indicate his expectation of moral change, and of communities that demonstrate the power of the gift in altered patterns of behavior. And in this light, we can understand why Paul speaks of judgment by works (e.g., Rom. 2:1–11; 2 Cor. 5:10) and can warn believers that those who sow to the flesh will reap destruction (Gal. 6:8). The judgment will scrutinize the evidence for the presence and power of the gift of grace: without that evidence it is clear that no gift has been received. The "good works" of the believer will not be instrumental in achieving a new grace; they are not forms of "merit" winning a new and final gift. All "walking in the Spirit" is dependent on the one gift, given in Christ, and in that sense it remains incongruous, externally sourced from the resurrection life of Christ. But the Spirit works to create a congruity between the life of the believer and the life of God, and Paul expects believers to "lead a life worthy of the kingdom of God, who calls you into his own kingdom and glory" (1 Thess. 2:12).[15]

This congruity arises from the transformative work of the Spirit; it is not a set of new obligations loaded onto the former self. Paul takes seriously divine agency in this transformation, but not at the expense of the believer's own agency, as if in some zero-sum calculation. It is the new self, sourced in and activated by the gift of God in Christ, that is busy at work "sowing to the Spirit," such that it is better to talk of "energism" (cf. Phil. 2:12–13) than to use the traditional alternatives of "monergism" and "synergism."[16] And at this point the "Gift Perspective" connects well with analyses of Pauline theology that elucidate salvation as "participation in Christ" or "union with Christ."[17] As 2 Corinthians 8–9 makes clear, the relationship between the gift of God in Christ and the gift-giving of believers is not simply that of example and imitation. If Christ's "richness" is his self-giving (2 Cor. 8:9; cf. 8:2) and his "poverty" is his becoming human (cf. Phil. 2:6), then his participation in the human condition grounds the participation of believers in the "richness" of Christ—that is, in the self-giving flow of χάρις (*charis*) that cascades through believers to one another. Caught up in this momentum of grace, the generosity of believers is energized and directed to one another and to all (2 Cor. 9:13; cf.

---

15. See further Barclay, *Paul and the Gift*, 449–519, with discussion of judgment by works in Rom. 2 at 461–74.

16. Barclay, *Paul and the Gift*, 439–42.

17. See, e.g., Michael J. Thate, Kevin J. Vanhoozer, and Constantine R. Campbell, eds., *"In Christ" in Paul: Explorations in Paul's Theology of Union and Participation* (Grand Rapids: Eerdmans, 2018); Grant Macaskill, *Union with Christ in the New Testament* (Oxford: Oxford University Press, 2013).

Gal. 6:10). The Christ-gift issues in such "good works" (Gal. 6:9–10; cf. Eph. 2:9–10; Titus 2:14) of necessity: the transformative power of grace remolds everything it touches.

The formation of new communities is therefore basic to the good news. Since they are "welcomed" without regard to their social or ethnic worth, believers create new types of community, which do not erase but do relativize their differences, allowing a new calibration of worth. Former systems of value that create competition out of the scarcity of honor are superseded by a new spirit of mutual support, in which the good to be supplied to one another and the honor to be shared are sourced in God and therefore without limit. The reformulations of community found in Galatians 5–6, Romans 12–15, Philippians, 1 Corinthians, and Philemon are expressly based on the gift-giving of God in Christ. It is because of their shared κοινωνία (koinōnia) in grace (Phil. 1:5–7) that Paul and the Philippians can enjoy the open-ended reciprocity of "giving and taking" that is expressed in material support (Phil. 4:10–20), while the novel form of gift from Paul's churches to the "saints" in Jerusalem (2 Cor. 8–9) is sourced in, and an expression of, the χάρις received in Christ.[18] Famously, the gift-language also shapes the way that Paul figures the mutual upbuilding of the church (1 Cor. 12; Rom. 12): what are shared in acts of mutual instruction and service are the χαρίσματα (charismata) that the Spirit distributes around the church (cf. 1 Cor. 1:4–7). Since these are gifts, they are not "owned" by those who possess them; they are designed for mutual benefit (1 Cor. 12:7). And since they are gifts, what matters is not just what is given but also how it is given; hence, Paul traces behind its proper distribution the necessary operation of love (1 Cor. 13:1–13).

As these examples show, the fulfillment of the divine gift takes place not primarily in one-way gifts but in the reciprocity by which believers are tied together in bonds of mutual gift and receipt (see 2 Cor. 8:13–15).[19] Gift-reciprocity is not straightforward: it can create unwanted obligations, misunderstandings, resentments, and oppressive patterns of power; there are times when Paul will accept such reciprocity with his own congregations and times

18. See David E. Briones, *Paul's Financial Policy: A Socio-Theological Approach*, LNTS 494 (London: T&T Clark, 2013); David J. Downs, *The Offering of the Gentiles: Paul's Collection for Jerusalem in Its Chronological, Cultural, and Cultic Contexts*, WUNT 2/248 (Tübingen: Mohr Siebeck, 2008).

19. For explorations of this reciprocity in Pauline gift-ethics, see John M. G. Barclay, "Manna and the Circulation of Grace: A Study of 2 Corinthians 8:1–15," in *The Word Leaps the Gap: Essays on Scripture and Theology in Honor of Richard B. Hays*, ed. Ross Wagner, Kavin Rowe, and Katherine Grieb (Grand Rapids: Eerdmans, 2008), 409–26; Barclay, "Benefiting Others and Benefit to Oneself: Seneca and Paul on 'Altruism,'" in *Seneca and Paul in Dialogue*, ed. Joseph R. Dodson and David E. Briones, APR 2 (Leiden: Brill, 2017), 109–26.

when he will not (1 Cor. 9:1–23; 2 Cor. 11:7–21; Phil. 4:10–20). But it can also be mutually enriching, since givers do not give themselves *away* in giving to others but give themselves *into* a relationship of shared benefit—what Paul's contemporaries called φιλία (*philia*) and what Paul preferred to call κοινωνία (*koinōnia*).[20] In such relationships of cointerest, it is not necessary to play off the benefit of one against the benefit of another: while selfishness is banished, the goal is not self-sacrifice or even "altruism" as we commonly understand that term but the flourishing of both giver and recipient in mutual benefit. And the reason each can benefit without competition is that in contributing to the other both parties draw from the measureless gift of God (2 Cor. 9:8–10; Phil. 4:19), finding fulfillment both in their giving and in their receiving. Gifts (broadly understood) constitute the sinews of the body of Christ, holding its diversity in unity; they are central to Paul's vision of the "common good."

The "Gift Perspective" in Relation to Others

The "Gift Perspective" carries echoes of other perspectives on Paul but is more than a compilation of their strongest points. It bears down on a theme (grace) that has been central to both Catholic and Protestant readings of Paul, but by more careful scrutiny of the meanings of this concept it enables us to understand conflicts between, and diversity within, these Christian traditions of reception of Paul. By distinguishing different perfections of grace, it combines an emphasis on the incongruity of grace with the integration of "ethics" as a necessary element of Pauline theology; hence, it has seemed to some readers highly "Lutheran" in tone, and to others deeply Thomist! Because of its fine-grained analysis of what is meant by "grace," it avoids negative stereotypes of Judaism as a "legalistic" or grace-less religion, and places Paul "within Judaism," participating in a Jewish debate about the mercy or goodness of God. Like the "New Perspective," it underlines the significance of Paul's work in founding communities (not just saving individuals), and of his mission to gentiles as the practical instantiation of his theology. But, crucially, it locates the root of that mission not just in a social concern for "unity" or "inclusion," nor just in Paul's biblical-historical conviction that the Abrahamic promises were coming to fruition but as the necessary expression of the Christ-gift, given without regard to preconstituted worth. It thus supplies a crucial theological dimension to the "New Perspective," a 3D depth to accompany its widescreen vision. It is not averse to learning from the history of reception

20. For the distinction between giving oneself *away* and giving oneself *into* a relationship, see the forthcoming Durham PhD thesis of Logan Williams.

of Paul (including the Reformation), but its critical scrutiny of that tradition entails that it is beholden to no single theological perspective.

Nonetheless, the historical and exegetical basis of the "Gift Perspective" is not divorced from an interest in the contemporary significance of Pauline theology. In fact, its implications are multiple and far-reaching. The communal dimensions of the gift suggest an ecclesiology in which the church is conscious of its difference from cultural norms of worth and thus able to form experimental communities that cross the still-pervasive boundaries of ethnicity, race, and social class. The good news that in God's economy everyone is of value to God in Christ, regardless of others' perceptions, is not only socially revolutionary; it also speaks to contemporary crises of worth and self-esteem. A missiology of gift thus forms a strong antidote to the many divisive and judgmental features of the current global and cultural scene, offering a daring welcome to those who, on various grounds, are considered of no worth by others or themselves. Here the individual and social dimensions of soteriology are united, and soteriology itself is integrated with pneumatology, ecclesiology, and ethics. Paul's policies of gentile welcome are found to be relevant to social conditions quite beyond the first century, while holding Jews and Judaism in the highest theological regard. The Pauline ethic of reciprocity has multiple applications to "charity" (global and local), which in a paternalistic, one-way form has a tendency to turn toxic. More broadly, if all creation is considered gift (cf. Rom. 1:18–25; 2 Cor. 9:8–10), responsibility for creation is given a strong theological foundation, while economic relations can be reconfigured, and reoriented.[21] In fact, placed into conversation with the outpouring of contemporary philosophy and theology of gift, this approach to Paul begins to hum with multiple contemporary resonances, without losing its historical foundation. And since any perspective on Paul has, among its multiple tasks, a responsibility to make sense within its contemporary conditions, a reading of Paul that has social, political, personal, ecclesial, and economic implications is well worth exploring further, as far as it can go.

---

21. See, e.g., the work of Jean-Luc Marion, John Milbank, and Kathryn Tanner.

Roman Catholic Perspective
Response to Barclay

BRANT PITRE

Let me begin by thanking John Barclay for his excellent essay on the Gift Perspective on Paul. Although Barclay's monograph *Paul and the Gift* was published only a few years ago, it has already been recognized as a watershed in Pauline scholarship.[1] In my opinion, time will show that *Paul and the Gift* may well prove to be as consequential as E. P. Sanders's *Paul and Palestinian Judaism*. I consider it a privilege to interact here with Barclay's more concise essay. With this in mind, I would like to begin by highlighting several points of agreement.

The "Six Perfections of Gift" and the Work of E. P. Sanders: Priority ≠ Incongruity

Although my own essay focuses on overlap between Catholic exegesis and E. P. Sanders's interpretation, I nevertheless agree with Barclay's critique of Sanders regarding "grace." In particular, Barclay's taxonomy of the six "perfections of gift" helps point out an important weakness of Sanders's view.[2] Barclay rightly points out that Sanders emphasizes the temporal "priority" of grace in the framework of "covenantal nomism" (e.g., "getting in" by grace) without

1. John M. G. Barclay, *Paul and the Gift* (Grand Rapids: Eerdmans, 2015).
2. See Barclay, *Paul and the Gift*, 66–78.

paying enough attention to the fact that "priority is only one of the possible perfections of grace" (224). He also rightly criticizes Sanders for assuming that the priority of grace also implies its "incongruity"; that is, the person receiving the gift of grace has done nothing in advance to be considered worthy of the gift. In short, by means of this taxonomy, Barclay has given scholars a tool by which they can be far more nuanced and precise in their discussions of "grace" in Paul than Sanders was able to do in his day.

Grace as "Unconditioned" but Not "Unconditional": Initial Justification versus Final Judgment

Equally significant is Barclay's concise and momentous conclusion that "grace, for Paul, is unconditioned, but not unconditional" (232). In my view, this constitutes one of *the* major contributions of Barclay's "Gift Perspective." Earlier in the essay Barclay explains that "grace" for Paul "may be a 'pure gift' in the sense of being unconditioned, but not in the sense that it carries no expectations and has 'no strings attached'" (223). With this assertion, Barclay provides a sophisticated and historically anchored explanation for what I was trying to outline in my essay: in patristic, medieval, and modern Catholic Pauline exegesis there is no conflict in the idea that the initial gift of justification is completely unmerited (i.e., "unconditioned"), and yet, at the same time, the final judgment of the believer will be according to "works" (i.e., not "unconditional"). Think here of the following passages in Paul:

> *Unconditioned:* So too at the present time there is a remnant, chosen *by grace*. But if it is by grace, it is *no longer on the basis of works*, otherwise grace would no longer be grace. (Rom. 11:5–6)

> *Not Unconditional:* For [God] will *repay* each person *according to his works*: to those who by patience in *good work* seek for glory and honor and immortality, he will give *eternal life*; but for those who are factious and do not obey the truth, but obey wickedness, there will be *wrath and fury*. (Rom. 2:6–8 AT)

How can Paul in the same letter speak of justification by unmerited "grace" (Rom. 11:5) and final judgment according to "works" (Rom. 2:6)? While there are lots of ways to interpret these texts, it seems to me that Barclay provides us with one extremely plausible explanation: although for Paul the initial "gift" or "grace" of justification is "unconditioned" (i.e., incongruous), the final judgment is not "unconditioned" (i.e., not without expectations of reciprocity). As Barclay has written elsewhere, "From this perspective, the old conundrum of justification by grace and judgment by works is perhaps less problematic than is commonly claimed. The works for which believers are accountable at the judgment seat of Christ are themselves the product of the grace that has transformed their agent and empowered their performance."[3]

If Barclay is right, this would at the very least provide a compelling explanation for why so many premodern—that is, patristic and medieval—Catholic commentators saw no difficulty interpreting Paul as saying that no one can merit the initial grace of justification *and* that the final judgment would be according to works.[4] Indeed, if Barclay is correct that "reciprocity is integral" to the "purpose" of gift giving and that "the gift/mercy of God is designed to elicit a response" (232), then a final judgment according to works performed by grace is to be expected.

Participation in Christ and "Energism"—Divine and Human Agency Not in "Competition"

As I outline in my essay in this volume, one of the pillars of a Catholic perspective on Paul is that salvation is not merely forgiveness of sins but a real and transformative "participation" in Christ. Along these lines, I agree with Barclay that for Paul, divine and human agency in Christ are not in "competition." This point is so important that I think Barclay's words bear repeating:

> Paul takes seriously divine agency . . . , but not at the expense of the believer's own agency, as if in some zero-sum calculation. It is the new self, sourced in and activated by the gift of God in Christ, that is busy at work "sowing to the Spirit," such that it is better to talk of "energism" (cf. Phil. 2:12–13) than to use the traditional alternatives of "monergism" and "synergism." And at this point the "Gift Perspective" connects well with analyses of Pauline theology that elucidate salvation as "participation in Christ" or "union with Christ." (233)

From a strictly exegetical perspective, it is puzzling that Barclay feels the need to avoid the language of "synergism" when Paul himself uses it: "We are coworkers [συνεργοί, *synergoi*] with God" (1 Cor. 3:9 [cf. 1 Thess 3:2]). Nevertheless, I agree that the language of "energism" does an excellent job of capturing Paul's understanding of how God acts (divine agency) in those

---

3. John M. G. Barclay, "Grace and the Transformation of Agency in Christ," in *Redefining First-Century Jewish and Christian Identities: Essays in Honor of Ed Parish Sanders*, ed. Fabian E. Udoh et al. (Notre Dame, IN: University of Notre Dame Press, 2008), 372–89, here 385.
4. For patristic and medieval examples of this view, see my essay "The Roman Catholic Perspective on Paul" herein.

who, through faith and baptism, are now in Christ. As Paul says elsewhere, "It is God who is at work in you [ἐνεργῶν ἐν ὑμῖν, *energōn en hymin*], enabling you both to will and to work for his good pleasure" (Phil. 2:13). Once again, Barclay's rich understanding of gift and reciprocity provides convincing readings of debated aspects of Pauline soteriology.

With that said, I do have three questions about Barclay's essay.

Grace and the "Necessity" of "Good Works"?

First, I am puzzled why Barclay says that for Paul, "the Christ-gift issues in such 'good works' (Gal. 6:9–10; cf. Eph. 2:9–10; Titus 2:14) of necessity" (234). I agree that for Paul, the gift of grace empowers good works, but in the first passage quoted by Barclay above, Paul's language is hardly that of "necessity":

> Do not be deceived; God is not mocked, for you reap whatever you sow. *If you sow to your own flesh, you will reap corruption from the flesh; but if you sow to the Spirit, you will reap eternal life from the Spirit.* So let us not grow weary in doing good, for *we will reap at harvest time, if we do not give up.* So then, whenever we have an opportunity, let us work good for all. (Gal. 6:7–10 NRSV adapted)

Notice here that Paul says that those who are in Christ will reap only "if" they "do not give up" but rather "work good" (ἐργαζώμεθα τὸ ἀγαθόν, *ergazōmetha to agathon*) (6:9–10). Indeed, the whole point of the passage seems to be to insist that the reaping of "eternal life" is directly contingent on whether believers "sow" to the "flesh" or to "the Spirit" (6:8). If believers "sow" to the "flesh" (σάρξ, *sarx*)—presumably by doing "the works of the flesh" (τὰ ἔργα τῆς σαρκός, *ta erga tēs sarkos*) such as "sexual immorality," "idolatry," "drunkenness," which Paul has mentioned just a few verses earlier (5:19–21)— they will reap "corruption" or "destruction" (φθοράν, *phthoran*) rather than "eternal life" (ζωὴν αἰώνιον, *zōēn aiōnion*) (6:8).[5] In short, would Barclay agree that, for Paul, it is possible for someone to fail to give the "return" that is "expected" and thereby "reap" destruction rather than eternal life?[6]

---

5. For more on this passage and other related texts, see Nathan Eubank, "Justice Endures Forever: Paul's Grammar of Generosity," *JSPL* 5 (2015): 169–87.

6. At least in one place Barclay himself seems to affirm that a person can fail to give a return. Commenting on Gal. 2:19–21, Barclay writes, "It [the self] is reconstituted in such a fashion that one has to speak thereafter of dual agency, and not simply of one operating in partnership with the other, but of Christ operating 'in' the human agent. *But this new power is clearly non-coercive. Paul entertains as a real possibility* (all too real in Galatia) *that one can reject the grace of God.*" Barclay, "'By the Grace of God I Am What I Am': Grace and Agency

Falling Away from Grace = "No Gift" Was Received?

Second, I completely agree with Barclay when he writes, "Christ died for the ungodly, but they are not intended to stay that way" (232–33). But what if a believer lapses back into "ungodly" behavior? What if he or she does not comply with the "expectation of moral change" implicit in the gift of grace? On the one hand, Barclay briefly mentions Paul's teaching on judgment according to works (Rom. 2:1–11; 2 Cor. 5:10). On the other hand, Barclay makes the following surprising claim about the final judgment: "The judgment will scrutinize the evidence for the presence and power of the gift of grace: without that evidence *it is clear that no gift has been received*" (233, emphasis added).

What is the exegetical basis for Barclay's interpretation here? Where does Paul ever say that the judgment will reveal that "no gift" was "received"? I for one can think of no text in which Paul uses such language. By contrast, there are multiple passages in which Paul describes the possibility of believers being cut off or falling away from grace:

> You who want to be justified by the law have *cut yourselves off from Christ*; you have *fallen away from grace*. (Gal. 5:4)

> So if you think you are *standing*, watch out that you do not *fall*. (1 Cor. 10:12)

> Note then the kindness and the severity of God: severity toward those who have *fallen*, but God's kindness toward you, provided you continue in his kindness; otherwise *you also will be cut off*. (Rom. 11:22)

Notice here that when Paul speaks of "falling away" (ἐκπίπτω, *ekpiptō*) from "grace" (χάρις, *charis*) (Gal. 5:4), it strains credulity to suggest that the person did not in fact receive the gift before falling away. Likewise, the language of "falling" (πίπτω, *piptō*) (Rom. 11:22; 1 Cor. 10:12) or being "cut off / estranged" (καταργέω, *katargeō*) (Gal. 5:4) or "cut off" (ἐκκόπτω, *ekkoptō*) (Rom. 11:22) surely implies that the person in question was once "standing" in grace and participating "in Christ." In light of such passages, would it not be more correct to say that if a believer does not reciprocate, then the relationship of being "in Christ" will not *continue*? As Barclay himself says, when it comes to ancient gift-giving, recipients who do not respond with the expected reciprocity fail to do something "necessary for the continuation of the relationship" (222). I see no exegetical foundation for concluding that one's lack of reciprocity means the relationship never existed to begin with.[7]

Divine and Human Agency—the "Reward" for Good "Works" Done in Christ

Finally, I wholeheartedly agree with Barclay that for Paul, divine agency and human agency are not a "zero-sum" equation (233). If this is true of grace, however, I am puzzled by what Barclay says about "good works": "The 'good works' of the believer will not be instrumental in achieving a new grace; they are not forms of 'merit' winning a new and final gift" (233). If Barclay is right that grace is not a zero-sum game (and I think he is), is it possible to speak of receiving a "reward" or "wage" (μισθός, *misthos*) according to the gift? To put the question exegetically: Why does Paul himself use the language "reward" or "wage" to describe how God will reciprocate the good "works" of the believer? Consider the following:

> According to *the grace* [τὴν χάριν, *tēn charin*] *of God* given to me, like a skilled master builder I laid a foundation, and someone else is building on it. Each builder must choose with care how to build on it. For no one can lay any foundation other than the one that has been laid; that foundation is Jesus Christ. Now if anyone builds on the foundation with gold, silver, precious stones, wood, hay, straw—*the work* of each builder [ἑκάστου τὸ ἔργον, *hekastou to ergon*] will become visible, for the Day will disclose it, because it will be revealed with fire, and the fire will test *what sort of work* [τὸ ἔργον, *to ergon*] each has done. *If the work* [τὸ ἔργον, *to ergon*] built on the foundation survives, the builder *will receive a reward/wage* [μισθόν, *misthon*]. If the work [τὸ ἔργον, *to ergon*] is burned up, the builder will suffer loss; the builder will be saved, but only as through fire. (1 Cor. 3:10–15 NRSV adapted)

Notice here that Paul does not hesitate to speak of building on "the grace [χάρις, *charis*] of God" that is Jesus Christ (3:10) with a "work" (ἔργον, *ergon*) that will earn a "reward" or "wage" (μισθός, *misthos*) (3:14). If we follow the implications of Barclay's own research, it seems to me that there is no reason to pit the incongruity of the initial gift against divine reciprocity and

---

7. For a full discussion, see B. J. Oropeza, *Paul and Apostasy: Eschatology, Perseverance, and Falling Away in the Corinthian Congregation*, WUNT 2/115 (Tübingen: Mohr Siebeck; Eugene, OR: Wipf & Stock, 2000); and more recently, B. J. Oropeza, *Jews, Gentiles, and the Opponents of Paul: The Pauline Letters*, vol. 2 of *Apostasy in the New Testament Communities* (Eugene, OR: Cascade, 2012).

"eschatological reward" for good works.[8] Precisely because participation in Christ is *not* a "zero-sum calculation" (233), the building up of eternal treasure through the "good works" of the believer in no way takes away from "the 'richness' of Christ" (to use Barclay's language, 233) (cf. 2 Cor. 8:9). Instead, I would suggest that to deny that the "good works" of believers in Christ are meritorious is to deny that Christ's own work is meritorious, since it is Christ himself working in the believer.[9] As Paul says elsewhere, "It is no longer I who live, but *it is Christ who lives in me*" (Gal. 2:20).

In sum, my question for Barclay is this: If divine and human agency operates on a noncompetitive basis and Paul himself connects "grace" and "wages" in 1 Corinthians 3, is it possible to speak of "wages" being given according to the "gift" (χάρις, *charis*)? If not, why does Paul speak of a "reward" or "wage" (μισθός, *misthos*) being given for the good "work" (ἔργον, *ergon*) done by someone in Christ (1 Cor. 3:10–14)?[10] I am grateful for all I have learned from Barclay's brilliant *Paul and the Gift*. But I for one would also like to read its sequel: *Paul and the Reward*.

8. Note Raymond F. Collins, *1 Corinthians*, SP 7 (Collegeville, MN: Liturgical Press, 1999), 159: "Paul uses 'wages' (*misthos*) as a metaphor for eschatological reward; elsewhere it indicates pay for a job well done (Rom. 4:4; cf. 1 Cor. 9:17, 18)."

9. See Michael P. Barber, "A Catholic Perspective: Our Works Are Meritorious at the Final Judgment Because of Our Union with Christ by Grace," in *Four Views on the Role of Works at the Final Judgment*, ed. Alan P. Stanley (Grand Rapids: Zondervan, 2013), 161–84, here 180.

10. Intriguingly, in his full-length study Barclay twice points out in passing that Paul uses "the term" μισθός (*misthos*) in 1 Cor. 3:14 in the sense of both "reward" and "pay" (Barclay, *Paul and the Gift*, 485n96, n98). Unfortunately, Barclay does not spend any time explaining how Paul's discussion in 1 Cor. 3 agrees with Barclay's denial of the meritorious character of good "work" (ἔργον, *ergon*) built on the foundation of Christ (cf. 1 Cor. 3:10–15).

Traditional Protestant Perspective Response to Barclay

A. ANDREW DAS

Professor Barclay has provided a helpful thumbnail sketch of his more detailed presentation in *Paul and the Gift*.[1] Starting with the widespread gift vocabulary in Paul's Letters, Barclay notes the stress on the *incongruity* of God's gift, its being granted without regard for human worth or works. Incongruity is just one of six ways a gift may be described or, as he puts it, "perfected" (221). A gift may be lavish or *superabundant*. It may take place *prior* to the action of the recipient. The giver may with *singularity* act out of sheer benevolence and without anger or judgment. A gift may or may not be *efficacious* in achieving its result. Finally, a gift may be *noncircular* if the giver does not expect reciprocity. Barclay has brought clarity to the varieties of grace within Second Temple Judaism. For Paul, grace is God's incongruous gift in Jesus Christ to all humanity, even non-Jews. Gentiles need not observe the law or be circumcised in the face of God's gift in Christ for humanity's sins. A law-observant life does not render one worthy of the gift.

Barclay unnecessarily defers to the "New Perspective" in defining "works of the law" as "adopting Jewish practices" or "Judaizing" (paralleled by circumcision) (226), despite Paul's alternation between "works of the law" and generalized human effort in Romans 3:28; 4:4–5.[2] Nevertheless, Barclay's em-

---

1. John M. G. Barclay, *Paul and the Gift* (Grand Rapids: Eerdmans, 2015).
2. See the critique of Barclay on this point in A. Andrew Das, "Paul and Works of Obedience in Second Temple Judaism: Romans 4:4–5 as a 'New Perspective' Case Study," *CBQ* 71

244

phasis on the incongruity of grace remains irrespective of human obedience or worthiness. As a result, Jewish identity is radically relativized since it is not salvific: "Jewish practices . . . are not the criteria of worth in the Christ-economy" (227). The Spirit is working in Christ to bring about a new creation as believers share in Christ's death and resurrection and are brought "into" Christ and thus into a new community based on what God has already graciously done for Israel in Christ.

God's sheer, gracious, undeserved gift is not without expectation of a response or reciprocity. Paul therefore emphasizes the good deeds of Christians worked graciously by the Lord (Phil. 2:12–13), and yet these works in response do not "merit" "winning a new and final gift" (233). The Spirit "energizes" a reciprocal behavior, and that reciprocity expresses itself in the generosity of a "gifted" community.

Less clear in Barclay's analysis is whether Paul is avoiding a negative stereotype of Judaism as "legalistic" or "grace-less" (235). Certainly, Paul's reasoning is Christ-centered, but his *defining* grace in terms of its incongruity and his regular contrasting of grace and works/doing appear to many *intentional*, targeting peers advocating *congruous* understandings that Paul did not view as truly gracious.[3] As Barclay has shown, such congruous notions of grace were indeed current in some sectors of Second Temple Judaism (e.g., Philo, Wisdom of Solomon, 4 Ezra [Uriel]).

In short, much of Barclay's analysis supports a traditional Protestant understanding of Paul. Luther, too, emphasized the expected response of appropriate conduct and thanksgiving for God's undeserved gift. As with modern apocalyptic readings of Paul, a "traditionalist" interpreter would heartily agree with much of Professor Barclay's analysis.

(2009): 795–812, here 804–5. It would also be helpful to stress in these verses the justified *sinner*. Barclay's solution-to-plight reasoning sometimes loses focus on the actual plight.

3. One need not wait with Barclay (*Paul and the Gift*, 571) until the disputed Pauline literature (Eph. 2:8–10; 2 Tim. 1:9; Titus 3:5) for "works" to serve also as moral achievements (Rom. 4:4–5).

New Perspective Response to Barclay

JAMES D. G. DUNN

It was a delight to read John Barclay's great book *Paul and the Gift*, with its exegetical discussion of Paul's Letters to the Galatians and the Romans in particular boiled down to a very modest amount of pages but packed with references to these key texts and exposition that stirred the soul as well as stimulated the mind.

Barclay's essay reflects one of the great values of his book in noting what he calls "The Diverse Dynamics of Grace in Second Temple Judaism" (chap. 10 of *Paul and the Gift*). But I could not help recalling that in the book the references to non-Pauline texts in the New Testament are very limited. To clarify our understanding of Paul in relation to his Jewish context is more than helpful. But given that Paul's theology of gift was the heart of his gospel, not least in defense of his gentile mission, and that it was this theology of gift as good news for gentiles that caused such turmoil within the early Christian mission (or should I rather say within early Christian missions), should there not be more room for relating Paul's gospel to other New Testament writings such as Matthew and James? The question of how Paul relates to the rich diversity of Second Temple Judaism is dealt with well. But how does Paul stand within the diversity of the New Testament writings, including the later writings attributed, rightly or wrongly, to Paul?

I couldn't help thinking in particular of Matthew 5:17–20 with its strong affirmation of the law, the striking warning that "whoever breaks one of the least of these commandments . . . will be called least in the kingdom of heaven," and the call for a righteousness that exceeds that of the scribes and

Pharisees. Would Paul have shared what would seem to be Matthew's understanding of these words? They seem to presuppose and envisage a situation that cuts across Paul's emphasis on grace as a gift and his sharp distinction of faith and works. Of course, Matthew was writing in what appears to have been a strong traditionalist Jewish context, whereas Paul was writing specifically as called to preach the gospel to gentiles. But does that not need to be brought out more clearly—the distinctiveness of Paul's gospel of gift even within the New Testament writings?

Similar issues arise when we include the Letter of James in the dialogue—particularly the latter's insistence on works as the necessary demonstration of faith (James 2:14–26). Of course, we can understand why a letter attributed to James, brother of Jesus and leader of the mother church in Jerusalem, should express such an emphasis. But this simply reinforces the issue of whether the New Testament believers were as united on grace and gift as the simple juxtaposition of these two terms implies. Was Paul a spokesman for the whole of the earliest church on this point, or was he using it primarily to defend his insistence that the gospel was for gentiles too, an insistence (gospel as gift) that he evidently felt he had to insist on even in confrontation with Peter?

And one cannot help wondering whether Paul's emphasis on gift and grace was too much for the successors of the first generation, with the increasing emphasis on office and hierarchy evident on through the second century and beyond. And did Luther's reassertion of Paul's gospel suffer the same fate? Is it the uncomfortable truth that Paul's gospel of gift is too discomfiting, even embarrassing for most human beings and institutions, so that it quickly loses its appeal and becomes obscured behind emphases on promotion, recognition, and reward? Gospel as gift certainly needs reemphasis today.

Paul within Judaism Perspective
Response to Barclay

MAGNUS ZETTERHOLM

John Barclay's essay on the "Gift Perspective" has much to commend it, in my view. I am pleased to note that he seems to share my conviction that Paul should be interpreted within Judaism "in a way that goes beyond Sanders's *Paul and Palestinian Judaism*, while building on Sanders's determination to refute Christian caricatures of ancient or modern Judaism" (220). As has been repeatedly noticed—although not everyone would agree—Christian theology has negatively influenced the effort to view the historical Paul as a late Second Temple Jew. And it had more than a little to do with increasing the social and political will to exterminate six million of Christian Europe's Jews. The more scholars who consciously aim at exposing unhistorical claims regarding Paul, the better. Perhaps Christians eventually will work out a theology that takes into account not only Paul's statement on righteousness through faith (Rom. 1:17) but also his ideas on the relation between Israel and the nations—"to the Jew first and also to the Greek" (Rom. 1:16).

I also appreciate as very illuminating Barclay's attempt to anchor the ideologies connected to gifts both in anthropology and in ancient social conventions; so too with his problematizing of the relation between "gift" and "grace." As many have noted,[1] Sanders was indeed onto something

---

1. See the essays in D. A. Carson, Peter T. O'Brien, and Mark A. Seifrid, eds., *Justification and Variegated Nomism*, vol. 1, *The Complexities of Second Temple Judaism*, WUNT 2/140 (Tübingen: Mohr Siebeck; Grand Rapids: Baker Academic, 2001).

when he characterized Judaism as a "religion" centered on God's grace, though, once alerted by Sanders, we now see that our evidence reveals a more complex situation. Thus, Sanders's reconstruction of ancient Judaism represented a gigantic leap forward, and *Paul and Palestinian Judaism* must be regarded as one of the absolutely most important works of the twentieth century in the field of biblical studies. However, as Barclay correctly observes, "Sanders's 'covenantal nomism' has offered a homogenized version of Jewish theology" (224). On this topic, Barclay certainly is correct in his attempt to position Paul within the thick context of contemporary first-century Judaism(s).

Barclay is also correct in focusing on Paul's mission to the nations. I fully agree with him that the issue at stake was not whether Jews within the Jesus movement thought that there should be a mission to non-Jews, but rather, a mission on what terms. It is clear, both from Galatians and from Acts, that by midcentury some within the movement argued that the mission to the nations should involve conversion to Judaism. In Acts 15:5 this is explicitly stated: "Some believers who belonged to the sect of the Pharisees [τῆς αἱρέσεως τῶν Φαρισαίων, *tēs haireseōs tōn Pharisaiōn*] stood up and said, 'It is necessary for them to be circumcised and ordered to keep the law of Moses [δεῖ περιτέμνειν αὐτοὺς παραγγέλλειν τε τηρεῖν τὸν νόμον Μωϋσέως, *dei peritemnein autous parangellein te tērein ton nomon Mōyseōs*].'" It is not entirely clear why some Pharisees would adopt this radical position given the vast range of possible accommodations to interested non-Jews that did not involve conversion.[2] Barclay, however, seems to be of the opinion that Paul's opponents quite naturally came to the conclusion that non-Jews should "adopt the mark of the Abrahamic covenant in male circumcision" (225).

The problem with this view is, however, that conversion is never mentioned in those texts from the Hebrew Bible that seem to have triggered the mission to the nations.[3] The impression given is rather that the nations will be part of the eschatological pilgrimage without changing their ethnic identity; that is, they are to remain members of the nations. They will, however, adapt to the ways of the god of Israel so that they will "walk in his paths" (Isa. 2:3). Some would call this Torah observance, which would make Paul's position hard to understand. Barclay's explanation of Paul's antithetical formulations in Galatians regarding, for instance, law versus grace, faith in Christ versus works of the law, is that "the Christ-event is interpreted as an unconditioned

2. See Terence L. Donaldson, *Judaism and the Gentiles: Patterns of Universalism (to 135 CE)* (Waco: Baylor University Press, 2007); Shaye J. D. Cohen, *The Beginnings of Jewishness: Boundaries, Varieties, Uncertainties* (Berkeley: University of California Press, 1999), 140–74.
3. See, e.g., Isa. 2:2–3; Mic. 4:1–2; Zech. 8:20–23; Tob. 13:11.

gift" (226). To me, it seems that Barclay here operates on a too advanced ideo-logical/theological level, and it is hard to avoid the impression that Barclay's Paul comes very close to a traditional Protestant version of the apostle.

I would rather assume that Paul's theology of grace, if there is such a thing, is not the starting point but the result of a problem on a more down-to-earth level that demands a certain rhetorical strategy. To reiterate what I argue elsewhere in this volume: I believe that the main problem that the early Jesus movement faced was related to the moral impurity of non-Jewish adherents to the movement. The fact that the eschatological pilgrimage now was a reality and not something to be implemented in the distant future entailed a new relationship between Israel and the nations. Thus, the issue at stake was to what degree these, potentially idolatrous, newly nonpagan gentiles could be trusted and to what extent it was possible for Jews to consort with non-Jewish followers of Jesus—for instance, eating (food acceptable for Jews) together. Against this background the strategy of "some believers who belonged to the sect of the Pharisees" (Acts 15:5) makes perfect sense: conversion and commitment to Torah observance would remove all obstacles for social relations.

Furthermore, with regard to the Antioch incident Barclay claims that Peter would have rendered the unconditioned gift conditioned if he had required the non-Jews to "live in accordance with Jewish meal regulations" (227). Here Barclay's dependence on the so-called New Perspective on Paul comes to the surface. According to this New Perspective, Paul is believed to have reacted against Jewish "identity markers" such as food regulations. As I have argued elsewhere,[4] it is highly unlikely that the ἐκκλησία (ekklēsia) in Antioch had abandoned Jewish traditional dietary regulations. Again, the problem in An-tioch most likely concerned not food but commensality. And is it correct to state that Paul was against "Judaizing" in every form, and, by extension, is it correct that God's gift is "unconditioned"?

While Jews who did not belong to the Jesus movement hardly expected non-Jews with whom they associated to refrain from "idolatry," this seems to have been an absolute demand within the Jesus movement. To refrain from "idolatry" is Torah teaching. To abstain from "what has been sacrificed to idols [εἰδωλοθύτων, eidōlothytōn] and from blood [αἵματος, haimatos] and from what is strangled [πνικτῶν, pniktōn] and from fornication [πορνείας,

4. Magnus Zetterholm, *The Formation of Christianity in Antioch: A Social-Scientific Approach to the Separation between Judaism and Christianity* (London: Routledge, 2003), 160. See also Mark D. Nanos, "What Was at Stake in Peter's 'Eating with Gentiles' at Antioch?," in *The Galatians Debate: Contemporary Issues in Rhetorical and Historical Interpretation*, ed. Mark D. Nanos (Peabody, MA: Hendrickson, 2002), 282–318.

porneias]" (Acts 15:29) is Torah teaching.[5] Thus, God's gift to the ungodly—
that is, the nations—was indeed given by grace, but indubitably it involved
adaptation to Jewish norms. According to Paul, trust in Christ made members
of the nations as holy and pure as Israel and created in them the ability to
live a holy and pure life. But let there be no doubt about how Paul expected
non-Jewish adherents to behave—in conformity with Torah teaching!

What precisely did Paul oppose with regard to non-Jews observing Torah?
This is indeed a question. My best guess, however, is that Paul faced non-
Jews who previously had been in contact with other Jews who argued that
Torah observance on Jewish terms would make them righteous before the
god of Israel. Again, as I argue in my essay in this volume, the assumption
that Paul was a nomistic exclusivist—that is, he believed that something like
"full" Torah observance was a Jewish prerogative alone—offers a satisfactory
explanation. This does not contradict the fact that Paul's teaching for non-
Jews is entirely built on the Torah. He is simply creating a form of Judaism
for non-Jews—built on the Torah.

Finally, I would add some observations about terminology. I believe that
Barclay's word choices work against his stated ambition to construct Paul
within Judaism. To use terms like "Christian," and "church" as a translation of *ekklēsia*, to denote members of this movement and their gatherings
undermines a historical first-century context. For example, on the one hand,
Barclay mentions the "Christian" interpretation that is responsible for the
contrast between "the grace of God in Christ" and the "religious character
of Judaism" (223); on the other hand, he speaks of "the Christian faith that
Paul sees adumbrated by Abraham" (229). Is Paul founding a new religion?
Barclay implies not, but the vocabulary sounds otherwise. It is true that the
word Χριστιανός (*Christianos*) occurs a few times in some New Testament
texts (Acts 11:26; 26:28; 1 Pet. 4:16), but these are late—written well after
Paul's lifetime—and they cohere more with the sensibility of that collection
of texts that we now call the Apostolic Fathers. Their postapocalyptic time
frame is not Paul's time frame. Their project is not Paul's.

There is simply no evidence that Paul, or any other Christ-follower contemporary with him, thought of themselves as "Christians." And while Paul's
social experiment of bringing Jews and members of the nations together
eventually gave rise to what we may call a "Christian" identity, this formative
process resulted in something quite different than Paul would have expected—
a Judaism without Jews, which basically is what Christianity is all about.
Thus, it is a good idea to follow Donald Akenson's advice and avoid "words

5. On this point, see also my response to James Dunn's essay, pp. 161–62.

that make us lie."[6] The same, of course, is true of "church." Whatever Paul's assemblies were, we can safely ignore "church" as an adequate English translation of *ekklēsia*.[7]

So, in conclusion: I sincerely appreciate Barclay's attempt to position Paul within Judaism, and I salute his ambition to avoid Christian caricatures of Judaism as the foundation for a reconstruction of the historical Paul. In my view, however, I would like to see him push his efforts a bit further.

6. Donald Harman Akenson, *Saint Paul: A Skeleton Key to the Historical Jesus* (Oxford: Oxford University Press, 2000), 55–67. See also Anders Runesson, "The Question of Terminology: The Architecture of Contemporary Discussions on Paul," in *Paul within Judaism: Restoring the First-Century Context to the Apostle*, ed. Mark D. Nanos and Magnus Zetterholm (Minneapolis: Fortress, 2015), 53–77; Magnus Zetterholm, "Jews, Christians, and Gentiles: Rethinking the Categorization within the Early Jesus Movement," in *Reading Paul in Context: Explorations in Identity Formation; Essays in Honour of William S. Campbell*, ed. Kathy Ehrensperger and J. Brian Tucker, LNTS 428 (London: T&T Clark, 2010), 242–54.

7. For an overview of the current debate on Paul's "Christ groups," see Richard Ascough, "Paul, Synagogues, and Associations: Reframing the Question of Models for Pauline Christ Groups," *JJMJS* 2 (2015): 27–52.

Gift Perspective Reply to the Respondents

JOHN M. G. BARCLAY

I am very grateful for the conversation that this project has brought about. It has created a forum for serious listening to alternative viewpoints—a phenomenon surprisingly rare in current scholarship! The responses to my chapter are acute and challenging, and I thank all my respondents most heartily. Overall, I am struck by the fact that the "Gift Perspective" has been so warmly appreciated on all sides, even if with some reservations. Scholars representing *all* the other perspectives seem to find here an approach they appreciate and can readily endorse. This is not because I have cherry-picked elements of their views, nor because I offer a "lowest common denominator" that everyone can accept. Rather, I think it is because the "Gift Perspective" has reconfigured a central issue—grace—that has divided Protestants from Catholics, New Perspective from Old, those who read Paul "within Judaism" and those who read him outside of Judaism. Turning the kaleidoscope in one crucial respect—clarifying the meaning of grace and the different "perfections" it can bear—I hope to have *solved* a lot of issues that have caused misunderstanding of Paul and difference among his interpreters. In other words, I think I have offered a way *beyond* many of our differences, or at least a means to remove some of the logjams in our thinking. As an additional benefit, the "Gift Perspective" also creates excellent dialogue between biblical studies and theology (both Catholic and Protestant), as is evident in the papers from a Durham colloquium published in the *International Journal of Systematic Theology*.[1] I will reply here to my respondents under three headings.

1. *Gift, condition, and reward* (Pitre). Although Brant Pitre and I are close on many things, I would like to reiterate what I wanted to make clear in my response to his chapter. I do not think that Paul would draw Pitre's distinction between an *initial* and a *final* salvation. Although the incongruous gift (of Christ) is designed to create (through the Spirit) the congruous fit between the life of the believer and the will/law of God—a fit that will be evident on the day of the Lord—what is awaited there is not *another gift*, a new or different grace, but the fulfillment and crowning of *the same gift* in its intended form. The gift of God, of eternal life, is already given in Christ (Rom. 6:23), because it is given to all who share the resurrection life of Christ (Rom. 6:1–11). There is not a *second gift* of eternal life to be given later. In this sense, the crowning of which Paul talks is not taking hold of a new prize but rather is the completion of the end for which the believer has already been "taken hold of" by God (Phil. 3:12–14).

Pitre is quite right (241), however, that Paul considers it possible for a believer to "fall from grace." That is clear enough in Galatians 5:4 and in the other texts that Pitre cites. Thus, he rightly corrects me when I said that, without the evidence of good works scrutinized at the judgment, "it is clear that no gift has been received" (233). What I should have said is this: "It is clear that the gift has been received in vain" (see 2 Cor. 6:1). I agree that if there is no evidence of the work of the Spirit in the response of the believer to the gift of grace, the "in Christ" relationship will cease, or has already ceased. I don't think one can take Paul's warnings seriously without reckoning with that possibility. But Paul is careful in the way that he words this matter. It is not, "if you cease to do good," or "if you do not work hard enough," but rather "if you do not remain in the kindness of God" (Rom. 11:22). What holds the believer through to salvation, from beginning to end, is the mercy or kindness of God. What matters is remaining *there*.

This helps us handle Paul's language of pay or reward (μισθός, *misthos*). Paul certainly uses this language, as Pitre insists, and it is the natural language to use for the recognition and recompense of work performed. But when Paul talks about reward, he is not talking about salvation. That, I think, is clear enough in 1 Corinthians 3:10–15, whether this passage applies to believers in

---

1. Mike Higton, Karen Kilby, and Paul Murray, eds., "Receiving the Gift: Ecumenical Theological Engagements with John Barclay's *Paul and the Gift*," special issue, *International Journal of Systematic Theology* 22, no. 1 (January 2020).

general or leaders in particular. The work that is high quality, Paul says, will receive a reward/pay (μισθός) (3:14). What is merely "wood, hay, and stubble" (3:12) will be burned up, and the worker will lose any reward/pay (3:15). Will he therefore lose his salvation? No: "If the work is burned up, he will suffer loss, but he himself will be saved, though only as through fire" (3:15 AT). If a person can lose his reward but still be saved, it is clear that reward supplements salvation but is not identical with it. Why will he be saved despite his terrible building work? Presumably because he was building on "the one foundation that can be laid, which is Jesus Christ" (3:11). That is what will survive the fire.

In the sowing-reaping metaphor (which is not the same as the metaphor of work-reward) it is clear that there are two fundamental life-directions, and those who do not "sow to the Spirit" are cutting themselves off from their vital life-source (Gal. 6:7–8). It is, indeed, possible to do that. But I do not find it helpful, or well founded in Pauline discourse, to talk of "meriting" (final) salvation, even if (on Pitre's terms) it is Christ who does the "meriting" (does Paul ever say anything like that?). What matters is remaining in the gift that has been given. That remaining will bear its proper—yes, its *necessary*—fruit. I mean "necessary" in this sense of integral, inseparable, or indispensable, in the way that it is necessary for those led by the Spirit to say "Jesus is Lord" and not "Jesus be cursed" (1 Cor. 12:3). This fruit, or that confession, is not the *basis* or *source* of salvation, but they are its necessary expression. The gift itself, the life of Christ "in me" (Gal. 2:20), remains the undeserved, incongruous gift, even while it aligns the life of the believer so as to make it congruous with Christ.

2. *Works and works of the law* (Das and Dunn). I fully recognize that in some places (Rom. 4:4–5; 9:11–12; 11:5–6) Paul uses "works" in antithesis to grace and thereby *generalizes* the concept of "works" in a sense broader than "works of the law." That change in Paul's language is carefully chosen (in the case of Abraham, there was no "law" for him to observe), and it is not a sign that in all cases we could substitute "works" for "works of the law," as if they meant just the same. I agree with Das (against some representatives of the "New Perspective") that where Paul uses "works" without qualifier, he does not restrict his sights to activities that distinguish Jews from gentiles. His purpose is to undercut all possible claims to symbolic capital, which some might find in their ancestry, some in their cultural traditions, and some in their achievements. You may make the categories as broad as you like, but there is nothing there, says Paul, on which we may take pride or consider ourselves worthy of God's grace (Rom. 4:1–8).[2] Such generalizations are continued in

---

2. See John M. G. Barclay, *Paul and the Gift* (Grand Rapids: Eerdmans, 2015), 484.

the subsequent Pauline tradition (Eph. 2:8–10; Titus 3:5), which at this point shows continuity with the Pauline ethos.

But—and this is a major "but"—I do not find evidence here that Paul is countering a characteristic Jewish tendency, or critiquing Jewish "legalism" in the sense of "a religion without grace." Paul may know of alternative Jewish readings of the stories of the patriarchs, in which their works, already performed or anticipated by God, made them worthy to receive God's favor. He certainly would have disagreed with those readings, but he is not targeting *Jews* or *Judaism* as such. At this point my reading of Paul joins those who critique that element of the classic Protestant reading of Paul, as if he were an opponent of "Jewish works-righteousness." Paul disagrees with some Jews on the incongruity of grace, but he agrees with others on this matter: there is no monolithic "Jewish perspective" in relation to which we must place him either in the same category or in a different one. On this topic, as on many others, he is part of an inner-Jewish *debate* about the operation of divine mercy or gift, and we should by all means resist figuring him as "anti-Jewish."

In fact, it is the Protestant reading of Paul as a refugee from Judaism and an advocate of "grace versus works" that has led to the unnecessary polarizations between Paul and James, or Paul and Matthew (see Dunn's response). To be sure, Paul could easily be misheard in his own day (as is clear in Rom. 3:8; cf. 6:1–2), and it is likely that the Letter of James is attacking a misunderstanding of Paul. But Paul, like James, was looking for the work that would result from faith (cf. Gal. 5:6: faith working through love), as a *necessary* expression of faith (in the sense of "necessary" outlined above). So, if Paul and the James of that letter had met to talk the matter through, I imagine they would have shaken the right hand of fellowship. Paul looks for righteousness as the fruit of baptism (Rom. 6:12–23) and expects "the obedience of faith" (Rom. 1:5). Matthew has a different sense of what "righteousness" and "obedience" look like, because he is operating within the frame of the Jewish law (writing largely for Jewish followers of Christ). But I am not convinced that the *structure* of his theology is wholly out of line with Paul's.

That still leaves Paul a radical, a discomforting figure who could clash with his contemporaries, just as he unsettles us. Why? Because he understood grace to undercut *all* the things on which we build our sense of worth. There is, for Paul, only one thing that gives us our true worth before God, and that is the gift of God in Christ. Paul saw the radical social implications of this belief, its capacity to create new communities that crossed distinctions of ethnicity, gender, and social status. That is equally unsettling today.

3. *Within Judaism* (Zetterholm). I am delighted to see the amount of common ground that Zetterholm and I share, and I think that some of our

remaining differences are terminological. I can understand that the terms
"church" and "Christianity" can be misleading. The problem is not so much
that they are anachronistic; we use lots of anachronistic vocabulary in describing the ancient world. But I can see that these particular anachronisms
may convey the sense of something that is *incompatible with* the Jewish
tradition, if we take "church" to be "non-synagogue" and "Christianity" to
be, by definition, something other than "Judaism" (as the term had become
by the time of Ignatius, in the early second century). Paul saw what was happening in Christ (the Messiah) as the fulfillment of what God had planned
for his people Israel, and as the centerpiece of Israel's future salvation (Rom.
9–11). Paul can distinguish the ἐκκλησία (*ekklēsia*) (perhaps better translated
as "assembly") from "Jews" and "Greeks" (1 Cor. 10:32), but "the assembly
of God" (Gal. 1:13; 1 Cor. 10:32) can hardly be alien to the Jewish people.
Those whom Paul describes as "in Christ" will later be called "Christians,"
and it is not necessarily misleading to call them such. "Christians" does *not*
mean non-Jews. In Paul's world, and for centuries thereafter, it was perfectly
possible to be a Jewish Christian, or a Christian Jew, and if we were to deny
that possibility (despite the reality of present-day messianic Jews), we would
be imposing our own definition on the terms "Christian" and "Jew." To use
a parallel question: In the current debate about the best translation of the
Greek term Ἰουδαῖος (*Ioudaios*), which some translate as "Jew" and others as
"Judean," one significant argument for keeping the translation "Jew" is that
this maintains the continuity between "Jews/Judeans" of the past and Jews
today.[3] By the same argument, one might say that we owe it to the first Christ-
followers to allow them the same label as their successors called "Christians."

Did Paul induce his gentile converts to "Judaize," as Zetterholm says (see
250–51)? Again, this is a question of whose language we use. The only time
Paul uses the term "Judaize," he *criticizes* Peter (Cephas) for requiring gentile
converts in Antioch to "Judaize" (Gal. 2:14).[4] We could override his usage
and insist that, from our perspective, asking them to give up idolatry is a
form of "Judaizing" or "adapting to Jewish norms." But that would be to use
our language instead of his, indeed, against his. When he expected gentiles
to "turn to God from idols to serve the true and living God" (1 Thess. 1:9),
what (in his terms) was he asking them to do? Not to turn to "the God of the

3. See John M. G. Barclay, "Ioudaios: Ethnicity and Translation," in *Ethnicity, Race, Religion: Identities and Ideologies in Early Jewish and Christian Texts, and in Modern Interpretation*, ed. Katherine M. Hockey and David G. Horrell (London: Bloomsbury T&T Clark, 2018), 46–58.
4. As I indicated in *Paul and the Gift* (367), I am quite open to the possibility that the issue in Antioch was commensality (meal intimacy with non-Jews) rather than whether the food was clean or unclean.

Jews," because there is only one God, who is God of both Jews and non-Jews (Rom. 3:29). He is asking them to turn to the God who is and was worshiped by Jews, but not to become Jews, or even to become "Jewish" in some other way. He is expecting them to recognize the truth that had always been true for everyone, but thus far had been acknowledged only by Jews. Like Philo, Paul would call worshiping the one true God just aligning oneself to the truth of the cosmos, not adopting a "Jewish" truth. To describe this as a cultural change ("Judaizing") is to override the truth claims that Paul was making, using a cultural-historical explanation of our own.

At the end of the day, I want to take Paul's theology seriously. I am not sure how one can read Romans 5–6 and complain that we would be operating "on a too advanced ideological/theological level" (Zetterholm's words, 250) to call the Christ-event an unconditioned gift. Paul was a Jewish theologian, just as were some of his Jewish contemporaries. And although their theologies were rhetorically charged and closely entwined with social realities, we should not reduce them to the level of social engineers.

Afterword

Pastoral Reflections on Perspectives on Paul: Five Views

DENNIS EDWARDS

To say that there is no shortage of books on the apostle Paul is an understatement. Some Christians might become paralyzed surveying the plethora of resources. For some, entertaining the possibility that previously held ideas about Paul may need to be refined or even abandoned is disconcerting. There are also pragmatic concerns for pastors. For instance, what might a change in perspective regarding Paul's theology mean for someone employed by a church if the congregation refuses to entertain any new ideas about Paul? My goal in this concluding chapter is not to rehash the issues addressed in this book but to urge pastors, teachers, and all thoughtful Christians—and especially leaders—to continue exploring academic discussions concerning the apostle Paul's theology. Paul is a model for Christian leaders, and I urge deeper reflection on his theology. I emphasize four areas of inquiry that emerge from the essays in this book. These issues relate to Second Temple Judaism and Paul's relationship to it. Increased understanding of this topic may lead to the reduction of anti-Semitism. I also reiterate the importance of reconsidering the topic of justification by faith. Furthermore, I suggest that there could be a reduction of antagonisms between Roman Catholics and Protestants when we discover aspects of Pauline theology that the two groups share in common. Certainly, there are more than four issues within Pauline theology worthy of examination, but I hope that the spotlight I put on these four topics will spur further inquiry and investigation of the life and writing of the apostle Paul.

Paul, the Model for Christian Leaders

Saint Paul is the patron saint of missionaries, evangelists, writers, and public workers. We pastors, who often are called upon to share the good news in the manner of missionaries and evangelists, who produce sermons and other spiritual writings, and who often supplement our income with employment outside the church, imagine a special connection to what we know of the apostle Paul. Although I earned a PhD in biblical studies, taught as an adjunct professor for many years, and currently teach full time, my primary professional identity was that of pastor throughout the vast majority of my adult working life. Twice I planted churches, one in Brooklyn, NY, and one in Washington, DC. I also twice served in established congregations, in Washington, DC, and in Minneapolis. In serving diverse populations in those urban settings, I felt a sort of kinship with the apostle Paul. He worked to bring Jews and gentiles together as one new humanity (Gal. 3:28; Eph. 2:15; Col. 3:11), and I worked to bring together people of different races, ethnic identities, genders, and income levels.[1]

Many of us pastors see ourselves in the apostle Paul when facing congregational, denominational, or neighborhood conflicts. We feel that we are "afflicted in every way, but not crushed; perplexed, but not driven to despair; persecuted, but not forsaken; struck down, but not destroyed" (2 Cor. 4:8–9). We might have intimate knowledge of the pain caused by personality cults as church members assert their allegiance to different leaders (see 1 Cor. 1:12). Church planters know the joys and sorrows of starting new congregations, planting seeds that others water, and trusting God for the growth (see 1 Cor. 3:6). We have personal stories of feeling abandoned because fellow workers deserted us (see Acts 15:36–40; 2 Tim. 1:15; 4:10, 16). Because of our shepherding instincts, our hearts are stirred when Paul lists horrendous hardships that befell him and concludes with these words: "And, besides other things, I am under daily pressure because of my anxiety for all the churches" (2 Cor. 11:28). We pastors intend not only to share God's good news with words but also, like Paul, to share our lives as well (1 Thess. 2:8). The Lord Jesus Christ certainly is our model for what it means to be a Christian believer, but the apostle Paul serves as the exemplar of professional ministry for many leaders. Therefore, we strive to understand Paul's humanity, his role as teacher, theologian, pastor, and even prophet. However, understanding Paul and his

---

1. I am aware of the scholarly disputes surrounding Pauline authorship of some of the letters that I cite in this essay. I am also aware that on a popular level, countless pastors and laypeople derive their perceptions of Paul's ministry from Acts as well as all the letters that bear Paul's name.

teachings seems increasingly complicated, as there are numerous schools of thought attempting to explain details about Paul, such as his relationship to Judaism; his view of the Torah; his meaning behind freighted terms such as "salvation," "justification," and "faith"; his ethical injunctions; and his eschatological insights.

Michael J. Gorman, at the start of his detailed study of Paul, quotes the genius Albert Schweitzer: "Paul is the only man of Primitive-Christian times whom we really know."[2] Gorman then asks, "Was Albert Schweitzer correct?"[3] Judging from Gorman's subsequent naming of ten different perspectives on Paul—which is not intended to be an exhaustive list—Schweitzer was not correct.[4] It seems we do not really know Paul. Decades earlier, F. F. Bruce asserted that Paul "has something worth saying, and in saying it he communicates something of himself; there is nothing artificial or merely conventional about the way he says it. And what he has to say is so important—for readers of the twentieth century as much as for those of the first—that the effort to understand him is abundantly rewarding."[5] We pastors hope that the effort to understand Paul—which seems increasingly complex—will indeed yield some reward. I confess that in my experience there are numerous pastors, and even some divinity school students, who do not have the inclination to explore more about Paul. Perhaps they trust that what they have already received from the traditional view of Paul is sufficient. Or maybe they do not want to run the risk of confusing people in their congregations. After all, the point of grasping Pauline theology is not simply to gain more knowledge but rather to try to embody it within Christian community. It is challenging not only to grasp new ideas about Paul but also then to teach them so that they may be manifested within congregations.

Pastors should be curious about the apostle Paul and do all they can to spark similar curiosity among their congregants. N. T. Wright recently asserted, "The Apostle Paul is one of a handful of people from the ancient world whose words still have the capacity to leap off the page and confront us. Whether we agree with him or not—whether we *like* him or not!—his letters are personal and passionate, sometimes tearful and sometimes teasing, often dense but never dull."[6] Indeed, Paul's writings are dense and never dull.

2. Michael J. Gorman, *Apostle of the Crucified Lord: A Theological Introduction to Paul and His Letters*, 2nd ed. (Grand Rapids: Eerdmans, 2016), 1. Gorman's quotation is from Schweitzer's *The Mysticism of Paul the Apostle* (London: Black, 1931), 332.

3. Gorman, *Apostle of the Crucified Lord*, 1.

4. Gorman, *Apostle of the Crucified Lord*, 1–2.

5. F. F. Bruce, *Paul, Apostle of the Heart Set Free* (Grand Rapids: Eerdmans, 1977), 457.

6. N. T. Wright, *Paul: A Biography* (San Francisco: HarperOne, 2018), xi.

Regarding Paul's Letters, the author of 2 Peter notes that "there are some things in them hard to understand" (2 Pet. 3:16). Therefore, we do our best to comprehend Paul and to apply his writings to our contexts.

Doing Our Best with Paul

Seven of the eleven New Testament occurrences of σπουδάζω (*spoudazō*) appear in letters attributed to Paul.[7] The word suggests haste, diligence, and conscientious effort. As a command, it is often translated as "do your best" or "make every effort." I recognize, respect, and relate to the busyness of pastors and other church leaders. Yet, I also know that zealous pastors would like to embrace the concept of σπουδάζω found in this Pauline admonition: "*Do your best* to present yourself to God as one approved by him, a worker who has no need to be ashamed, rightly explaining the word of truth" (2 Tim. 2:15), bearing in mind that the meaning of "the word of truth" now includes Paul's writings. Consequently, part of doing our best is wrestling with and refining ideas found in Paul's writings and preparing ourselves to adjust some of our attitudes and actions. The essays in this volume touch on several concepts that we pastors do well to reconsider. Based upon my experience, I emphasize these from the five perspectives presented: (1) the alleged legalism of Second Temple Judaism; (2) Paul's relationship to Judaism; (3) Paul's understanding of justification; and (4) the possibility that Roman Catholics and Protestants are not far apart when it comes to Pauline theology.

1. As for the alleged legalism of Second Temple Judaism, it is important to see that all the essayists in this book interact with E. P. Sanders's seminal work, *Paul and Palestinian Judaism: A Comparison of Patterns of Religion*. A. Andrew Das, who advances the traditional Protestant view of Pauline theology, acknowledges, "Not all Second Temple Jews affirmed a legalistic or works-based approach, but at least some did, and Paul is responding to that claim" (85). It may be surprising to some that an advocate of the traditional, or Lutheran, view of Paul would admit that not all Jews during Paul's time were legalists. Magnus Zetterholm asserts the likelihood that most scholars have accepted Sanders's basic view of Judaism. However, popular preaching often creates caricatures of legalistic, self-righteous Pharisees during the times of Jesus and Paul, and such depictions fan the flames of anti-Semitism.[8] At

---

7. Gal. 2:10; Eph. 4:3; 1 Thess. 2:17; 2 Tim. 2:15; 4:9, 21; Titus 3:12; the other four are in Heb. 4:11; 2 Pet. 1:10, 15; 3:14.

8. See Magnus Zetterholm, *Approaches to Paul: A Student's Guide to Recent Scholarship* (Minneapolis: Fortress, 2009), 62–63.

the very least, contemporary students of Paul must not be flippant in their discussions and portrayals of Judaism. Beyond that, we will need to learn how to give a more nuanced treatment of the expression "works of the law," recognizing that perspectives on the Torah varied within Judaism. It is possible to assert the centrality of Christ without turning a hateful or condescending eye toward Judaism.

2. Paul's relationship to Judaism is related to the debate over whether "call" or "conversion" is the best word to describe what happened when Saul of Tarsus encountered the risen Jesus of Nazareth on the Damascus Road (Acts 9:1–22). North American Christianity routinely refers to the Damascus Road event as the apostle's conversion. The language of conversion suggests to some that Paul abandoned Judaism. The fact that the name "Paul" eventually replaces "Saul" in Luke's narrative reinforces the notion of conversion, especially to many Christians who have grown accustomed to stories of dramatic conversions. Evangelical worship services are modeled after American tent meetings and revivals that focus on personal testimonies. The altar call— a staple in many evangelical churches—assumes that sudden and exciting conversions should be normative. Conversion implies abandoning one's old way of life, and many assume that Paul did precisely that. Paul's reflection on his past in contrast to his current zeal for Christ, described in Philippians 3:4–11, may suggest to some that Paul rejected Judaism in favor of a new way of life. However, some scholars describe what happened to Saul on the way to Damascus as a call rather than a conversion. The language of call emphasizes that the former persecutor of the Way had become an apostle to the nations (Acts 22:4; 1 Cor. 15:9) but did not have a complete change in his theological beliefs.[9] The essays by John M. G. Barclay and Magnus Zetterholm push us to acknowledge that Paul operated within Judaism, and both authors address how Paul's mission to the gentiles fits into their perspectives. Paul's relationship to Judaism is related to my previous point regarding Jewish legalism. If Paul is firmly situated within Judaism, yet preaches Christ—the Messiah— crucified according to Israel's Scriptures and raised from the dead by Israel's God (1 Cor. 15:3–4), then there may be ways for Christians to remain faithful to their convictions without demeaning Jews.

3. Paul's articulation of justification by faith is a topic of considerable debate. James D. G. Dunn's essay in this book, as well as many of his other writings, addresses the topic of justification along with the terms associated with it, such

9. See Michael J. Gorman, *Reading Paul* (Eugene, OR: Cascade, 2008), 14–17; Michael F. Bird, *Introducing Paul: The Man, His Mission and His Message* (Downers Grove, IL: IVP Academic, 2009), 34–37. Bird strikes a mediating chord, asserting, "Paul was converted from the Pharisaic sect to a messianic sect *within Judaism*" (35 [emphasis original]).

as "righteousness of God" and "works of the law." On a popular level, when the forensic idea behind justification by faith is accentuated, Christians run the risk of minimizing upright behavior related to conversion. This is to say that some Christians regard faith in Christ as verbal assent to certain propositions about Christ (i.e., death and resurrection). That assent then gives these confessors "fire insurance" from eternal punishment in hell. We pastors have umpteen stories of people who confessed faith in Jesus Christ but for years did not demonstrate any desire to be conformed to the image of Christ (Rom. 8:29). Conversely, the popular perception of justification that emphasizes behavioral change is associated with Roman Catholicism and therefore rejected by many Protestants. Love for God and others, which includes upright actions and attitudes, is viewed as *works* that have nothing to do with one's status before God. We pastors need ways to communicate justification as providing both divine acquittal (i.e., forgiveness of sins) and participation in God's righteousness. Craig S. Keener connects differing perspectives on justification when he argues that "Galatians 2:11–21 addresses both forensic justification and union with Christ. . . . God, who puts people in the right forensically, also transforms them."[10] The more we, as pastors, preachers, and teachers, can help people reconcile their beliefs with their actions, the better it will be for churches.

4. Keener's efforts to reconcile differing views of justification relate to my final issue that emerged from the essays in this book. Pastors and other teachers must consider that Roman Catholic and Protestant perspectives of Paul may be closer to each other than what people think. As part of my doctoral studies at the Catholic University of America, I frequently sat under the instruction of Joseph A. Fitzmyer, including a seminar in Romans and a separate course in Pauline theology. Brant Pitre's essay in this book draws on the work of Fitzmyer, as well as many other scholars, along with statements from the Council of Trent. Pitre argues that in Roman Catholicism "justification involves both the remission of sins and a real participation in the death and resurrection of Christ" (27). This observation resonates with that of Keener noted above, and it may come as a surprise to some Protestants. In fact, Pitre finds much overlap between Catholic interpretations of Paul and those emerging from the New Perspective on Paul. Of course, there are still significant differences between Roman Catholic and Protestant theologies, but there may be important points of agreement, particularly with regard to Paul's writings. These points of agreement may serve well to foster or strengthen good relationships between Catholics and Protestants.

---

10. Craig S. Keener, *Galatians: A Commentary* (Grand Rapids: Baker Academic, 2019), 176. Keener offers what he calls a "closer look" at justification in an excursus (173–77).

Conclusion

From my vantage point as a pastor and student of Scripture, I have observed the need for all readers and teachers of the Bible to reexamine their views of Pauline theology. The landscape is vast, so I have tried to use the essays in this book to highlight topics where such reexamination might start: (1) legalism and Second Temple Judaism; (2) Paul's relationship to Judaism; (3) justification; and (4) the similarity of Roman Catholic and Protestant perspectives regarding aspects of Pauline theology. There certainly are other issues that require continual study, such as Pauline ethics and eschatology. For example, there are Christians in the Majority World, along with ethnic minorities in the United States and women throughout the world, who are suspicious of the household codes in the disputed Pauline letters, especially regarding admonitions for slaves to obey human masters (e.g., Eph. 6:5; Col. 3:22) and instructions that marginalize women's voices (e.g., 1 Tim. 2:9–15).[11] Furthermore, the New Perspective's emphasis on reconciliation might help with contemporary discussions of racial harmony in North American Christianity. N. T. Wright somewhat dismisses contemporary discussions of slavery and racial harmony when he comments on Paul's Letter to Philemon, noting that Paul's failure to denounce slavery is a matter of concern for "post-Enlightenment moralists, for whom the issue of slavery has become something of a moral touchstone, not least due to the great abolitionist movements of the nineteenth century and the link of the slavery then abolished with colonialism and racism, neither of which had anything to do with slavery in Paul's world."[12] Despite those words, Wright points out that "for Paul the *reconciliation* and *mutual welcome* of all those 'in the Messiah' took precedence over everything else."[13] Pauline theology should be able to help us heal racial division, as well as divisions caused by other issues in our time. As for eschatology, pastors may need help communicating Pauline ideas regarding the parousia of Christ, the nature of the human body after its resurrection, and what redemption looks like for nonhuman creation (see Rom. 8:19–23).

There is also continual need for books and other resources to help make Pauline theology practical. If, as I argue, preachers and other Christian leaders

---

11. See, e.g., Grace Ji-Sun Kim and Susan M. Shaw, *Intersectional Theology: An Introductory Guide* (Minneapolis: Fortress, 2018); Abraham Smith, "Paul and African American Biblical Interpretation," in *True to Our Native Land: An African American New Testament Commentary*, ed. Brian K. Blount et al. (Minneapolis: Fortress, 2007), 31–42; Brian K. Blount, *Then the Whisper Put On Flesh: New Testament Ethics in an African American Context* (Nashville: Abingdon, 2001), 119–57.

12. N. T. Wright, *Paul and the Faithfulness of God*, COQG 4 (Minneapolis: Fortress, 2013), 1:12.

13. Wright, *Paul and the Faithfulness of God*, 1:12 (emphasis original).

might need to adjust some aspects of their thinking regarding Paul, then these contemporary communicators need examples that illustrate how their day-to-day ministry might be impacted. Scot McKnight, an editor of this volume, is one who has been involved in providing such resources.[14] Several times the apostle Paul writes, "I/we do not wish you to be ignorant" (Rom. 1:13; 1 Cor. 10:1; 12:1; 2 Cor. 1:8; 1 Thess. 4:13). We church leaders gladly respond to Paul's wish; we want to continue learning what Paul has to say even if that requires changing or adjusting previous ideas.

14. E.g., Scot McKnight, *Pastor Paul: Nurturing a Culture of Christoformity in the Church*, TECC (Grand Rapids: Brazos, 2019); Scot McKnight and Joseph B. Modica, eds., *Preaching Romans: Four Perspectives* (Grand Rapids: Eerdmans, 2019); Scot McKnight and Greg Mamula, eds., *Conflict Management and the Apostle Paul* (Eugene, OR: Cascade, 2018).

Author Index

Abernathy, David, 14n67
Achtemeier, Paul, 100
Akenson, Donald, 251–52
Aletti, Jean-Noël, 44n89
Allman, James E., 3n6
Anderson, Garwood, 6n25, 20
Ascough, Richard, 252n7
Augustine, 29n19, 30, 32, 35, 36, 37, 39n64, 40, 42–43, 44, 49–50, 192n98
Aune, David E., 27n11
Avemarie, Freidrich, 14n67, 15n68

Bachmann, Michael, 14nn67–68, 17n90
Bandstra, A. J., 2n6
Barber, Michael B., 51, 52n118, 55n136, 76n1, 77nn2–5, 78n6, 78n8, 80nn13–14, 111n8, 195n1, 199n5, 200n6, 243n9
Barclay, John M. G., 3n6, 13n64, 13n66, 15, 21, 23, 65, 66, 70n4, 72n11, 75, 81n15, 81nn17–18, 82nn19–22, 84, 100, 122n1, 122n3, 125n6, 127, 164n2, 166n6, 166n8, 168n, 173n10, 211n1, 214n7, 217–18, 219n1, 220n3, 222nn4–5, 223n6, 224nn7–8, 225n10, 227n11, 230n13, 232n14, 233nn15–16, 234n19, 237–43, 244–45, 246–47, 248–52, 255n2, 257nn3–4, 263
Barr, James, 57n3
Barrett, C. K., 144n12, 180–81
Bassler, Jouette, 101–2, 125
Bates, Matthew, 77n4
Baugh, S. M., 14n68
Baur, F. C., 164
Beilby, James K., 103n56, 133n3

Beker, J. Christiaan, 21n116
Benedict XVI (pope), 26n8, 31–32, 33, 38, 39, 40, 44–45, 51, 54
Bernard of Clairvaux, 36n52
Bertschmann, Dorothea, 178n35
Betz, Hans Dieter, 202n4
Billerbeck, Paul, 174n16, 174n18
Billings, J. Todd, 21n110
Bird, Michael F., 2n6, 11n54, 17n88, 18n94, 18n96, 20, 39n63, 80–82, 263n9
Blackwell, Ben C., 22n116, 30n23
Blount, Brian K., 265n11
Boccaccini, Gabriele, 19n101
Boer, Martinus de, 21n116, 219n1
Bousset, Wilhelm, 174n16
Bovati, Pietro, 105n60
Bozung, Douglas C., 3n6
Brawley, Robert L., 95n29
Briones, David E., 234n18
Brooks, David, 163
Bruce, F. F., 2n6, 261
Buch-Hansen, Gitte, 13n67
Bultmann, Rudolf, 172n2, 174n16
Byrne, Brendan, 11n57, 18n94, 44n89

Campbell, Constantine R., 21n110, 233n17
Campbell, Douglas, 17, 21–22, 77n4
Carson, D. A., 15, 85n7, 119n4, 175n20, 248n1
Cerfaux, Lucien, 4n15
Chancey, Mark A., 2n6, 5n23
Chester, Stephen, 20, 21n110, 36n54, 70n5, 71n7, 122n1, 164n2, 219
Cohen, Shaye J. D., 192n100, 249n2

267

Scripture Index

Subject Index